The THEORY and PRACTICE of CHALLENGE EDUCATION

by

Thomas E. Smith

Christopher C. Roland

Mark D. Havens

Judith A. Hoyt

KENDALL/HUNT PUBLISHING COMPANY
2460 Kerper Boulevard   P.O. Box 539   Dubuque, Iowa 52004-0539

Table of Contents

Acknowledgements

To our colleagues, students, workshop participants, practitioners, mentors, and family and friends who have helped guide us through this writing journey. We are most thankful for your caring, sharing, feedback and support. Because of your involvement, the roots of challenge education continue to spread throughout the numerous professional disciplines.

A special nod goes to our contributing authors: Bill Quinn, Dan Creely, Gary Robb, Mike McGowan, Dick Wagner, Gail Ryan, Warren Schumacher and Steve Proudman. Thanks also go to the following organizations and associations with whom we have developed many of our roots:

Association for Experiential Education, Denver, Colorado
Association for the Support of Human Services, Westfield, Massachusetts
Boston University, Boston, Massachusetts
Bradford Woods Outdoor Center (Indiana University), Martinsville, Indiana
Camp Allan, Bedford, New Hampshire
Human Environment Institute (Boston University), Peterborough, N.H.
Portland State University, Portland, Oregon
University of Wisconsin-Madison, Madison, Wisconsin
University of Massachusetts, Amherst, Massachusetts
Vinland National Center, Loretto, Minnesota

Credits

Editing & Design
Lynda DeTray

PREFACE

Our purpose is to define and overview the evolving orientation to the facilitation of growth and learning which can be summarized as "challenge education." Challenge education is a complex synthesis of a variety of therapeutic, educational, recreational, rehabilitative, and enrichment strategies. The challenge education methodology has now been applied in a variety of settings, and has evolved to a point where there is a considerable body of relevant literature. Our attempt will be to overview this innovative alternative for guiding people toward a deeper understanding of, and appreciation for, themselves, all other persons, the total universe, environment, the self/other interdependency, and the self/environment interdependency.

As the orientation of concern has evolved through the past decade, it has not always been called "challenge education." Quite often, programs which we consider reflective of, and contributory to, the challenge education orientation, and which are certainly quite similar to the challenge education approach, are considered as "outdoor education," "adventure education," "risk recreation," "affective education," "experiential learning" or adventure based counseling. It is important, therefore, to distinguish the challenge approach from those other, perhaps more common, educational and therapeutic orientations.

Perhaps the concept of "Gestalt" is relevant in that the whole is greater than the sum of the parts. Challenge education involves methodologies and philosophical perspectives drawn from many other approaches to education, counseling, recreation, and rehabilitation, but it is more than a simple cumulative collection of those many contributing strategies and ideologies. About two years ago, the idea for a book which would attempt to show how there are many parts to the evolving whole of challenge education was formulated. The authors sought feedback on the concept from other professionals, and there was much encouragement to proceed with the task. Gary Robb, Director of Indiana University's Bradford Woods noted:

> It's important to show all of those who are at work with the various sequences of challenge methodology how they fit into the big picture—or else they tend to think their particular approach is the big picture.

One of the major influences on challenge education is that of outdoor education. However, by definition and development, outdoor education involves "the outdoor classroom." L. B. Sharp, often considered the father of formalized outdoor education, argued that curriculum sequences which could be *best* taught in the out-of-doors *should* be taught in the out-of-doors. Much of the challenge education methodology can be best applied in the outdoors, and some definitely requires the "outdoor classroom." However, there is a considerable number of exercises, curriculum sequences, and programming alternatives of challenge education which can be offered indoors. Outdoor education could not unfold without the out-of-doors; challenge education could—but definitely should not as the out-of-doors is such an important place for achieving many of the programming goals.

Challenge education also has historical roots in common with adventure education. The unique strategies of the ropes and teams courses, outdoor initiative tasks and "new games," and adventure activities such as climbing, caving, canoeing, and camping, are very often a part of the challenge sequence. However, just as outdoor education relies on the outdoors, so does adventure education rely on those strategies associated with ropes courses and outdoor adventure and recreation activities. Challenge methodology includes these activities, but involves much more. It should also be noted that the concept of adventure education is closely tied to the Outward Bound approach—the guiding of clients to high risk and high adventure, and utilization of the teams and ropes methods as educational and therapeutic adjuncts. The approach called challenge education seems to have broader perspective, and should not be misidentified as another adventure education alternative.

Challenge education recognizes that people need to grow emotionally, socially, and spiritually, as well as cognitively. The challenge sequence is usually designed to impact on selfconcept, interpersonal relationships, and, consciously or unconsciously, on the spiritual awareness of all that is and should be for humankind and the world. As such, challenge education is like affective education, humanistic education, and holistic education. Still, the strategies of the challenge approach are only partially drawn from those

educational orientations. The innovative methodologies of adventure, initiatives, new games, and outdoor journey are seldom a part of the affective education curriculum. Yet these methodologies, which are an important dimension of the challenge sequence, can have considerable impact on the psychological and social development of clients.

Finally, it is recognized that there is much historical overlap between challenge education and experiential education. Experiential education, however, is a theory of procedure; it recommends emphasizing the "hands on" approach to education, or "learning by doing." This is one of the important procedural guidelines for challenge education. It might be said that challenge education is one pattern of experiential education; but it should be recognized that there are other approaches which follow the experiential theory.

Organization of the Book

Chapter One provides an overview to the historical roots of the challenge education methodology. There are brief historical summaries of the various influential methodologies, with references to guide the reader in follow-up. The historically defined fields of "outdoor education," "adventure education," "humanistic education," and "experiential education" are overviewed in terms of their contributions to challenge education. Other influential fields of education or "movements" of ideology, less frequently recognized as important in the evolution of the challenge methodology, such as "awareness education," "camping education," and "recreation education" are also overviewed. Finally, there is attention to influences which can be grouped as unique educational approaches, such as "somatic education," "play education," "holistic health education," "family education," and "native American Indian education." As indicated, there are over 250 references for further exploration of the history of the evolving field of challenge education. Challenge education has developmental roots in such a wide variety of methodologies for facilitating growth and learning that there is no singular philosophy for the methodology. Also, as the professionals who utilize challenge methods tend to be "doers" as opposed to "thinkers," there has not been a great deal of attention paid to the question of philosophical foundations. Chapter Two is concerned with providing some philosophical roots for challenge professionals to consider as they develop a philosophy for their practice. The reader will find brief introduction to the ideas of E. F. Schumacher, Arthur Combs, George Brown, Roberto Assagioli, Teilhard de Chardin, Jack Gibb, and Jiddu Krishnamurti, as well as ideas from "existential theory," "experiential education," "neo-humanism," "trust level theory," and what can be considered as "connectedness and belongingness theory." The reader will be introduced to a wide variety of thinking, which the authors think relevant for consideration by challenge education professionals. Again, there are over 250 references for further exploration.

Chapter Three offers a summarization of the basic operational guidelines for challenge education. Since the challenge methodology has been adopted and adapted by so many different professionals in so many different settings, any standardization of procedure is most difficult. However, there are a number of guidelines which are apparent in the best of the challenge programs, and which the authors feel should be applied in all applications of the challenge methodology. Some of these

programming guidelines should be considered as "mandatory" and they should be an important part of any challenge education sequence. For example, if the program does not attend to safety, does not emphasize experiential learning, does not provide opportunity for participants to process or debrief their experiences, and does not utilize a sequential approach, then that program is not truly in line with the challenge education approach. Other operational guidelines can be considered as "highly desirable," in recognition that they cannot always be a part of the challenge sequence. Examples include the recommendation for attention to research and evaluation, the utilization of "solo" sequences, and efforts to have pre-program and postprogram involvement with the client population.

Chapter Four offers a collection of original papers, dealing with some of the important issues facing the evolving field of challenge education. The authors attempted to seek out recognized challenge education experts, and assigned them to prepare a paper on a particular issue. Some of the contributions are more theoretical, some are argumentative, and some provide a case study example of the problem of concern. There are papers on the issues of leadership training, research, interdisciplinary communication, and environmental ethics, all of which should stimulate thought in the reader. The collection is recognized as limited in scope and analysis of the many issues confronting the challenge education professionals; however, the references provided should enable the reader to probe more deeply into the issue of concern.

Clarification

There are a number of points of clarification which the authors feel are important.

Challenge Education as an Alternative: The challenge methodology is often described as "alternative." The authors agree that the challenge curriculum offers a viable alternative for education, corporate training, counseling, rehabilitation, and recreation. Whenever one is offering ideas and strategies that are innovative and different from traditional approaches, there is a tendency to consider them "alternative." However, there is some question as to whether or not the conceptualization of challenge education methodology as alternative gives clear focus to the orientation of the various professionals who utilize these strategies. Most might prefer usage of the term "supplemental curriculum," "adjunctive curriculum," or "curriculum enrichment," in describing challenge methodology. In the attempt to promote the utilization of challenge curriculum in the schools, many are careful to avoid any direct challenge to the approaches of the traditionalists. One must certainly recognize that the 1980's brought a conservative educational reaction to the humanistic and affective educational explorations of the 1960's and 1970's. Many argued for a return to the basics, with emphasis on "reading, writing, and arithmetic." Others suggested that there were too many alternatives about, and that the schools should not be concerned with frivolous curricula emphasizing social and emotional development of the child, and teaching children "how to learn" as opposed to content. Certainly, there was good reason to move cautiously in recommending any educational "alternative."

In clinical settings there was a similar problem. Psychiatrists and psychologists tended to control the basic therapy program of clients. While the traditional psychoanalytic approaches were in decline, both the psychotropic therapies and the many different "talk therapy" approaches were still in the hands of the doctors and professional therapists. Those who had other ideas about therapeutic intervention were viewed as providing "adjunctive" or "ancillary" services. Thus, "occupational therapy" "vocational therapy," "therapeutic recreation," and a number of other approaches became supplemental offerings. Again, there was caution to avoid any direct challenge to the medical-psychological profession.

The authors of this book wish to advocate the challenge education approach as truly "alternative." Our challenge is not to the content of traditional education, nor to the goals of traditional therapy and rehabilitation, but to the methodology. We recognize that the best traditions of education influence curriculum to impact on life values and life skills as well as to teach knowledge of history, philosophy, literature, and science. The best traditions of education are holistic, and humanistic, and are concerned with the education and development of the whole child. We recognize that the best traditions of counseling do emphasize the development of the whole person, body, mind, personality and spirit. Our suggestion is that challenge education offers a methodology which is not only different from, but more effective than, the traditional methodologies. Thus, we advocate that challenge education theory and practice offers a true alternative of process or methodology. It is, we think, a better way to accomplish the most noble goals of humanistic and holistic education, therapy, and rehabilitation. We think it is time to move beyond viewing the challenge education approach as "adjunctive" or "ancillary," and recognize the whole methodology as a potent and desirable "alternative."

Development of self as opposed to acquisition of skills: Some would view the process of becoming a challenge education professional as one of acquiring a package of skills for facilitation of the growth and learning of others. They may tend to view this collection as a "cookbook" of ideas and strategies for utilization. This is not the intent of the authors, although we certainly recognize the importance of skill development.

This book is offered in an effort to expand the total development of challenge education leaders and students. We think it is time for all those who are part of this unfolding orientation to expand their ideas about the methodology, its potential philosophical foundations, its issues, and its operational procedures. The collection is offered to stimulate thought, to provoke discussion, and to facilitate the overall development of challenge education and the challenge education professional. It is not a "cookbook" and readers are encouraged to explore their own ideas and strategies in relation to the overview provided rather than simply mimic anyone else's suggestions. Our position parallels that of Carl Rogers, who wrote about his ideas on person-centered counseling:

> ...but I have no illusions that my analysis is correct or that it is the only correct one. I hope that you will build your own.

About the Ever-Changing Nature of Challenge Education: We are aware that by the time our book gets into print, there will be many other developments in the fast-changing field. The authors recognize their own changes, each and every day, and many of our learnings relate to our whole conceptualization of the theory and practice of challenge education. If we were to start the book over again, there might be differences in summarization and orientation. We also recognize the quick-changing nature of any new orientation to facilitation of growth and learning. We suggest this book is more a history of the evolution of the field than a statement of the state of the art. It is a reference point for future development of the challenge education methodology, and will hopefully serve as a valuable resource for all challenge educators.

CHAPTER ONE

THE HISTORICAL ROOTS OF THE CHALLENGE EDUCATION METHODOLOGY

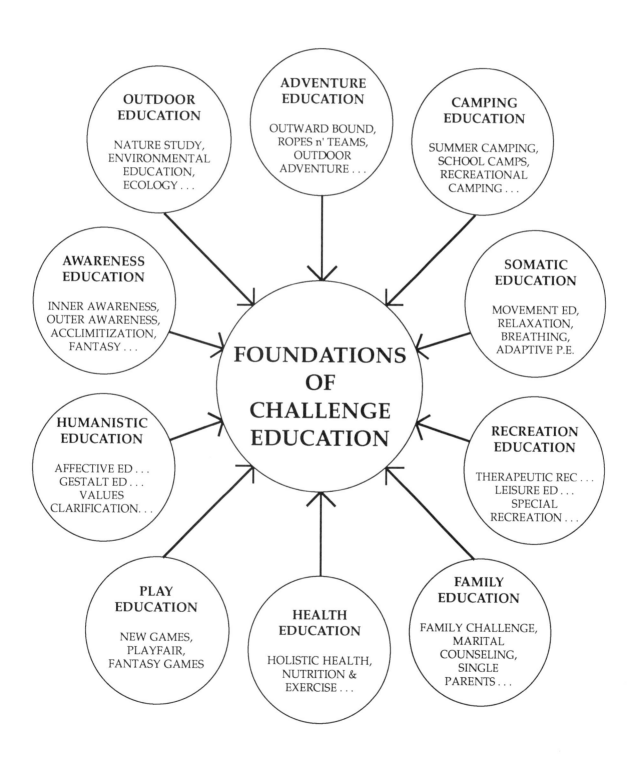

OUTDOOR EDUCATION

NATURE STUDY, ENVIRONMENTAL EDUCATION, ECOLOGY . . .

ADVENTURE EDUCATION

OUTWARD BOUND, ROPES n' TEAMS, OUTDOOR ADVENTURE . . .

CAMPING EDUCATION

SUMMER CAMPING, SCHOOL CAMPS, RECREATIONAL CAMPING . . .

AWARENESS EDUCATION

INNER AWARENESS, OUTER AWARENESS, ACCLIMITIZATION, FANTASY . . .

SOMATIC EDUCATION

MOVEMENT ED, RELAXATION, BREATHING, ADAPTIVE P.E.

FOUNDATIONS OF CHALLENGE EDUCATION

HUMANISTIC EDUCATION

AFFECTIVE ED . . . GESTALT ED . . . VALUES CLARIFICATION . . .

RECREATION EDUCATION

THERAPEUTIC REC . . . LEISURE ED . . . SPECIAL RECREATION . . .

PLAY EDUCATION

NEW GAMES, PLAYFAIR, FANTASY GAMES

HEALTH EDUCATION

HOLISTIC HEALTH, NUTRITION & EXERCISE . . .

FAMILY EDUCATION

FAMILY CHALLENGE, MARITAL COUNSELING, SINGLE PARENTS . . .

Chapter One

The Historical Roots of the Challenge Education Methodology

The roots of the challenge education methodology are numerous and complexly interwoven. They can be overviewed as shown in Figure 1. The major methodological contributions to challenge education are the nine interrelated fields of outdoor education, adventure education, camping education, somatic education, awareness education, humanistic education, play education, recreation education, and experiential education. Other fields of education which have had considerable impact on the evolution of challenge education are holistic health education, group dynamics education, family education, spiritual education, and Native American Indian education. However, through the past decade each of these methodologies has expanded to incorporate strategies and techniques from many other fields. In addition, challenge education itself draws from a wide variety of alternative methodologies. Therefore, what can be considered "challenge education" is a complex blending of a number of different approaches to the facilitation of growth and learning.

In 1979, the youthful Association for Experiential Education (AEE) themed its annual conference "Unity in Diversity" in an attempt to find common threads in the many different methodologies of experiential education. By 1989 the AEE group had matured, and there was recognition of the value of the many different clusters of theory and practice. The conference theme for 1989 was "Celebrating Diversity." It had become obvious that there was a wide range of program sequences which contributed to experiential education; the same is true for challenge education.

Each of these approaches can be considered as educational fields or orientations in the broadest sense, implying that they are collections of theory and practice which have some common denominators and are supported by educators and other professionals of similar orientation. Some of these fields of education have historic identity, while others can be clustered under less recognizable labels because of their similarity of theory and/or practice. Most of the identified educational orientations, and some of the subfields within them, have an ongoing identity and development quite apart from the field of challenge education. Still, they have made, and continue to make, contribution to the theory and practice of challenge education.

Some of the listed foundations for the challenge education alternative are recognizably rooted in psychology, psychotherapy, rehabilitation, and recreation as opposed to education. However, if education is defined from a holistic perspective, with emphasis on psychological and social growth as well as cognitive development, then all of these orientations can be considered as education. If education is defined from such a holistic/humanistic perspective, there is no need to distinguish between challenge education, challenge therapy, challenge rehabilitation, and challenge recreation; one of the exciting realities of the challenge alternative is that the activities and sequences can be educational, therapeutic, rehabilitative, and recreational at the same time.

Any attempt at summarizing the many influences on challenge education may result in errors of both omission and over-inclusion, and may reflect the personal bias of the summarizer. Many may not agree with the summarization as shown in Figure 1, and others may not agree with the chosen labels for the various threads of influence. For purposes of understanding the broad scope of the theory and practice of challenge education, it is more important that the historical influences be recognized and understood than agreeably labeled.

A. OUTDOOR EDUCATION

One of the strong influences on challenge education is that of outdoor education, especially as that field expanded and redefined through the 1970's and 1980's. Outdoor education has a half century of organized interaction with the schools (Hammerman, 1980). The theory behind outdoor education can be traced back to the philosophies of Rousseau and Pestalozzi, some two hundred years ago (Meyer, 1956). Important influences in America developed in the late 1800's, through the philosopher/naturalists Whitman, Emerson, and Thoreau. John Dewey's emphasis on learning by doing, and on teaching the child to deal with real life, was supportive of those who advocated utilization of the "outdoor classroom" (Dewey, 1938).

Rey Carlson, a long-time leader in the field of outdoor education, noted that nature study was brought into adjunct with the

schools in the early years of this century. There were "Junior Naturalists Clubs," as developed by L. H. Bailey, and the New York and New England development of "Children's Museums" (Carlson, 1980). Nature study became a part of the school curriculum in the 1920's, with the classic handbook by Anna Botsford Comstock adopted by many educators (Comstock, 1919). However, most of what would have been considered as outdoor education was a study of the outdoors, not a study in the outdoors.

Lloyd B. Sharp, (1930) is often cited as the father of formalized outdoor education, which dates to the 1930's. He completed his doctoral dissertation on "Education and Summer Camps," which gave rationale for moving students into the outdoors. By the end of the 1930's, Sharp had been involved with the training of hundreds of classroom teachers, and significantly influenced many of the future leaders in the field of outdoor education. Sharp's basic point was simple: Those subjects, topics, and courses that can best be taught out-of-doors, and learned out-of-doors, should be taught and learned out-of-doors (Robb, et al., 1983).

4

In the 1930's and 1940's, the "Life Camps" of the East, and the "Boy's Camps" sponsored by the Texas Salesmanship Clubs, brought residential camping programs into interaction with the school. Most of those educators who did recognize the value of outdoor education associated the field with camping education and camping experiences. It was the l950's before there was true acceptance of the field of outdoor education as a part of school curriculum. A major statement about, and in support of, the developing field was provided by the Association for Health, Physical Education, and Recreation (Smith, 1957). Still, there was only limited impact on school curricula until the mid-1960's. A 1963 publication on school curriculum, nearly 700 pages long, devoted but sixteen lines to the topic of outdoor education (Fleming, 1963). While there was recognition of the potentials of the field, there was not much in the way of actual curriculum to provide. Most of what had been the historic focus on nature study had been absorbed by the science curricula, and there had not been alternatives for outdoor education.

In one of the early textbooks on outdoor education, which provides rationale for teaching in the outdoors, suggestions for school curriculum, and ideas on preparation of outdoor education teachers, the authors suggest:

> One purpose of outdoor education is to compliment content areas of school curriculum by means of first hand observation and direct experiences outside the classroom. Extending the learning process into these instructional settings beyond the classroom provides opportunity for bringing greater understanding, deeper insight, and clearer meaning to those areas of knowledge which, all to often, are merely read about and dis-cussed, but which are seldom experienced. (Hammerman, et al., 1964)

This essential emphasis on outdoor education as an extension and enrichment of the standard curriculum continued into the 1970's (Hug & Wilson, 1966; Schramn, 1969; Gross & Railton, 1972). Meantime, a number of things were happening that would redefine outdoor education: Rachel Carson's classic *Silent Spring* laid groundwork for "environmental education." The roots of "awareness education" were developing in mainstream education and were impacting on outdoor teaching strategies (Perls, 1969; Stevens, 1971; Van Matre, 1972). There was also development of "adventure education," after the strategies of Outward Bound and Project Adventure (James, 1964; Rohnke, 1977; Miner & Bolt, 1981; Wilson, 1981). Meantime, there had been over ten years of explorations with "affective education" curricula, as supported by the humanistic psychologists and educators. Those who were advocating outdoor education as just an extension of the nature studies dimension of the regular curricula, or a simple transposing of the regular curricula to the more appropriate outdoor setting, were soon in the minority. New patterns of outdoor education were unfolding.

In the forward to the third edition of Hammerman's book (1985), it was noted that there had been many changes in the years since the first edition (1964):

> A great many things have happened with regard to outdoor education. Innovative programs, such as adventure programming, stress-challenge, high-risk education, environmental awareness, acclimatization, values clarification, new games, cultural journalism, have appeared on the scene. (Thomas Rillo, in Hammerman, et al., 1985)

These new ideas for outdoor education, or of adjunctive interest to outdoor educators, did not just "appear on the scene"—they dominated the scene, and outdoor education became a complexity of methodologies. The new outdoor educators stated goals for teaching students about self, others, the environment, and the desired awareness of person-planet interdependency. The goals were often quite independent from the regular school curriculum (Staley, 1979; Ford, 1981; Link, 1981; Van Matre; 1974,1979; Knapp & Goodman, 1981). Soon into the 1980's there was also advocation for outdoor education for special populations (Brannan, 1981; Roland & Havens, 1981; Frant, 1982; Robb, et.al., 1983).

As the 1980's unfolded, Paul Yambert, a leader in the field of outdoor education through those developing years of the 1960's and 1970's, projected that there would be even greater interdisciplinary efforts in the future, that there would be further refinement of the ideas about impacting on human values through outdoor experiences, and that outdoor programming would be used to do more than just enhance awareness—it would be a methodology for helping students to "transcend awareness" (Yambert, 1985).

In many ways, the same forces of the 1960's and 1970's which brought so many changes to outdoor education were laying foundations for challenge education. Certainly, there have been many common threads of influence, and a long history of interaction between outdoor education and challenge education. Many who consider themselves challenge educators or challenge therapists as the 1990's unfold would have considered themselves outdoor educators just a few years back. However, just as awareness education and adventure education stand separate from outdoor education, so should challenge education stand apart. A major difference is that challenge education does not require the out-of-doors, although may often sequence activities between the indoors and the outdoors.

B. CAMPING EDUCATION

Camping education involves encouraging others to the values of camping, and teaching them the skills involved. While closely related to outdoor education, camping education can be distinguished because there is seldom a direct connection to the schools. However, as Rey Carlson has noted:

> Education is not regarded solely as the prerogative of the schools, but as the sum total of experiences, whether at home, school, work, play, or in the many group associations available to youth. Camp as an educational institution has a unique aspect in that it is a total community in itself, a 24-hour-a-day adventure outdoors organized for the benefit and joy of childhood. (Carlson, 1975)

Although some camping programs were organized by private schools, churches, and youth service groups prior to 1900, the 20th century saw the real development of organized camping programs. During the first third of the century the number of operating camps became so great as to warrant standards and national organization. The American Camping Association (ACA) was organized in 1935. It was 1940 when the W. K. Kellogg Foundation gave a summer camp to the public schools in Michigan, and it was near mid-century by the time there were a significant number of camps that were really connected to the schools. Prior to that time, the camps were owned and operated by religious organizations, youth organizations (Y.M.C.A.,

Scouts, etc.), or private citizens (sometimes educators or human service professionals who designed their camps for specialized populations). Carlson noted that most camps have program goals that include some of the following:

1. Learning to live outdoors and become acquainted with the outdoor environment.

2. Experiencing individual growth and development.

3. Learning to live and work together.

4. Practicing health and safety.

5. Developing new skills and interests and perfecting old ones.

6. Developing spiritual meanings and values.

7. Enjoying a recreational experience.

(Ibid.)

He further suggested that the camp can be designed to address a number of the needs of children, including:

• Need to learn through direct experience.

• Need to develop a feeling about the universe and man's place in it.

• Need to live in a community with a concern for basic moral and ethical values.

• Need for freedom to play, explore, act, sing, and create.

• Need to accept responsibility for personal and group actions.

• Need to be exposed to a natural environment of harmony and beauty. (Op. cit.)

Residential camping can be viewed as unfolding in the 1920's, with a major impact being the camp at Woodland Springs, Texas, sponsored by the Texas Salesmanship Club of Dallas. That program provided a year-round camp and school program for emotionally disturbed boys. A summary of the first thirty years of that program is considered a standard overview to the process of residential school camping (Loughmiller, 1965).

In parallel to the development of summer camps, school camps, and residential camps, there has been a steady increase in the number of families and individuals who "go camping" every vacation. A former director of the ACA estimated that by the middle of the 1970's there were tens of millions of campers in America. It was suggested that there were over thirty-million hikers and backpackers, five-million canoeists, and approximately eight-million families who camp (Schmidt, 1977). Others have suggested that the 1980's was the decade of greatest increase in Americans outdoors. It may be safe to suggest that nearly half of the American population uses the outdoors for recreation, adventure, camping, and personal enjoyment.

The scope of organized camping and the less organized vacation camping movement brought forth a number of issues as the 1970's and 1980's unfolded. There were environmental issues, concerned with the intensity of impact on the ecological balance, and the requirements of "low-impact" camping. This issue was summarized in the often quoted recommendation to "take nothing but pictures, leave nothing but footprints." There were also issues involved in making parks, campgrounds, and wilderness areas accessible to all persons. The Federal Rehabilitation Act of 1973 mandated public properties to be accessible to the handicapped, and the White House Conference on Handicapped Individuals, held in 1978, gave recommendations for making state parks, historic sites, campgrounds, and some wilderness areas accessible.

The traditional summer camps were also facing problems. Basic economic issues resulted in many camps closing, and those that survived had to find new ways to balance budgets. Two solutions were developed. First, there were a number of camps that developed yearround programming. They either developed ongoing school year contracts, offering day trips, and short-term overnight packages, or opened their doors to community groups for special outdoor programs. Baker offered suggestions for "year-round camping through adventure education programs," noting that such a program could set goals that were in the area of "socialization, education, recreation, and/or personal growth." He also suggested that camps should reach out to discover markets for their facility and program, attempting to develop contracts with "private schools, public schools, colleges and universities, business and industry, and programs for special education, youth-at-risk, and other target groups" (Baker, 1978). The second solution for camps was to consider the new outdoor adventure alternatives, and begin to operate more as an outdoor adventure center (Moore, 1987).

Challenge education methodology has been influenced by, and is certainly influential on, the whole camping movement. Many of the strategies and experiential sequences offered in the challenge education program require the outdoor environment, and challenge leaders need to work with the outdoor centers and the camps. As challenge theory and practice has evolved, it has been economically and programmatically valuable for many camps. As camps have moved in new directions—building teams and ropes courses, stocking appropriate equipment for new games and initiatives, developing modified and accessible trails and challenge courses, and even offering special training programs for teachers and other professionals—challenge education has profited.

C. ADVENTURE EDUCATION

Any overview of the field of adventure education must start with attention to Outward Bound. According to their own histories, Outward Bound was founded in the early 1940's, in Wales, as a program for survival training for British seamen. The founder and director of the program was Kurt Hahn, an educator who saw the survival training as both the teaching of basic skills for emergency situations and cultivating "the will to survive" in the individual (Rohrs, 1970).

Many have considered the Outward Bound schools "survival training," but this is only part of the underlying motivation for the programs. Biographers have noted that while Hahn's program was designed to prevent men from dying in lifeboats when their ships were sunk, he had a much deeper educational philosophy. He was indebted to Plato, and while still a student at Oxford he proposed a school patterned after the principles set forth in the *Republic* (James, 1980). Hahn's desire was to create educational programs which would stimulate students to a passion for life and growth, and would also cultivate social vision. He was working in the sense of Rousseau's "awakening" of the spirit of students for collective concern; he was a personal growth facilitator, a builder of character, more than a teacher. It is this very distinction that links the whole Outward Bound movement to the challenge education movement.

Almost twenty years after World War II, an Outward Bound program was organized in Colorado, and worldwide expansion followed. By the 1960's there were a half-dozen training schools around the United States and the world (James, 1964; Miner & Bolt, 1981; Wilson, 1981). It was a concern for the character of young Americans that brought Outward Bound to the U.S.A. in 1962. As the 1950's ended, the optimism, the energy, the idealism and the social consciousness that was to become synonymous with youth was still ahead. There was concern, at that time, for the apathy of young Americans, a general declining of the concern for others which was such an important part of American history, and the developing feelings of individual impotence within society. Also, the results of research studies on prisoners-of-war from Korea had suggested a surprisingly high percentage of collaborators. Under the leadership of F. Charles Froelicher, founding president, the Colorado Outward Bound School began.

The Colorado program was not started to teach people how to live in the mountains, nor develop wilderness survival skills. The idea was to use the mountains and the Outward Bound sequence as a classroom to produce better people—to build character. The program was designed "to instill that intensity of individual and collective aspiration on which

the entire society depends for its survival" (James, 1980).

John Breeding has also argued for "truly powerful survivors," individuals who are "both serious and playful, hardworking and lazy, self-confident and self-critical." He suggests that this new breed of survivors will know of the need for humankind's connectedness to the earth, and love and concern for each other.

> The earth does need our wisdom to heal. The people of this planet are moving forward; there is no other way. It is up to us to help emerge new human beings who are synergistic and who are survivors, who know how to exercise true and loving power (Breeding, 1985).

An early Outward Bound manual states that "the aim of education is to impel young people into value-forming experiences." That manual was quoted by H. L. Foster, an urban educator who recognized the potentials of Outward Bound after participating in the sequence and admitting that it had "profound effects." He quoted that early Outward Bound manual further, noting that the program is designed:

> ...to insure the survival of these qualities: an enterprising curiosity; an undefeatable spirit; tenacity in pursuit of goals; readiness for sensible selfdenial; and, above all, compassion. (Foster, 1974)

As the Outward Bound programs moved through the 1970's there were explorations of impact on adjudicated youth, city gangs and other youth-atrisk. There were also programs for special education students, mentally dysfunctional adults, and college level leadership courses. There are, of course, variations of the Outward Bound program depending on geog-

raphy, time span, and the characteristics of the group involved.

Basically, the Outward Bound curriculum involves initial experiences for group building, physical conditioning, goal setting, basic skill training and basecamp utilization of ropes and teams courses. Then the group moves to adventures and challenges for the individual and the group (climbing, caving, canoeing, etc.). There is also a component of the experience that involves "solo" journeys, emphasizing a time for reflection and introspection about the other aspects of the program. Outward Bound places considerable emphasis on physical challenge, not as an end in itself but as an instrument for training the individual's will to survive and master.

Early in the 1970's, an educator involved in the human potential movement noted the possible significance of the Outward Bound program:

Its primary ingredient is will training. The participant forces himself to do things he did not believe possible...rock climbing, living off the land, diving into icy waters. The spirit of the group and the organization of the experience heightens his motivation to do these difficult and unpleasant things, but these would be insufficient without great individual efforts. (Mann, 1972)

Very early in the 1970's, a group of innovative educators in Hamilton, Massachusetts, most of whom had prior involvement with Outward Bound, sought to develop a school-based program along the same lines. Application of the full Outward Bound sequence was untenable because of time and expense, but the group was able to develop a sequence of "adventure activities" patterned after Outward Bound. "Project Adventure" was initially funded under a Federal Office of Education grant, and has been the prototype for adventure education programs across the country. The very usage of the term "adventure education" can most likely be traced to Project Adventure.

The first major publication of Project Adventure was *Cowstails and Cobras,* which was a guide to ropes courses, initiative games, and other adventure activities (Rohnke, 1977). That publication served as a guidebook for the development of ropes and teams courses across the nation in the late 1970's and early 1980's. A later publication outlined an "adventure curriculum" for the schools (Rohnke, 1979). The Project Adventure staff began training teachers and adjunctive educators in adventure programming late in the 1970's. During the next decade they trained over 10,000 professionals in education and human services, and consulted with over 1000 school systems to help them develop adventure programs. Adventure leaders trained by Project Adventure moved out into the field to develop the methodology in schools, camps, hospitals, and social services agencies. In the last few years they have also expanded consultation and training services to mental health and chemical dependency hospitals (Schoel, et. al, 1988).

Rohnke has summarized the basic learning goals of Project Adventure:

1. To increase the participant's sense of personal confidence.

2. To increase mutual support within a group.

3. To develop an increased agility and physical coordination.

4. To develop an increased joy in one's physical self and in being with others. (Rohnke, 1986)

In a historical review of Outward Bound, it is noted that:

> No other innovative educational proposal spinning off from Outward Bound has enjoyed a greater success with the educational establishment than Project Adventure. (Miner & Bolt, 1981)

As more and more educators and youth leaders developed interest and skills in the basics of teams tasks and initiative activities, there was increasing demand for access to the equipment that would enable facilitation of such sequences. Through the 1980's there were hundreds of ropes and teams courses built around the country and the world (Darst & Armstrong, 1986). As the 1980's ended, "portable ropes courses" were introduce for both inside and outside utilization. The developers of this "ropes course alternative," note that "people learn better when their whole body is involved and when they can use a

hands-on trial-and-error process" (Roland, 1989).

Outward Bound concepts have also influenced other programs for training educators for outdoor leadership. The Council on Outdoor Education of Ontario, Canada, recognized the need for training teachers and counselors to use outdoor adventure sequences because of their potentiality for impacting on the psychological and social aspects of the students. Both Outward Bound and Project Adventure recognized the overlap of their programming and that of the counseling group, but the Canadian task force report states it most clearly:

> We see obvious overlapping with sociological and psychological forces...the facts require that we deal with interpersonal interaction, small group dynamics, values, decision making, consensus, etc. (Rogers, 1979)

The evolution of adventure programming has also been toward recognition of the overlap with all of outdoor education, and all of affective education. It is this blending of ideologies and methodologies which evolves toward challenge education theory and practice. The challenge educator may utilize initiatives, teams courses, and even outdoor adventure expeditions as part of a sequential unfolding of curricula for a group. The adventure educator, conversely, attends to the dynamics of the group, the processing of feelings, and steering the student towards introspection.

As mentioned, one of the important strategy contributions of Outward Bound is that of the "solo" experience. Most adventure and challenge programs now utilize this pattern of experience for participants, although most often it would involve time at a "special place" or a "secret spot," and not a day or two excursion to the wilderness alone. When the humanistic, existential, and awareness educators advocate experiences such as "centering" and "focusing," they recognize that looking inward and looking outward add up to the same vision. John Muir recognized the connection between taking time to search inward, and the value of solo time when he wrote: "Only by going alone, in silence, without baggage, can one truly get into the heart of the wilderness" (Muir, in Teale, 1954).

Webster defines adventure as "an undertaking involving danger and unknown risks." Adventure education recognizes that there is adventure in many tasks that involve newness, risk, trust, sharing, and exploring the unknown. Adventure education recognizes that schoolyard and outdoor center sequences can be "adventures," just as much as mountain climbing, whitewater rafting, backpacking, and cold-weather camping, etc. Furthermore, most adventure educators support the argument that there is also "adventure" when one journeys to the wilderness within. This brings all of adventure education into parallel philosophy with challenge education.

D. AWARENESS EDUCATION

Webster defines awareness in terms of "having knowledge of something, and especially of something that is not generally known or apparent." It is the search for this deeper knowledge, this less readily apparent information about ourselves and our world, that guides the practices of awareness education. We can say that the advocate of awareness education recommends learning by impacting on the full sequence of sensation-perception-emotion, and is also concerned with the consequent behavioral expression. Expose the student to diverse stimuli, having them touch, smell, and listen, and they will discover the complexities and delicate balances of the natural world; and they will ultimately behave with improved regard for themselves, others, and the environment. Have the student look inward, seeking the wisdom of balance and interrelatedness of all things, and ultimately they will behave in greater harmony with all that is about them.

This argument for developing and applying keen awareness to the total learning process is not new. The ancient practices of yoga, meditation, and suffism were, in part, procedures for enhancing and awakening one's awareness of self, others, world, and beyond. However, awareness methodologies did not really impact on American education until the middle of the twentieth century. Before that, educational learning theory had been most influenced by the early twentieth century psychological orientations which disallowed introspection and awareness processes. The realities of the external world create sensations which result in behavior; change the input and you change the output. Science was not to be concerned with what went on "inside" the person, for that could hardly be quantified and studied by scientific methodology.

Actually, at the very roots of modern psychology, the research of Weber, Fechner, and Helmholtz, in "psychophysics," had attempted to show the relationships between outside stimuli and the subjective experiences triggered. However, there soon came the impact of behaviorism (Wundt, Watson, etc.) and the reflexologists (Pavlov, etc.) who made the argument for study of antecedent stimuli and consequent observable responses, without regard for complex intervening processes that require subjective interpretation.

Classic textbooks on psychology offer full chapters on the study of the five senses, but do not offer any focus on the subject of "awareness."

Some of those who advocate awareness education might find some agreement with the behaviorists. After all, it is the ultimate changes in behavior that are the goal. If students are guided through sensory awareness exercises, and later behave with greater regard for self, others, and world, then we have accomplished our goal. This argument would not be acceptable, of course, to those who advocate the value of the process of seeking awareness itself, apart from any observable goalpoint.

By the middle of the century, psychologists opened doorways to focusing attention on the processes of awareness. The voices of psychologists and biologists arguing for recognition of the complexity of the human machine, and the qualities of total human-being-ness, became much stronger (Snygg & Combs, 1949, 1959; Eckstein, 1969). There was increasing attention to individual differences in perception, emotional reaction, and motivational state, as psychology developed a more holistic overview to the person. P.T. Young, essentially of the physiological psychology approach, recognized both perceptual and affective internal processes, and noted that they are "much influenced by knowledge, information, training, and past experiences" (Young, 1961).

C. W. Erickson, while agreeing with tradition that the senses are only receptors of information which ultimately influences the behavior, noted that even those basic processes "are not automatic cameras, simply recognizing what is presented." He recog-

nized that, "we can focus, attend, improve, and enhance our sensory awareness," and he advocated more careful attention to the internal processes of awareness (Erickson, 1958).

Awareness educators evolved in parallel to these changes in psychological orientation, and became interested in facilitation of exercises which would enhance the students sensory processes, and improve overall learning.

Even as the scientist-psychologist was evolving toward re-attention to the awareness processes of people, there were other forces stimulating the development of awareness education. The concepts of the "third force" psychologists in America (Allport, Maslow, Rogers, etc.) and the focus of the existential philosopher-psychologists of Europe (Jaspers, Binswanger, etc.) brought considerable emphasis to the complex inner dimensions of the person. The 1960's also brought great interest in the ancient Eastern philosophies and practices (yoga, meditation, t'ai chi, suffism, etc.), and that impacted on many educators. It might be summarized in noting that by the end of the 1960's psychoeducational thought had seemed to arrive at a point where many leaders were keenly aware of awareness.

Also at the roots of awareness education stands Rachel Carson, who stirred the conscience of the world in the classic *Silent Spring*, which announced the imminent dangers of man destroying the very world he is dependent upon (Carson, 1957). She later recommended a solution for the problem, based on the cultivation of an emotional awareness of, and appreciation for, the environment and the person-world interdependency. She wrote in *The Sense of Wonder*, "It is not half so important to know as to feel" (Carson, 1959).

She was arguing that we must cultivate an awareness that rises from our totality, not just our brain.

Two patterns of awareness psychology/education have evolved over the past two or three decades. The first has to do with ideas on how to develop and enhance our awareness in general, or how to improve our "inner awareness." The second has to do with applying keen awareness practices to the study of the world about us, or how to improve our "outer awareness." The first can be viewed as a body of theory and practice for making the person more aware of self, in the here-and-now existence, as an evolving bundle of personal potential. For some, this inner search is advocated as the avenue towards spiritual development. The second type of awareness education has to do with using our totality to grasp the realities, complexities, intricacies, and beauty of our world; and thus guiding us to a passionate understanding of the necessity of person-planet interdependency.

These two patterns of awareness education are interwoven. If one senses the totality of it all, then humankind is nature, nature is humankind; the inside is the outside, and the outside is the inside. To fully understand the world about us, and enhance our appreciation for all that is, leads to an understanding of ourselves in balance with that environment.

Conversely, understanding the world within us, sensing all that we are and can be, leads to an understanding of that same person-world totality. It can be stated: "There is a wilderness beyond... ...and there is a wilderness within..." (Smith, 1981). We go to the outside to learn about the inside, and we go to the inside to learn about the outside. The two

starting points are on the same circle that can be considered as awareness education.

1. Environmental Awareness. The exemplifying force in the development of activities and complete school curricula for this pattern of awareness education is Steve Van Matre and *Acclimatization* (Van Matre, 1973, 1973, 1979). Although the early American Naturalists (Whitman, Emerson, Thoreau, Muir, etc.) must be recognized as advocates of an approach to learning about the environment by being with that environment, they did not sequence any sort of curriculum or educational plan. John Muir noted the necessity for experiencing the natural world with full awareness. He concluded his writings on his youth by summarizing his rationale for leaving college: "I was only leaving one University for another, the University of Wisconsin for the University of the Wilderness" (John Muir, in Teale, 1954).

Van Matre's work on acclimatization has had much influence on educators and outdoor leaders. He offers suggestions for activities and curricula that enhance awareness and emphasize the very basis of awareness education.

> Natural awareness is a many sided quality; it is an illuminating beacon, stabbing through a foggy understanding of life. (Van Matre, 1974)

There were others who moved toward using awareness methods for teaching students about the personplanet interdependency. Joseph Cornell even considered himself a "nature awareness instructor," and in the preface to his book on sharing nature with children he notes, "children understand and remember concepts best when they learn from direct personal experiences" (Cornell, 1979).

14

Cornell has authored a trilogy of environmental awareness books (1979, 1987, 1989). In his last work, he states as one of his basic principles: "If we want to develop an attitude of reverence for life, we need to begin with awareness, which in turn can lead to loving empathy."

Observation of the 1980's would find awareness educators (and, also, the outdoor educators and the challenge educators) facilitating "blind-walks," "tree hugging," solo time to "special places," and a host of other activities developed for enhancement of awareness. It should be noted that most of those who develop an educational sequence concerned with environmental awareness understand the relatedness of the outside to the inside.

Van Matre expresses interest in both en-

vironmental awareness to guide the student to keen understanding of the essentials of ecology and conservation, and in the fostering of individual growth and development. He sum-

marizes: "I feel that self-awareness follows natural awareness" (Van Matre, 1974).

> Awareness of the earth, consciousness of its proximity, of its inescapable influence—even when not obvious—presents aesthetic and psychological possibilities largely overlooked or forgotten. Each individual, in canyons and beyond, is deeply affected by his physical surroundings. If it can reach him, knowledge of the earth as reality, rock as material of the universe, landscape as momentary expression of natural process, is a rich and vital source of sanity and calm for modern man. (Leveson, 1972)

2. Inner Awareness. Fritz Perls, father of Gestalt Therapy has been quoted:

> The task of all deep religions—or of really good therapy—is the *satori*, the great awakening, the coming to one's senses, waking up from one's dream. When we come to ourselves, we start to see, to feel, to experience. (Fritz Perls, in Csaky, 1979)

Perls was a leader in the field of awareness education, even though his personal emphasis was on facilitation of growth through psychotherapeutic intervention, not school curriculum. One of his students, who was also his editorial advisor and friend, authored a book of theory and exercises for enhancing personal awareness. John Stevens recognized the activities as tools for usage by the therapist, the group facilitator, the self-searcher, and the educator.

> It's incredible how much you can realize about your own existence by simply paying close attention to it and becoming more deeply aware of your own experiencing. Awareness is basic, and you can discover this through your own experiencing... The revolution of awareness is happening because more of us are insist-

ing on living our own lives. You can join us by living your own life fully, with awareness. (Stevens, 1971)

Many others did join the "revolution of awareness," some with more direct focus on education (Selver, 1966; Jones, 1970; Rubin, 1973; Ludell,1978). One special education teacher applied Gestalt awareness methods in work with emotionally disturbed children (Lederman, 1969). Two humanistic educators provided a manual of selfconcept enhancement strategies for the classroom, and noted their debt to Gestalt ideology and practice (Canfield & Wells, 1976). The methods of "transactional analysis" were offered for educational application with "Gestalt Experiments" (James & Jongeward, 1971).

Fritz Perls would be considered a major theorist of the whole human potential movement, and had impact on challenge theory and practice from that perspective as well. However, his attention to awareness stands out as very significant, and may be his most important contribution. Teachers concerned with fostering personal growth and social development of students, adventure leaders seeking to guide clients toward getting more out of their experiences, and environmental educators seeking to enhance student awareness of ecological relationships, utilize awareness methods that were developed by Perls and his colleagues.

The concepts and recommended activities of the awareness theorists are reflected in much of contemporary educational and psychological literature. Interestingly, this whole thread of impact on challenge education theory and practice came quite separate from the works of Van Matre, which has also had an influence on challenge practices via the out-

door education connections. A review of the literature finds few cross references; in other words, the works of the Acclimatization theorists make little mention of the Gestalt theorists, and vice versa. However, in both cases there is often mentioned recognition of the circular nature of inner and outer awareness.

Early in the 1980's there was a marriage of the ideas about environmental awareness and personal awareness. A book, *Humanizing Environmental Education,* which was subtitled "A guide for leading nature and human nature activities," tapped both bodies of data (Knapp & Goodman, 1981). The senior author, Cliff Knapp, had a background in outdoor education and the teaching of science in the outdoors. The second author, Joel Goodman, was a humanistic educator who had previously authored books on values clarification, non-competitive play, and creative problem solving. Each of the authors brought an appreciation of awareness activities, but from different perspectives. Interestingly, to solidify the marital bond, there were two forwards written to the book. The first was authored by Joseph Cornell, respected outdoor educator who utilized many awareness activities similar to those of Van Matre; and the second was offered by Jack Canfield, a leader in the humanistic and transpersonal education movement, who was concerned with awareness in the traditions of the Gestalt practitioners.

Knapp and Goodman offer an entire chapter on the topic "Coming to your senses: environmental and people awareness." As the relationship between outer awareness and inner awareness became more recognized, the distinctions disappear.

The word "awareness" is used freely and broadly in writing today. Awareness occurs when you combine the sensory input from the outer environment with thoughts and feelings from the inner environment to produce meaning. (Knapp & Goodman, 1981)

As the 1980's unfolded there was an obvious trend toward the inclusion of awareness activities in all of education, and the trend was toward no separation of person awareness and nature awareness. Some would argue for starting the awareness cycle with a careful look to the world without, breathing in sensitivity to all that is, and then focusing on inner awareness. Most recognize the circular pattern of the awareness process, as the inside and the outside blend.

The circle of awareness has been summarized as follows:

So you want to learn? To grow?
To understand? To know?
Then do not run wildly through the
    trails of life.
Slow down. Come to Center. Breathe
    deeply.
Sense the colors of the world around
    you.
Hear the sound of the environment.
Reach down and touch the environment.
Reach down and touch the Earth.
Reach up and draw forth the energy of
    the Sun.
Look. Better even, stare,
At all the little things in the world,
At all the big things in the world,
At all the living things of the world,
And at all the dying things of the world.
As your eyes fill, rest them in closure,
But keep on looking, inward, deep at
    your Center.
That is where the wisdom is to be
    found." (Smith, 1981)

E. SOMATIC EDUCATION

If one observes a typical sequence of challenge education there will most likely be exercises that involve relaxation, body movement, explorations of body boundaries, and focusing on the mind-body-world relationships. There does not appear to be any particularly encompassing identification for the many theories and practices of this nature, but they could perhaps be clustered as procedures for "somatic education." The encompassing nature of our somatic existence has been summarized by philosopher Thomas Hanna in a statement which might well serve as an overview to "somatic education."

Soma does not mean "body"—it means "Me, the bodily being." "Body" has for me the connotation of a piece of meat—a slab of flesh laid out on the butcher's block or the physiologist's work table, drained of life and ready to be worked upon and used. Soma is living; it is expanding and contracting, assimilating and accommodating, drawing in energy and expelling energy. Soma is pulsing, flowing, squeezing and relaxing—flowing and alternating with fear and anger, hunger and sensuality. Somas are unique things which are yearning, hoping, suffering, tensing, paling, cringing, doubting, despairing. Human somas are convulsive things: they convulse with laughter, with weeping, with orgasms. Somas are the kind of living, organic being which you are at this moment, in this place where you are. Soma is everything that is you, pulsing within your fragile, changing, growing, and dying membrane that has been chopped off from the umbilical cord which linked you—until the moment of that severance—with millions of years of organic genetic history within this cosmos. The umbilical cord has been severed, and now you stand separated from the chain, a unique membranous bag of living bone and muscle and

17

nervous tissue and blood—a collection of structured, breathing offal that is somehow you.

Somas are you and I, brothers of a common membranous enclosure, a common mortality, a common environment, a common confusion, and of a common opportunity, right now, to discover far more than we have ever known about ourselves. Somas are you and I, at this moment and at this place we are in, beings whose evolutionary history has brought us to the revolutionary stage of realizing that the brave new world to be discovered is no longer "out there" but is the here and now of our immediate organic being. The brave new world to be explored by the twenty-first century is the immense labyrinth of the soma, of the living, bodily experiences of human individuals. And we of the latter third of the twentieth century have been appointed discoverers and the early cartographers of this somatic continent. (Hanna, 1970)

Some might be tempted to package the various strategies of the somatic approach as alternative "physical education," but the procedures seem to be at too great a variance with standard P.E. practices. It should be noted that the 1960's and 1970's did bring some arguments for redefinition of the goals and practices of physical education. In the 1970's a definition of fitness that included body, mind, and emotion was offered; Zen had infiltrated the traditions of the physical education curriculum (Millman, 1979). The human potential movement and the alternative play strategies of "new games" and "noncompetitive sports" had some influence on some teachers of physical education, but basic theory and practice changed very little. So it does not seem proper to package the alternative somatic approaches as variations in the traditions of physical education.

However, the programming called "Adaptive Physical Education" does warrant attention. This educational specialty developed from a blend of special education and physical education, and by design was concerned with the alternative methods for enhancing physical growth and well-being. As the special education field expanded so rapidly in the 1960's and 1970's there was an increasing dissatisfaction with the methodologies of traditional P.E. Not only were basic calisthenics and competition sports ineffective for persons with disabilities, they were often counterproductive to the educational and psychological goals as outlined in each child's 'Individualized Educational Plan (IEP).' Special educators, in conjunction with physical therapists and professionals who had background in adventure education, awareness education, and various aspects of somatic education (movement, relaxation, etc.), helped develop appropriate strategies for the adaptive P.E. programs.

Historically, there was mention of Adaptive P.E. as far back as the 1950's, when there was first growth of special education programming. The basic argument at that time was to avoid exclusion of special students from the P.E. curriculum, but rather to lower standards and modify activities so that they could be included (Daniels & Davis, 1954). It was not until the 1970's when there was same attention to developing alternative P.E. programs that were better for the special students. The field of Adaptive P.E. developed quite rapidly in the next decade, and by the middle 1980's there was clear definition of the specialty (Arnheim & Sinclair, 1985; Auxter & Pyfer, 1989). However, review of the standard textbooks for this new field does not reveal a strong attention to the alternative strategies of adventure, challenge, awareness, and somatic education.

Very few of the professionals who have been involved with the development of the somatic education strategies for growth and learning have been from the field of physical education: more have backgrounds in psychology, dance, drama, recreation, and the study of Eastern philosophy and practice. In spite of the variations in backgrounds of the facilitators and leaders, there does seem to be some common threads to the recommended activities. It is reasonable to package them as somatic education. It should be noted that most of the advocates of these alternatives have a holistic overview to humankind, and would certainly view their offerings as contributory to the total development of the student.

1. Movement Education. A strong thread of influence on challenge education has been that of music and dance teachers, especially those who consider themselves "movement educators" and/or "movement therapists." One of the earliest of contemporary references is Gladys Andrews, who advocated the value of body movement quite independent of preparation for future dance training (Andrews, 1954). Through the 1970's the terms "movement therapy," "dynamic play," and "active learning," began to appear in music and dance education fields (Sweeney, 1970; Cratty, 1971; Gell, 1973; Witkin, 1979; Peck, 1979; Torbert, 1980; Curtis, 1982; Sullivan, 1982).

Lowen has stressed the intimate relationship between movement and the cognitive and emotional functioning of the person:

The functional identity of thinking and feelings stems from their common origin in body movement. Every movement of the body that is perceived by the conscious mind gives rise to both a feeling and a thought...they provide the very substance for our feelings and thoughts. We are accustomed to see movement as a result of thinking and feeling, rather than the other way around. (Lowen, 1971)

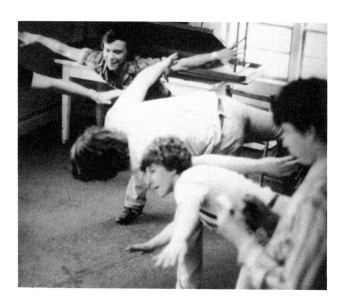

In the introduction to her book *Leap to the Sun*, Judith Peck connects the whole movement education ideology with psychology and challenge education by noting:

Self-expression, if encouraged, leads to self-confidence. Self-confidence leads to a continued desire to learn, to produce, and to succeed. (Peck, 1979)

Dance itself has been recognized as important for holistic growth, and the exercises suggested in dance training are often quite similar to those used by the challenge education facilitator.

Have the students find three different ways to move from place to place in the room. Have them create shapes with their bodies, individually, with partners, or in small groups. (Hypes, 1978)

Some movement and dance therapists suggest free movement and exploration of body rhythms can facilitate spiritual awareness. They would find interest in the comments of Lame Deer, a Native American Indian:

All of our dances have beginnings in religion, they started out as spiritual gatherings—dancing and praying, it's the same thing. (Lame Deer, 1972)

2. Awareness Through Movement. A parallel focus can be traced to the philosophy and methodology of Moshe Feldendrais, whose concept is that there can be an increasing awareness of personal potential through exercises of body movement. He argues that students doing the recommended movement exercises will find considerable improvement in "all functions essential to life" (Feldendrais, 1972). Two of his students, who developed a program for stimulating awareness, imagination, and creativity in children, wrote:

Our approach to movement is directed not only at teachers of movement and drama...but at anybody interested in developing clear and meaningful ways of using the body and increasing human perceptiveness through development of imagination and creativity. We want to understand the body-mind relationship underlying human behavior, and the basic expressive impulses inherent in humans and animals. The nearer a person is to his own instincts, the better able to turn himself into a flowing instrument in touch with the inner nature he has in common with all other human beings. (Bartal & Ne'eman, 1975)

The Feldenkrais philosophy attempts to demonstrate that nothing is permanent about a person's behavior patterns, and very practical exercises of movement can expand the boundaries of human possibility. Feldenkrais argues that we act in accordance with our self-image, and that a strong contributing factor to self-image is "self-education." Self-education progresses in the developing person, parallel to imposed education. He continues:

Self-education alone is to some extent in our own hands. Self-education...is appreciably subject to will. Education makes each of us a member of some definite human society and seeks to make us as like every other member of that society. ...Self-education is the active force that makes for individuality...for every person who feels the need for change and improvement it is within the limits of practical possibility...but it must be recognized that the acquisition of a new set of responses is a step-by-step process. Correction of movements is the best means of self-improvement. (Feldenkrais, 1972)

When challenge group facilitators stress the importance of basic body warm-ups prior to more rigorous tasks, they are starting at the beginning as outlined by Feldenkrais and other movement educators. The emphasis on stretching, breathing and energizing for the journey to new awarenesses and new learnings is really a beginning of that new awareness and new learning.

3. T'ai Chi Ch'uan. T'ai Chi is a unique Chinese system, dating back to A.D. 1000, but still practiced widely in China and throughout the world today. It has been defined as "soft-intrinsic exercise" (Delza, 1961). T'ai Chi is a sequence of 108 different movements designed to improve mental and physical coordination, and bring the individual to a state of harmony between mind and body. As physical exercise, it increases blood circulation, glandular activity, joint-action, and stimulates the nervous system, without increasing the activity of the heart or breathing rhythm; it thus differs from the traditions of the "aerobic workout." It is also recognized as a healing art, but most importantly it is a stimulant for the mind.

> T'ai Chi Ch'uan aims at "the motivation of temperament." The balance of movements and the way of using slowness, lightness, and calmness relax nervous temperaments, give one an easy pace and therefore good disposition, and rid one of arrogance and conceit. Because every movement is anticipated by the mind, patience and control of temper develop without effort, and a consistent equilibrium is established between the heart and mind. (Delza, 1961)

The Chinese philosopher and physical therapist Da Liu is often quoted by those summarizing T'ai Chi:

> Many of the movements are named for animals that have displayed wisdom in the art of survival. Yin stands for softness, inactivity, passive femaleness, and night; Yang stands for firmness, activity, male strength, and day. Interaction of these cognates is said to explain all change in the universe. To unite them successfully is grand terminus, consummate embodiment of softness and firmness; retreat and advance. If you practice T'ai Chi every day, your temperament changes. You grow still like mountain, active like flowing waters. (Ruben, 1970)

Interestingly, in addition to studying the techniques of Feldendrais, Bartal and Ne'eman were also students of T'ai Chi and incorporated those strategies into their programming (Ibid.). Many others of the human potential movement were influenced by the

teachings and the practices of T'ai Chi (Huang, 1977). The progression from internal harmony to harmony with others and the environment is a natural one. There was even emphasis on international communication and relationships, and for many years, Sophia Delza taught T'ai Chi at the United Nations.

Although the potentials of T'ai Chi for the challenge education sequence have not been fully explored, and may be difficult to incorporate because of the limited time frame of most challenge programs, many of the facilitators of the challenge methodology have been influenced by this beautiful Chinese system of attaining harmony and balance. Modifications of various T'ai Chi movements have been adopted by some challenge leaders.

4. Exercises from the Native American Indians. The Native American Indians tended to a cosmological overview which emphasized the interconnectedness of all things, a common awareness goal of most of challenge education. Most of their ceremonies for seeking energy, wisdom, health, and awareness, and for giving thanks to the "Great Spirit," have remarkable parallel to the traditions of the orient (Yoga, T'ai Chi, Suffism, etc.). Although they were not sun worshippers, the Indians did recognize the potentials for stretching, breathing, relaxing, healing, and praying in the sun. The literature of challenge education, and the influential strands of summer camping and outdoor education, make many references to the ideology and ceremonial practices of the American Indians (e.g., Neihardt & Black Elk, 1961; Storm, 1972; LaChapelle, 1978; Sun Bear & Wabun, 1980).

A sequence of sun stretches and group energizing exercises adapted from the practices of the Native Americans has been offered for challenge group facilitators (Smith, 1981). The author notes that these exercises have been successful as basic warm-up, energy toning, and in building group cohesiveness; they may also contribute to both environmental and spiritual awareness. These exercises have been reported valuable as a part of the whole challenge sequence when applied to special populations (Robinson & Skinner, 1985).

Observation of challenge group facilitators at work might find a wide range of individual and group activities based on the practices of the Native Americans.

>...
"sun lofting" or "bird lofting," which involves the group raising each member in turn high overhead and rocking them slowly back to the earth...
>...
"touching faces," which involves pairs from the group risking a warm contact with each other by making solid eye contact and then finger touching the face of the partner...
>...
"raccoon and the eagle," which is a sequential stretch beginning on hands and knees close to the ground, and moving from a "smell" of the earth upwards to a "touch" of the sun"... (Smith, 1990)

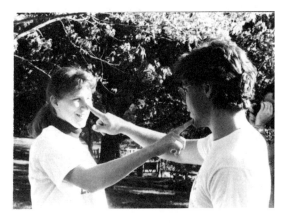

There is definitely opportunity for enhancement of awareness in the movements. The parallels to other aspects of "movement education," are obvious: these exercises can enhance body awareness, teach of the body's potentialities, and demonstrate the relationship of body-in-action and body-in-quiet to the environment. They can even increase awareness of one's spiritual self and one's relationship to the cosmos.

5. Relaxation. Somatic education involves attention to stillness as well as action. Relaxation and breathing are important parts of T'ai Chi, Feldenkrais, the Native American Indian exercises, and most other aspects of somatic education. The goal is to seek understanding of the energy and the potentialities of action and reaction, and also to tune in to the wisdom of silence and the energy therein.

>By studying the speeds of vibrations, I realized that everything in the uni-verse is vibration, and the only dif-ference between phenomena is the varying speeds of vibration. Material objects vibrate at slower speeds than invisible phenomena like sound and light. There is no one key or scale for any particular person or entity. All scales are contained within all entities, and when all sounds combine they equal silence, which is the total sound of the universe. Just as clear light is the source of all colors, silence is the source of all sound. (Stanistreet, 1973)

It is possible to trace the educational and psychological concern for relaxation quite a few years back in history. From the ideas on "progressive relaxation" offered by Jacobsen (1929, 1957) until the end of the third quarter of the century, there were more than twenty different approaches to teaching others the skills involved with total relaxation (Gunther, 1968, 1973). A review of these many methods concludes with advocation of their potentiality for work with groups, educationally and psychologically (White & Fadiman, 1976).

Few educators were inclined to adopt these methods for classroom usage until the Human Potential movement of the 1960's, and the Challenge Education movement of the 1980's.

Often, the Challenge Educator utilizes the relaxation procedures as a methodology for readying the individual and the group for further journeys of adventure, awareness and growth. The procedures have also been suggested as an alternative approach to the processing of Challenge experiences (Smith, 1987). In the sequential unfolding of the challenge group, one of the basic skills for the adventure is the ability to move from action and "energy up," to quiet and "energy down." By the 1980's, basic introductory manuals on relaxation were offered for adventure/ challenge facilitators, and the exercises were being modified for application to groups of special populations (Fensterman, 1981).

There are three closely-related orientations which warrant attention. Among many others, Dr. Bruno Hans Geba, whose background was in psychology, physical education, and physical rehabilitation, suggested a program of relaxation and breathing. He noted that these basics are the antithesis of movement, and one must tap both energies as advocated by the Chinese "Yin" and "Yang" (Geba, 1973). Evelyn Loewendahl was a professor of physical rehabilitation, working with groups of patients in a traditional physical therapy activity room, when she proposed a sequence in stretching. She advocates a program of balancing, stretching and relaxation movements, with the goal of increasing physical and mental powers (Loewendahl, 1977). The meeting of East and West was further emphasized by those who recognized the potentials of meditation. Beginning in the

1960's, educators, psychologists, and group facilitators found interest in meditation, and it was suggested that basic relaxation is a state of readiness to progress into deeper states of attention to self, others, the environment, the universe, and the beyond (Naranjo & Ornstein, 1973). The 1970's also brought attention to the methods of "Transcendental Meditation."

> Growth is accomplished through a series of changes. Without change there can be no development. Life is eter-nally changing and the inevitable flow of life from one event or state to ano-ther is an eternal truth... Every man wants to extend the range of his experience, to know more of life, to expand the very boundaries of his knowledge and strengthen his ability to act. The natural tendency of life is to overcome limitations, to move toward unbounded love, unbounded awareness and unrestricted freedom of activity... In order to experience the full field of Being, states Maharishi, it is only necessary to move within. (Forem, 1974)

The whole process of meditation has often been associated with Eastern philosophies and religions, and misinterpreted by many as a mystical attempt to attain enlightenment. This is not the case, for meditation can be a procedure to enhance basic awareness and indulge in simple introspection as well.

> Not all systems of meditation lead to enlightenment. In many systems, instead of serving as a method for establishing contact with higher self, it has often been a simple process for quieting the mind and relaxing the body. (Leichtman & Japikse, 1984)

Be it the Maharishi's ideas on meditation, Loewendahl's sequence for stretching, Geba's program on breathing, Feldenkrais' awareness through movement, or the long traditions of Chinese T'ai Chi or Native American Indian sun exercises, the parallels are quite remarkable.

6. Centering. Probably the most significant book of ideas on movement and relaxation, as far as classroom teachers, youth workers, and challenge group facilitators were concerned, was *The Centering Book* (Hendricks & Wills, 1975). The authors offer a whole sequence of practical activities for relaxation, stretching, movement, guided imagery, and storytelling—all based on a beginning with "centering." They state their viewpoint, which they consider as based in the theory of "transpersonal education":

> Most of us agree that education needs new directions. Schools should help people become more responsive to their environment... Schools should teach meaningful skills... One of the most meaningful skills is the process of psychological integration that we call centering. Centering helps people develop a pool of inner stillness that facilitates appropriate action. To feel centered is to experience one's psychological center of gravity—a solid integration of mind and body. The authors believe that knowing how to feel centered is as important to young people as knowing how to read. (Hendricks & Wills, 1975)

The Centering Book is an outstanding resource book for challenge educators, and should be found on the bookshelves of many who facilitate groups of people in challenge sequences. The success of the book was such that the authors offered the *Second Centering Book* (1982), which provides additional exercises that are readily applicable to the challenge group.

George Leonard had written some years before:

> Reading and figuring are undoubtedly important...but exercises in fundamen-tal states of being, something as basic as sensitivity to and union with others, something as simple as merging identity with that of a tree (an exercise in Tibetan mysticism) are far more important. (Leonard, 1972)

Such a simple exercise, but one might find it as part of a great many different methodological orientations. It could follow from "centering," or be a movement in parallel to T'ai Chi; it might be recommended by the advocates of relaxation, or meditation. One might observe a similar exercise in the practices of the Native American Indians. It could be a part of an outdoor awareness sequence, or be designed as a "tree-me" exercise in the sequence of a challenge therapy program.

There are, no doubt, other alternative psychoeducational methods which might be considered somatic education. More and more psychologists and educators have recognized the value of guiding the person toward awareness of totality—body, emotion, mind, spirit. Certainly, the challenge group facilitator of the 1990's will continue to explore the ideas and exercises of those who create and adapt somatic sequences. It has been suggested that a holistic approach to facilitation of growth and learning for others is like bringing a full orchestra to symphonic harmony.

> Perhaps the human organism may be considered analogous to a symphony orchestra, consisting of a multitude of energies and vibrations. However, under the ordinary conditions of living, the organism is seldom properly tuned, integrated, organized, and it operates in a random, erratic fashion. Meditation, chanting, ritual dancing, and other specialized exercises and movements are designed to tune the organism. (Payne, 1970)

F. HUMANISTIC EDUCATION

About fifty years ago there was a developing attitude of dissatisfaction with the evolving traditions of American psychology and psychiatry. The historical trends had been twofold. First, there was Psychoanalysis and psychodynamic theory and practice, with roots in Freud and the neo-Freudians (Jung, Horney, Sullivan, etc.). This ideology prevailed in psychiatry, psychiatric social work, and the developing field of clinical psychology. A full review of the various "schools of psychoanalytic thought" notes:

> Each psychoanalytic school offers some insights peculiarly its own which, when considered in proper perspective, may prove of especial import to other disciplines. (Monroe, 1955)

On the other hand, in terms of the broader range of theories of personality, development, and behavioral breakdown, the range of psychoanalytic overview is quite similar, whoever the theorist.

The second tradition of American psychology was that of Behaviorism and the scientific theories of personality and learning. (Wundt, Pavlor, Watson, Skinner, etc.) The behavioristic psychologists were dominating university programs, and while there were a number of different theories (cf., Koch, 1959), these approaches based on scientific orientation tended to study the person solely as a biophysical or biosocial being. At midpoint of the century, American psychological theory was predominantly behavioristic.

Voices of discontent began to appear as the century halved. The more recognized leaders of what was to become the third force in American psychology were Allport, Maslow, Rogers, Perls, and May. Allport was an influential personality theorist, whose classics *Personality* (1937) and *Becoming* (1955) recognized the inner spirit of the person. Maslow studied the selfactualizing personality, creativity, and the nature of "peak experiences." His most influential work was *Toward A Psychology of Being* (1961). Rogers was a psychotherapist, whose "personcentered" approach was in sharp opposition to the authoritarian medical model of the psychoanalysts. He wrote of the process (*On Becoming A Person*, 1961), and the life pattern (*A Way of Being*, 1980), for growth and learning. Perls is considered the father of "Gestalt Psychology." He developed strategies for counseling which have had a major impact on psychology and education. Gestalt therapy is a technique of personal integration which is based on the idea that all of nature is a unified and coherent whole (gestalt). Interestingly, his studies in young life included psychodrama, body awareness, bioenergetics, Taoism, Zen, and the Living Theatre. Much of his influential writing was published posthumously (Perls, 1971, 1972). May began as a psychoanalyst, but then was very influenced by the Existential Psychologists of Europe. He contends that modern man is plagued by feelings of emptiness and loneliness, which are part of the greater experience of anxiety. He advocates the cultivation of creativity, courage, and sensitivity as an important part of the growth process (1953).

There were others, lesser known, who had a strong influence on the evolving third force of American psychology. Strong theoretical foundations were provided by the perceptualphenomenological theory of individual behavior as offered by Donald Snygg and Arthur Combs (Snygg & Combs, 1949, 1959;

Combs, et al, 1976). Combs also edited a collection, *Perceiving, Behaving, Becoming,* published as a "new focus for education," by the Association for Supervision and Curriculum Development of the National Education Association (Combs, 1962). Sidney Jourard was well recognized by his peers, having offered a study of *Personality Adjustment: An Approach Through The Study of Healthy Personality* (1958), and writing an excellent overview to the principles of the new psychology (1974). George Isaac Brown, a student of Fritz Perls, provided a penetrating analysis of *Human Teaching For Human Learning,* an overview to "confluent education" which attempts to provide an integration or flowing together of the affective and cognitive elements in individual and group learning (1971). Brown recognizes that he is using the term "confluent education," whereas "humanistic education" would also reflect his approach. He does seek to differentiate his approach from that of "affective education," as he sees a focus on feelings as only part of the confluent approach.

"Affective Education" is the term usually applied to curricula that emphasize teaching the child about emotions and their behavioral impact. A number of humanistically oriented educators have advocated the value of guiding children toward greater understanding of feelings, and this must be recognized as a part of humanistic education. Classroom focus on emotions can be implemented very early, with simple exercises such as the "feeling square," which has students talk about the four basic emotional states of "mad," "sad," "glad," and "scared" (Smith & Tangy, 1980). As the developmental years unfold, there can be attention to the "language of emotions," and feeling adjective card packs developed for the

level of the language of the group. These can be used to teach about emotions, and as valuable aids for alternative processing procedures (Smith, 1987).

Lawrence Kubie summarized the child's "right to know" the language of emotions:

> A child's fifth freedom is the right to know what he feels...this will require new mores for schools, one which will enable young people from the early years to understand and feel and put into words all the hidden things which go on inside of them, thus ending the conspiracy of silence with which development of the child is now distorted both at home and school. If the conspiracy of silence is to be replaced by the fifth freedom, children must be encouraged and helped to attend to their forbidden thoughts, and put them into words. (Kubie, 1960)

Some psychologists and educators argued that even the humanistic view of growth and learning was not inclusive enough. They advocated "transpersonal education," which would include teaching about altered states of consciousness, self-transcendence, parapsychology, and spiritual growth; as well as put greater emphasis on relaxation, guided fantasy, imitation, and the ideas of Gestalt psychology. It was noted:

> Freudian, behavioral, and humanistic psychologies are seen as useful, but incomplete psychologies. The new transpersonal psychology offers a more inclusive vision of human potential, suggesting both a new image of man, and a new world view... An underlying assumption of transpersonal psychology is that physiological, emotional, intellectual, and spiritual growth are interrelated, and the optimal educational environment stimulates and nurtures the intuitive as well as the rational, the imaginative as well as the practical, and the creative as

well as the receptive functions of each individual. Transpersonal psychology has focused attention on the human capacity for self-transcendence as well as self-realization, and is concerned with the optimum development of consciousness. (Roberts & Clark, 1976)

Is this a "fourth force" in American psychology? Perhaps there is more emphasis on body awareness, consciousness discovery, and transcendence, but much of what is claimed for the curriculum is also very much incorporated into the broader scope of "humanistic psychology." A brochure from the California Institute of Transpersonal Psychology, in 1975, suggested that graduate students would study in five areas of concentration. "Body work" would include learning Yoga, T'ai Chi, the Feldenkrais method, and dance and movement therapy. "Group work" involved study of Gestalt therapy, psychodrama, Rogerian group work, and problem-oriented group work. "Individual work" meant exposure to systems of individual therapy, and a sequence of personal growth involving Psychoanalysis, Jungian analysis, psychosynthesis, or client-centered therapy. "Intellectual work" implied academic in depth study of a complete system of philosophy and of psychology. "Spiritual work" would include study and practice in group meditation, chanting, concentration exercises, and the study of Buddhist, Yogic, Jewish, and Christian traditions (Frager, 1976). The majority of such a curriculum is certainly included in a holistic-humanistic approach to psychology and education. There is hardly enough uniqueness in the approach of "transpersonal education" to consider it as a field or methodology distinct from that of "humanistic education."

Transpersonal approaches should be recognized, however, as an important part of the "third force" in psychology and education. These "third force" theorists sought an identity separate from the scientifically dominated American Psychological Association (APA). So the early 1960's brought a new national organization to champion the alternative approach to individual and group counseling, education, group work, health, and life. The Association for Humanistic Psychology (AHP) was formed as an interdisciplinary organization, and provided a rallying point for many others who were advocating alternative strategies for growth, learning, and the development of human potential. National and regional conferences of the AHP offered workshops in alternative counseling and educational procedures, but also included workshops in yoga, guided fantasy, T'ai Chi, Native American Indian "vision quests," movement strategies, Sufi dancing, "out of body" experiences, Teilhardian practices, "wilderness therapy," etc. Many professionals from business and industry, sociology, medicine, religion, and mainstream education joined AHP, and were influenced by the whole Human Potential Movement. In an excellent summary of the roots and directions of the whole movement, Marilyn Ferguson wrote:

> A leaderless but powerful network is working to bring about radical change in the United States. This movement is the Aquarian Conspiracy. It is a new mind—a turnabout in consciousness in critical numbers of individuals, a network of power enough to bring about radical change in our culture. (Ferguson, 1980)

Carl Rogers' book titled *Freedom To Learn*, was offered as a view of "what education might become" (Rogers, 1969). He did not anticipate the wide range of strategies for teaching and facilitating the holistic growth of children which unfolded as part of the human potential movement through the 1970's and 1980's. In an overview to the human potential movement in education, *Learning To Be*, the author noted a number of significant trends:

> ...teachers have become more like guides and less like instructors...in schools which stress the freedom of the individual to follow his own interests rather than stretch or shrink him to fit the demands of an externally imposed curriculum...
>
> ...the curriculum has been redefined...the variety of offerings expanded...
>
> ...interest has shifted from content to process...the traditional teaching emphasizes mastering a specific content... in contrast, process instruction teaches how to use the resources at disposal... and how to understand his own capacities and use them. (Mann, 1972)

There were other summarizing texts on the methodologies of the new patterns of education, all emphasizing the goal of teaching the students how to understand, direct, and develop themselves (Faust & Feingold, 1969; Postman & Weingartner, 1969; Jones, 1970; Borton, 1970; Brown, 1971). Many humanistic educators found wonderful ideas for the holistic classroom program in the offbeat collection of activities published as *Big Rock Candy Mountain* (1970).

George Brown summarized the need for schools to adopt these alternative methodologies:

> The greatest potential for change and significant improvement in our individual predicaments and in our dilemma as a society lies in the school. It is the one institution in Western civilization outside

the family that most profoundly affects the human condition. It is also the institution that, though resistant, is the most practical in which to innovate. (Brown, 1971)

It was in this spirit of innovation that educational alternatives which emphasized environmental awareness, selfawareness, movement, adventure, and challenge unfolded in the late 1970's and into the 1980's. Table 1, on the following page, offers a comparison of humanistic education and traditional education. It is obvious that the groundwork developed by humanistic education is of significance for challenge education, and that the basic orientations of challenge educators is quite parallel to that of the humanistic educators. Challenge educators are, indeed, humanistic educators.

Courtesy of Alpine Towers, Jonas Ridge, N.C.

TABLE 1: Comparison of the characteristics of humanistic education and traditional education

Characteristics of Traditional Education	Characteristics of Humanistic Education
emphasis on content, book knowledge	emphasis on learning how to learn, applied knowledge...
learning as a product, a destination...	learning as a process, a journey...
learning the answers, the solutions to problems...	learning the procedures, how to solve problems...
structured curriculum, step-by-step sequences...	flexible curriculum, modified to needs of individuals...
emphasis on cognitive process, affective and social processes often viewed as interfering with learning...	attention to affective and social processes, blending cognitive and emotive...
teacher as authority figure, passing knowledge on to the students, teacher knows...	teacher as facilitator, releasing knowledge from the students, teacher also a learner...
classroom orders, designed for efficiency and keeping order...	classrooms open, flexible, using outside environment, circles of interaction...
students get most from interaction with teacher, peer interaction discouraged...	students encouraged to share learning experiences and to interact with others...
study of personal values, emotions, social behavior patterns not included in the curriculum...	curriculum includes offerings for value exploration, understanding feelings, working on interpersonal behaviors...
education/school is viewed as an early life necessity, what the young do before they join adult world of work...	education/school viewed as a lifelong process, students encouraged to view learning as a never-ending process...
learning is viewed as taking place in the school, as a "job" one must put hours in at...	learning occurs everywhere, all the time, and is exciting, 24-hour-a-day adventure...
students must be taught to learn, and they need discipline and structure to do so..	human beings have natural potential to learn, and are curious to seek new knowledge...
best learning occurs in a quiet environment, with passive and receptive students waiting to be filled with knowledge...	significant learning occurs by doing, with active involvement from the learner...

G. PLAY EDUCATION

In his book emphasizing the process of transformation of humans toward a greater actualization of their own being, George Leonard discusses the inappropriate emphasis of values in the modern world. With regard to games and sports, he notes:

> Competition and individualism, aggression and acquisition: It would be rare indeed to spend time observing classroom, playground, sporting event, or television scene without seeing these values glorified to the full.   (Leonard, 1972)

In an earlier book on the future goals of American education, Leonard had described a future scene of children at "play." He wished for games of "expansion" and "creativity," designed to stimulate free expression and interpersonal harmony. He fantasized a full play sequence that would involve "ten children running wildly from one crest of a gently rolling playfield to another, then sitting down in a circle." After sharing their feelings about the joy of play and of sharing, the children would design their own next sequence. Then, "they creep catlike to the next crest, and sit again in that sharing circle" (Leonard, 1968).

Later, in his book *The Ultimate Athlete*, Leonard criticized the very traditions of physical education and our procedures for teaching children how to play. He noted that observation of a standard physical education class would reveal:

> A few students in each class, already good at sports, excelling, and so going on to a lifetime of rewarding physical activity... But many of the boys, and a clear majority of the girls, are simply confirmed in their feelings of ineptitude, turned away from the potentials of their own bodies. In the old-model P.E., children in the lower grades are likely to be playing games or running relays. This means a great deal of the time they are just standing or sitting around. In some games (dodgeball, for instance), they stand or sit around after being eliminated. In other games (kickball and other forms of baseball), they stand or sit around waiting for their turns to strike or catch the single ball that is shared by two whole teams. In still other games (capture the flag), they stand or sit around in "jail" waiting to be rescued by their more agile teammates. Almost always, they spend time milling about while the game or relay is being organized. And under these peculiar and inefficient circumstances, they are to learn whether they are winners or losers. (Leonard, 1974)

By the time of that last book, Leonard had became familiar with new approaches to play, emphasizing cooperation, sharing, joyful interaction, and movement. He recognized that expressive play was right for young children, and voiced support of the alternative ideas of the movement educators:

> Movement education, on the other hand, tries to cut the win/lose knot, while systematically teaching the basic movement skills that are needed in sports and in life. For one accustomed to the games-and-relays approach, a large room full of young children in movement education makes a striking picture. In a class devoted to ball play, for example, every child has a ball and every child is moving. (Ibid.)

In much of Western civilization, play involves competition. The basic psychology and sociology of play was not studied until the middle of this century, although there had been some earlier cross-cultural comparisons of play behavior. One of the early overviews to play in our culture noted that it might even

30

be appropriate to consider our species as "Homo Ludens," meaning "man, the player," since we are so concerned with our free time, and seek to leave our attention to work behind (*Homo Faber: Man, the Maker*, Huizinga, 1950).

What developed as the concept of play in our culture was competition, and sometimes overt aggression. A classic turn-of-the-century compilation of playground games for the school, which served as a guidebook for thousands of educators during the first two or three decades of the century, offered the following suggestions:

> ...teach players to play to win—with all their might.
> ...teach children that they must abide by the rules of the contest.
> ...young players will need to be helped to learn how to attack the opponents' weak points. (Bancroft, 1909)

After mid-century, there was some attention given to the exaggeration of competition and aggression in play and sports. There was argument for the psychological and sociological problems created by competition, especially the damaging effects to the self-concept of those who were not as capable (Basser, 1967; Bruner, et al., 1976). Still, in a compilation of games from the 1950's, a very prominent professor of physical education suggested as part of the very definition of games that it be recognized that: "Games always involve competition and are always played according to some definite rules" (Hindman, 1978).

George Leonard's recognition that play could be a shared and joyful interactional process, without aggression, without competition, and without "losers," was in parallel with the development of new formats for recreation, play, and physical education. He argued that play could foster values of peace and harmony as opposed to "acquisition and aggression," an argument that lies at the root of the movement towards non-competitive "new games."

Leonard's thought was influenced by, and no doubt influential on, Stewart Brand, the founding father of the "new games" theory and practice. Brand had started exploring "peace games" during the middle 1960's, with war resistors, war protestors, and other "peaceniks" around the San Francisco area. By the late 1960's he had become friends with Leonard, through involvement with the Esalen Institute, a think tank for leaders of the human potential movement. Seminar leaders at Esalen during the early years included Rollo May, Carl Rogers, Arnold Toynbee, Linus Pauling, Norman Brown, Alan Watts,

Fritz Perls, Will Schutz, and Carlos Castaneda (Ferguson, 1980).

Philosophers, psychologists, educators, and other thinkers of vision at Esalen were recognizing the need to educate the public in the potentials of alternative play techniques, which could contribute to healthy growth and evolutional development for the 21st century. Together with Michael Murphy, one of the founders of Esalen, Brand, Leonard, and others founded the Esalen Sports Center in 1973. Murphy had published *Golf In The Kingdom* (1971), Leonard was at work on *The Ultimate Athlete* (1974), and Brand was at work on activities for play that were to become the "New Games." Later, Leonard gave this overview:

> The time has come to move on, to create new games with new rules more in tune with the times; games in which there are no spectators, and no second-string players, games for a whole family and a whole day, games in which aggression fades into laughter—new games. (Leonard, 1975)

Under Stewart Brand's leadership, "new games tournaments" began in 1973. The "New Games Foundation" followed shortly, and the first book of "New Games" was published in 1976 (Fluegelman, 1976). In the second book of new games, published in 1981, it was reported that over 14,000 people, mostly teachers, counselors, youth workers, recreational therapists, and other human service professionals, had been trained over a five-year period. Many of the early adventure/challenge facilitators recognized the potential of the new patterns of play, and the parallels to some of the developing initiative tasks and teams courses, so they became educated about new games strategies. The early

years of development also brought increasing awareness of the whole process of non-competitive, creative, and joyful play as a therapeutic alternative. Fluegelman noted:

> We've found that new games can be a tool that will assist human services professionals in a variety of settings... For the disabled, new games can be a therapeutic tool. (Fluegelman, 1981)

Other recreational specialists and educators wrote in full support of the non-competitive humanistic systems of play. There were a number of books that offered ideas about play education which were contributory to the whole new games movement. The titles of the books speak for themselves: *Initiative Games* (Simpson, 1978), *Playfair: Everybody's Guide to Non-Competitive Play* (Weinstein & Goodman, 1980), *The Cooperative Sports Book* (Orlick, 1981). Our society began to teach people how to play games and enjoy activities that would contribute to humanistic growth and development (Oppenheim, 1984). The new games training program even advertised as "a leadership workshop in humanistic recreation."

Those advocating new play procedures and new physical education programs to develop cooperative, harmonious, and humanistic spirit as opposed to the aggressive, competitive, and teamcentered traditions, had much in common with the advocates of "movement education." George Leonard had early recognized the potentiality of movement as the major vehicle for elementary school P.E., and others made similar arguments.

William Schutz, who authored an early book about the human potential movement's interactional groups providing opportunity for expanded awareness (1967), later turned to the whole question of "education and the body" (Schutz, 1973; Schutz and Turner, 1976). He noted how full potentiality of the physical dimension of many students is blocked by three factors: physical trauma, emotional trauma, and limited use. The first two factors related to children with special problems, and therefore give suggestion for alternative "adaptive P.E." orientations. The many children who are blocked from full awareness of their bodies (and subsequent limitation of creativity and imagination) because of limited utilization of body movements, need expressive play sequences that enable them to learn about their bodies in space and bodies in motion. Schutz actually suggests that activities such as those developed by Feldenkrais might well be offered as "playground activities."

Alexander Lowen, a psychoanalyst, made significant contributions to the understanding of body-mind relationships, and his perspectives provide some theoretical base for both movement education and play education. His concept of "Bioenergetics" is based on the principle that "you are your body," and suggests that the pleasures of movement are related to freeing up the very spirit (soul) that is a part of the physical being. He suggests that appropriate play and movement can lead to ability to move "in harmony with the universe" (Lowen, 1970, 1971, 1972, 1974, 1975).

Everett Shostrom, a psychologist, authored *Freedom To Be: Experiencing and Expressing Your Total Being* the same year as the first "new games tournament." He also notes the desirability for providing free movement activities in play sequences, so that the individual can get into better touch with emotions. In order to understand dynamic play, Shostrom seeks definition for the "joy" and "pleasure" of flowing movement. He interviewed Lowen, and asked for a definition of "pleasure."

> Pleasure is a feeling of the energy flow within your own body. That flow, of course, has to harmonize with the flow outside. But when the flow of feeling in your body, when the easy rhythm of breathing in, breathing out, moving left foot, right foot, swinging along, when that movement and easy rhythm of that movement become blocked, this flow becomes painful. We tend to block these rhythms, these natural, flowing sensations from our body to gain control. We try to gain control over ourselves just as we try to gain control over others, over nature, and over environment. Once a person is locked into these patterns of control and holding, his body becomes frozen in a sense, and it is this that is the basis of his inability to have pleasure. He cannot let himself go, he does not feel free within himself to be himself. (Alexander Lowen quoted in Shostrom, 1972)

33

The observations on play and movement as related to body awareness and the full functioning of the person, as reported by Leonard, Schutz, Lowen, and Shostrom, are quite parallel with those of Csikzentmihayli, who is quite frequently cited as providing theory for new play procedures. He suggested the concept of "flow," defined as "a dynamic sensation that people feel when they act with total involvement" (Csikzentmihayli, 1974, 1975, 1990). He argues for "synergistic forms of enjoyment."

Many recreation leaders, outdoor educators, and summer camp program directors also advocated attention to participation by all, and developing games and activities that would expand the individual rather than cause withdrawal and contraction. In a collection of games for the camp and school, Jack Pearse suggested that leaders set goals to:

> ...encourage team effort and participation by all, and discourage the centering of attention on who wins and who loses...
> ...develop an awareness of life and its processes...
> ...enhance understanding of the ways of nature and a sense of responsibility for the living things in the world.
> (Pearse, 1981)

As challenge/adventure education unfolded through the 1980's, there was increasing attention to the ideas and activities suggested by those involved with teaching people new ways to play and grow. Challenge educators concerned with development of programs for persons with disabilities offered ideas on both creative adaptations of traditional teams courses and special play activities for special populations (Roland & Havens, 1981). *Project Adventure* offered a quarterly newsletter, "Bag of Tricks," which provided an idea exchange for those working in the field and continually developing new initiative activities and new games for challenge and adventure. Adventure educators often focused on the development of activities that involved risktaking, trust building, and group development. Although there were goals beyond basic play and free flowing movement, these activities were definitely "fun." In the forward to the Project Adventure collection of "initiative problems, adventure games, and trust activities," *Silver Bullets*, John Cheffers wrote:

> There is little doubt of the value nor of the effect of this kind of activity on students; they love it, they search for it, and their wish to participate illustrates clearly that people will respond to challenging, enjoyable, and meaningful activity curricula.
> (John Cheffers, in *Silver Bullets*, 1984)

There was a second pattern of play education which also had influence on challenge education methodology. As the human potential movement unfolded, with increasing attention to people's need for expanding sensory awareness, personal awareness, social awareness, environmental awareness, and awareness in general, usage of fantasy games for play and enjoyment was advocated. It was the approach of the Gestalt psychologists and educators which emphasized the potentials of imagery, and recognized that from a state of relaxation students could be "guided" in imagery journeys. One of the earliest books on utilization of imagery as games for growth was even playful in title: *Put Your Mother on the Ceiling* (DeMille, 1967). Since that time there has been an abundance of literature on usage of "guided imagery" and "creative visualization" in growth and learning groups.

Many challenge educators use these methods for warmup activities or as part of an experiential sequence.

There was also the recognition of fantasy games and fantasy encounter games for play and for improving interpersonal relationships. Herb Otto, (1967) who had earlier authored a book on activities for classroom groups and counseling groups that would foster actualization of human potential suggested a series of fantasy games:

> Fantasy games are for enjoyment. Life is a journey into fantasy and imagination. By nourishing and developing our capacity to fantasize, we enrich and expand life itself. Our horizons are limited only by imagination.
> Adult play is important. We need to play to recreate ourselves, to regenerate, to allow ourselves pleasure and to recharge our energies so we can then actualize more of our human potential.
> Fantasy encounter games are a new and revolutionary way of interpersonal gaming. They are designed not only to enlarge the horizon of our fantasy, but to offer new adventures in communication.
> (Otto, 1972)

It might be argued that the new educators of play behavior for our society are taking the process all too seriously. Is all of our "play" designed for developing new energies, new awareness, trust relationships, personal growth, or spiritual enhancement? Can we not just play for the sake of playing? The counter to that argument might be a recognition of Robert Merton's distinction between "manifest" and "latent" functioning of groups. As play behavior unfolds, people's conscious awareness of purpose would be "manifest," and might well be stated as "just to have fun." However, the game facilitator might have purposes for the activities which the players are not fully conscious of. These "latent" purposes might be for personal growth, group development, reorientation of values, or even spiritual enlightenment.

The common challenge activity of "lofting," which involves the group lifting each member high overhead, gently rocking them to and fro, then slowly lowering them to the ground, might serve as example. The instructions for this exercise are sometimes, "be as a bird...free...stretching your wings in the wind...flying high in the sky." The participants typically report the experience as "fun," "exciting," "exhilarating," or "as if I was flying up in the sky." The facilitator might well have had other purposes in mind, such as building trust or group cohesiveness. Some facilitators might even be seeking to give each group member an opportunity to enhance spiritual awareness.

> Man is like a bird with two wings that potentially lift him to the pathway of the stars (spiritual life). Too often, however, he is like a bird with a broken wing. One wing is the physical conscious thinking process, and the other is the spiritual. When both wings are functioning with the rhythm of the beauty path (spiritual path), they have mighty power, and can carry the soul to joyful heights.
> (David Villasenor quoted in LaChapelle, 1973)

35

After facilitation of a group in the "bird lofting" sequence, it might be tempting to ask, "Was it as if your very spirit was being lifted high into the sky? Did you become aware of the very beauty and connectedness of all that is?" Most likely, the answer would be, "Huh?" This does not mean, of course, that the experience did not provide the person with an awareness of spiritual dimensions, but only that they could not, at that moment in time, consciously recognize that significance. Leaders must recognize that the games and activities often have "latent" impact on clients; and besides, these exciting new games and play alternatives are, indeed, fun.

It might also be argued that play education is really a part of physical education, recreation, and/or leisure education. However, professionals from those disciplines were not historically involved with the development of the play alternatives, although many have now incorporated the strategies into their programs. Perhaps the movement toward teaching people games that are appropriate for the 21st century, games of sharing, caring, and positive interaction between people, will be incorporated into the fields of recreation and physical education. However, it might be predicted that psychologists, sociologists, anthropologists, and philosophers will continue with attention to the play behavior of our society; and that the new adventure educators and challenge educators will continue to utilize and create alternative play strategies. Play education deserves a multi-disciplinary approach; that is the heritage, and that should continue to be the trend.

The alternative play strategies, the new games, the fantasy games, the initiative tasks, and the interactional group procedures that have been developed as the play education movement has unfolded are certainly an important influence on challenge education.

H. RECREATION EDUCATION

The classification "recreation education" can be used to encompass a number of different professional and programmatic approaches. This force of influence on challenge education includes specialists in community recreation, leisure education, special recreation, therapeutic recreation, and those involved with recreation through the park and forest services. All of these professionals are concerned with teaching and guiding others towards making good use of leisure time and resources, and how to develop the skills necessary for meaningful recreation. Some have special concern for the rehabilitative and psychosocial therapeutic aspects of recreation.

It should be recognized that there is no particular methodological sequence of activities which are unique to the broad field of recreation. Rather, there is an organizational and leadership orientation which seeks to stimulate clients to utilization of the many methodologies and activities which are available. In addition, recreational leaders develop working relationships with various societal institutions (schools, hospitals, clinics, rehabilitation centers, retirement homes, criminal justice institutions, social service agencies, etc.), and assist those programs in development of significant recreational activities.

Most of these professionals are part of the broad field of recreation, but there has been a long history of conflict and identification struggle between various components of that profession. The three most identified orientations to recreation are often considered therapeutic recreation, leisure education, and special recreation. The problems of dis- tinction between these professional orientations arises, in part, because of the wide variety of settings within which they apply their expertise, and the vast array of clients with whom they work (Fry & Peters, 1972; Compton, 1981).

The history of organized recreational services, and the various components of this approach, have been documented often (E. G. Avedon, 1974; Butler, 1965; McCall & McCall, 1977; Weiskopf, 1982). It was about one hundred years ago when Joseph Lee, who is considered the father of what has been called "The American Playground Movement" sought to develop play equipment and play opportunity for the children of Boston (Hartman, 1937). Other historical figures considered to be influential on recreation theory and practice include Luther Gulick, who was founder and early president of the Playground Association of America, Dorothy Enders, who was in charge of Milwaukee's famous "lighted schoolhouses" and Josephine Randall, director of the San Francisco Recreation Department, who supported dance and drama programs as important recreational offerings (Butler, 1965; Russell, 1986).

As with most of the human service professions, recreation has been influenced by societal changes and problems. There have been a number of influential factors and forces through the past quarter-century:

(1) The Community Mental Health Act of the 1960's, paralleled by the societal trend toward deinstitutionalization and normalization had impact on recreation in general, and especially on the approach of those in Therapeutic Recreation (TR). The TR professionals had traditionally worked in hospitals and large residential treatment center settings, and as the clients were moved back toward the community, they had to re-orient their approach and develop new patterns for recreational intervention. This, of course, clouded the distinction between more traditional community recreation.

(2) There was also the changes in Special Education programs in our society, especially with enactment of Public Law 94-142, which mandated local school districts to provide "least restrictive" educational programming for all children, and emphasized "mainstream" placement as often as possible. This movement gave impetus to the unfolding recreation specialization of "Special Recreation," but also resulted in service conflicts with the community recreation and TR professionals.

(3) Since mid-century, there has been ever-increasing amounts of leisure time available within our society, and this has meant increasing attention to development of quality recreational programming. In addition to citizens having more leisure time, there was an attitudinal change in our society. Historically, the influence of the "Protestant Ethic," with emphasis on work and productivity, meant that time off from the work station was simply for rest and regeneration of energy for the return to production. As the century unfolded, value orientations changed, and people became more concerned with playtime than with the time at work (Kaplan, 1975).

(4) There has also been a shift in the balance between youth and the aged in our society. Early retirement and longer life has resulted in increasing numbers of older adults seeking recreational opportunity. Whereas much of the focus of recreational leaders dur-

ing the first half of the century was on youth, there is now increasing focus on adult recreation. The challenge of new programming faces recreational theory and practice as we move into the 21st century. Modern society the world over is calling on the leadership expertise of many men and women who are employed in leisure-related settings.

(5) Finally, recreational theory and practice has been greatly influenced by the creative and innovative new methodologies which have been introduced by adventure education, outdoor education, somatic education, awareness education, play education, and challenge education. Conversely, recreation leaders have often been very involved in the development of these new strategies for facilitation of growth and learning.

Certainly, as the century moves into the last decade, recreation education has became a multi-methodology orientation. In a text on development of recreation leadership, there are appendices suggesting that the facilitators of recreational programming must have familiarity with, and skills in, sixteen different methodologies and strategies:

1. game leadership
2. new games leadership
3. song leading
4. leading dramatic exercises
5. arts and crafts
6. guiding the dance experience
7. tournament conducting
8. coaching sports
9. leading aquatic programs
10. leading group fitness sessions
11. leading nature activities
12. leading adventure activities
13. leading trips
14. special event programming
15. planing and conducting parties
16. leading children in free-play experiences. (Russell, 1986)

The multi-disciplinary aspects of recreational programming are further emphasized by philosophical orientations of the recent years. There has been a significant trend toward recognition and advocacy of the recreational rights of persons with disabilities (O'Morrow, 1976; Kraus, 1983), and Federal legislation has mandated accessibility. There has been argument for a more humanistic perspective on the practice of therapeutic recreation, with greater attention to the psychological and social growth potential of the recreational sequence (Austin, 1982). There have been suggestions for increasing interaction between recreation leaders and special education programs (Brannan, 1975), physical education programs (Mobility, 1982), and environmental education (MacNeil, 1982).

Recreation education is a changing, socially responsive, and important focus for the future. Recreation leaders often bring a wide variety of skills and client knowledge to the setting wherein they work. Most of the recreation leaders are continually seeking to expand their knowledge of new methodologies. A regional conference for professionals in the field of TR has offered training workshops in a variety of strategies. Review of the program outline for the Midwest Symposium on Therapeutic Recreation for 1988 reveals reference to: "new games for a new age," "exercises from the East, the West, and the Native American Indian," "breathing relief" and relaxation methods, "creative dramatics for special populations," "trust activities," and "challenge education."

There has been a history of interaction between professionals in recreation and the evolving orientation of challenge education. Both tend to develop program sequences that involve strategies from a wide range of alternative approaches. For the past couple of decades, recreation has tended to be more concerned with offering programs that may stimulate growth and learning as well as provide meaningful free-time experiences. Early in the 1970's, Brian Sutton-Smith, a recognized expert on the psychology of recreation, noted that productive use of leisure time can contribute to well-being and self-satisfaction.

> Other things being equal, there is some optimal level of play participation, which contributes to the subject's greater autonomy, greater enjoyment of life, a greater potential repertory of responses, and a greater potential flexibility in the use of resources. (Sutton-Smith, 1972)

One very important thrust of recreational educators has been to involve those with physical disabilities in meaningful activities for leisure time. Recognition and research on the social psychology of physical disability began about mid-century (Barker, 1948; Barker & Wright, 1952; Wright, 1960). The therapeutic importance of having the client re-involved in meaningful work and play activity was recognized.

> The rehabilitant needs to be immersed in purposeful activities at the earliest possible time in order to (1) minimize brooding about the irreversible past, (2) reduce boredom by giving him a structured and well-organized day, and (3) prepare him—physically, emotionally, and vocationally—for rehabilitation. As the program of activities becomes an integral part of the patient's existence, he is in position, with guidance, to evaluate his resources and to affirm or modify his life

goals as he learns more about his actual functioning. Emphasis should be on purposeful activity if the client is to become ego-involved and well motivated. (Neff & Weiss, 1965)

Until the 1960's recreational programming for persons with disabilities had typically been limited to indoor activities that did not require risk or physical mobility (e.g., table games, arts and crafts, spectator sports). Opportunities in outdoor pursuits, adventure, and more active sports (e.g., skiing, canoeing, kayaking, rock climbing) were somewhat restricted for persons with disabilities, partly because of problems of accessibility, and partly because of the lack of knowledge about equipment modification and special techniques. In the 1970's a valiant band of creative explorers began to move forward into the wilderness (literally) with persons with disabilities. Wilderness Inquiry, a Minneapolis group of recreation, education, health, and adventure professionals, began a program of integrated (ablebodied and disabled) adventure trips. Since that time, Wilderness Inquiry has conducted hundreds of trips, and has expanded services to those individuals with cognitive and emotional handicaps as well. Wilderness Inquiry programming has been duplicated in other parts of the country with equal success.

One of the major reasons for the success of year-round outdoor adventure programming with persons who are disabled has been the creative adaptation of equipment and methodology. About the time Wilderness Inquiry began exploring the potential for mixed-group adventures, another Minneapolis program was unfolding. The Vinland National Center, funded in part by a bicentennial gift to the United States from Norway, and in part by a grant from the U.S. Department of

Health and Human Services, sought to develop methodologies for the disabled to utilize traditional outdoor sports. The Vinland program was influenced by the "Healthsports" movement of Northern Europe. Vinland was staffed by both able-bodied and disabled professionals, and early emphasis was on developing equipment and modifying procedures for outdoor recreation sequences. As experimentation unfolded, the developing experts published manuals to aid others in development of outdoor recreation programs for the disabled: *Pulk Skiing, Sled Skiing, and Ice Sledding for Persons With Mobility Impairments* (Orr, 1981), *An Introduction to Kayaking for Persons With Disabilities* (Galland, 1981) and *CrossCountry Skiing for Persons With Disabilities* (Opel, 1982).

Challenge educators, who were concerned with development of alternative growth and learning sequences for all populations, early recognized the special populations. The Vinland Center called upon challenge education professionals to explore modifications in initiatives, new games, movement exercises, and ropes courses. An exploratory "accessible ropes course" was developed in the early part of 1981. Training programs explored movement, relaxation, and interactional games as modified for the disabled. Two additional manuals soon became available: *An Introduction to Adventure: A Sequential Approach to Challenging Activities with Persons Who Are Disabled* (Roland & Havens, 1981) and *Relaxation: An Introduction to Relaxation Techniques With Adaptations for Persons With Disabilities* (Fensterman, 1981).

The working interaction between recreation, rehabilitation, therapeutic, and challenge education professionals in this whole situation demonstrates the value of interdisciplinary efforts. All of these professionals had orientation to provide exciting and stimulating activity sequences which may contribute to psychological, social, and spiritual growth. It also exemplifies the historic working relationship between those in recreation education and those involved in the unfolding new alternative of challenge education.

I. EXPERIENTIAL EDUCATION

Like "recreation education," this important influence on challenge education does not have a particular package of strategies, but rather offers a theoretical and methodological approach to education in general. The influence of experiential education on challenge education cannot be understated. First of all, challenge educators recommend experiential learning—learning by doing. This is, in fact, one of the basic operating principles for the challenge educator (see Chapter 3). Second, the very philosophy of challenge education is partly rooted in experiential education theory (see Chapter 2). Third, throughout the development of challenge education the professionals involved with challenge education were often associated with the nationally active Association for Experiential Education

(AEE), as there was no other professional education organization as receptive and supportive to the innovative approach of the challenge methodology.

Challenge education is one variety of experiential education. Experiential education implies that the student is actively involved in the learning sequence. The tradition of learning by experience is often tied to the educational theory of John Dewey. The emphasis on process, on the constant changes of the truths of reality, on the whole child, and the words "experience" and "experiment" as necessary to learning, can be traced to Dewey's theory of progressive education. He wrote:

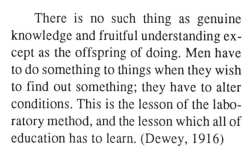

> There is no such thing as genuine knowledge and fruitful understanding except as the offspring of doing. Men have to do something to things when they wish to find out something; they have to alter conditions. This is the lesson of the laboratory method, and the lesson which all of education has to learn. (Dewey, 1916)

Kneller has summarized six assertions of Dewey's progressivism as it evolved through time and the interpretations of others. The experiential educator and the challenge educator would most likely agree with these six points:

1. Education should be life itself, not a preparation for living.
2. Learning should be directly related to the interests of the child.
3. Learning through problem solving should take precedence over the inculcating of subject matter.
4. The teachers' role is not to direct but to advise.
5. The school should encourage cooperation rather than competition.

6. Only democracy permits—indeed encourages—the free interplay of ideas and personalities that is a necessary condition of true growth. (Kneller, 1971)

It should be noted that many experiential educators would tend to misinterpret Dewey's emphasis on experience, in parallel to the error of the "child activity movement" of the 1930's and 1940's. Although all activity may lead to learning, it is not sufficient for the educator to simply stimulate free activity and personal choices for the learner. Dewey would argue that growth itself cannot be self-justifying, as there is need to move towards some fixed goal. The process is of utmost importance, but there must be consideration of the direction of the movement. Dewey wrote:

> Growth is not enough; we must also specify the direction in which growth takes place, the end toward which it tends.
> Every experience is a moving force. Its value can be judged only on the grounds of what it moves toward and into.
> They (students) should know how to utilize the surroundings, physical and social, that exist, so as to extract from them all that they have to contribute to building up the experiences that are worthwhile. (Dewey, 1938)

J. J. Nold, a former director of Colorado Outward Bound, and an active participant in the early formation of AEE, followed Dewey's theory through to a very significant endpoint. He noted that Dewey is the guru of experiential education, and that the scientific method is the basis of his theory of learning. This implies that:

> Learning begins with a stimulus, an impulse, a problem, a question... The stimulating impulse creates interest, arouses curiosity... The stimulus also raises the question of how should I re-

spond? What do I want to happen? This Dewey calls desire, a consideration of means and ends. Where do I go now? How do I want to get there? What are the alternatives?...These desires are then acted upon experimentally and the alternatives tried out... resulting in consequences. Dewey applies the pragmatic test, does it work or doesn't it? If it doesn't, try again... If it does, I can generalize from the experience and form a theory...the generalization is available to me as new learning for future experience. I have learned something... Learning is thinking about experience. (Nold, 1977)

It is from this theory of experiential education that challenge education draws a second important operating principle. There must be post-experience reflection; in the facilitation of challenge groups there is strong emphasis on debriefing/processing of the experiences.

There is more to the contribution of the experiential education movement to challenge education than philosophy and focus on doing and reflecting about that doing. In the early 1970's when the advocates of alternative methods for education and for social service programs sought professional organization, they found none. The National Education Association (NEA) was not only quite conservative and tied to traditional educational methodologies, but required certification as a teacher or educational specialist for membership. Likewise the Council for Exceptional Children (CEC), which was organized for special education teachers and adjunctive professionals. Some of the advocates of alternative education methodology found value in membership with the Association for Humanistic Psychology (AHP), which had no particular credential requirements and was extremely innovative and interdisciplinary. However, many did not recognize that the whole experiential education movement had significant overlap with the human potential movement which was associated with AHP. Professional organizations for physical education, dance and movement education, therapeutic recreation, camping, and outdoor education were basically for those with particular professional background training. Furthermore, most of those working with the innovative approaches found that the more traditional organizations were simply not receptive to their more radical ideas.

There were also a growing number of people who considered themselves as outdoor leaders, adventure guides, and wilderness instructors. Some had been trained by the Outward Bound Schools, Paul Petzhold's National Outdoor Leadership Schools (NOLS), or other outdoor programs that trained their own staffs. These professionals had come to recognize that they were, in part, dealing with clients from both educational and psychological perspectives.

There was a growing desire on the part of these alternative educators to tap the many resources of other outdoor leaders, and to find a forum for exchange of ideas. So, in the early 1970's, as the outdoor adventure leaders and those of other alternative education approaches shared concerns about their needs

for professional identification, interdisciplinary interaction, and a way to network, the seeds for a national organization were planted.

Ron Gager, a past president of AEE, has summarized the history:

> In 1973, less than 100 people gathered at Appalachia State University for the Conference on Outdoor Pursuits in Higher Education. By the Fall of 1976, Estes Park, Colorado and Mankato University in Minnesota had already hosted the second and third gatherings...and a fourth Conference on Experiential Education was about to attract almost 700 people to Kingston, Ontario...
> At the Kingston conference, the 1977 steering committee was charged with the task of building both a 5th annual conference...and an association which would continue developing future conferences as an expression of a more serious alliance of dedicated professionals in the field of experiential learning. (Gager, 1977)

AEE has since operated and grown as a focal point for a variety of alternative methodologies for learning and growth. The organization publishes a quarterly journal offers a periodic newsletter, provides a jobs clearinghouse for those of alternative orientation, and has published a number of books that are significant for the experiential educator and many other professionals. In addition, AEE sponsors national and regional conferences, which provide a rallying point for adventure educators, outdoor educators, risk recreation professionals, challenge educators, and hundreds of experiential leaders from outdoor adventure and urban adventure programs. It is under the umbrella of AEE that challenge educators and challenge therapists exchanged theory and methodological procedures, dreams, problems, creative strategies, and ethical issues—with those many other professionals who were a part of the influential forces in the unfolding of a theory and practice of challenge education.

J. OTHER INFLUENCES ON CHALLENGE METHODOLOGY

There are a number of additional influences on the evolution and focus of challenge education theory and practice. While it would be tempting to cite these as "lesser" influences than those heretofore discussed, it should be recognized that for some challenge professionals and some challenge programs they are very important factors. In parallel to those influences already discussed, these additional orientations will be considered as educational, in that they are concerned with teaching others. There are, no doubt, approaches that have had some impact on challenge education but will not be discussed because their influence has been relatively limited. The orientations summarized here seem most important, as they have had an impact on a considerable number of challenge education professionals.

1. Holistic Health Education. Over the past few decades there has been a significant development in opposition to traditional medical practice. Just as the human potential movement was influenced by reactions against the clinical-medical models of psychology and psychiatry, so a band of theorists and practitioners have offered alternatives to the traditions of medicine. The movement was cited as "The End of Medicine," with this suggestion:

> A holistic approach to improving the health of human beings, either as individuals or in groups, requires placing them in

a larger and richer context than that medicine typically assigns. (Carlson, 1981)

Stuart Miller, an editor of the Psychosynthesis Institute's journal for "realization of the self," had early called for "a new humanism in medicine." He emphasized the need for health and growth professionals working together to develop new approaches. He summarized:

> Groups of investigators must begin to concern themselves with the person—not only with the patient, but the underlying humanness. Not just with his or her disease, but with the body as a whole, with the feelings, the mind, and the spirit—even the spirit—of the patient. (Miller, 1974)

America's loss of faith in the traditional medical approach led to a paradigm shift from reliance on body technicians and the large institutional medical complex to attention to the potentials of self-help. John Naisbitt listed this whole shift in orientation as one of the "Megatrends" in our society's shift from the old to the new, and notes that there has been new attention to the whole concept of wellness.

> The new holistic health approach has opened up a new area in the search for health and wellness: the human mind. What constitutes a basic wellness program is simple and uncontroversial: regular exercise, healthy diet, no smoking, adequate rest, and stress control. Personal habits are the key element in the new health paradigm, so personal responsibility is critical...and that represents a real turnabout. In the past we believed our health was the doctor's responsibility. (Naisbitt, 1982)

The holistic health movement was described by Marilyn Ferguson as "Healing

Ourselves," because the new approach puts major emphasis on the complex body-mind relationship and the self-responsibility involved in both prevention and cure of disease and disability. This new approach should be recognized as an important part of the "Aquarian Conspiracy," which is concerned with guiding the transformation of human beings to higher order of existence. Ferguson lists some of the assumptions of the new paradigm for health as opposed to the traditional model, which include:

> ...recognizing the body as a dynamic system, a field of energy within other fields...
> ...focusing on the mind as a primary or coequal factor in all illness...
> ...viewing prevention of physical and mental breakdown as synonymous with wholeness, the healthy person will be concerned with prevention...
> ...recognition of the patient as autonomous... (Ferguson, 1980)

The American Holistic Health Association was formed in 1978. By that time there was a considerable body of literature emphasizing the potentials of the body-mind approach to health and healing (Samuels, 1973; Frank, 1974; Bromberg, 1975; Jaffee, 1976; Dychtwald, 1977; Pelletier, 1977; Ballentine, 1978). Holistic health centers had developed about the country, and there were nationwide workshops, seminars, retreats, conferences, and health fairs, devoted to educating the public about health alternatives and the mind-body factors in disease and wellness. There was attention to many of the methodologies which were already having an influence on challenge/adventure methodology: relaxation, awareness, breathing, stretching, centering, T'ai Chi, meditation, rituals of the Native American Indians, etc. The new orientation also focused people's attention on nu-

trition (including food selection, food preparation, organic gardening,etc.), fitness (aerobics, jogging, etc.), birth alternatives (midwives, home births, birthing centers, etc.), and cross-cultural practices (herbalism, acupuncture, etc.). The new orientation recognized the psychology of the person, the complexity of the mind-body dynamics, and self-responsibility for well-being (Fadiman & Gordon, 1980; Pelletier, 1980; Cousins, 1981).

Naisbitt, like Ferguson, and many others, related our society's attention to these new ideas about health and wellness to the whole human potential movement; but he also suggested that both movements were rooted, in part, in a dissatisfaction with the schools. He wrote:

> We have suspected that the schools were failing to educate our young. As we became more disillusioned we asked ""what, or whom, can we trust?" The resounding answer was "Ourselves." We recognized the need to become more self-sufficient. Motivated by mutual self-interest, we started to help each other and ourselves... Medically, self-help is taking responsibility for health habits, environment, and lifestyle; and it is demanding to be treated holistically. It is asking to be treated as a whole person; body, mind, and emotions.   (Naisbitt, 1982)

Challenge education is concerned with the total health state of clients, and those developing the theory and practice of challenge education have a history of interaction with professionals from the holistic health movement. One reason for the interaction was quite pragmatic. When evolving challenge and adventure programs needed medical consultation, it was typically those doctors and health professionals of alternative orientation who responded, for they recognized the potentials of the challenge methodology. When outdoor adventure challenge programs wanted medical consultation in programs with disabled clients, it was the holistic medical practitioner who helped.

An outstanding example of this cooperative interaction is that of the Vinland Center of Minnesota, Vinland was concerned with providing a comprehensive program of health, growth, rehabilitation and recreation for persons with disabilities, with special emphasis on outdoor sports and adventure recreation. The program was designed to guide the participants towards holistic health and positive lifestyle (Saari, 1981). The consulting physician for Vinland authored a manual, "Health Promotion, Wellness, and Medical SelfCare," noting:

> The concept of Vinland is that it is not composed of discrete programs of recreation or sports or arts/culture or social/personal development; but offers a comprehensive program linking them all together.   (Sehnert, 1981)

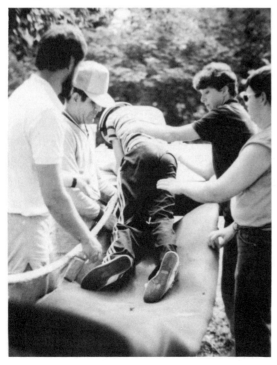

In recent years, many psychiatric, chemical dependency and rehabilitative programs have recognized the potential of the challenge methodology. The challenge leaders have become an integral part of interdisciplinary teams working to accomplish total treatment goals for clients. The involvement is more than as a simple "adjunct" to the psychiatric, rehabilitative, or medical goals; the challenge professional has come to be recognized as offering an important therapeutic and rehabilitative alternative. When challenge professionals are working with interdisciplinary teams, it could be said that they are having *direct connections* with professionals of the holistic health movement. However, all programs of challenge education have *indirect connections* with the holistic health movement, in that they seek to enhance the self-concept of clients, and guide them toward assuming self-responsibility for their life patterns. In many ways, challenge leaders can be considered holistic health educators.

Challenge education offers alternative strategies that can contribute to accomplishment of client goals in the holistic medical/rehabilitative program; and challenge educators have learned much from the alternative approaches of the holistic health professionals. It might be predicted that the relationship between challenge education and holistic health education will become even more complex in the future. It must be recognized that the goal is more than simply teaching others that a healthy mind means a healthy body, or that a healthy body means a healthy mind. The challenge is to guide others to know that there is only one process, that of developing a healthy *mindbody*.

2. Family Education. Psychologists, counselors, social workers, educators, and other human service professionals often utilize therapeutic and educational approaches for the family to better meet client goals. As counselors and educators, challenge leaders have also became involved with the family constellation. This has led to interaction with the more professionally trained family therapists and family educators. Challenge facilitators have sought to expand their personal skills, and improve their program offerings, by cultivating family involvements.

At least three different patterns of attention to families have had some impact on the development of challenge education.

(a) Family Therapy.

Some challenge programs have developed sequences that are essentially designed as therapeutic for families. This involves attempts to facilitate sequences of experiential activity that will lead to insights, improved trust and communication, and better problem solving and decision making skills, not only in the tasks-at-hand, but in the day-to-day functioning of the family unit. Sometimes, these offerings are not intensely psychodynamic, but simply offer the opportunity for the family to play together, explore together, and enjoy each other in exciting and challenging activities outdoors. This is, of course, still quite therapeutic for the total family constellation.

The practice of family therapy has been dated to the 1950's, when there was expanded recognition of the interplay between the individual and the social situation as influential in development of problems. Actually, even Freud had involved parents, as in the case of "little Hans," when he involved the father (Grotjahn, 1950). However, appropriate attention was not given to the family until the 1950's (Ackerman, 1958; Bateson, 1959). Theoretical overviews and therapeutic constructs developed thereafter.

Salvador Minuchin offered an approach called "Structured Family Therapy" inspired, in part, by the ideas of Bateson (Minuchin, 1974). This approach emphasized the process of communication and feedback, as the therapist and family "work together" to reorganize structured roles and functioning behaviors. The therapist is actually viewed as "joining" the family in tasks that can provide "mutual support, nurturance, and socialization" for the various members. The therapist has the role of introducing new ways of communicating and sharing feedback. This general model of family therapy can be recognized as having much potential for the challenge approach to activities and processing.

A second major orientation to family therapy is that of Virginia Satir, (1967) called "Conjoint Family Therapy." This is a more insight-searching orientation, with the therapist more of an observer of the process of family interaction. However, the therapist assumes responsibility for "creating a setting in which the family members can observe themselves and their actions objectively." Satir later authored a book written for parents, *Peoplemaking* (1972), which has often been recognized as valuable for the new student of family therapy. To Satir, problems and challenges are not something terrible, but the very stuff from which life is made. As families come to recognize their capability for dealing with problems, they move forward as a unit that can contribute to positive growth for all members.

Throughout the 1980's there was increasing attention given to the therapeutic impact of the challenge approach. As mental health clinics, psychiatric hospitals, drug treatment centers and rehabilitation programs incorporated challenge sequences into their total treatment package, challenge professionals have interacted with the other treatment specialists. Challenge leaders were exposed to, involved with, and impacted by orientations of individual, group, and family therapy. In turn, the challenge facilitators have educated those other professionals in the therapeutic potentials of challenge for individuals, groups, and families.

(b) Family Guidance/Education.

Sometimes, challenge educators have sought to help the family understand the problems and the world of the client with whom the challenge program is working. This approach would traditionally have involved didactic method, with lecture and discussion of information. The professionals would be teaching the family unit about the nature of the client's problem and potentials. As challenge professionals have become involved in this approach, they have brought their experiential orientation, and involved the total family in interactional learning.

There is a fine line between family therapy, and programs for family guidance, family education, and family enrichment. (There is parallel overlap between the so-called "personal growth experience," and procedures for psychotherapy.) However, the approach of educating the parent to better understand the child, the uniqueness of each child, and the potentialities of each child, has a history that is separate from that of family therapy.

Child psychology, as a field of scientific specialization, was an early subfield of psychology in America. By the 1940's, there was a significant body of information available, and professionals began to pass that information along to parents (Gesell, 1943). A predominant influence on parents and parenting practices in the 1950's was the classic work of Dr. Benjamin Spock (1957). In the 1960's, Haim Ginott had major impact with his *Between Parent and Child* (1965), and *Between Parent and Teenager* (1969). There were also important contributions from "Transactional Analysis" (T.A.) (Berne, 1964) and from "Parent Effectiveness Training" (P.E.T.) (Gordon, 1970). Less recognized, but important in retrospect, were the contributions of Dodson (1970), and those of Salk (1973).

Lee Salk made important observations on the importance of activity for learning. He would have been an advocate of the potential of challenge methodology for family education, as he had noted that parents should be careful not to interfere with the child's free play and exploration of body potentials, since "toys and the activity of play are the tools of education." He also noted that a reciprocity of love and respect must develop in the relationship between parent and child (Salk, 1973).

It was also in the 1970's that there was attention given to the special problems of parenting a child with disabilities (Poznanski, 1973). This area of focus has had significant impact on those challenge educators who have worked with special populations. One parent of a child with cerebral palsy recognized the potentials of challenge practice for building family unity. Judy Hoyt not only worked with her own son and family, but early in the 1980's initiated a program of "family challenge" for other families. There developed a comprehensive approach to "families as partners" in the basic rehabilitation and growth program for the disabled child (Roland & Hoyt, 1983; Roland, et al., 1986).

Challenge leaders have recognized that their methodology can contribute to enrichment of all families. A brochure from a social service agency, which offers a "Family Challenge" program, suggests:

The family challenge is a unique program combining adventure activity and professionally-facilitated discussion. Through challenging but achievable tasks your family can grow and experience the thrills of success—together. Attention is focused on how the family solves problems, how its members communicate, and how it adjusts to challenges. In the course of working, learning, and having fun together, the family becomes a more effective and confident unit. (Protestant Social Service Bureau, 1988)

Programs of family education and family enrichment are one of the many exciting applications of challenge methodology. As the 1990's unfold, challenge educators and family educators are, indeed, working together and having interactional influence.

(c) Alternative Family Education

Another area of "family" focus that has impacted on challenge education theory and practice is that of surrogate parents and alternative family models. There is a movement" in our society toward redefinition of the family and extension of the boundaries of "family connections. In spite of ongoing suggestions and efforts to restore the basic family constellation, from argument that this is the only way to overcome many of the complex problems of our society, it must be recognized that such hope is quite idealistic. The reality is that millions of children and adults in our society do not have, and will never have, connections with their blood-genetic family. Virginia Satir recognized this, and addressed the problem of "adapting the system to meet the challenge of redefinition of the family." (Satir, 1984)

Psychologists have recognized that human beings have complex needs for "belongingness," "connectedness," "sharing," and "love." Fulfillment of these needs is extremely important to the adjustment and actualization of every individual. Therefore, there must be attention given to alternative family models; without them many, many individuals would live lives of loneliness and incompleteness. Becoming an adequately adjusted and fully functioning human being means being connected to significant others. There are millions of children, adults, and senior citizens, living in foster homes, group homes, halfway houses and residential centers, who have no intimate connection to others. Challenge leaders have recognized this need, and have suggested that the challenge methodology offers promise for building alternative family systems (Smith, 1988).

As the 1990's unfold, there is a challenge before all society. How can we meet the needs of the individual for belonging and sharing just as the traditional family constellations become less frequent? The historical emphasis on the challenge methodology as building cohesive, caring and meaningful group affiliation, would certainly seem to have potential. It might be predicted that challenge educators and family educator/philosophers who are concerned with alternative family systems will find increasing value in interaction and exchange of ideas in the near future.

3. Group Dynamics Education

As development of the unique and multidimensional groupwork methodology that became challenge education unfolded, the leaders recognized the need for deeper understanding of group dynamics, and greater skills in group processes. The groupwork strategies associated with group psychotherapy, and with the alternatives recognized through the human potential movement, made contributions to challenge education. In addition, challenge professionals were influenced by the theoretical and strategic ideas of social psychologists and sociologists who focused on group dynamics. It was still the 1970's

when one experiential educator suggested the potential for "application of small group theory to adventure programs" (Jensen, 1979).

Two broad bodies of theory and research about group organization and group function can be identified. The first is mainly associated with social psychology, and the second offers a blend of sociological theory and concepts of organizational psychology.

(a) Social Psychology

Social psychological study of groups has a long history in the academic environment, but there has been limited application of many of the principles researched because there is no real profession of "applied social psychology." Much of the focus of social psychology can be traced to the "field theory" of Kurt Lewin (1959). However, all who work with groups, in education, counseling, recreation or elsewhere, can find value in the theory and research of the social psychologists. A list of the problems that have been given attention by social psychologists demonstrates the possibilities for attention by challenge educators. For example, social psychologists have written on "leadership," "group problem solving," "group cohesiveness," "role playing in groups," "group goal setting," "building of trust in groups," "heterogeneous vs. homogeneous group composition," and the process of "scapegoating." All of these phenomena are a part of the groups facilitated by challenge leaders. Three classic texts on social psychology provide a good starting point for the curious challenge leader: Lindzey, 1954; Maccoby, et al., 1958; Cartwright & Zander, 1968.

Other professionals have taken the research findings of the social psychologists into the field, and there are suggestions for developing groupwork skills that draw upon that research (Bonner, 1959; Stratford, 1977; Bolton, 1979; Larson, 1984).

(b) Interactional Theory

Two different theoretical approaches can be viewed as coming together in the work of the laboratory group (T-group) concepts of the 1960's. Symbolic Interactionism is rooted in the sociological theory of George Herbert Mead, and places emphasis on three elements of social phenomena: communication processes, interaction patterns, and the subjective meaning of these phenomena to the individual. Basically, the individual conducts himself/herself in terms of the meanings assessed to the various communications and interactions (Mead, 1934; Blumer, 1969). The psychoanalytic approach of Harry Stack Sullivan is offered as Interpersonal Theory, with emphasis on social interaction as important to the development and functioning of personality (Sullivan, 1947, 1949).

When Kurt Lewin worked at the Massachusetts Institute of Technology in the 1940's, he offered the idea that training people in human relations skills was an important, but often overlooked, dimension of education. It was shortly after his death that the first T-group (T stood for training) developed. Lewin's colleagues and students carried on the concept, and the National Training Laboratories were formed (Bradford, et al., 1961). The primary thrust of the NTL program was toward business and industry, but through the years the methods for cultivation of human relations skills was extended to educators, counselors, and all persons who worked with groups.

It was in the tradition of NTL that professors at MIT suggested a new field of theory and research, separate from the traditions of sociology, social psychology, industrial psychology, and other fields which had made contributions to the new orientation. Interpersonal Relations was offered as an interdisciplinary field, and the goal of a first textbook was to "sketch out the conceptual territory and boundaries of the field...more clearly, coherently, and integratively than has been done before" (Bennis, et al., 1964). The authors recognize the major contributions of Mead's theory, and the works of Sullivan, and also suggest that the new orientation draws from other neo-Freudians who emphasized social interactions (Melanie Klein), and from the existential psychologists and psychiatrists. Their overview to the text summarizes:

> We can divide the problems Man faces into two classes, the noninteractional or the man-in-relationship-to-nature, and the interactional or man-in-relationship-to-man. (Bennis, et al., 1964)

The topical focus of these interpersonal relations theorists are, indeed, different from those of traditional social psychology. Instead of dealing with the patterns of group dynamics studied by the social psychologists (leadership, role behavior, etc.), they focus on the more reality-based concepts of "intimacy," "loneliness," "establishing identity," "trust," etc. It was suggested that the whole laboratory method, and the emphasis on interpersonal relations, "does not fit into the conventional categories of education or therapy . . . it contains elements of both processes but maintains its uniqueness" (Schein & Bennis, 1966).

The attention to questions of trust, openness, sharing, and the many other real-life phenomena which were often deemed too abstract to be studied by scientific approach, should be of great concern to challenge education professionals. Some challenge leaders have already found ideas in the applications of interpersonal relations theory as suggested by Jack Gibb (Gibb, 1971, 1972). TORI is the name Gibb gives to a new view of personal and organizational development; TORI is an acronym for the four core processes of the group

"Trust-being,"
"Opening-sharing,"
"Realizing-growing," and
"Interdependency-teaming."

Gibb considers his approach "Trust Level Theory," and recognizes it as a dynamic and "flowing" model, which parallels the nature of human beings. His concept of life and living as an unfolding process of activity and flow has much overlap with the approach of challenge education (See Chapter 2 for a further overview of Trust Level Theory). He writes:

> The essence of living, both experience and behavior, seems to be that it flows. The body/mind that functions best seems to be one that is into the flow, the continual movement of energy, the bioenergetic systems, the internal symphony of flowing processes. The mind/body is glorious process. It is a oneness in mind, body, spirit. It enters into synchronic and harmonious flow with other living organisms in the environment. Some flow models seem to fit human systems best. The river of life, the stream of consciousness, the ebb and flow of feeling, the rhythms of the body. The experiences of sailing, skating, dancing, and flying seem to strike a kind of polyphony with the inner rhythms of the spirit and physical body. The TORI discovering processes happen, emerge, flow, and arise

out of the field of interaction between the person and the world.   (Gibb, 1978)

In his examples of flowing experiences, Gibb might well have included skiing, climbing, group lifting experiences, and other challenge exercises.

4. Spiritual Education. Life as journey is a common metaphor. Journey as adventure, or adventure as journey, are often discussed by challenge and adventure leaders. The journey is one of searching about the "wilderness beyond" and the "wilderness within." The search is a spiritual quest, as each person seeks personal answers to the age-old questions of "who am I?," "why am I?," "where am I going?," and "what is my relationship to all that is?"

This "Journey of Faith," as it has been called, has been a part of all people, all cultures, through all time—although for many, sometimes or always, it is an unconscious journey. Each generation, each culture, each religious orientation, has offered commentary on the journey. As summarized by Jerome Berryman:

> Lao Tzu talked of the Tao, which in one translation has been translated as *The Way*. Buddhists speak of the *Mbhayana*, which is translated as the *Great Way*. The Hindus refer to the *Devayana*, of the *Way of the Gods*. Christ said, "I am the Way." Moses showed the people of Israel the way out of bondage into the *Promised Land*. In Islam, the Prophet Mohammed led the *Way to Mecca*. There is the *sirat almustaquim*, sometimes translated as the *Straight Way*, and there is the Sufic *taruqagm* or *Way*. The *Straight Way* is the theme in both the Psalms and the Gospels. The Sioux trod the *Red Road*, and the Japanese sought the *Shondo*, or Holy

52

Path. The image of the journey is universal. (Berryman, 1978)

Since mid-century, the quest for spiritual faith has tended to shift from the church-related, organized-religion-sponsored, authoritarian model to a more personalized, self-responsibility methodology. This trend was outlined in the writings of a number of theologians and philosophers who were of the existential, humanistic, holistic orientation (Tillich, 1952, 1957; Vahanian, 1957; Buber, 1958, 1961; Smith, 1963; Keen, 1970; Neibuhr, 1972).

The challenge education movement acknowledges relationship to that trend presently unfolding in our society. To the extent that the American system has brought most people beyond focus on basic biological needs, and moved beyond the attention to social interactional needs of the 1960's and 1970's, there has been increasing attention to what can be considered as "spiritual education." A number of attitudinal surveys of the 1970's reflected the changes. In 1978, *McCalls* magazine reported an overwhelming skepticism about organized religion; and this was supported by a Gallup poll later in the same year. It was noted that over 60% of churchgoers agreed with the statement: "Most churches have lost the real spiritual part of religion." Yet, another Gallup poll showed that nearly 80% of college students wanted "spiritual meaning" (Ferguson, 1980). It was suggested that the journey has become more personalized, more self-directed, and that people were reaching out to new experiences that could guide them in the search.

Many leaders of the human potential movement, concerned with humanistic and holistic education, also made references to spiritual education. In a summarization of reflections on the theory and practice of Carl Gustav Jung, it was noted that becoming a whole person means finding ourselves beyond ourselves:

> The divine paradox is this—becoming complete, becoming whole as individuals, means that our completion is not limited to the bag of skin in which we live. Rather, it makes us open and porous, utterly permeable to the universal source of strength outside ourselves. The source is not really "outside," although it may in the beginning be so experienced. It is the great Self, of which our experiential self is a part, a participant, an integral part of the very ultimate order. (Singer, 1972)

James Fowler and Sam Keen offered suggestions of "Life Maps" for the journey of faith, based on the developmental theories of Erickson (1963) and Kohlberg (1969). They suggest a process view of faith, with the metaphor of the human journey, noting:

> We form and reform who we are as persons making our way... Faith development occurs as the result of an individual's interaction with his environment. (Fowler & Keen, 1978)

Such a quotation is remarkably parallel to the thinking of those who advocate environmental and social interaction to enhance awareness of self, others, environment, and other. In fact, to the extent that the challenge group facilitator has drawn from the traditions of outdoor education and environmental education there is long history of the wilderness journey as a journey of the spirit (Emerson, Whitman, Thoreau, Muir, etc.). Emerson had suggested that man would find the answers to those important questions of the journey if he opened himself to nature: "Man should take up the universe into himself. Yonder mountain must migrate into his mind" (Emerson, 1929).

This same sentiment has been restated with direct attention to the relationship between sensing nature and sensing the morality of humanity: "To recover the moral sense of our humanity, we would need to recover first the moral sense of nature" (Kohak, 1984).

The strategies of challenge education, especially those which cultivate the individual's sense of potency and confidence to meet new situations, also relates to spiritual education. Emerson, in fact, noted that the individual must rely on personal resources and personal strengths in the search for personal meaning. Teachers could guide, but the individual is ultimately self-responsible:

> Tis little we can do for each other. We accompany the youth with sympathy to the gate of the arena, but it is certain that not by ours but only on strengths of his own he must stand or fall. (Emerson, 1929)

Challenge education's emphasis on guiding the individual and the group to new adventures and innovative activities that involve commitment, risktaking and stretching of personal expectations, encourages the individual to self-responsibility, and thus contributes to the personal quest for faith. Speaking of experiential programs that involve challenge and adventure, one experiential educator wrote:

> Experiential programs help us manage our fear; we learn to realize that growth in life involves risks—and living with new people is part of the risk-taking—the stranger without teaching the stranger within us. The extent to which the stran-ger threatens us and we are un-comfortable with ourselves, to that extent we are ripe for growth. (MacArthur, 1985)

The author goes on to suggest that the very risk-taking skills that are cultivated by the experiential program can ready one for the spiritual quest. In that sense, experiential education is spiritual education. He quotes Parker J. Palmer, who seems to relate risk-taking and explorations of new and frightening experiences with the world and with others even more directly to the journey of faith.

> The religious quest, the spiritual pilgrimage, is always taking us into new lands where we are strange to others and they are strange to us. Faith is a venture into the unknown, into the realms of mystery, away from the safe and comfortable and secure. (Palmer, 1983)

It has been suggested that the rituals and cosmological perspectives of the Native American Indians have made contribution to challenge education methodology. This will be discussed in greater detail in the next section, but it is important to note that there is also contribution to spiritual education. The prime example would be the "Vision Quest" of the plains Indians, which can certainly be considered a spiritual journey. This practice plays a central role in the popular novel *Hanta Yo* (Hill, 1979). It has been related to the emphasis on solo journey in the wilderness, or to a quiet "special place" for introspective reflection. The "vision quest" was designed as a time for what Rudolf Steiner has called "inner work," which is a necessity if one is to "unlock the divine within."

Erich Fromm, (1950) long ago suggested that maladjustment in individuals, and pathology in cultures, could be traced to the failure to provide for the development of the "moral and spiritual potentials." As our society comes to understand this, and seeks to develop meaningful strategies for spiritual education, challenge education methodology may make significant contributions.

5. Native American Indian Education.

There is a body of information on the rituals, customs, ceremonies, beliefs, games, healing exercises, and general life patterns of the Native American Indians. This wealth of data has been recorded by historians, ethnologists, anthropologists, journalists, naturalists, and by the Indians themselves. This information can be considered the content of "Native American Indian Education," and it must be recognized as having considerable impact on the developing theory and practice of challenge education. Many of the methodologies which have contributed to challenge education have also been influenced by this package of knowledge. Outdoor education, camping education, awareness education, somatic education, recreation education, adventure education, humanistic education, health education, and spiritual education have all been influenced by Indian education; one can find references to the Native Americans in the literature of every one of those interrelated fields.

The American Indians tended to have a conceptual overview of life that stressed man in harmony with the universe, man in balance with the world he was a flowing part of, and man in balance within himself. There were obvious differences in belief and practice from tribe to tribe, and historians have noted that there were even some myth and ritual changes from time to time within the same tribe. Also, it may be that any common denominator value orientation of the Indians has been romanticized by those who recognize the appropriateness of seeing the interconnected-

ness of all things. In any case, over the past few decades there has been a good deal of attention paid to the rituals, ceremonies, and cosmological belief systems of the Indians.

Three books published in the 1970's received attention by professionals in education, and also by the public at large. Dee Brown's *Bury My Heart At Wounded Knee* (1971) summarized the difficulty of the American Indians' attempts to hang on to their heritage and customs as the white man impacted. The historical novel, *Hanta Yo*, covered a century of lifespan for the Indians of the Plains, and was widely read (Hill, 1979). Many likened the saga of *Hanta Yo* to the story of the Blacks in America, *Roots* (Haley, 1976).

Probably the most influential book in terms of attention by eduators and growth

facilitators, was *Seven Arrows*. (Storm, 1972) *Seven Arrows* offers an adventure based on the Plains Indians' view of life and the universe, which reads in format for growth and learning. Based on the tenants of the "medicine wheel," the book acts as a manual for a personal growth journey for the reader. The medicine wheel schema was recognized as having potential as the format for a personal growth group sequence (LaChapelle & Bourque, 1976; Smith, 1979, 1981). As more and more environmental educators reacted to the challenge of guiding students toward a greater understanding of the earth and the interdependency of person and earth, the ideas and wisdom of *Seven Arrows*, the medicine wheel, and the teaching stories were widely adapted.

There were other books about the Native Americans that were often found in the hands of evolving challenge educators. *Touch the Earth* offered perspectives on the earth, the spiritual journey of the people, and the interactional problems created by value orientation conflicts between the red man and the white man. The words of prominent and poetic Native Americans of the past flow with wisdom for the present and the future (McLuhan, 1971).

Rolling Thunder is the story and teachings of an American Indian medicine man–spiritual leader, philosopher. With sponsorship from the Menninger Foundation, Doug Boyd studied both Far Eastern Hindu traditions of health and medical practice, and the procedures for growth and healing of the Native American Indians. The words of Rolling Thunder have relevance to much of contemporary environmental education.

> The earth is a living organism, the body of a higher individual who has a will and wants to be well, who at times is less healthy or more healthy. People should treat their own bodies with respect. It's the same thing with the earth. Too many people don't know that when they harm the earth they harm themselves, nor do they realize that when they harm themselves they harm the earth. (Boyd, 1974)

Of relevance to the holistic health orientation, and the potentials of sun energy for well-being, Rolling Thunder said:

> You can take a glass of water, pray over it in the morning when the sun's coming up. When the sun is rising in the morning, vibrations—what you would call vibrations of the earth, we call it the Great Spirit's power—are the strongest, and they're bringing forth new life. Let the rays of the sun hit that water and you can make medicine out of it. (Ibid.)

And, of relevance to the whole process of knowledgeable leaders working to facilitate personal growth, learning, and consciousness expansion in the young and the seeking:

> There are a lot of people who want to do something and they don't know what to do, and we have to get it together. There are a lot of people ready to learn something, and they don't know where it's at. If the people can come together to really learn, people who have a real purpose, there is a lot to be done. (op.cit.)

Lame Deer, Seeker of Visions, was a holy man of the Lakota Sioux, whose story in autobiographical style tells of the sacredness of the rocks and the earth, the way of the dance, the value of darkness, and the meaning of many ceremonials and rituals (sun dance, sweat lodge, heyokas, etc.). Somatic educators, awareness educators, and adventure educators, as well as outdoor educators and environmental educators, have found relevance in Lame Deer's words. For example, of concern to those seeking to enrich growth and learning by expanding sensory awareness, Lame Deer offers these words:

> Let's sit down here on the open prairie. Let's have no blankets to sit on, but feel the ground with our bodies—the earth, the yielding shrubs. Let's have the grass for a mattress, experiencing its sharpness and its softness. Let's listen to the air. You can hear it, feel it, smell it, taste it. (Lame Deer & Erdoes, 1972)

Black Elk Speaks, was originally published in 1932, and was reissued to acclaim in 1972. Black Elk was also a Sioux, who had witnessed as a boy of thirteen the Battle at Little Big Horn. He tells of his own "vision quests," and the wisdom he found there (Neihardt, 1972). Some years later, Black Elk gave a more detailed account of the seven major ceremonial rites of the Oglala Sioux (Brown, 1971). One of the rituals, the Tapa Wanka Yap (Throwing of the Ball), was an interactional game, remarkably parallel to some of those suggested by the new games education. A large ball, which represents the universe, is passed about by four groups in an attempt to move it through goals placed in the four directions of wisdom. Black Elk noted that, "Everybody was able to have the ball, as all of us are part of the Universe."

One of Black Elk's commentaries is about the significance of the circle. It has been used as a "reading" at the start of challenge education workshops for personal growth journeys, in order to emphasize the importance of the basic "tribal circle" which the group settles into after experiences for purposes of sharing thoughts and feelings (Smith, 1979, 1983).

> You have noticed that everything an Indian does is in a circle, and that is because the Power of the World always works in circles, and everything tries to be round. In the old days, when we were strong and happy people, all our power came to us from the sacred hoop of the nation, and so long as the hoop was unbroken, the people flourished. The flowering tree was living center of the hoop, and the circle of the four quarters nourished it... Everything the Power of the World does is done in a circle. The sky is round, and I have heard that the earth is round like a ball, and so are all the stars. The wind, in its great power, whirls. The sun comes forth and goes down in a circle. The moon does the same, and both are round. Even the seasons form a great circle in their changing, and always come back to where they were. (Black Elk)

Frank Waters interpreted Native American life and behavior in a number of books and stories, and is a recognized expert on the Indians of the Southwest (Hopi, Pueblo, Zuni, Navaho, etc.). His book, *Masked Gods*, first appeared in 1950, but was reprinted in 1970 at the time of great interest in the wisdom of the Native Americans. He later wrote the following words on the connectedness of all that is:

> Nothing is simple and alone. We are not separate and alone. The breathing mountains, the living stones, each blade of grass, the clouds, the rain, each star, the beasts, the birds, and the invisible spirits of the air—we are all one, indivisible. Nothing that any of us does does but affect us all. (Waters, 1970)

Francis Densmore was another scholar of the Native Americans, and through the first half of this century many of his papers were published by the U.S. Government's Bureau of Indian Affairs. LaChapelle (1973) offers a quotation from one of Densmore's interviews, which relates to the relationship between people and the animals. Many challenge sequences involve exercises, fantasies, games, and interactions that attempt to cultivate the participant's consciousness about self and about the important interdependency of all creatures. This quotation can serve as a cognitive stimulus to parallel the emotional learning of such experiences.

> I have noticed in my life that all men have a liking for some special animal, or plant, or spot of earth. If men would pay more attention to these preferences and

seek what is best to do in order to make themselves worthy of that toward which they are so attracted, they might have dreams which would purify their lives. Let a man decide upon his favorite animal and make a study of it, learning its ways. Let him learn to understand the sounds and the motions. The animals want to communicate with man, but Wakan-Tanka does not intend they shall do so directly— man must do the greater part in securing an understanding. (Brave Buffalo)

Many environmental educators and challenge educators have been influenced by Tom Brown, author of *The Tracker* (1978) and *The Search* (1980). His background of tutorial interaction with an elderly Apache, Stalking Wolf, helped him develop a "teaching school" for tracking, wilderness survival, and environmental awareness. Brown believes that he was "chosen" by Stalking Wolf, in order to pass along the ancient teachings and skills. One journalist spent a week in the Tom Brown School of Tracking, Nature, and Wilderness Survival, and offers this comment from Brown:

> I believe that teaching survival gets to people's hearts, that when a person learns how to enter the world purely, unencumbered by society, where you live a hand-to-mouth existence with the earth, a connection develops. That's why I run this school, to bring as many people as possible back to the earth, and to send them out to teach other people. I hope that when you go home you will have a new love and respect for the earth, that you will have a full commitment to help save it... Please...Time is running out. (Tom Brown, in Krautwurst, 1988)

That author summarized his experience with the Tom Brown School:

> I've gained a greater sense of my place in the world, and a heightened awareness of the life around me. I have begun, in a small way, to feel what the Native Americans called "the spirit that moves in all things." (Krautwurst, 1988)

Dover Publications, a company that reproduces historic books in demand by educators, offered a series of texts on the Native Americans, many of which have made contributions to the evolving methods of challenge education (e.g., Curtis, 1968; Densmore, 1974; Cullin, 1975; Parker, 1975). These publications provide a wealth of information on rituals, ceremonies, games, dances, songs, chants, and stories, many of which have been blended into challenge sequences. The University of Nebraska Press also reissued books, including a series of teaching stories and folk tales originally collected by George Bird Grinnell. The series includes *Pawnee Hero Stories and Folk-Tales* (1961), *Blackfoot Lodge Tales* (1962), and *By Cheyenne Campfires* (1971).

In the 1980's, a concept of psychotherapeutic intervention called Hakomi was offered as a system for "creating change on a deep emotional level." The system is based on an ancient Hopi belief about the importance of standing in good relationship to the many realms of being. The main belief behind Hakomi Therapy is that each person forms basic value orientations about self, others, and the world in early childhood, and these become adult "maps" that must be discarded for improved growth and expanded consciousness (Kurtz, 1985).

There have also been some noteworthy theoretical and methodological offerings based on the Indians of Central America and South America. ARICA, which means "open door" in the language of Bolivian Indians, was a training center founded by Oscar Ichazo. ARICA offered a sequence of leadership training and personal growth to a higher consciousness, and emphasizes usage of "solo time" in order to develop skills of self-observation (Ichazo, 1976).

Another approach, from the Chilean psychiatrist, Claudio Naranjo, put emphasis on meditation, sensory awareness, and psychotropic search for "peak experiences" (Nar-

anjo, 1976). Naranjo was influential on the thinking of Robert Ornstein, with whom he authored a book on meditation (Naranjo & Ornstein, 1971). Ornstein later produced his theory of right brain/left brain consciousness (1972), which evolved into his theory of "multimind" (Ornstein, 1986).

Finally, one must mention the influence of Carlos Castaneda, whose five years as a pupil of a Yaqui Indian shaman of Mexico produced the classic series that began with *The Teachings of Don Juan* (Castaneda,

1968). Challenge education facilitators, as well as many other educators and therapists, have often been inspired by the wisdom of that series (Castaneda, 1971, 1972, 1974). While the journey is recorded as an intellectual one by Castaneda, he admits that there is need to "put forth dramatic exertion" in order to meet the challenge of change. The ultimate goal is to become a part of the process of learning, and growing, and becoming.

At the academic level, the 1970's and 1980's brought development of special curricula in "Native American Studies" to many colleges and universities. Graduate students in other fields also attended to the ways of the Native Americans, and there were studies of relevance from students in outdoor education, recreation, physical education, and experiential education. Many focused on the potentials for applying Native American practices to their own field (e.g., Quinn, 1988).

Starting in the 1970's and continuing on to the present, professional conferences and training symposiums have offered workshops and instruction on the ritual and ceremony of the Native Americans, as adaptable for educational, counseling, and adventure groups. There have been presentations at national meetings of the Association for Humanistic Psychology, the Association for Experiential Education, the Council for Exceptional Children, the American Camping Association, the Association for Health, Physical Education, Recreation and Dance, and many other groups.

There is no doubt that the wisdom, the philosophy, the ritual, and the cosmological consciousness of the Hopi, the Yaqui, the Apache, the Lakota and Oglala Sioux, and many other Native American cultures, as reported by the medicine men, the storytellers, and the chroniclers, offer a tradition of "Native American Indian Education" which has relevance to challenge education. The ideas and the methodologies must be modified and adapted to meet the needs of the new approaches. Rolling Thunder noted:

> I want to warn you not to copy me, but to work out your own method. Our people tell us to be original. If you can watch the method, though, maybe that would give you some thoughts to follow... then you work out your own songs, your own prayers, and things to go with it. (Boyd, 1974)

The interaction between those who offer Native American Indian education and those developing challenge education has a meaningful history. Challenge educators have creatively adapted the rituals and ceremonies of the Indians, and these adaptations have had meaningful influences on the challenge methodology.

REFERENCES

Ackerman, N. (1958). *Psychodynamics of Family Life.* New York: Basic Books.

Allport, G. (1955). *Becoming: Basic Considerations for a Psycholoqy of Personality.* New Haven: Yale University Press.

Andrews, G. (1954). *Creative Rhythmic Movement For Children.* New York: Prentice-Hall.

Arnheim, D. D. & Sinclair, W. A. (1985). *Physical Education for Special Populations.* New York: Prentice-Hall.

Assagioli, R. (1965). *Psychosynthesis: A Manual of Principles and Techniques. New York: Hobbs, Dorman, & Company.*

Assagioli, R. (1974). *The Act of Will.* New York: Viking Press/Penguin.

Austin, D. (1982). *Therapeutic Recreation: Processes and Techniques.* New York: John Wiley & Sons.

Auxter, D. & Pyfer, J. (1989). *Principles and Methods of Adapted Physical Education and Recreation.* New York: Times-Mirror/Mosby College Press.

Avedon, E. M. (1974). *Therapeutic Recreation Service: An Applied Behavior Science Approach.* Englewood Cliffs, NJ: Prentice-Hall.

Baker, C. W. (1978, January). Year 'round camping through adventure programming. *Campinq Magazine.*

Ballentine, R. (1978). *Diet and Nutrition: A Holistic Approach.* Honesdale, PA.: Himalayan International Institute.

Bancroft, J. (1909). *Games for the Playground, Home, School, and Gymnasium.* New York: Macmillan Company.

Barker, R. G. (1948). The social psychology of physical disability. *Journal of Social Issues, 4* (1).

Barker, R. G. & Wright, B. A. (1952). The social psychology of adjustment to physical disability. In J. F. Garrett (Ed.), *Psychological Aspects of Disability.* Washington, DC: U.S. Dept. of Health, Education, & Welfare.

Bartal, L. & Ne'eman, N. (1975). *Movement Awareness and Creativity.* New York: Harper & Row.

Bateson, G. (1959). *Individual and Family Dynamics.* New York: Grune & Stratton.

Bennis, W., Schein, E., Berlew, D., & Steel, F. (1964). *Interpersonal Dynamics: Essays and Readings in Human Interaction.* Homewood, IL: Dorsey Press.

Berne, E. (1964). *Games People Play.* New York: Bantam Books.

Berryman, J. (1978). The life/faith journey. In *Life Maps: Conversations On the Journey of Faith.* Minneapolis, MN: Winston Press, 1978.

Big Rock Candy Mountain. (1970) Menlo Park, CA: Portola Institute.

Binswanger, L. (1958). The existential analysis school of thought. In May, R. (Ed.), *Existence.* New York: Basic Books.

Blumer, H. (1969). *Symbolic Interactionsis.* Englewood Cliffs, NJ: Prentice-Hall.

Bolton, R. (1979). *People Skills.* Englewood Cliffs, NJ: Prentice-Hall.

Bonner, H. (1959). *Group Dynamics: Principles and Application.* New York: Ronald Press.

Bradford, L., Gibb, J., & Benne, K. (Eds.) publication date? *T-Group Theory and Laboratory Method.* New York: Wiley.

Brannan, S. (1975). Trends and issues in leisure education for the handicapped through continuing education. In Fanchier, E. & Neal, L. (Eds.) *Common Unity in the Community.* Portland, OR: University of Oregon, Center for Leisure Studies.

Brannan, S. (1981). *The EXPLORE Program.* Portland, OR: University of Oregon, Explore Program.

Brannan, S. (1981). *A Holistic Approach to Outdoor Education and the Handicapped.* Lexington, KY: University of Kentucky Press.

Brannan, S, Rillo, T., Roland, C., & Smith, T. (1984). Current issues in camping and outdoor education with persons who are disabled. In Robb, G. (Ed.) *Bradford Papers, 4.*

Breeding, J. (1985). Hope for the people and the planet: truly powerful survivors. *Journal of Experiential Education, 8.*

Bromberg, W. (1975). *From Shaman to Psychotherapist.* (reprinted from the first edition, 1937) Chicago, IL: Henry Regnecy Co.

Brown, D. (1972). *Bury My Heart At Wounded Knee.* New York: Bantam Books.

Brown, G. I. (1971). *Human Teaching for Human Learning: An Introduction To Confluent Education.* New York: Viking Press.

Brown, J. E. (1971). *The Sacred Pipe.* (reprinted from the first edition, J. E. Brown recording Black Elk, 1953). New York: Penguin Books.

Brown, J. E. (1982). *The Spiritual Legacy of the American Indians*. New York: Crossroad Press.

Brown, T. (1978). *The Tracker*. Englewood Cliffs, NJ: Prentice-Hall.

Brown, T. (1980). *The Search*. Englewood Cliffs, NJ: Prentice-Hall.

Buber, M. (1958). *I and Thou*. (translated by R. G. Smith). New York: Charles Scribners & Son.

Buber, M. (1961). *Between Man and Man*. Boston: Beacon Press.

Canfield, J. & Wells, H. (1976). *One Hundred Ways To Enhance Self-Concept In The Classroom*. Englewood Cliffs, NJ: Prentice-Hall.

Carlson, R. (1975). The values of camping. (Occasional Paper.) Martinsville, IN: American Camping Association.

Carlson, R. (1980). Innovations for the future: where have we come and where are we going? In Robb, G. (Ed.), *Bradford Papers, l.* Bloomington, IN: Indiana University Press.

Carlson, R. J. (1975). *The End of Medicine*. New York: John Wiley.

Carlson, R. J. (1981). Health care: 21st century. In Villoldo, A. & Dychtwald, K. (Eds.), *Millennium: Glimpses Into the 21st Century*. Los Angeles, CA: J. P. Tarcher, Inc.

Carson, R. (1957). *Silent Spring*. New York: Harper & Row.

Carson, R. (1959). *The Sense of Wonder*. New York: Harper & Row.

Castaneda, C. (1968). *Teaching of Don Juan*. New York: Simon & Schuster.

Castaneda, C. (1971). *A Separate Reality*. New York: Simon & Schuster.

Castaneda, C. (1972). *Journey to Ixtlan*. New York: Simon & Schuster.

Castaneda, C. (1974). *Tales of Power*. New York: Simon & Schuster.

Cartwright, D. & Zander, A. (Eds.). publication date? *Group Dynamics: Research and Theory. 3rd Edition.* Evanston, IL: Row, Peterson, & Co.

Cohen, M. (1986). *How Nature Works: Regenerating Kinship With Planet Earth*. New York: World Peace University.

Combs, A. & Snygg, D. (1959). *Individual Behavior: A Perceptual Approach to Behavior*. New York: Harper & Row.

Combs, A., Richards, A. & Richards, F. (1976). *Perceptual Psychology: A Humanistic Approach to the Study of Persons*. New York: Harper & Row.

Combs, A. (Ed.). (1962). *Perceiving, Behaving, Becoming*. Washington, DC: Yearbook ASCD, National Education Association.

Compton, D. (1981). Therapeutic recreation at the crossroads. In Hitzhusen, G. (Ed.), *Expanding Horizons in Therapeutic Recreation* (vol. 9). Columbia, MI: University of Missouri Press.

Comstock, A. (1919). *Handbook of Nature Study*. Ithaca, NY: Comstock Publications.

Cornell, J. (1979). *Sharing Nature With Children*. Nevada City, CA: Ananda Publishing.

Cornell, J. (1987). *Listening to Nature*. Nevada City, CA: Dawn Publications.

Cornell, J. (1989). *Sharing the Joy of Nature: Nature Activities for All Ages*. Nevada City, CA: Dawn Publications.

Cousins, N. (1981). *Anatomy of An Illness*. New York: Bantam Books.

Cratty, B. (1971). *Active Learning*. Englewood Cliffs, NJ: Prentice-Hall.

Csaky, M. (1979). *How Does It Feel: Exploring the World of Your Senses*. New York: Harmony Books.

Csikszentmihayli, M. (1975). *Beyond Boredom and Anxiety*. San Francisco, CA: Josey-Bass.

Cullin, S. (1975). *Games of the North American Indians*. (reprinted from the 1902 edition). New York: Dover Publications, Inc.

Curtis, N. (1968). *The Indians' Book*. (reprinted from the 1907 edition). New York: Dover Publications, Inc.

Curtis, S. (1982) *The Joy of Movement in Childhood*. New York: Teachers Colleqe Press.

Daniels, A. & Davies, E. (1954). *Adaptive Physical Education*. New York: Harper & Row.

Darst, P. & Armstrong, C. (1986). *Outdoor Adventure Activities for Schools and Recreation Programs*. Minneapolis, MN: Burgess Publishing.

Delza, S. (1961). *T'ai Chi Ch'uan: Body and Mind in Harmony*. North Canton, OH: Good News Publishing.

DeMille, R. (1967). *Put Your Mother On The Ceiling: Childrens' Imagination Games*. Chicago, IL: Walker Press.

Densmore, F. (1974). *How Indians Use Wild Plants for Food, Medicine, and Crafts*. (reprinted from the 1928 edition). New York: Dover Publications, Inc.

Dewey, J. (1938). *Education and Experience*. New York: Macmillian & Co.

Dewey, J. (1956). *Philosophy of Education* (1956 edition). New York: Littleford, Adams, & Co.

Dodson, F. (1970). *How To Parent*. New York: New American Library.

Dychtwald, K. (1977). *Bodymind*. New York: Jove Press.

Eckstein, B. (1969). *The Body Has A Head*. New York: Harper & Row.

Emerson, R. W. (1929). *Complete Writings of Ralph Waldo Emerson.* New York: William Wise and Company.

Ericksen, C. (1958). Unconscious processes. In Jones, M. R. (Ed.). *Nebraska Symposium On Motivation.* Lincoln, NE: University of Nebraska Press.

Erickson, E. (1963). *Childhood and Society* (revised edition). New York: W. W. Norton Co.

Fadiman, J. & Gordon, J. (Eds.) (1980). *Health for the Whole Person.* Boulder, CO: Westview Press.

Feldenkrais, M. (1972). *Awareness Through Movement.* New York: Harper & Row.

Fensterman, K. (1981). *Relaxation: An Introduction to Relaxation Techniques With Adaptations for Persons With Disabilities.* Loretto, MN: Vinland National Center.

Ferguson, M. (1978). *The Aquarian Conspiracy.* New York: Harper & Row.

Flemming, R. (Ed.) (1963). *Curriculum for Today's Boys and Girls.*

Columbus, OH: Charles E. Merrill, Inc.

Fluegelman, A. (1976). *The New Games Book.* Garden City, NY: Doubleday.

Fluegelman, A. (1981). *More New Games.* Garden City, NY: Doubleday.

Ford, P. (1981). *Principles and Practices of Outdoor/Environmental Education.* New York: John Wiley & Sons.

Fowler, J. & Keen, S. (1978). *Life Maps: Conversations of the Journey of Faith.* Minneapolis, MN: Winston Press.

Frant, R., Roland, C., & Schempp, D. (1982). Learning through outdoor adventure. *Reaching Exceptional Children, 14.*

Fromm, E. (1950). *Psychoanalysis and Religion.* New Haven: Yale University.

Fry, V. & Peters, M. (1972). *Therapeutic Recreation: Its Theory, Philosophy, and Practice.* Harrisburg, PA: Stackpole Books.

Gager, R. (1977). Experiential education: strengthening the learning process. *Journal of Experiential Education, 1.*

Galland, J. (1982). *An Introduction to Kayaking: For Persons With*

Disabilities. Loretto, MN: Vinland National Center.

Gallwey, W. (1974). *The Inner Game of Tennis.* New York: Random House.

Geba, B. (1973). *Breathe Away Your Tension.* New York: Random House/Bookworks.

Gell, H. (1973). *Music, Movement, and the Young Child.* Erasmas, PA: Volkwein Brothers.

Gesell, A. & Ilg, F. (1943). *Infant and Child in Culture Today.* New York: Harper & Row.

Gibb, J. (1971). TORI community. In Egan, G. (Ed.) *Encounter Groups: Basic Readings.* Belmont, CA: Brooks/Cole.

Gibb, J. (1972). TORI: theory and practice. In Pfeiffer, J. & Jones, J. (Eds.) *Annual Handbook for Group Facilitators.* Iowa City, IA: University Associates.

Gibb, J. (1978). *Trust: A New View of Personal and Organizational Development.* Los Angeles, CA: Guild of Tutors Press.

Ginott, H. (1965). *Between Parent and Child.* New York: Macmillan.

Ginott, H. (1969). *Between Parent and Teenager.* New York: Macmillan.

Gordon, T. (1970). *Parent Effectiveness Training.* New York: New American Library.

Grinnell, G. B. (1961). *Pawnee Hero Stories and Folk-Tales.* (reprinted from the 1889 edition). University of Nebraska Press.

Grinnell, G. B. (1962). *Blackfoot Lodge Tales.* (reprinted from the 1892 edition). University of Nebraska Press.

Grinnell, G. B. (1971). *By Cheyenne Campfires.* (reprinted from the 1920 edition). University y of Nebraska Press.

Gross, P. & Railton, E. (1972). *Teaching Science in an Outdoor Environment.* Berkeley, CA: University of California Press.

Grotjohn, M. (1950). *Psychoanalysis and the Family Neurosis.* New York: Norton.

Gunther, B. (1968). *Sense Relaxation.* New York: Macmillan/Collier Books.

Gunther, B. (1973). *Sense Relaxation: Below Your Mind.* New York: Pocket Books.

Haley, A. (1976). *Roots.* New York: Scribners.

Hammerman, D. R., Hammerman, W. M., & Hammerman, E. L. (1964-1985). *Teaching In The Outdoors.* Danville, IL: Interstate Printers and Publishers, Inc.

Hammerman, D. R. (1985). Outdoor Education: Then, Now, Tomorrow. In Robb, G. (Ed.). *The Bradford Papers, 5.*

Hammerman, W. E. (1980). *Fifty Years of Residential Outdoor Education: 1930-1980.* Martinsville, IN: American Camping Association.

Harris, T. (1969). *I'm O.K. - You're O.K.* New York: Harper & Row.

Havihurst, R. (1961). The nature and value of meaningful free time activity." In Kleesmeier, R. (Ed.). *Aging and Leisure*. New York: Oxford Press.

Henderson, C. (1975). *Awakening: Ways to Psycho-Spiritual Growth*. Englewood Cliffs, NJ: PrenticeHall.

Hendricks, G. & Wills, R. (1975). *The Centering Book*. Englewood Cliffs, NJ: Prentice-Hall/Spectrum Books.

Hendricks, G. & Fadiman, J. (1976). *Transpersonal Education*. Englewood Cliffs, NJ: Prentice-Hall.

Hill, R. (1979). *Hanta Yo*. New York: Doubleday.

Hindman, D. (1956). *Kick the Can: And Over 800 Other Games*. Englewood Cliffs, NJ: Prentice-Hall.

Huang, A. (1977). *Embrace Tiger, Return to Mountain*. New York: Bantam Books.

Hug, J. & Wilson, P. (1966). *Curriculum Enrichment Outdoors*. New York: Harper & Row.

Huizinga, J. (1950). *Homo Ludens: A Study of the Play Element in Culture*. Boston: Beacon Press.

Hypes, J. (Ed.) (1978). *Discover Dance*. Washington, DC: Alliance for Health, Physical Education, and Recreation.

Ichazo, 0. (1973, July). Conversations with Oscar Ichazo," by Sam Keen, *Psychology Today*.

Ichazo, 0. (1976). *The Human Process for Enlightenment and Freedom*. New York: The Arica Institute.

Jacobsen, E. O. (1929). *Progressive Relaxation*. Chicago, IL: University of Chicago Press.

Jacobsen, E. O. (1957). *You Must Relax*. New York: McGraw-Hill.

Jaffe, D. (1976). *Healing From Within*. New York: A. A. Knoff.

Jaffe, D. (1980). *Mind, Body, and Health*. New York: A. A. Knoff.

James, D. (1964). *Outward Bound*. London: Rutledge Co.

James, M. & Jongeward, D. (1973). *Born To Win: Transactional Analysis With Gestalt Experiments*. Reading, MA: Addison-Wesley.

James, T. (1980). *Education on the Edge*. Denver, CO: Colorado Outward Bound.

Jensen, M. (1979). Application of small group theory to adventure programs. *Journal of Experiential Education, 2*.

Jones, R. (1970). *Fantasy and Feeling in Education*. New York: Harper & Row.

Jourard, S. (1974). *Healthy Personality*. New York: Macmillan.

Kaplan, M. (1975). *Leisure: Theory and Policy*. New York: John Wiley & Sons.

Keen, S. (1970). *To A Dancing God*. New York: Harper & Row.

Knapp, C. & Goodman, J. (1981). *Humanizing Environmental Education*. Martinsville, IN: American Camping Association.

Kneller, G. (1971). *Introduction to the Philosophy of Education*. (2nd ed.) New York: John Wiley & Sons.

Kohak, E. (1984). *The Embers and the Stars*. Chicago, IL: University of Chicago Press.

Kohlberg, L. (1969). Stages and sequence: the cognitive development approach to socialization." In Goslin, D. (Ed.). *Handbook of Socialization Theory and Research*. Chicago, IL: U. C. Press.

Kraus, R. (1978). *Therapeutic Recreation Service: Principles and Practices*. Philadelphia: W. B. Saunders Co.

Krautwurst, T. (1988, March). The Tom Brown School. *Mother Earth News*.

Kubie, L. (1960). The rights of children for education. In Jones, R. (Ed.). *An Application of Psychosynthesis to Education*. Springfield, IL: C. C. Thomas.

Kurtz, R. (1985). *Hakomi Therapy*. Boulder, CO: Ron Kurtz Publications.

LaChapelle, D. (1973). *Earth Wisdom*. Silverton, CO: Finn Hill Arts.

LaChapelle, D. & Bourque, J. (1974). *Earth Festivals*. Silverton, CO, Finn Hill Arts.

Lame Deer, J. & Erdoes, R. (1972). *Lame Deer: Seeker of Visions*. New York: Simon & Schuster.

Larson, E. (Ed.). (1984). *Teaching Psychological Skills: Models for Giving Psycholoqy Away*. Belmont, CA: Wadsworth.

Lederman, J. (1969). *Anger and the Rocking Chair: Gestalt Awareness With Children*. New York: McGraw-Hill.

Leicthtman, R. & Japikse, C. (1984). *Active Meditation: The Western Tradition*. Columbus, OH: Ariel Press.

Leonard, G. (1968). *Education and Ecstasy*. New York: Dell/Delta Books.

Leonard, G. (1972). *The Transformation*. New York: Dell/Delta Books.

Leonard, G. (1978). *The Ultimate Athlete*. New York: Viking Press.

Lewin, K. (1959). *A Dynamic Theory of Personality: Selected Papers*.
(reprinted from the 1935 edition). New York: McGraw-Hill.

Lindzey, G. (Ed.) (1954). *Handbook of Social Psychology*. Cambridge, MA: Addison-Wesley Publishing Co.

Link, M. (1981). *Outdoor Education: A Manual for Teachinq in Nature's Classroom*. Englewood Cliffs, NJ: Prentice-Hall.

Lowen, A. (1966). *The Betrayal of the Body*. New York: Macmillan.

Lowen, A. (1970). *Pleasure*. New York: Lancer Books.

Lowen, A. (1971). *The Language of the Body*. New York: Collier Books.

Lowen, A. (1975). *Bioenergetics*. New York: Coward, McCann & Geohaugen.

Lowendahl, E. (1977). *The Power of Positive Stretching*. Pasadena, CA: Ward Ritchie Press.

Loughmiller, C. (1965). *Wilderness Road*. Anton, Texas: Hogg Foundation.

Loughmiller, C. (1979). *Kids In Trouble: Adventure in Education*. Tyler, TX: Wildwood Books.

Ludell, J. (1978). *Sensation*. New York: W. H. Freeman.

MacArthur, R. (1985). The stranger without and the stranger within: transplanting the liberal mind. *Journal of Experiential Education, 8*.

MacNeil, R. (1981). Environmental congruence and recreational programming. In Hitzhusen, G. & Peterson, B. (Eds.). *Expanding Horizons in Therapeutic Recreation, IX*. Columbia, MO.: University of Missouri Press.

MacNeil, R. (Ed.). (1982). *Perspectives on Leisure Education in a Changing Society*. Columbia, MO: Univeristy of Missouri Press.

McLuhan, T. C. (1971). *Touch the Earth*. New York: Simon & Schuster/ Touchstone Books.

Maccoby, E., Newcomb, T. & Hartley, E. (Eds.). (1958). *Readings In Social Psychology* (3rd Edition). New York: Henry Holt & Co.

Mann, J. (1972). *LearningTo Be: The Education of Human Potential*. New York: Macmillian, Free Press.

Maslow, A. (1968). *Toward A Psychology of Being*. New York: Van Nostrand.

Maslow, A. (1973). *Dominance, Self-Esteem, Self-Actualization: General Papers of A. H. Maslow*. (Edited by Lowrey, R.) Monterey, CA: Brooks/Cole Publishing.

May, R. (1953). *Man's Search For Himself*. New York: W. W. Norton & Co.

May, R., Angel, E. & Ellenberg, H. (Eds.). (1958). *Existence: A New Dimension In Psycholoqy and Psychiatry*. New York: Basic Books.

May, R. (1969). *Love and Will*. New York: W. W. Norton & Co.

Mead, G. (1934). *Mind, Self, and Society*. Chicago, IL: University of Illinois Press.

Meyer, A. (1956). *The Developments of Education in the Twentieth Century*. Englewood Cliffs, NJ: Prentice-Hall.

Miller, S. (1974) A new humanism in medicine." *Psychosynthesis: The Realization of Self*. San Francisco, CA: Psychosynthesis Institute Press.

Millman, D. (1979). *Whole Body Fitness*. New York: Clarkson N. Potter, Pub.

Miner, J. & Bolt, J. (1981). *Outward Bound, U.S.A.* New York: William Morrow & Co.

Miner, J. (1984). *Outward Bound*. Greenwich, Connecticut: Outward Bound Inc.

Minuchin, S. (1974). *Families and Family Therapy*. Cambridge, MA: Harvard University Press.

Mobily, K. (1982). Physical activity and aging. In MacNeil & Teague. (Eds.) *Perspectives on Leisure and Aging in a Changing Society*. Columbia, MO: University of Missouri Press.

Moore, G. (1987). *The Regional Outdoor Adventure Education Center: A Link To the Practioner*. Unpublished Paper.

Murphy, M. (1969). *Golf In The Kinqdom: The Psychic Side of Sports*. Esalen, CA: Esalen Press.

Naisbitt, J. (1982). *Megatrends: Ten New Directions Transforming Our Lives*. New York: Warner Books.

Naranjo, C. & Ornstein, R. (1971). *On the Psychology of Meditation*. New York: Viking Press.

Naranjo, C. (1973). *The Healing Journey: New Approaches to Consciousness*. New York: Ballantine Books.

Naranjo, C. & Hoffman, B. (1976). *Gettinq Divorced from Mother and Dad: The Discoveries of the Fisher-Hoffman Process*. New York: Dutton.

Neibuhr, R. (1972). *Experiential Religion*. New York: Van Nostrand.

Neihardt, J. & Black Elk. (1961). *Black Elk Speaks*. Lincoln, NE: University of Nebraska Press.

O'Morrow, G. (1976). *Therapeutic Recreation: A Helping Profession*. Reston, Virginia: Reston Publishing Co.

Oppenheim, J. (1984). *Kids and Play*. New York: Ballantine Books.

Orrlick, T. (1978). *The Cooperative Games and Sports Book*. New York: Partheon Books.

Ornstein, R. (1972). *The Psychology of Consciousness*. San Francisco, CA: Freeman.

Ornstein, R. (1986). *Multimind*. Boston, MA: Houghton-Mifflin.

Orr, L. (1981). *Pulk Skiing, Sled Skiing, and Ice Sledding for Persons With Mobility Impairments*. Loretto, MN: Vinland National Center, Inc.

Otto, H. (1966). *Exploration in Human Potentialities*. Springfield, IL: C. C. Thomas.

Otto, H. & Mann, J. (Eds.). (1968). *Ways of Growth*. New York: Grossman.

Otto, H. (1970). *Group Methods to Actualize Human Potential*. Beverly Hills, CA: Horlick Press.

Otto, H. (1972). *Fantasy Encounter Games*. Los Angeles, CA: Nash Publishing.

Palmer, P. (1983). *The Company of Strangers: Christians and the Renewal of Americans' Public Life*. New York: Crossroads.

Parker, A. (1975). *The Indian How Book*. (Reprinted from the 1927 edition) New York: Dover Publications.

Payne, B. (1973). *Getting There Without Drugs*. New York: Viking Press.

Pearse, J. (1981). *Clouds on the Clothesline and 200 Other Great Games*. Huntsville, Ontario: Camp Tawengo Publishing.

Peck, J. (1979). *Leap to the Sun: Learning Through Dynamic Play*. Englewood Cliffs, NJ: Prentice-Hall.

Pelletier, K. (1977). *Mind as Healer: Mind as Slayer*. New York: Delta.

Pelletier, K. (1980). *Holistic Medicine*. New York: Delacorte.

Perls, F. (1951). *Gestalt Therapy*. New York: Julian Press.

Perls, F. (1969). *Gestalt Therapy Verbatim*. Moab, UT: Real People Press.

Postman. N. & Weingarten, C. (1969). *Teaching As A Subversive Activity*. New York: Delacorte.

Poznanski, E. (1973). Emotional issues in raising handicapped children. *Rehabilitation Literature, 34* (ll).

Protestant Social Services Bureau. (1988). *Family Challenge*. (Program Brochure). Wollaston, MASS.

Quinn, W. (1988). *Native American Hunting Practices as Outdoor Education Content*. Unpublished Doctoral Dissertation, Boston University.

Richards, M. (1980). *Towards Wholeness: Rudolph Steiner Education in America*. Middleton, CT: Wesleyan University Press.

Rillo, T. (1985). Preface. In Hammerman, et.al. *Teaching in the Outdoors*. Danville, IL: Interstate Printers and Publishers.

Robb, G. (Ed.). (1980-1986). *The Bradford Papers*. Martinsville, IN: Indiana University Press.

Robb, G., Havens, M. & Wittman, J. (1983). *Special Education Naturally*. Martinsville, IN: Indiana University Press.

Robb, G. & Hamilton, E. (Eds.). (1985). *Issues in Challenge Education and Adventure Programs*. Martinsville, IN: Indiana University Press.

Robb, G. (Ed.). (1987–1989). *The Bradford Papers Annual*. Martinsville, IN: Indiana University Press.

Roberts, T. & Clark, F. (1976). Transpersonal psychology in education. In Hendricks, G. & Fadiman, J. (Eds.). *Transpersonal Education*. New York: Prentice-Hall.

Robinson, F. & Skinner, S. (1985). *A Holistic Perspective on the Disabled Child*. Springfield, IL: C. C. Thomas.

Rogers, C. (1951). *Client Centered Therapy*. Boston, MA: Houghton Mifflin.

Rogers, C. (1959). A theory of therapy, personality, and interpersonal relationships. In Koch, S. (Ed). *Psychology: A Study of a Science, Vol. III*. New York: McGraw-Hill.

Rogers, C. (1961). *On Becoming A Person*. Boston, MA: Houghton Mifflin.

Rogers, C. (1969). *Freedom To Learn: A View Of What Education Might Become*. Columbus, OH: Charles E. Merrill Publishing Co.

Rogers, C. (1970). *Carl Rogers on Encounter Groups*. New York: Harper & Row.

Rogers, C. (1980). *A Way of Being*. Boston, MA: Houghton Mifflin.

Rohnke, K. (1977). *Cowstails and Cobras*. Hamilton, MA: Project Adventure.

Rohnke, K. (1977). *Teaching Through Adventure*. Hamilton, MA: Project Adventure.

Rohnke, K. (1984). *Silver Bullets*. Hamilton, MA: Project Adventure.

Rohnke, K. (1986, May/June). Project adventure: a widely used generic product. *Journal of Physical Education and Recreation*.

Rohrs, H. (1970). *Kurt Hahn: Biography*. London: Routledge & Kegan Paul.

Roland, C. (1989). *The Teams Kit Instructor's Manual*. Lake Mills, WI: Learned Enterprises.

Roland, C. & Havens, M. (1981). *An Introduction to Adventure: Sequential Approaches With Persons Who Are Disabled*. Loretto, MN: Vinland National Center.

Roland, C. & Hoyt, J. (1983). Family adventure programming. *Bradford Papers, 4*.

Roland, C., Dunham, T., Hoyt, J. & Havens, M. (1986). Families as partners with disabled youth. *Journal of Experiential Education, 7* (1).

Ruben, W. (1970). *T'ai Chi*. New York: Lancer Books.

Ruben, L. (Ed.). (1973). *Facts and Feelings in the Classroom*. New York: Viking/Compass Books.

Russell, R. (1986). *Leadership in Recreation*. St. Louis, MO: Times Mirror/Mosby College Publishing.

Saari, J. (1981). Positive health: physical fitness and disabilities. In Hitzhusen, G. (Ed.). *Expanding Horizons in Therapeutic Recreation, IX*. Springfield, MO: University of Missouri Press.

Salk, L. (1973). *What Every Child Would Like His Parents to Know*. New York: Warner Paperback Library.

Samuels, M. & Bennett, H. (1973). *The Well Body Book.* New York: Random House.

Satir, V. (1967). *Conjoint Family Therapy* (Rev. Ed.). Palo Alto, CA: Science and Behavior Books.

Satir, V. (1972). *Peoplemaking.* Palo Alto, CA: Science and Behavior Books.

Satir, V. (1984). *Adapting the System to Meet the Challenge in Redefinition of the Family.* [Lecture]. KWEN Family Institute, IL.

Schein, E. & Bennis, W. (1966). *Personal and Organizational Change Through Group Methods.* New York: John Wiley & Son.

Schmidt, E. (1985). Perspectives on camping: Today and tomorrow. *Bradford Papers, 5.*

Schramn, W. (1969). *Classroom Out-of-Doors.* Kalamazoo, MI: Sequoia Press.

Schurke, P. & Lais, G. (1982). Wilderness inquiry, II: Bringing people together in the wilderness. *Bradford Papers, 2.*

Schutz, W. (1967). *Joy.* New York: Grove Press.

Schutz, W. & Turner, E. (1976). *EVY: An Odyssey into Bodymind.* New York: Harper and Row.

Sehnert, K. (1981). *Health Promotion, Wellness, and Medical Self-Care.* Loretto, MN: Vinland National Center.

Selver, C. & Brooks, V. (1966). Report on work in sensory awareness. In Otto, H. (Ed.). *Explorations in Human Potentialities.* Springfield, IL: C. C. Thomas.

Sharp, L. (1930). *Education and the Summer Camp: An Experiment.* Unpublished Doctoral Dissertation. Teachers College, Columbia University.

Shostram, E. (1972). *Freedom To Be: Experiencing and Expressing Your Total Being.* New York: Prentice-Hall.

Simpson, B. (1978). *Initiative Games.* Butler, PA: Simpson.

Singer, J. (1972). *Boundaries of the Soul: The Practice of Jung's Psychology.* Garden City, NJ: Doubleday & Co.

Smith, J. (1957). *Outdoor Education for American Youth.* Washington, DC: Association for Health, Physical Education & Recreation.

Smith, T. (1977). Wilderness adventure. *Proceedings of the Conference on The Family—Spectrum of Cooperative Living.* University of Illinois.

Smith, T. (1978). Wilderness beyond, wilderness within. [Paper] *Midwest Conference of Association for Humanistic Psychology.*

Smith, T. (1979). Medicine wheels and teaching stories. [Paper] *School for the Healing Arts Conference.* Minneapolis, MN.

Smith, T. (1990). *Wilderness Beyond...Wilderness Within.* McHenry, IL: McHenry Press.

Smith, T. (1981). Vision quest: 2001. [Paper] *Proceedings of the Fifth American Imagery Conference.* Chicago, Illinois.

Smith, T. (1983). Outdoor Leadership and Endu Consciousness. *Bradford Papers, 3.*

Smith, T. (1984). Therapeutic recreation, outdoor education, and special Eeducation. *Bulletin.* Chicago, IL: International Committee of the National Therapeutic Society.

Smith, T. (1987). Foster families and challenge therapy. *Bradford Papers Annual, 1.*

Smith. W (1963). *The Meaning and End of Religion.* New York: Mentor Books.

Snygg, D. & Combs, A. (1949). *Individual Behavior: A New Frame of Reference for Psychology.* New York: Harper & Row.

Spock, B. (1957). *Child Care.* New York: Duell, Sloan, & Pearce.

Stainstreet, E. (1973). The Amazing Mister Stanistreet. *East/West Journal.*

Staley, F. (1979). *Outdoor Education for the Whole Child.* Dubuque, IA: Kendall Hunt Publishing Co.

Stanford, G. (1977). *Developing Effective Classroom Groups: Exercises for Problem Solving and Group Decision Making.* New York: Hart.

Stevens, J. (1971). *Awareness: Exploring, Experimenting, Experiencing.* Moab, UT: Real People Press.

Storm, H. (1972). *Seven Arrows.* New York: Ballantine Books.

Sullivan, H. (1947). *Conceptions of Modern Psychiatry.* Washington, DC: W. A. White Psychiatric Foundation.

Sullivan, H. (1949). Psychiatry: Introduction to the study of interpersonal relations. In Mullahy, P. (Ed.). *New Contributions to Psychiatry.* New York: Hermitage Press.

Sullivan, H. (1953). *The Interpersonal Theory of Psychiatry.* New York: W. W. Norton & Co.

Sullivan, M. (1982). *Feeling Strong, Feeling Free: Movement Exploratons for Young Children.* Washington, DC: National Association for the Eduation of Young Children.

Sutton-Smith, B. (1972). "Play As A Transformation Set." *Leisure Today.* Washington, DC: Association for Health, P.E., & Recreation.

Sweeney, R. (Ed.). (1970). *Selected Readings in Movement Education.* Reading, MA: Addison Wesley Publishing Co.

Teale, E. W. (Ed.). (1954). *The Wilderness World of John Muir*. Boston, MA: Houghton Mifflin.

Tillich, P. (1952). *The Courage to Be*. New Haven, CT: Yale University Press.

Tillich, P. (1957). *The Dynamics of Faith*. New York: Harper & Row.

Torbert, M. (1978). *Follow Me: A Handbook of Movement Activities for Children*. Englewood Cliffs, NJ: Prentice-Hall.

Vahanian, G. (1957). *The Death of God*. New York: George Braziller.

Van Matre, S. (1972). *Acclimatization*. Martinsville, IN: American Camping Association.

Van Matre, S. (1974). *Acclimatizing*. Martinsville, IN: American Camping Association.

Van Matre S. (1979). *Sunship Earth*. Martinsville, IN: American Camping Association.

Waters, F. (1970). *Masked Gods* (reprinted from 1950 ed.). New York: Ballatine Books.

Watts, A. (1968). *Psychotherapy, East and West*. New York: Random House.

Watts, A. (1972). *In My Own Way*. New York: Random House.

Weinstein, M. & Goodman, J. (1980). *Playfair: Everybody's Guide to Non-Competitive Play*. San Luis Obispo, CA: Impact Press.

White, J. & Fadiman, J. (1976). *Relax*. New York: Confucian Press.

Witkin, K. (1977). *To Move: To Learn*. Philadelphia, PA: Temple University.

Wright, B. (1960). *Physical Disability: A Psychological Approach*. New York: Harper & Row.

Yambert, P. (1985). Outdoor education: The next fifty years. *Bradford Papers, 5*.

Young, P. (1961). *Motivation and Emotion*. New York: John Wiley & Sons.

CHAPTER TWO

PHILOSOPHICAL FOUNDATIONS FOR CHALLENGE EDUCATION

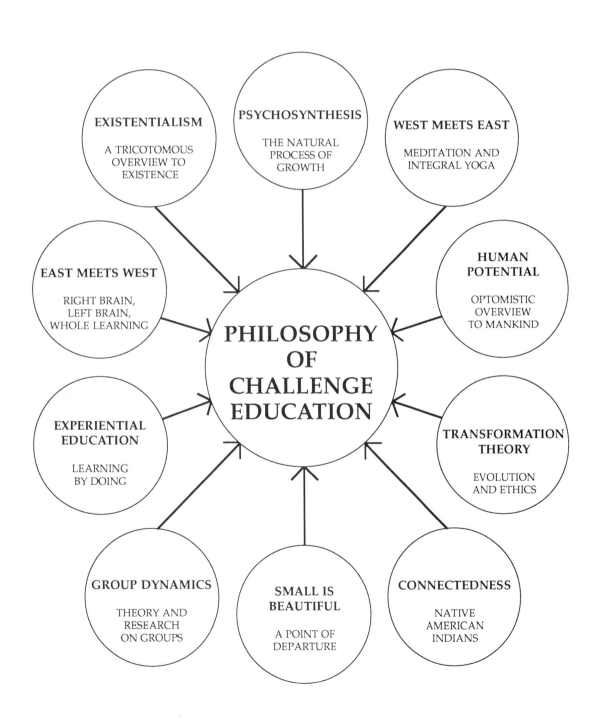

Chapter Two

Philosophical Foundations for Challenge Education

Challenge education has developmental roots in a wide variety of methodologies for facilitation of growth and learning. It has evolved from the orientations of many different professional disciplines, often with creative interdisciplinary teamwork. It has been explored and developed in a great number of educational, rehabilitative, recreational and therapeutic settings, with attention to the needs of many different client populations. It would be expected, therefore, that there is no simple philosophical base for challenge education. Instead, there would be—and should be—a variety of theoretical ideologies which could contribute to a philosophy of challenge education.

It should be recognized that the professionals who utilize the challenge methodologies tend to be "doers." They are most usually involved with providing direct services to their clients or, in some cases, are concerned with the organization and administration of programming. There are a few professionals in academic positions who understand the potentials of the challenge methodology, and offer courses which include an overview and/or experiential introduction to some of the strategies. Typically, these individuals are in academic positions reflective of their professional background; i.e., outdoor education, physical education, recreation, counseling, or experiential education.

In other words, there are few professionals who would consider themselves "philoso-phers of challenge education." Rather, the various working professionals who are continually exploring and developing challenge methodology in the field periodically turn to the task of reflection on the practice and the identification of various philosophical underpinnings for the approach. What exists as a philosophy of challenge education has developed from the ground up as the working professionals search for ideas that support their strategies. Contrary to any expectation that such a system for development of challenge philosophy would bring only a fragmented and conflictual philosophical base, the result has been a dynamic and meaningful evolution of theory—the very sort of philosophical base that a system of strategies so complex and variable, with applications in such a wide variety of situations, warrants.

Certainly, no defining theory of challenge education has yet been developed. Perhaps there will be none; perhaps there *should* be none. What is to be presented in this chapter is not a philosophy *of* challenge education but a series of brief summaries of a variety of philosophical orientations that seem to warrant attention from concerned professionals. These are ideas to be considered *for* challenge education philosophy.

The ideas to be discussed are summarized on page 69. Some of these philosophical foundations for challenge education are identified by a definitive historical orientation, such as "holistic education," "humanistic education" or "experiential education." Others are identifiable with a particular individual, such as E. F. Schumacher, Teilhard de Chardin, or Roberto Assagioli, although it should be recognized that many others have explored and expanded their initial work and there are other individuals who may have developed parallel viewpoints. Finally, some of the overview categorizations have been labeled by the author to provide some clustering of some philosophical ideas that seem to have potential for a theory of challenge education, such as "connectedness theory" and "East Meets West."

These various philosophical focal points are but briefly summarized, and so the task ahead is for challenge education professionals to determine value and explore more deeply. References are by no means complete, but should provide a starting point for those who wish to delve further into the various ideas. There is no particular order to the sequence of ideas discussed, and each package of philosophical thought is presented to be "self-contained." For this reason, some of the points for thought may be restated in the various sections of the chapter. The reader should be able to see the interconnectedness of some of the philosophical orientations. Many of the ideas presented bear a relationship to the various strategies and methodologies of challenge education as summarized in Chapter One, and cross-checking should lead to an even better understanding of that particular orientation. This seems important, for any developing philosophy of challenge education should certainly be as flexible and flowing as the methodology itself, and there should be constant blending of the two.

At the end of the chapter, some summarization points are offered. While they should not be viewed as a philosophy of challenge education, they would appear to be important points for any developing philosophy to consider. The main intention of this chapter is to provide ideas for exploration, to suggest a number of possible starting points for anyone seeking to develop a philosophy of challenge education.

SMALL IS BEAUTIFUL— E. A. SCHUMACHER

It has often been suggested that the grand purpose of education should be "preparation for life." More idealistic and visionary educators have suggested extension of that definition to the goals of "preparation for life, as it ought to be." E. A. Schumacher was an economist, not an educator, but his analysis of the way the world *is* evolved into a vision of the way life *ought to be*. Accordingly, his thinking has some significant implications for the goals of education.

Schumacher's most significant publications were *Small is Beautiful* (1973) and *A Guide for the Perplexed* (1977). In *Small is Beautiful*, he challenged modern "economic science" by calling its basic metaphysical and psychological foundations into question. His ideas proved anything but "small" and had a major impact not only on economics but on all of social science. It was noted:

> *Small is Beautiful* woke many people from a sound sleep. Concern for our environment, for nature, and for peace were signs of this awakening. The hallmarks of Schumacher's thinking were a search for wholeness and quality, together with the realization that the movement for an alternative to industrial society may have many facets, but that all of those facets are closely interlinked. (Kumar, 1984)

Born in Germany, Schumacher immigrated to England in the late 1930's after being there as a Rhodes scholar. He worked as a farm laborer and developed a feeling for the soil which stayed with him thereafter. By the end of the 1940's and throughout the 1950's he worked for the British government as an economic advisor. His work took him to Burma and he studied Buddhism while there, which also influenced his thinking on economics. He began to see the appalling effects of pouring aid in the form of advanced technology into an underprivileged country: the rich get richer and the poor get poorer. He concluded that without human and social development, technology can achieve nothing. He became an advocate of development of human resources and his ideas evolved toward the psychological, educational, environmental and ethical aspects of economics. He first became known professionally when he published papers on "Intermediate Technology," a theory for helping the underprivileged countries in a step-bystep sequence. He was already in his sixties when *Small is Beautiful* was published. In the early pages of that book, he made the following observations:

On nature: "Modern man does not experience himself as a part of nature, but as an outside force destined to dominate and conquer it."

On technology: "Wisdom demands a new orientation of both science and technology towards the organic, the gentle, the nonviolent, the elegant, and the beautiful."

On peace: "How could peace be built on a foundation of reckless science and violent technology?"

On economics: "We may suspect that meta-economics consists of two parts—one dealing with man and other dealing with the environment. We may say that economics must derive its aim and objectives from a study of man—and from a study of nature."

On spirituality: "Spiritual health and material well-being are not enemies: they are natural allies." (Schmacher, 1973)

Perhaps most importantly, Schumacher recognized that "education is the most vital of all resources."

The task of education should be, first and foremost, the transmission of ideas of values, of what to do with our lives. There is no doubt also the need to transmit know-how, but this must take second place, for it is obviously somewhat foolhardy to put great powers into the hands of people without making sure that they have a reasonable idea of what to do with them. At present, there can be little doubt that the whole of mankind is in mortal danger, not because we are short of scientific and technological know-how, but because we tend to use it destructively, without wisdom. More education can help us only if it produces more wisdom.

The essence of education is the transmission of values, but values do not help us to pick our way through life unless they have become our own, a part, so to say, of our mental make-up. This means that they are more than mere formulae or dogmatic assertions: that we think and feel with them, and that they are the very instruments through which we look at, interpret, and experience the world.

When people ask for education, they normally mean something more than mere training, something more than mere knowledge of facts, and something more than a mere diversion. Maybe they cannot themselves formulate precisely what they are looking for: but I think what they are really looking for is ideas that would make the world, and their own lives, intelligible to them. When a thing is intelligible, you have a sense of participation; when a thing is unintelligible you have a sense of estrangement. (Ibid.)

For Schumacher, to the extent that education does not produce "whole persons" who have a firm understanding of their basic convictions and of their view on the meaning and purpose of life, it fails. He stated it in terms of the person having to find personal values, wisdom, strength, and a feeling of "inner certainty." When one does not possess that "inner certainty" and does not know of the smallness and allness of their own "centre," they stand alone. Schumacher recognized the basic human needs for belongingness and connectedness. Without a reasonably small and definable social reference group, the individual loses touch with, and faith in, personal potency. When the individual only has involvement with large, impersonal, over-structured society groups, there is great danger that the resultant feelings of impotency, insignificance, and uncertainty will lead to alienation and isolation. He notes that the person without "inner certainty" and a sense of balance at "centre" is...

> ...as a person in a strange land ...without maps or signposts or indicators of any kind. Nothing has any meaning for him; nothing can hold his vital interest; he has no means of making anything intelligible to himself. (op.cit.)

Almost twenty years before the publication of *Small is Beautiful*, Colin Wilson had been drawn to the problems of the individual becoming alienated from society because of feelings of unimportance and personal impotence. His publication of *The Age of Defeat* (1955) attracted the attention of prominent humanistic psychologist Abraham Maslow. Shortly thereafter, these two scholars became friends and exchanged a series of letters and papers. Ten years later, Wilson wrote a book about Maslow and his ideology, *New Pathways in Psychology* (1967).

Wilson appreciated Maslow's attention to the hierarchy of human needs and the idea of the "self-actualized personality." He realized that the healthy personality was one that did not feel overwhelmed by society, but held to a strong sense of inner security and personal potential. In his book *The Outsider* (1959), Wilson explored the whole process of alienation in more detail. The "Outsider" was a man struggling to find some sense of personal potential, but in his feelings of futility he drifted alone, apart, outside of the mainstream. In his search the Outsider thinks about the classic novel *Steppenwolf* by Herman Hesse (1929). Steppenwolf, the main character of the novel, is a successful writer, fairly wellto-do, with a nice house, books, music, and a girlfriend, but still he is "lost." He feels bored, frustrated, lukewarm to life, and quite unable to tap into the emotional intensities of living. He even contemplates suicide, until an unexplainable experience with a glass of wine, a moment of deep relaxation, and a sudden burst of special new awareness. Wilson later equated what happened to Steppenwolf with Maslow's "peak experience" and suggested that it may be a viable solution to the problem of many "outsiders." Perhaps, thought Wilson, a "peak experience"—that moment of sudden bubbling of happiness, that moment of relaxation-awarenessexcitement when the individual seems most open to new feelings of personal confidence and personal potential— could stir the alienated to feelings of potency to move within, and against, the society which held that terrible blend of inappropriate value orientation and awesome power. He later wrote:

> If only there were a way in which you could push a button and induce that experience instantly—then we would have solved the basic problem of modern civilization. (Wilson, 1984)

There is no doubt that in our society all too few people achieve that highest step of Maslow's hierarchy: self-actualization. There are, indeed, all too many "outsiders," feeling alone, confused, and lost amid the demands of that seemingly unconcerned society. Psychologists and sociologists have related most of the problems of our time—from drug abuse to child abuse to lack of motivation in the workplace—to this basic problem of the individual feeling unimportant. Too many people do not find that feeling of "inner certainty" that Schumacher talked about.

Colin Wilson discovered Schumacher in the 1970's and recognized that his ideas for a reorientation of the psychological, social and economic concepts of society would also tackle the basic problem of the modern world. It was in "smallness" of groups and experiences that one could reach down and find potency—that one could even, perhaps, find significant and meaningful "peak experiences." He wrote:

> As soon as I read Schumacher's *Small is Beautiful*, I could see it was a logical extension of Maslow's ideas— that the healthy person is the person who does not feel overwhelmed by the environment. He doesn't feel helpless, he doesn't feel a cog in the machine; he preserves a sense of drive, of individuality, of creativity. And clearly the problem of the whole of civilization is this problem of how to keep

> things "small" enough so that as many people as possible can experience this sense of individuality. (Ibid.)

Soon after publication of *Small is Beautiful*, Schumacher became a hero of all those proposing alternatives to technocratic society, an influence on the ideas about development of third world countries, and an appealing speaker for young audiences—especially the alienated. His ideas provided a rallying point for those who understood intellectually and/or emotionally the plight of the lonely "outsider," with those feelings of futility and smallness. He spoke to those many who felt insignificant and unimportant, who felt threatened by the bigness of government, and who had fears of nuclear holocaust and scientific technology gone wild. He was saying that "Small is Beautiful" much as the civil rights leader Malcolm X was declaring "Black is Beautiful" to those Blacks who had lost faith in self and system. Definitely, Schumacher was speaking to the psychology of individuals, not to the economics of society.

Schumacher recognized the problems of modern man in *Small is Beautiful*. His conclusion was simple: improving society had to start with improving the individual. Improvement for the individual meant turning inward, finding significance in smallness, in a few intimate connections with others, and in cultivation of a sense of balance with the small things of the world. He turned to prescription for change in *A Guide for the Perplexed*, which he completed shortly before his death. He recognized that as people go "clamoring for solutions," they frequently become angry when told that the restoration of society must come from within, not from without. His recommendation to begin by turning within was no doubt influenced by his earlier training in

Eastern thought, but his views of the journey to self-discovery are more complex than simple meditation. For one thing, he tends to an appreciation for cognitive expansion, and sees basic learning of facts as important for full development. He also recognized the necessity for basic faith and the development of moral character. He suggests that there is need for "a new moral basis of society, a new foundation of ethics." One of his closing statements in *A Guide for the Perplexed* is: "There really is no economic problem and in a sense there never has been... But there is a moral problem."

In the epilogue to *A Guide for the Perplexed*, Schumacher quotes Dorothy Sayers on the subject of Dante's *Inferno*. Sayers had noted that Dante depicts the human condition as one of sin and corruption, a description quite parallel to that of many who analyzed the human situation of the 1950's in America. The problems, as outlined by Dante, are our problems, according to Sayers.

> Futility; lack of living faith; the drift into loose morality, greed, consumption, financial irresponsibility, and uncontrolled bad temper; a self-opinioned and obstinate individualism; violence, sterility, and lack of reverence for life and property; the exploitation of sex, the debasing of language by advertisement and propaganda, commercializing religion; these are the all-toorecognizable stages that lead to the cold death of society and the extinguishing of all civilized relations. (Dorothy Sayers, in Schumacher, 1977)

Schumacher goes on to note that these were still our problems twenty years after Sayers wrote about them. (It could now be argued that they are still our problems twenty years after Schumacher wrote about them!)

Certainly, these are the problems to which education must attend as we come to the end of the twentieth century.

Schumacher's writings reflect his own breadth of being. His ideas are in support of meditation, organic gardening, nature, classical literature, tree planting, alternative energy sources, peace, Buddhist Economics, personal growth, ethical reflection, and the challenge facing education. *A Guide for the Perplexed* has been described as a "manual for survival," and as a guidebook for attaining that feeling of inner certainty or self-validation. This wisdom at "centre" provides an anchor against alienation and feelings of impotence.

For education, the challenge is obvious. People need small and significant connectedness, which provides them the opportunity to feel relevant and involved. (Is this not the typical challenge program group?) People need the opportunity to test themselves, and to push themselves to the upper limits of accomplishment, which provides them with the opportunity to feel "I'm O.K." and "I can do it." (Is this not the typical challenge sequence?) People need to be guided to new awarenesses of self, others, environment and the joyous connectedness and importance of all that is. (Is this not challenge education?)

Schumacher's thinking has been summarized:

> He advocated a strong alliance between peace with oneself, peace with the peoples of the world, and peace with Nature. He was part of a process of holistic thinking, putting forth ideas on ways and means for living in harmony with Nature and limiting our material needs. According to him, a simple ecological and spiritual lifestyle is not only necessary for the survival of the human species, it is also more fulfilling and satisfying. (Kumar, 1984)

Long ago, William Blake expressed an understanding of the concept of "small is beautiful" when he wrote the first stanza of *Auguries of Innocence*.

> To see a world in a grain of sand,
> And a Heaven in a wild flower,
> Hold infinity in the palm of your hand,
> And Eternity in an hour.
>   (William Blake, in Untermeyer, 1955)

EXISTENTIALISM

Existentialism has been considered the philosophy of our times. Although there are roots back to the nineteenth century, with Soren Kierkegaard's alternative to Hegel's rationalism usually considered the foundation of existential thought, the essential refinements and impact of the existential approach was after World War II. In retrospect, the German philosopher Friedreich Nietzsche, who published in the latter half of the nine-

teenth century, has been considered influential in the development of existential thought. At least one American philosopher, John Wild, with a somewhat different interpretation of existential history, has suggested that William James was "the first American existential philosopher." (Wild, 1963) James' works were also published in the later years of the nineteenth century.

The modern German philosophers, Karl Jaspers and Martin Heidegger, wrote in the first half of the twentieth century, as did the French philosophers Gabriel Marcel and Jean-Paul Sartre. However, translations of the works of these prominent European thinkers did not appear in English until the 1940's and 1950's. The theologian-philosopher Martin Buber published in the 1930's but was not recognized as an existential thinker until later, when the historical body of writings by the significant others came to focus. The most prominent of the "existential analysts" who had diverted from their training with Freud and Jung was Ludwig Binswanger. He published in the 1930's, but again, translations were not available until after World War II.

So it was in the 1950's that existential thought gained widespread attention in America. It was, in fact, more than attention—it was an enthusiastic and often controversial explosion into the American consciousness. The Great Depression, the tragedies of World War II, and the new fears resulting from the nuclear age hung a great cloud of concern over humankind. Many were inclined to seek refuge from what W. C. Auden called "the Age of Anxiety" by burying their heads in the sand and avoiding the issue of personal responsibility for self and world.

American humanistic psychologist Gordon Allport had suggested a literary portrait of the person hiding in the business of everyday life. His description of "Citizen Sam," whose life was a sequence of sleeping, working so as to take care of basic needs, and periodically plunging into some diversion as with movies or drinking, outlined an escape pattern that tended to keep one from having to contemplate life's problems or dealing with the question of personal responsibility for what is happening in the environment.

Take for example "Citizen Sam," who moves and has his being in the great activity wheel of New York City. Let us say that he spends his hours of unconsciousness somewhere in the badlands of the Bronx. He wakens to grab the morning milk left at the door by an agent of a vast dairy and distributing system whose corporate maneuvers, so vital to his health, never consciously concern him until there is a strike of dairy workers... At the factory he becomes a cog for the day in a set of systems beyond his ken. To him (as to everybody else) the company he works for is an abstraction... Unknown to himself he is headed next week for the surplus labor market... At noon the corporate monstrosity swallows him up, as much as he swallows up one of its automatic pies. After more activity in the afternoon, he seeks out a standardized daydream produced in Hollywood, to rest his tense, but not efficient mind. At the end of the day he slinks into a tavern and, unknowingly victimized by the advertising cycle, orders in rapid succession Four Roses, Three Feathers, Golden Wedding, and Seagrams, which men who plan beyond tomorrow like to drink. (Allport, 1950)

Unfortunately, as pointed out by David Bradley, there was *No Place to Hide* (1948). A look at the state of the world as the nuclear age unfolded brought the individual to realization that the task of improving civilization

was in his/her hands. This simply compounded the anxiety, for it implied awesome responsibility for each individual. Many sought refuge from this anxiety by hiding in the security of the group; but as argued by David Riesman, one soon discovered that *The Lonely Crowd* (1950) affords no real escape or peace of mind.

Paul Tillich's *The Courage to Be* (1952) addressed the issue. He suggested that the anxiety of the mid-century came from the loss of the meaning of life. Granting the developing feelings of impotence in a nuclear age and an everexpanding technocratic and powerful societal superstructure, there is no choice but to come to grips with our anxiety and to seek to discover ourselves and our place in the world.

Sartre had recognized that man seeks to evade his responsibility by living marginally and not in accord with his full potential. While man is free to shape his existence, he often falls victim to feelings of despair, impotence, and unconcern. He comes to feel that "nothing makes any sense, nothing makes any difference" (Sartre, 1947). His observation of the reality of many people's lifestate as quite parallel to that of "Citizen Sam" brought a good deal of pessimism to Sartre, and resulted in his thinking being considered "existential pessimism." Actually, such interpretation is erroneous, for Sartre is simply observing a clear reality, which is what all must do in order to develop the faith, hope, and optimism upon which a meaningful life can be built.

One of the reasons for the popularity of existentialism (among students and intellectuals-at-large, if not in American philosophical circles) was its message that philosophy is for everyone. Each person can peel back his own layers of defensive armor and risk the search into the depths of personal being. In fact, say the existentialists, it is each person's responsibility to seek, to find, and to bring forth the actions which they are. Everyone can discover what it means to be human, and what it means to assume responsibility for choosing values and subsequent actions. Existentialism offered mid-century man, so filled with anxiety and despair, a new optimism and new courage based on facing the hard facts of life such as the certainty of death. One student of existentialism reportedly defined the implications of the philosophy as follows: "It means that I must become aware of two basic facts: I will be dead someday...and I am not dead now. What happens between now and then is my responsibility."

A decade after existentialism splashed onto the American scene, Gayer (1961) summarized:

In spite of the advance of science—perhaps because of it—we no longer think progress inevitable. Catastrophe is at least as likely. Technology appears to be mastering us. Knowledge is running amuck, proliferating faster than we can contain it. And man has disappeared within the mass. He is anxiety-ridden and without the guidelines of cherished values. He wonders whether science is enough. He will not renounce science; it has done so much for him, and he believes in it. But he would like to supplement his belief in science with something that will give him a comforting sense of identity and personal worth.

Contemporary existentialism enters, bombarding us with reminders that we are human and that we are very unique individuals. Its mentors continuously pose the question of Being versus Nothingness, an appropriate topic for a society which knows it has the means of destroying itself speedily, without recourse, and even quite accidentally.

Yet, it is not so much that technical philosophical focus which gives existentialism its burgeoning appeal. It is, rather, the entry into a technological world of philosophy based on the individual, the very one whom technology has seemingly made expendable, his importance diminished by machine-like methods of organizing men. Existentialism poses a new interpretation of truth, allowing man to believe or disbelieve in God as he chooses, without needing to come to grips with rigorous, logical proofs. It holds that valid solutions are found in man's emotions as much as in his cerebrations. Existentialism reaffirms man's priority and importance, and the desirability of his becoming an authentic person. It introduces man to the use and value of philosophizing as an everyday, do-it-yourself way of life. It posits a conception of history which tells man that it is up to him to save the world, or to destroy it.   (Gayer, 1961)

The responsibility of each individual to remake themselves and their world was even reflected in American folk music. Joan Baez, (1965) writing for the album cover of her collection *Farewell Angelina*, summarized eloquently:

Only you and I can help the sun rise
    each morning.
If we don't, it may drench itself out in
    sorrow.
You–special, miraculous, unrepeatable,
    fragile,
fearful, tender, lost, sparkling ruby
    emerald jewel, rainbow splendor
    person.
It's up to you.

Vanguard Album "Farewell Angelina" (V79200) by Joan Baez

There are a wide variety of existential philosophies, and any listing of "basic principles" would no doubt be long discussed and debated among those who consider themselves existential thinkers. However, there does seem to be some basic agreement on a number of points.

1) The individual must become keenly aware of who he is and how he would like to exist in that short time span between birth and death.

2) The knowledge sought must include more than mere cognitive reflection; emotional "knowing" and awareness based on the real experiences of life must be admitted as evidence. In fact, without experience there really is no evidence.

3) The individual must accept and assume full responsibility for his/her existence. People who tend to avoid dealing with this assumption of personal responsibility are doomed to a life of loneliness and despair, estranged from themselves and their world, living a life at lesser stages of existence and as inauthentic beings.

4) Once individuals open themselves to the full range of their awareness and knowledge, and assume responsibility for their personal values, actions, and being, they are free to make of themselves whatever they choose.

At the philosophical level, existentialism attempts to provide a model that can help understand each person in his/her reality and totality. Most of the existential thinkers attend to that branch of philosophy called "ontology," the science of being. This leads them to address the problems of mind–body dualism. Rollo May, (1958) has defined existentialism as:

> The endeavor to understand man by cutting below the cleavage between subject and object which has bedeviled West-

ern thought and science since shortly after the Renaissance.

This cleavage that dichotomizes man as mind and body—as having a mental existence and a physical existence—has been considered "the cancer of all psychology up to now" by Ludwig Binswanger, (1956) prominent spokesman of the early existential analysts. Historically, the existential analysts were reacting against Freud's limited biological view of man. They claimed that it was experientially obvious that human beings could not be reduced to a biological bundle of impulses, motivations, and drives. In many ways, they were reacting against Freud over the same issues as the neo-Freudians (Fromm, Horney, Sullivan, etc.) and the American humanistic psychologists (Allport, Rogers, Maslow, etc.).

It is the existentialists' view of the person as a being of existence in three modes or realms that contributes much to the correction of the errors of mindbody dualism, and thereby offers all of psychology and education a more encompassing orientation to the complexity and totality of the human being. There is biological existence in a biophysical world; this is the *Umwelt* or the "world around." There is a social existence in a social world; this is the realm of the *Mitwelt* or the "world with." Finally, there is that realm of unique, private, introspective identity awareness—the world of "self" or "spirit." This is the *Eigenwelt* or "world within" (May, 1958). One can only understand man in the *Lebenswelt* or the "life-world" if there is attention given to all realms of existence.

American philosopher John Wild has considered the existentialists' attention to the *Lebenswelt* their most significant contribution, for the trichotomous view expands the horizons of the study of man to include both objective and subjective data. Both types of thought are indispensable to philosophy, and the phenomenological exploration of the *Lebenswelt* heals the breach between the two (Wild, 1963).

The existential trichotomy recognizes the human being as a biological pile of cells, a psychological interactional being, and as a being with an existence in the phenomenological field of self-awareness. The trichotomy has been summarized by Rollo May as follows:

> There is a world of biologic drive, fate, and determinism (Umwelt) the world of one's responsibility to fellow men (Mitwelt), and the world in which the individual can be aware of the fate he alone at the moment is struggling with (Eigenwelt). (May, 1958)

While the postulation of existence in three modes improves our overview of man, it is important to recognize that the totality of the person involves dynamic interaction and interdependency across all three realms. We must be careful not to "fragment" our understanding of the human being by overattention to, or exclusionary thinking about, any of the three modes.

> It should be clear that these three modes of world are always interrelated and always condition each other. The human being lives as *Umwelt, Mitwelt,* and *Eigenwelt* quite simultaneously. There are by no means three different worlds, but three simultaneous modes of being in the world. (Ibid.)

Freud's emphasis was on the *Umwelt*. Critics and subsequent analysts, especially Sullivan, recognized that there must be atten-

tion paid to the social interaction of the person (Sullivan, 1953). Existential theologian Martin Buber focused attention on the person in the *Mitwelt*, analyzing interaction in his *I and Thou* (1958). It is the *Eigenwelt* that has been least under-stood in modern psychology; in fact, in the traditions of American Behaviorism there is overt denial of the value or necessity for postulating any concept of "self." The existential view attempts to provide a framework within which psychology and education can recognize and work with the realities of the wholeness of each person.

As existential thought gained attention in the 1950's, educational philosophers turned to ascertaining the implications for education. It was found that few of the historical or contemporary existential philosophers had attended to the questions of education. Kneller, (1964) wrote:

> I must mention that existential philosophers have written very little on education as such. Martin Buber is an exception. Gabriel Marcel frequently refers to education in passing, JeanPaul Sartre has defined the educational significance of literature. Karl Jaspers has published a book on *The Idea of the University*. This neglect of education is surprising when one considers how many of the traditional philosophers, such as Plato, Locke, Kant, and Dewey, have addressed themselves to educational problems.
>
> It becomes all the more surprising when one reflects that as a philosophy of personal life, existentialism is bound to yield insights into education, a process in which the person can either be made or make themselves. Perhaps the explanation is that a new school of thought is almost bound to concentrate on the theoretical problem it has raised and leave till later or to others the application of its principles in realms where thought and

practice converge, such as politics, law, and education. Be that as it may, the opportunity is all the greater for educators themselves to explore and synthesize the educational insights with which existentialism abounds.   (Kneller, 1964)

Soon after that commentary, George Kneller authored a major work of interpretation on the importance of existentialism for education titled *Existentialism and Education*. One of his important points was that many existentialists would disagree with the American educational curriculum's emphasis on the world, as opposed to the person, and the person-in-the-world (Kneller,1965).

Two other early contributions to exploration of the implications of existentialism for education were *Existentialism in Education* (Morris, 1966) and an edition of selections of educational relevance from the existential thinkers, *Existential Encounters for Teachers* (Greene, 1967). In a later review and scholarly study of *Existentialism and Creativity* (Bedford, 1972), the author argued that the existential theories must have significant educational implications. He quoted John Dewey: "If a theory makes no difference in educational endeavors, it must be artificial."

In his study, Bedford proceeds to organize a list of nearly three hundred statements about man, knowledge, life, teachers, choice, and change, and then seeks to determine whether there are arguments of agreement in the writings of four prominent existential thinkers—Kierkegaard, Buber, Jaspers, and Sartre. He defined the study:

> The essential problem of this study was to discern whether existentialism as a philosophical system contains within it the seed of an educational philosophy which might contribute something of

value to the great educational debate of the 20th century. (Bedford, 1972)

The investigation resulted in a number of findings about an existential overview of education:

1) The first conclusion of this study is that there are traits of authentic becoming which are inherent in existential thinking. The word "becoming" is very important, for the existentialists agree that an individual does not attain the authentic stage in a gigantic, once and forever, leap.

Bedford discusses the nature of authenticity in detail, and suggests that much of the existential ideology is quite parallel to the thinking of Carl Rogers.

2) The elementary school atmosphere must be one which develops in the child a feeling of confidence and trust in the learning experience. It is important that the school atmosphere be one which maximumly stimulates the spontaneity of the child, and encourages him/her to express themself openly and without fear of intimidation.

3) Learning must not merely involve cortical functioning. Learning experience must be translated into action—into doing. The

student must see how what she is learning is applicable to her life.

With regard to this conclusion, Bedford notes that the existentialists would agree with Dewey in the belief that the learning situation involves active reconstruction of one's own experiences and the society in which one's existence is engaged.

4) In the education of the adolescent, the teacher will be charged with the responsibility of studying each student to learn their strengths and weaknesses, so that they may bolster them during the times of crisis.

Existential theory does, indeed, have implications for education, and challenge education theorists may find much of relevance as they attend to the task of developing a theoretical perspective on activities and methodologies which offer a challenge for growth and learning.

HUMANISTIC PSYCHOLOGY

The methodology of challenge education has many roots in the theory and practice of the "third force" in American psychology. As the twentieth century unfolded, there was increasing criticism of both the academic-scientific psychological orientation toward "behaviorism" and the clinical-biological orientation of the psychoanalytic approach to dealing with personality development and the treatment of behavioral dysfunction. Actually, the criticisms of the strict biological model of Freud and "psychoanalysis" were first raised by his own colleagues, students, and secondgeneration analysts (e.g., Rank, Horney, Jung, Fromm, Sullivan, etc.). They suggested that the biomedical view of the person was too restrictive, and did not provide

sufficiently for the importance of social influences on personality and development.

The behaviorists of the academic world, in their efforts to steer psychology closer to the standards of scientific methodology, were also criticized as limiting the perspectives on humankind. Distinctions were made between the scientific study of human-kind and the study of persons from a broader perspective, recognizing their complexity and totality. For a number of years, there was debate and discussion about the necessity and desirability of a concept of "self" for psychological science. The debate ended, in part, as many theorists recognized that the issue was based on inappropriate questions. The experiential fact was obvious—that persons did indeed possess awareness, and whether the concept of self belonged in psychology or not, it was real. It was not only appropriate to seek an understanding of the nature and function of "self," but it was necessary to any comprehensive overview of the totality of the human being. Through the late 1930's and into the 1940's, the philosophical foundations of what was to become that "third force" in psychology were formed. Even as the new theory was unfolding, laboratory psychologists were focusing on self-concept, and validating it empirically (Wylie, 1961).

The new "humanistic psychology" had parallels in the European thinking about "existential psychology" (May, 1958; Kneller, 1965; Morris, 1966; Greene, 1967; Bedford, 1967). It was also recognized as having roots in the phenomenological philosophies (Husserl, 1936; Merleau-Ponty, 1942, 1945; Ricoeur, 1967; Giorgi, 1970; Zaner & Ihde, 1973).

The new model for psychology also bore a relationship to "General Systems Theory" as set forth by Ludwig von Bertalanffy, a biologist, who had an interest in making psychology and psychiatry more relevant to the true nature of the human being (Bertalanffy, 1950, 1955; Bertalanffy & Rapport, 1956). His thought paralleled that of other critics of historical psychology:

Let us face the fact: a large part of modern psychology is a sterile and pompous scholasticism which, with the blinders of preconceived notions or superstitions on its nose, doesn't see the obvious; which covers the triviality of its results and ideas with preposterous language bearing no resemblance either to normal English or normal scientific theory; and which provides modern society with the techniques for progressive stultification of mankind.

The famous battalions of rats working innumerable Skinner boxes have little to tell about the human condition, our sorrows and the problems of our age. The question to modern psychology and sociology, it seems, is whether they can be *human* — concerned with the issues, temporal and eternal, of man and society; and at the same time scientific — true to fact and guided by that discipline of method that has developed over the past few centuries.

Psychology, in the first half of the twentieth century, was dominated by a positivistic-mechanistic-reductionistic approach which can be epitomized as the robot model of man.

I believe that there are certain principles in common in an emerging psychology of man or, we should rather say, in a new science of man or general anthropology, because this will obviously be an interdisciplinary enterprise including biology, psychiatry, sociology, linguistics, economics, the arts, and other fields. Against the robot model of the primary reactivity of the organism a conception emerges which, in psychological language, can be termed that of man as an active personality system. I arrived at these notions long ago from my biological background. They now seem to become central in various recent developments in psychology. (Bertalanffy, 1967)

Most of the critics of the traditional model recognized that there would be no rapid shift in the orientation of the academic psychologists, who tended to cling to the behavioristic and learning theory models. The humanistic psychologists, frustrated by the rigidity of the academic American Psychological Association (APA), began efforts in the late 1950's to organize an alternative professional organization. The Association for Humanistic Psychology (AHP) was organized in the early 1960's. AHP offered a rallying point for the "third force" psychologists, but also opened membership to educators, philosophers, social scientists, clergymen, and interested laymen. The "Human Potential Movement" was underway; the years from 1960 to 1980 were fully chronicled as "The Aquarian Conspiracy" (Ferguson, 1980).

The tenants of an educational orientation based on humanistic psychology have often been summarized. One of the most meaningful compilations of basic principles has been presented by humanistic outdoor educator Cliff Knapp and humanistic educator Joel Goodman in their book *Humanizing Environmental Education.*

1) It is important to address the "whole person" in any educational endeavor. In addition to cognitive learning, it is crucial that we acknowledge the affect areas of human experience. The two areas cannot be separated as we learn.

2) People learn best when they feel safe, respected appreciated, motivated, challenged, when they have opportunities

to make choices in their lives, and when they have chances to identify and build on their own strengths and interests.

3) There is a universe within each of us that can be a legitimate and exciting subject matter for exploration. Humanistic education seeks to help people develop self-scientist skills — learning about and from our own thoughts, feelings, and behaviors.

4) We must help people to develop a sense of identity, a sense of connectedness, and a sense of mastery or locus of control. Identity involves one's selfimage and feelings of self-worth. Connectedness involves one's relationship with other people. Mastery or locus of control involves the extent to which one is in charge of what happens to him/ her.

5) We must create learning environments that encourage; pluralism and respect for differences, collaboration and cooperation, nourishment and support among people, and opportunities to generate alternative solutions to problems.

6) Learning will be internalized to a greater extent when: both the experiential (actively participating) and reflective (relating to one's own life experience) modes are employed; different learning styles are incorporated in the program (e.g., listening, observing, reading, touching, discussing, notetaking, playing, working alone, and working cooperatively with a group.

7) Humanistic education is an approach to creating positive learning environments that encourage people to develop life skills that they find valuable in addressing personal and society concerns. Humanistic education helps people develop life skills in four areas: the cognitive (thinking), the affective (feeling), the active (behaving), and the interpersonal (human relations). (Knapp & Goodman,1981)

Humanistic education has also addressed itself to the issue of guiding human-kind to a new image of what it means to be human, and

to an awareness of the responsibility that comes with living in a participatory democracy. The humanistic educator recognizes that evolution toward the world as it ought to be involves challenging each and every person to modify values and behavior, and move in a direction consistent with the appropriate vision of humankind. In a 1970 article in a book on the implication of social and technological change for education, Willis Harman described two alternative future societies. One was based on a continuous transition of the twentieth century technological society into the twenty-first century, and the second alternative involved a significant break with the past, in parallel to what Thomas Kuhn had called a "paradigm shift" (Kuhn, 1962). The basic orientation of this second alternative for the future would be that of the "personcentered" society. Harman's thinking has been influenced by Carl Rogers, and he presented the two visions of the future with a bias toward the latter alternative.

Two years later, the Worth Commission on Educational Planning, of Alberta, Canada, drew heavily from the Harman article in offering suggestions for educational curricula (Worth Commission, 1972). Based on the argument that it would be careless and undesirable for the world to simply arrive at either of the two alternatives without having given careful forethought to the desirability of them both, the Commission suggested:

> Both types of society assume that most activities (i.e., education, legal and social functions, economic and political affairs) will continue to be carried out by large-scale centralized organizations. However, traditional values, congenial to the second phase of industrial society, favor a highly bureaucratic organizational structure. Such values are based on a hi-

erarchy of authority and communication, clearly specified roles and many rules to guide daily activity.

Conversely, the person-centered society's humanist values support a more flexible structure, which better enables the organization to recognize, adjust and adapt to changing conditions. There would be more emphasis on a two-way flow of communication between superior and subordinate, creating a greater emphasis on participation in decision-making by those at lower levels of the organization. (Ibid.)

In addition to this difference between a less-and-more participatory society, the Commission summarized other conceptual and functional differences between Harman's two alternatives. They concluded that the personcentered society was, indeed, more desirable. They argued that such an alternative could be realized if there was an appropriate reorientation of values in the near future. This could come from choosing between two images of the human being, and the appropriate choice would be along the lines of the humanistic psychology perspective. This, then, implies that educational programs should alter their orientation and give greater consideration to the suggestions of the humanistic psychologists.

The distinction between the approach of humanistic psychology and that of mainstream psychology in the academic world became more defined through the 1960's. In 1973, I. L. Child wrote of the differences in the two images that psychology presented to the world:

One is the concerned effort to understand persons. Here, like the humanities, psychology is centered on individuals and, like other humane endeavors, is aimed at promoting personal welfare and

growth. The second image is the quest for abstract knowledge about human behavior. As in the other sciences, the object of study is looked at as object, and is considered not for its own sake but for the generalizations that can be based on it. Psychology, in this second image, may forget the person in order to study only the processes occurring within him. The first image is represented in an extreme form by the movement known as humanistic psychology, but it emerges from a long tradition of centering psychology on humanity.The second image is represented in an extreme form by the experimental study of behavior, with its restrictive emphasis on method and evidence. (Child, 1973)

Challenge educators have long recognized their relationship to the humanistic psychologists, and to the whole historical tradition of seeking to improve the quality of life for human beings. Two of the important psychological theorists that influenced the whole human potential movement were Carl Rogers and Abraham Maslow. Their ideas about, and suggested techniques for, humanistic growth, development, and learning are often discussed in the writings of challenge educators, experiential educators, adventure educators, and outdoor educators. Many of their methodologies are utilized in the challenge education perspective. Challenge educators seeking philosophical foundation for their programming can find value in the writings of Rogers (c.f., 1951, 1958, 1959, 1961, 1969, 1980) and Maslow (c.f., 1954, 1956, 1968, 1971, 1973).

One of Carl Rogers' papers was published in a collection of articles that afforded "glimpses into the 21st century" (Villoldo & Dychtwald, 1981). He recognized the importance of education in the total process of human-kind growing toward the future. He suggested that an educational system based on the concepts of humanistic psychology might contribute to a culture of trust, openness, creativity, and productivity. He outlines what might be achieved by education in the future:

- It could build a climate of trust in which curiosity, the natural desire to learn, could be nourished and enhanced.

- It could free students, faculty, and administrators alike to participate in decision making about all aspects of learning.

- It could develop a sense of community in which the destructive competition of today would be replaced by cooperation, respect for others, and mutual helpfulness.

- It could encourage students to prize themselves, to develop self-confidence and self-esteem.

- It could enable both students and faculty increasingly to discover the source of values in themselves, coming to an awareness that the good life is within, and is not dependent on outside sources.

- It could imbue students with an excitement in intellectual and emotional discovery, which would lead them to become lifelong learners, in a community of learners.

- These are not "pie-in-the-sky" statements. We have the know-how for achieving every one of these goals. Whether as a culture we choose to bring them about is the only uncertain element. (Rogers, 1981)

Many other approaches that were given significant impetus by the human potential movement have also been recognized as important for challenge education theory and practice; they have been discussed in professional papers and training workshops. This includes the work of Sid Simon on "values clarification" (Raths, et al., 1966; Simon, et al., 1972; Simon & Kirschenbaum, 1978), the classic book of strategies for enhancing self-concept in the classroom (Canfield & Wells, 1976) and many articles and books on "affective education" (Krathwohl, 1956; Leonard, 1968; Jones, 1968; Weinstein & Fantini,

1970). The theoretical base of these practices deserves exploration by the challenge education philosopher.

Two very important contributors to the humanistic education movement, perhaps less known to challenge educators, deserve attention in any discussion of the philosophical roots of programming. They are Arthur Combs and George Brown.

PERCEPTUAL PSYCHOLOGY – ARTHUR COMBS

In 1949, two respected academic psychologists, Donald Snygg and Arthur Combs, published an overview of a new psychology. They titled the book *Individual Behavior: A New Frame of Reference for Psychology* (Snygg & Combs, 1949). They did not call it "perceptual psychology," but noted that their orientation was phenomenological, thus differing from the traditions of the majority of American psychology with roots in the behavioristic ideology. Their publication received only moderate attention, and was apparently considered too far afield from the mainstream to warrant critical attention.

By the time of the second edition of the book ten years later, the movement of humanistic psychology was unfolding rapidly, and the relationship between the phenomenological and humanistic approach was recognized. Both of the authors had begun to recognize the truly alternative nature of a psychology based on the way the person perceives the world, and had actively published theoretical and research papers through that ten-year period. For the second edition, the title was changed to *Individual Behavior: A Perceptual Approach to Behavior* (Combs & Snygg,

1959). In the forward to that edition, Arthur Combs noted:

> In the last few years new developments in perceptual psychology have occurred with such rapidity that like Alice in Wonderland, one must run as fast as he can just to keep up. Almost every psychological journal reports new and intriguing studies bearing on some aspect of the personal frame of reference.

Fifteen years later, perceptual psychology had indeed come of age, and a third edition of the text was offered, in light of "two new understandings."

> 1) Perceptual psychology is not just the study of the internal lives of persons or the study of behavior; it is the study of persons. Historically, psychology began with the study of mental processes, and the earliest psychologists were almost exclusively preoccupied with such matters. Later psychologists, including most of those in the United States, took a different tack. They were deeply impressed with the control and prediction of events achieved in the physical sciences and sought to apply that model to psychology. As a consequence, they focused attention on the study of behavior, especially behavior that could be precisely observed and manipulated. In that preoccupation, the internal life of persons was largely ignored, passed over as "unscientific," or rejected outright as a legitimate area of study because it was inaccessible to direct methods of observation.
>
> 2) Perceptual psychology is both product and process of the humanistic movement. The humanistic movement finds expression in humanistic psychology, sometimes called the third force. This emphasis in psychological thought began about the same time perceptual psychology was formulated in the late 1940's. Since then, dozens of new humanistic approaches to understanding persons and human functioning have come into being as increased numbers of psychologists and practitioners have turned attention to humanistic matters. Among these are psychologists calling themselves transactionalists, existentialists, phenomenologists, self-psychologists, humanists, and, of course, perceptual psychologists. Perceptual psychology is more than an expression of the humanist movement. It is also a frame of reference specially designed to deal with questions raised by the movement and to contribute to its implementation in the solution of human problems.
>
> The humanistic movement requires a person-centered psychology, one capable of dealing not only with behavior, but with the meanings and perceptions that constitute the internal experience of persons as well. A perceptual psychology is uniquely suited to provide this kind of understanding. (Combs, et al., 1976)

The third edition of the book was titled *Perceptual Psychology: A Humanistic Approach to the Study of Persons.* At that time, the authors recognized that when one accepts a basic scientific paradigm or frame of reference, then the problems selected for study are also defined. In the spirit of Thomas Kuhn's work on scientific revolutions (Kuhn, 1962), the authors noted:

> The great human problems of our time press upon us and we need the best possible understanding we can acquire about the nature of persons and their behavior. In adopting any frame of reference or any theory of human functioning, however, we need to be keenly aware that all such theories are always only an approximation of the nature of events. Sooner or later, the best of theories is likely to be superseded by something a bit better, simpler, more accurate, more comprehensive, or more useful for accomplishing our major purposes. This should not dismay us. Rather, it should give us courage to make the very best attempt we can to

achieve the best approximations to the gossamer threaded "truth" of which we are capable in our time.(Combs, et al., 1976)

Combs and his co-authors note that the third edition involves review of the research and theoretical perspectives of thousands of psychologists, social scientists, and philosophers interpreted within their perceptual frame of reference. Basically, they postulate that all behavior, without exception, is determined by the individual's perceptual field at that moment of action. "The perceptual field is the entire universe, including himself, as it is experienced by an individual at the instant of action." It is each person's perceptual field of awareness, the field of meanings and values, which determines his behavior. In the course of a person's growth and learning, and as the result of all the experiences with the world around him, certain aspects of the perceptual field become more or less clearly defined, differentiated, valued, and sought because they satisfy needs. These differentiations are considered *goals*. Also, during that course of growth and development the individual develops personalized *techniques*, or patterns of behavior to achieve the goals desired. For each individual, some goals and techniques are considered more positive, more satisfying, and hence are recognized as *values*. Throughout life, individuals seek for basic maintenance and enhancement of themselves and their life by attending to their personally perceived goals, techniques, and values (Ibid.).

Although the emergence of behaviorism in American psychology in the 1920's and its dominance of the field until mid-century had brought arguments against the inclusion of the concept of self in the science of human behav-

ior, there were early voices that suggested its importance. The voices of George Herbert Mead (1935), Kurt Lewin (1935), Gordon Allport (1937), and Kurt Goldstein (1939) laid early groundwork for the self-concept psychologies to follow from Gardner Murphy (1947), Carl Rogers (1947), A. H. Maslow (1954) and Clark Moustakas (1956), as well as the work of Snygg and Combs. Review of theory and research that covers such to-pics as adequacy feelings, group membership, peak experiences, perceptual fields, values clarification, self discovery, and introspection make up the context of the third edition of the Snygg and Combs book, and would provide valuable historical perspective for the challenge educator.

Combs and Snygg call for educational programs which will involve:

> Utilization of new approaches to education which will emphasize the development of self-learning skills in the person and creation of conditions which will foster spontaneous learning. Diversity in educational pursuits together with less emphasis on grading and credentials. (Combs et al.,1976)

In summary, they noted that:

> Our tendency to use our vast technological power for both good and ill has resulted in one of the most critical periods in human history. Possessing the resources to improve greatly the human situation both now and in the future, we have confronted the fact that we may not have a future at all. We have come to realize, too, that our emphasis upon quantity rather than quality, the tendency toward dehumanization of individuals, and the pollution of the environment are not the inevitable consequences of our technological development, but the product of our values, attitudes and beliefs. We have

come more and more to realize that the future we may experience will be the product of the goals we strive for and the beliefs we hold about ourselves and our possibilities. (Ibid.)

The challenge for the future is obvious, but the authors tend toward optimism. They wrote:

> Perceptual psychology provides us with an essentially hopeful view of persons. For several generations we have lived with a conception of persons as almost exclusively the products of the forces exerted upon them, prisoners of the past. In such a view the responsibility of human beings lies always outside themselves and human potentiality lies largely at the mercy of forces over which an individual has little or no control. The perceptual view is far more hopeful. It sees the dynamics of behavior as inside each person; therefore, in far greater measure the human being is architect of his own existence. (Op. cit.)

Shortly after the publication of the second edition of the Snygg and Combs text, Arthur Combs served as chairman and editor of the National Education Association's "Association for Supervision and Curriculum Development." In that role, he was responsible for the ASCD's yearbook, published in 1962. It was titled *Perceiving, Behaving, Becoming: A New Focus for Education*, and opened with a question:

> How can it be timely, in a period in which attention in education is riveted on the technological revolution, alternative proposals for organizational structure, and updating knowledge in government-favored academic areas, to offer a "new focus for education?" (Combs, 1962)

The yearbook answered the challenge by providing papers by Earl Kelly, Abraham Maslow, and Arthur Combs himself, followed by their discussion of the nature of a perceptual-humanistic approach to education. They review such topics as:

> ...increasing openness to experience...
> ...trust and trustworthiness...
> ...development of self-concept...
> ...human interaction...
> ...attitudes toward the handicapped...
> ...horizontal versus vertical organizations...
> ...self-actualization...
> ...the learning of values...
> ...leadership...
> ...protection of group participants...
> ...the process of becoming...
> ...the challenge of experience...

Eight years later, in 1970, Arthur Combs was a contributor to another of the ASCD yearbooks titled *To Nurture Humaneness: Commitment for the 70's* (Socobey & Graham, 1970). Combs took a more action-recommending stance than in the earlier theoretical textbooks. He wrote:

> If humanism is to take its place as a prime objective of education, that fact must be spelled out in our procedures and practices. It makes a great deal of difference through what pair of glasses one looks at the schools. If one looks through a pair marked "Providing Information," the schools look very good. Common practices and procedures are clearly related to those goals and make a great deal of sense. Looked at through the glasses marked "Valuing Humanism," schools look decidedly different. In fact, some of the very procedures required for the business of giving information get in the way of achieving humanism. If humanism is to be given the kind of central position this volume calls for, then a careful, system-

atic search of our goals and practices is needed to weed out those whose effects are destructive to human values.

If increasing humanness is to be a major function of the schools, it will be necessary for us to find much better ways than we have to get students involved in the whole educational process. To meet the needs of students it will be necessary to involve them deeply. This will not be easy, for traditional practices have done their work well, our students are thoroughly brainwashed into the belief that learning is a passive process in which you are not learning anything unless someone is telling you something and that independent action gets you nowhere.

Responsibility and self-direction, we need to remind ourselves, are not learned from withholding these things. It is hard, however, to give young people responsibility and independece because we are so afraid they might not be able to handle it. This fear prevents us from giving students responsibility; it is never learned from having it withheld.   (Combs, 1970)

Again, in 1978, Combs took on the task of editing a collection of papers for ASCD. This edition provided an even deeper look at the nature of the objectives of the humanistic alternative in education, and offered an assessment of progress over the previous two decades (Combs, 1978). Challenge education was beginning to develop by that time, mainly through the methodologies of adventure education (Project Adventure), outdoor leadership training and programming for juvenile offenders (Outward Bound), and new approaches to environmental education (Acclimatization). Also, there had been formation of a new national organization of educators concerned with experiential learning (Association for Experiential Education), which provided considerable impetus to the development of challenge education. However, there were few recognitions of the parallels be-

tween these approaches and the already unfolding programs of humanistic education. In a very few years, humanistic educators would be involved with the experiential education movement, and those advocating experiential education were recognizing the value of the humanistic education strategies.

As challenge education unfolded-with emphasis on providing students with innovative, experiential, and exciting learning situations, learning problems, group interactions, and opportunities for self-discovery there was significant attention paid to the ideas of the humanistic psychologists and humanistic educations. Now as the search commences for appropriate philosophical foundations for the challenge education orientations, the works of the "perceptual psychologists," as reflected in the work of Arthur Combs, would appear to be very significant.

Confluent Education - George Brown

One of the important influences on the whole human potential movement, because it provided a gathering point for many of the thinkers and doers, was California's Esalen. The list of prominent speakers, workshop facilitators, seminar leaders, and think tank participants, provides a veritable who's who of the human potential movement. The list included: Rollo May, Carl Rogers, B. F. Skinner, Arnold Toynbee, Abraham Maslow, Aldous Huxley, George Leonard, Linus Pauling, Paul Tillich, Carlos Castaneda, Alan Watts, Buckminster Fuller, John Lilly, Colin Wilson, Fritz Perls, Roberto Assagioli, Ashley Montagu, Joseph Campbell, Victor Frankel, S. I. Hayakawa, J. B. Rhine, Robert Ornstein, and George Leonard.

In addition, Esalen provided the setting for a number of special research and development projects. One of these projects, funded by the Ford Foundation, was the Ford-Esalen Project in Affective Education, headed by George Isaac Brown, who had been a student of Fritz Perls, leader of the school of Gestalt Therapy. After a final report on the project, Brown authored a book (Brown, 1971) and edited a collection of papers (Brown, et.al, 1975). The first book, *Human Teaching for Human Learning,* was subtitled "An Introduction to Confluent Education." In the editor's introduction to that book, Stuart Miller summarized the Ford-Esalen Project's goal as:

> ...Beginning a serious attempt to renew one of the oldest traditions in education, the central tradition of Western education—education for the whole man. We must reinvent the great tradition by renewing it. One of the primary ways for such renewal is found in the concept of "affective education"— that is, the identification for specific educational concern of the nonintellectual side of learning: the side having to do with emotions, feelings, interests, values, and character. (Miller, in Brown, 1971)

It is interesting to note that while the purported focus of the Ford-Esalen Project was "affective education," George Brown did not consider that an appropriate description of the ideas the project generated. He explains his position in the early pages of the book:

> Confluent education is the term for the integration or flowing together of the affective and cognitive elements in individual and group learning. Affective refers to the feeling or emotional aspect of experience and learning. How a child or adult feels about wanting to learn, how he feels as he learns, and what he feels after he has learned are included in the affec-

tive domain. Cognitive refers to the activity of the mind in knowing an object, to the intellectual functioning. What an individual learns and the intellectual process of learning it would fall within the cognitive domain—unless what is learned is an attitude or value, which would be affective learning. It should be apparent that there is no intellectual learning without some sort of feeling, and there are no feelings without the mind's being somehow involved.

> We are now at a new threshold. Simultaneously emerging in our time are a number of approaches to the extension of human consciousness and the realization of human potential. Some are dangerous, some are irresponsible, and some are exciting, holding great promise. There are a variety of exploratory practices and theories that can be grouped under the taxonomic umbrella of humanistic psychology. These have been the largest resource for work in the area of confluent education. To reiterate, confluent education describes a philosophy and a process of teaching and learning in which the affective domain and the cognitive domain flow together, like two streams merging into one river, and are integrated thus in individual and group learning. (Brown, 1971)

The Ford-Esalen project involved a group of educators and psychologists exchanging ideas for affective techniques and sensory-awareness exercises; and the group spent many hours actually experiencing activity sequences. One of the teachers in the core group was Janet Lederman, who later published her own book on her experiences, and her ideas for incorporating some of the strategies into the school curriculum (Lederman, 1969).

Many of the activities of the workshop group are described and discussed in Brown's book, and would be quite familiar to leaders of challenge education sequences. For example:

> ...dyads for communication
>   enhancement...
> ...guided fantasy...
> ...trust walks...
> ...improvisational drama...
> ...mirroring...
> ...trust circles...
> ...animal fantasy...
> ...contemplation...
> ...decision by consensus...

Brown summarized the whole approach of confluent education with discussion of significant issues, such as the necessity for the development of responsibility in parallel to the delegation of freedom. He argues that the implementation of affective and confluent curricula in the schools will be an evolutional process, and should not be expected to rapidly reverse the conservative traditions of the mainstream of education. His elaboration of the following ideas provide insights for any challenge educator:

- No one should be coerced to do anything he does not want to do.

- The teacher must get in touch with himself, and experienced group leaders are skillful at avoiding that responsibility.

- The teacher must take the child where he is, and then bring him as far as he can go.

- We must be committed to the thesis that an individual is the expert on himself.

- Well-intentioned persons can ultimately do more harm than good, especially if they rush in as leaders while still in the euphoria of their own exciting experiences.

- The teacher who cannot provide on demand an intelligent, understandable rationale for his work in this area if not only heading for trouble himself; he will also create many problems for those who do know what they are doing.

- There is still strong justification for having content for students to learn.

- Getting in touch with oneself is invaluable in knowing how far one should go when teaching in the affective domain. It is not difficult to sense when one is getting in over his head. This is the time to stop.

- The good teacher knows what is happening NOW. And he knows how his students are responding NOW. And he knows what he is doing NOW, and how he feels about doing it. Experiencing the NOW and taking responsibility for the NOW is essential for successful teaching in confluent education. (Ibid.)

The Ford-Esalen Project was followed by the project for "Development and Research in Confluent Education" (DRICE), also funded by the Ford Foundation. The empirical research was summarized in a publication by John Shiflett and George Brown (1972), and there was a theoretical and programmatic collection of articles edited by Brown. The book of readings was titled, *The Live Classroom: Innovations through Confluent Education and Gestalt* (Brown, et al., 1975). Brown writes in the introduction about the title description of a "live classroom:"

> What is the difference between a dead and a live classroom? The real way to tell is to experience both of them. In the dead classroom learning is mechanistic, routine, over-ritualized, dull, and boring. The teacher is robotized, and the children are conceived of as containers or receptacles whose primary function is to receive and hold subject matter. This is essentially the consequence of the misuse of the industrial model. The efficiency of the process, when there is such concern, is usually also based on technological or business constructs.
>
> The live classroom, on the other hand, is full of learning activities in which students are enthusiastically and authentically involved. Students take on as much responsibility for their learning as their capabilities allow. Each student is genu-

inely respected and treated as a human being by his teacher. He, in turn, participates in the learning-teaching process as one who structures strategies for learning, as individualized as possible, while focusing on process as well as subject matter. There is frustration in the live classroom, but at a level which is perceived by the learner as a challenge rather than as an overwhelming obstacle.

In the live classroom, the learning involves living. In the dead classroom, the learning turns destructively on itself and on the learner. To survive this, the student must numb himself, his real self, for he is caught between the pressures of socialization and the grim irrelevance and inertia of his lessons. He may drop out. At best, he plays the learning game wherein he creates a role or subpersonality called the "me as student" that has little or no relation to the rest of himself. (Brown, 1975)

The major thrust of the second of Brown's books is to elaborate the meaning and the process of confluent education. The effort is colorfully described:

Essentially we are attempting, through the development of confluent approaches to education, to pour back some juice into dehydrated educational practices. As a result, the dried-up prunes of classroom process become plums of learning plump, sweet, and nourishing. We want to help change those schools in which teachers and students are bored with routine into exciting, challenging places, where content comes alive, generating the curiosity and excitement we all once had as children discovering a world full of wonder and marvels. (Ibid.)

The book provides readings that deal with the practices of Gestalt therapy as they can be applied to educational programs, and there are ideas on the educational curriculum, including examples of instructional units, and course outlines. Classroom teachers discuss

their efforts to include the principles of confluent education into their classrooms, and write of the successes and the failures. In his concluding comments, Brown again offers some significant thoughts that challenge educators should contemplate, and there is special concern for teachers copying the techniques without appropriate training and personal development.

Our first caution is that the reader who is a teacher not be seduced into using any of the techniques or approaches without somehow making them a part of his own total teaching approach and philosophy. Unless he does this he will simply be using a gimmick and today's gimmick disappears tomorrow. In all our work with teachers and others, we have found that there are essentially three stages of training and professional development. We begin the initial stage by introducing the techniques experientially in the training, and then having them utilized by the participants themselves. The next stage seems to be when these techniques become an integral part of a person's philosophy and behavior, through emphasis not just on the techniques themselves but also on an appreciation of the philosophy and understanding underlying the techniques.

This has been described as moving from a teacher who uses confluent techniques to one who becomes a confluent teacher. Finally, being a confluent teacher incorporates a third stage wherein the teacher takes the techniques or approaches learned in stage one and uses them to create new approaches or new techniques himself for his own classroom situation. (Op.Cit.)

One of the most fascinating aspects of George Isaac Brown would appear to be his blend of optimism and patience. Challenge education, as with humanistic education, recognizes the need for the human being to get about the process of becoming more human.

The technocratic, materialistic, human chauvinistic orientation of twentieth-century human-kind leads many to prediction for self- and-planet destruction in the future. The first result of an awareness of the potential for man to became, as visioned by humanistic psychology, can be an increasing optimism and hope. However, as the scope of the challenge for change is perceived, many who hold cognitive awareness of human-kind's potential have trouble emotionally believing that change will come in time. This often leads to pessimism, and to an impatience for people to quickly and completely transform. Then there is cry of "Grow or Die" (Lockland, 1973), and "before it is too late." All would do well to sense the wisdom of George Brown:

> The happiest way to think about it is that mankind is evolving gradually, that there is some kind of collective consciousness as well as unconscious, and that there is a wisdom in people they don't know about. They behave in certain ways; they know how fast they're ready to move. (Brown, 1974)

PSYCHOSYNTHESIS - ROBERTO ASSAGIOLI

As challenge education programming has concerns for facilitation of personal growth, there may be value in attention to the theory and practice of Psychosynthesis, as developed by Italian psychiatrist Roberto Assagioli. Although he studied in psychoanalysis in the early 1900's, Assagioli was quick to find the limitations of Freud's biological model of growth and development. In his doctoral study, he maintained that Freud had not given sufficient weight to the higher aspects of human personality, and recognized the need for a broader conceptualization of the person. In many ways, his thinking was parallel to that of other Freudian critics (Sullivan, Horney, Fromm, Jung, etc.), and also had overlap with the ideas of Abraham Maslow, who some forty years later would write on "the further reaches of human nature" (Maslow, 1968).

Throughout the 1930's and the 1940's, Assagioli impacted on many students in Italy and throughout Europe, but it was not until the 1950's that his thinking became influential in America. In a relatively short time, his writings were translated, he came to the States to lecture and exchange ideas with others who were seeking new models for life and growth, and he spent time at Esalen in California, the "think tank" for the whole human potential movement. His ideas were well received, and ten years later, when Marilyn Ferguson surveyed people involved in the human potential movement (which she summarized as "the Aquarian Conspiracy"), she found that Roberto Assagioli was one of the top ten listed "influences" on their thinking and practice (Ferguson, 1980).

Like the challenge education sequence leader, Assagioli sought to develop an approach to growth facilitation that encompassed the whole person, including the higher processes of creativity, joy, wisdom, and the will, as well as basic impulses and drives. He was eclectic in his search for integrative strategies, and experimented with many different procedures. Like the existential thinkers, Assagioli saw the person as always in process of change and becoming. Basic to his whole theory was the postulate that there is an internal tendency towards positive growth in the human personality. In quite simple terms, his theory of Psychosynthesis advocates that the person should attend to, and cooperate with, this natural tendency towards new learning, new awareness, and personal growth (Assagioli, 1971).

Psychosynthesis is a process, an approach, to the revelation of the self. While individuals may cultivate practices which will allow this natural process to unfold, there may be need for learning appropriate ways to cooperate with the growth process from a skilled teacher or therapist. Assagioli suggests that the most appropriate designation for the person who is in this leadership role would be "guide." Psychosynthesis focuses on the concept that the person is in a constant state of change, seeking to actualize their hidden potentials in balance with their underlying personal values (ethical, aesthetic, religious), and the responsibility they take for making choices and decisions. Obviously, value conflicts, life-stress situations, emotional problems, and other developmental factors can stifle the natural growth process, as can the person's withdrawal from personal responsibility.

Maximization of growth and learning involves the person assuming full responsibility for themselves, actively participating in mapping and exploring their personal depths, and accessing the personal value of the many strategies which are available. Psychosynthesis places much emphasis on the uniqueness of each person, and recognizes that the process of growth and learning involves different patterns for different persons. Because of this the strategies of the approach are eclectic, and draw from many other approaches. The more typically recommended procedures for personal growth include relaxation, meditation, guided imagery, personal journaling, trust building, cognitive analysis, humanistic groupwork, and creative exploration. The whole approach blends into ongoing growth theories and practices, which might vary from country to country or group to group. In other words, the argument of Psychosynthesis is simply, "Grow...in your own fashion, with the strategies that work for you and are available to you...but, in any case, grow."

According to Assagioli, the process of growth unfolds through four stages. First, there is the requirement of learning about oneself. This involves explorations of values, conflicts, interpersonal relationships, and the various levels of consciousness from lower to higher. The second stage is that of seeking reasonable control over the total self discovered at stage one. Thus, there must be attention to resolution of conflicts, clarification of incongruent values, more honest and open interpersonal relationships, and procedures for attending to higher order consciousness. Third, there is the stage of integration of all discovered at stage one and two, finding basic harmony, balance, and the nature of one's center. Finally, there is the stage called "Psychosynthesis" which involves turning to self-actualization. There must be both a personal and a transpersonal synthesis. The personal self is the worldly self, and synthesis at that level means learning how to be more personally integrated and effective in usage of personal energies. At the level of transpersonal selfexpression, the person becomes involved with values, psychosocial harmony, global perspectives, environmental awareness, and spirituality. The seeking of transpersonal synthesis implies dealing with higher goals of cooperation, altruistic love, social and planetary responsibility, and spiritual expression.

Psychosynthesis puts emphasis on striving to attain transpersonal synthesis, for there at, one finds highest human functioning. In defining the transpersonal domain, Assagioli writes:

96

From this region we receive our higher aspirations—artistic, philosophical, scientific or ethical imperatives, and urges to humanitarianism and heroic action. It is the source of the higher feelings, such as altruistic love, and of genius and the states of contemplation, illumination, and ecstasy. In this realm are latent the higher of the psychological functions and the spiritual energies. (Assagioli, 1971)

Assagioli's suggestion of the basic tendency for evolutional growth and change, a driving force within the person seeking expression, provided a very dynamic model for growth counseling. There was not need for "teachers" so much as for "releasors," who could guide the person to break through their own barriers and let their growth tendencies propel them forward. This argument about human beings caught the attention of Albert Szent-Gyorgi, famed biologist twice awarded the Nobel Prize. In a journal of the theory and practice of Psychosynthesis, Szent-Gyorgi presented a paper on the nature of "drive in living matter to perfect itself." The paper outlines his research data suggesting a process of "syntropy," which involves the evolution of cells toward "higher and higher levels of organization, order, and synamic harmony." He suggests that this is apparently an innate "wisdom" within living matter, probably more complex as organisms evolve along the scales of genetic complexity. Assagioli's suggested "natural tendency toward growth" may well have a biological basis (Szent-Gyorgi, 1974).

A primary focus of the whole approach of Psychosynthesis is the "will." Assagioli's second book, published through the Esalen Institute while he was teaching there, was *The Act of Will* (Assagioli, 1973). He noted that the existential experience of "willing," or exercising "will power," has been little attended in psychological literature. He noted that his attention to the development of the inner potentials of the human being led him to recognition of the importance of the will among inner powers:

Fundamental among the inner powers, and the one to which priority should be given, is the tremendous, unrealized potency of man's own will. Its training and use constitute the foundation of all endeavors. There are two reasons for this: the first is the will's central position in man's personality and its intimate connection with the core of his being—his very self. The second lies in the will's function in deciding what is to be done, in applying all the necessary means for its realization and in persisting in the task in the face of all obstacles and difficulties. (Assagioli, 1973)

Assagioli's attention to the will as a central aspect of the person's basic selfconcept, and thus a key element of the very personality and character of the person, was reflective of the psychology of William James, who argued for the individual's freedom of choice. Also, and apparently with no awareness of the other's thought, Assagioli's discussions of the will and recommendations for training for the will bear a resemblance to the ideas of educator Kurt Hahn, founder of the Outward Bound schools. It is understandable that these two did not know of each other. Assagioli was a psychotherapist, working in Italy; Hahn was an educator, working in England. Yet both were concerned with the facilitation of personal growth, and both noted the importance of development of the individual's will. Challenge educators looking for philosophical perspectives might find value in detailed study of their writings on cultivation of will.

Although Assagioli did not write about education to any great degree, he did make some observations that challenge educators may find of relevance. In *The Act of Will*, he suggests that the purpose of education is apparent from the word. Educere means to "draw out," so education is the process of providing students with opportunity to "release their latent possibilities" and "activate their internal energies." He suggests that education is one very important focal point for implementation of will training, although it should be recognized that training of the will is certainly not limited to the formal education program, since "the training of the will is a lifetime task" (Assagioli, 1973).

Psychosynthesis recognizes the potentiality of the small group to develop an increased power, especially when there is an atmosphere of open communication and interactional support to the growth of all members. In a psychosynthesis workbook, one of Assiagoli's most prominent students, Vargiu (1977):

> When a number of individuals form a harmonious group, and thus become psychologically close to one another, there is much energy to be released, which can then become available and can be turned outward to useful purposes. (Vargiu, 1974)

The whole process of Psychosynthesis involves the individual developing strategies which can help tap into the hidden energies and resources which are seeking expression, then releasing them for productive, imaginative, humanitarian, and self-actualizing accomplishment. Each person has capacity to unleash vast personal energies and creative expressions, to deal with old problems and to face new challenges, to explore personal ho-

rizons and become all that one wishes to become. The role of the educator/therapist/facilitator is simply that of guiding the person to activities and exercises which will enable exploration of those inner potentialities, and which provide opportunity for their expressive release. Assagioli summarized shortly before his death:

> We can perform any role that life requires of us or that we decide to play. In a large variety of life situations there is always in the human-being the latent possibility to do anything within reasonable limits, to choose freely, to deliver themselves from social pressures, prejudices, and obstacles in order to reach their higher goals. (Assagioli & Servan-Schreiber, 1974)

HOLISTIC EDUCATION

The overview to education that is considered "holistic" provides for a broad range of strategies and curriculum formats. An historical review of holistic education notes:

> What is holistic education? It is not any one teaching method but a social philosophy based on reverence for life and profound respect for human potential. (R. Miller, 1988)

Holistic education is founded on the belief that the human species is, indeed, moving toward transcendence of the narrow world view of science and technology. Such a shift in perspective demands a new design for education.

> The last 400 years of scientific and intellectual progress contain a gigantic paradox. Every great advance, every profound insight in the sciences and other intellectual disciplines, has torn down the barriers of distinction between those disciplines; and yet the institutional result of each of these achievements has been fur-

ther fragmentation and specialization of the academy. (Turner, 1986)

Our aim is not merely to make the child understand, and still less to force him to memorize, but so to touch his imagination as to enthuse him to his inmost core. We do not want those complacent pupils, but eager ones; we seek to sew life in the child rather than theories, to help him in his growth, mental and emotional as well as physical, and for that we must offer grand and lofty ideas to the human mind, which we find ever ready to receive them, demanding more and more. (Montessori, 1949)

The emphasis on the uniqueness, totality, and complexity of each child, which is the focus of holistic education, is parallel to that of challenge education. It is appropriate to consider the challenge education methodology as a variety of holistic education. As such, challenge education theory can be developed, in part, from the same philosophical ideologies that are considered basic to holistic education.

Although the word "holistic" has been applied to educational theory for only a few decades, there have been centuries of philosophical thought which is now relevant to the thinking of holistic educators. In 1988, there was first publication of a professional journal devoted to explanation and summarization of historic and contemporary thinking of relevance to holistic educators. In the first issues of the "Holistic Education Review, " the editor noted:

The holistic approach starts with the realization that the human being is wholly and innately connected to the universe; we are part of the same process which made the stars, and we are made of the same stuff. All facets of human experience—intuitive, aesthetic, imaginative, emotional, and spiritual, as well as ratio-

nal intellect—are needed to fully grasp the awesome depth of our existence. But schooling in modern societies, say holistic educators, has neglected this organic and vital connection between ourselves and Nature, and has forgotten that true learning involves not just academic discipline, but also wonder and awe, spontaneity and joy. This is a minority view, however, and holistic educators have always been found on the romantic and mystical fringes of Western industrial civilization.

Yet something has occurred since the 1960's to give the holistic approach new emphasis and new hope. A small but provocative group of thinkers, frequently called the "new age" movement, has begun to stir Western culture. Inspired by humanistic psychology and brain research, non-Western and esoteric spiritual traditions, the ecology movement, as well as the 1960's counterculture, writers like Theodore Roszak, Marilyn Ferguson, Jeremy Rifkin, Fritjof Capra, and Robert Theobald, to name a few, have opened a frontal assault on modern industrial culture.

It (holistic education) is at odds in many ways with the predominant materialism of modern industrial culture, and until now has flourished only in small, counterculture enclaves. But there are indications that holistic education is an idea whose time has come. (R. Miller, 1988)

Any historical overview to the traditions of holistic education includes consideration

99

of the ideas of Rousseau, Pestalozzi, Dewey, Montessori, and Steiner. More recent thinkers of influence include John Holt, Carl Rogers, George Leonard, George Brown, and many of the others who wrote on education as part of the whole "human potential movement." Many of the contemporary writers would have considered themselves under a different label of educational theory and practice (e.g., humanistic education, confluent education, affective education, transpersonal education, etc.), but it is possible to umbrella them all under the broad scope of holistic education. Miller suggests that all of these approaches shared a romantic, enthusiastic, passionate, and visionary appreciation for the potential of human beings.

Rudolph Steiner, in particular, has been recognized by holistic educators as an important thinker and program developer. As founder of the "Waldorf Schools," he argued that the Western mind was too enthralled by the materialistic comforts to willingly move in the direction of spiritual essence and earth-saving orientations. The learning environment must be structured to provide the child with opportunity for holistic development, and this means that teachers must develop a spiritual wholeness themselves, and that they must choose curriculum materials and methods which contribute to appropriate development. Steiner's thinking has been influential in the home schooling movement, the development of private schools, and even as a guideline for "spiritual parenting." Parents, as well as teachers, need to be sensitive to the physical, emotional, social, intellectual and spiritual needs of the child at each step of development, and must try to "provide them with the space to be themselves, to experience

and grow, and try on the world" (Baldwin, 1989).

Most of the holistic thinkers have alternative world views and radical ideas on the desirable purposes and methodologies of education. They are critical of the shortcomings of traditional education, and suggest new methods, new goals, and new visions for the Twenty-First century.

> Deprived of a holistic understanding of human life and growth, modern societies breed personal disintegration, fanomie, and despair. There is an urgency in many of the new age writings, warning that if materialism continues to dominate modern consciousness, then personal alienation will inevitably reach the point of global selfdestruction.
> The new age writings may not be the last word, but they are an earnest invitation to examine our cultural prejudices and the educational system which reinforces them. Holistic education is not another new batch of methods, not another chapter in the endless cycle of reform/back-to-basics/reform which has characterized American education for 150 years. Holistic education offers a new image of human nature and human possibilities, and a new way to define the relationship of individuals to society and to the world. To avoid these issues—to assume that the educational establishment will be able to continue its traditional practices into the next century is itself sentimental and unrealistic, and in this period of cultural malaise, amounts to moral default. (R. Miller, 1988)

According to advocates, Holistic Education represents the new-age overview to the whole process of growth, learning, and self-directed evolutional unfolding for humankind. It is the desirable educational format for the future; it represents a shift in the educational paradigm which must parallel the shift in scientific-technological orientation and the shift in the economicpolitical orientation as now unfolding in our culture. These new patterns of education must occur in order for humankind to survive and fulfill heretofore unrealized potentials.

As the twentieth century moves towards its concluding years, prognosticators from around the world and from many different walks of life are speaking about the dawn of a new age. There are associations and journals dedicated to life in this new age and the number of books written about the period is growing rapidly. Fritjof Capra, Alvin Toffler, Marilyn Ferguson, John Naisbitt, Buckminster Fuller, Robert Muller, Jose Arguellas, George Leonard, Gary Zukav, and Joseph Pearce are just a few writers who are telling us about the changes that are in process. An education based on these ideas would accelerate humanity's path to wholeness. Such a method will evolve through new and different approaches to teacher preparation—approaches that help adults create new meaning for, and new relationship to, the process of education.   (Gang, 1988)

A major paradigm shift is taking place. The chances are that by the year 2000 we will have a vastly different system for educating our children. If this is to occur, however, we must explore both the old and the new assumptions relating to every facet of the educational process. Only then can we determine those which are most inappropriate to the needs of young people who will spend most of their lives in the twenty-first century. (Clark, 1988)

Traditional education, like modern culture, is fragmented and atomistic. A holistic education emphasizes relationships—between thinking and intuition, mind and body, individual and community, personal self and higher Self (spiritual dimensions of experience). Holistic education seeks for transformation—that

is, the continuing growth of the person and society. (J. Miller, 1988)

In the first two years of publication of the *Holistic Education Review*, there were articles spanning a variety of theoretical and programmatic approaches. The editor of the journal suggested that holistic educators need to look beyond the boundaries of any one movement, noting that

...each of us, no matter what our particular training, orientation, or special interests, is something larger. Let us honor that vision. Let us share our insights with one another and work together to bring about that vision of a humane, nurturing, culture. (R. Miller, 1989)

The journal did, indeed, seek to provide a format for seemingly diverse orientations to seek common denominators. Review of the published articles finds reference to many different concepts, including:

...alternative schools, creative writing, neo-humanistic models of education, meditation, wonder and ecstacy...
...rites of passage, vision quests, Outward Bound, C4R, experiential education, Quaker education, Montessori and spiritual education, Krishnamurti, and T'ai Chi...
...free schools, simulation games in learning, imagination, the Walden within, environmental education, teacher empowerment, bilingual learners, learning styles...

It was suggested that a number of common themes were reflected in the diverse body of material, and this helps define Holistic Education:

1. Holistic education seeks to nurture the development of the whole person. It is not enough to educate for academic achievement and vocational skills alone;

the human personality is an integrated complex of intellectual, physical, social, moral, emotional, and spiritual possibilities. All of these must be taken into account in the education of children.

2. Holistic education involves a new relationship between teacher and student—and, in more general terms, between the adult generation and the young. Authoritarian practices are replaced by dialogue, cooperation, respect, and friendship. In holistic education, students are valued for their individuality, not solely for their conformity to authoritative standards. Their distinct styles of learning and their personal interests and questions need to be honored.

3. Holistic education is a spiritual worldview rather than a materialist one. It is a belief in, and a reverence for, a self-directing life force that lies beyond our rational, intellectual understanding. It seeks to support and nourish the natural unfolding of the human soul within the lives of individuals. But spirituality does not imply particular religious beliefs and rituals; a more empirical spirituality may use terms such as "selfactualization" or "creativity" to refer to the same natural unfolding of human personality.

4. Holistic education is, at least implicitly, a critical perspective on modern culture. Once we seek to nurture the finer potentials of the human spirit, it becomes evident that the competitive, hierarchical, violent, materialistic, and hedonistic tendencies of contemporary Western world are highly destructive of these potentials. (R. Miller, 1989)

Challenge education is concerned with the holistic growth and learning of students. Many of the strategies that contribute to the methodology of challenge education are rooted in a philosophical orientation that can be considered as holistic. In parallel to challenge education, holistic education represents an attempt to synthesize philosophical ideology after the fact of many program innovations (Armstrong, 1987; LePage, 1987; Kline,1988; Miller, J., 1988; Miller, R., 1989; Perrone, 1989). As the process of formulation of an encompassing philosophy for holistic education unfolds, challenge educators will find considerable value in a meaningful summarization of their own theoretical perspectives.

EAST MEETS WEST

Through the past few decades there have been many suggestions for American educators and personal growth facilitators to "look to the East" for philosophical ideologies and supportive ideas. Those educators advocating challenging procedures which can stimulate holistic growth and development in students, and guide them toward personal balance and harmony with others and the world have attended to the teachings of Yoga. For example, it has been pointed out that the stretching exercises as offered under Hatha Yoga can help in the release of physical and psychological tensions, can stimulate basic circulation and blood flow as required for more strenuous activity, and can guide students toward a "natural state of balance in body, mind, and spirit (Vishnudevananda, 1960). Adventure educators, with advocation of special experiences in climbing, caving, and "solo" journeys, take note of the fact that for many centuries, in the Hindu and Buddhist traditions, people have gone to caves, mountaintops, and other remote places to practice yoga, or to meditate, or to seek inner awareness of balance between self and the universe (Yogananda, 1981).

Certainly, as challenge educators seek to develop philosophical bases for their innovative methodologies, there is wisdom to be found in the teachings of the East. However, it is important to be aware of the suggestion attributed to Carl Gustav Jung. Shortly before his death, on observation of the vast number of young Americans who were bandwagoning with the ideologies and practices of Yoga, the Tarot cards, the schematics of the *I Ching* and the writings in *The Tibetian Book of the Dead*, Jung warned that there was danger in Western man mimicking the practices of traditional Eastern man. He noted that while the basic practices of relaxation, stretching, balancing, and meditating are valuable for personal growth, there must be consideration of the development of a "Yoga of the West," appropriate to our culture in our times. The values that contemporary education finds in the philosophy and practices of the East must be carefully adapted to this place and these times, and to the 21st century to come. With this in mind, there are a number of different systems of philosophy from the East that warrant consideration in the search for appropriate philosophical bases for challenge education theory and practice.

Krishnamurti

One of the most influential minds of the East, who was partially educated in England, and taught some in the United States, was Jiddu Krishnamurti. In contrast to many of the teachers from the East, Krishnamurti wrote and spoke a good deal about education; accordingly he had considerable influence on both the human potential movement and the holistic education movement. In a recent overview of Krishnamurti's ideas about education, it has been suggested that the essence of his approach to education can be summarized by a simple quotation: "The man who knows how to split the atom, but has no love in his heart, becomes a monster" (Krishnamurti, 1981).

In his article, "Krishnamurti, Education, and Wholeness," Edward Murray suggests:

At a time when our classrooms are being criticized for turning out students who are academically inferior to students in many other countries, and who are more concerned with financial success than with a significant philosophical or spiritual understanding of life, Jiddu Krishnamurti offers a challenge to our customary ideas on education. (Murray, 1989)

Krishnamurti was early groomed by the Theosophical Society (a group devoted to investigation of ancient religions and promotion of brotherhood for all mankind), to become their spiritual leader. However, by age 30 he had begun to form an attitude which was to soon result in his departure from that position. He began to feel that the old cultures of both the East and the West were outdated and ineffective. Furthermore, to seek to blend East and West would prove ineffective; so Krishnamurti moved in his own directions. He founded schools in various parts of India, in England, and in the United States. His personal development, and the unfolding of his ideas, was a lifelong process, and, according to a major biographer, he changed and responded to the times and the problems at hand (Lutyens, 1984, 1985, 1988).

Krishnamurti was a teacher, and throughout his life he spoke of the value of education in cultural development. He saw the educator's task as that of providing an environment of safety and stimulation within which the student can explore, experiment, increase awareness, and understand life. He suggested that: "To understand life is to understand ourselves, and that is both the beginning and the end of education" (Krishnamurti, 1981).

In order to know yourself, you must rid yourself of impatience and allow yourself time to observe. Self-knowledge includes understanding how you think, how you are conditioned, why you believe in aspects of your culture, and what more you need to know. You must be alert and sensitive to all the intricacies of your thought patterns. If you are able to understand yourself, you can be meaningfully active and give yourself creative happiness. He suggests there is value in meditation, once one has achieved good understanding of themselves, because the meditative mind "sees, watches, and listens."

In order to prevent self-destruction, which is imminent if humans continue to destroy their air, water, planet, and each other, teachers should try to cultivate in students a sensitivity to others and to the earth. While all learning begins with the self-search, this first phase of knowledge must give way to the unfolding of a "new mind." Basically, Krishnamurti argues that the proper process is to grow from thinking that is dominated by the "I" and the "me," toward thinking dominated by the "we" and the "us." He recognizes that this is a shift that will not come easily, as people tend to cling to the old ways, to the "old mind." There is risk in giving up the known and moving into the unknown; but teachers must challenge students to make that transformation. Changing the world requires that we first change ourselves, though we often don't really want to change, even when we say that we do. We tend to have special interest in things staying the way they are, and so we do nothing. As people become more irresponsible, the State steps in to assume the responsibility. The end of this is certainly crisis, but it is not a political crisis, nor an economic crisis; it is a crisis of education.

An important ingredient of the solution, according to Krishnamurti, is the appropriate education and development of teachers who are themselves "whole persons." If our world is to survive, we need a vision of wholeness. If our youth are to develop such a vision of the interdependence of all that is, then they must be taught by teachers who have cultivated that vision in themselves. Krishnamurti's position would define the primary problem of education as the educator.

> If students are to be inwardly free, teachers also must be inwardly free— free to pursue truth wherever it may take them. Where such freedom exists there is a better opportunity for change to occur, and for wholeness to become a reality. (Murray, 1989)

The responsibility for guidance of students toward education about the totality of themselves, and their relationship to the world, which will lead them to desire for increasing their knowledge of all that is, lies with the teacher.

> The function of your teachers is to educate not only the partial mind but the totality of the mind; to educate you so that you do not get caught in the little whirlpool of existence but live in the whole river of life. This is the whole function of education. The right kind of education cultivates your whole being, the totality of your mind. It gives your mind and heart a depth, an understanding of beauty. (Krishnamurti, 1974)

Maharishi Yogi

A most notable influence from the East, with extensive impact throughout the West, was that of Transcendental Meditation, spearheaded by Maharishi Mahese Yogi. At the height of development in the late 1970's there were over 300 "World Plan Centers" established throughout the United States, as the Maharishi offered workshops and published in English. An international research center and university program was founded in California, and those touched by the methodology of Transcendental Meditation (TM) gave suggestions for education (Levine, 1972; Rozman, 1975).

The Maharishi defined the purpose of education as follows:

> ...to culture the mind of a man so that he can accomplish all his aims in life. Education should enable a man to use the full potential of his body, mind, and spirit. It should also develop in him the ability to make the best use of his personality, surroundings, and his circumstances, so that he may accomplish the maximum in life for himself and for others. (Yogi, 1965)

In a review of ten years of the TM movement, Jack Forem noted the potential for the usage of Transcendental Meditation to enhance health, stimulate creativity, improve interpersonal communication, and make overall contribution to personal growth and wellbeing (Forem, 1973). Critics have made arguments that these elaborate goals are beyond the potential of the simple practice of meditation, but advocates have held to higher visions. In any case, there was much recognition of the value of meditation, and the whole TM movement gave support to practices of relaxation, breathing, centering, private time, introspection, and journaling in educational programs. Some of those who were earlier influenced by the TM movement have been influential in the development of humanistic education, holistic education, transpersonal education, and challenge education.

Interest in developing meditation curricula for the school continues as the 20th century moves through the last decade. The value of meditation as a tool for opening the door to all of education has been summarized:

> Modern education, grounded in the empiricism of the Western industrial world view, fails to address the deeper levels of human consciousness. Meditation reveals that these levels are the true source of all learning, creativity, and compassion. Meditation techniques are easily taught to children and have great value for them. (Winkelried-Dobson, 1988)

Of course, it must be recognized that while meditation and other patterns of relaxation, energy focusing, and introspective contemplation are not only valuable in their own right, but can contribute to further learning. One of the major impacts will be on the behavior of teachers.

> Adding meditation to the standard curriculum is certainly a step in the right direction, although our new awareness must be augmented by a change in our outdated approach to learning. Through self-awareness, teacher guides will not teach, but rather allow learning to happen.
>
> Meditation, a method by which the student's mind is led from the gross level of experience to the deeper states of consciousness, awakens the Selfconscious which is the foundation, the stable component of all knowledge. A student must first experience himself as the knower of knowledge. Meditation can lead him beyond the self-imposed physical and linear boundaries of education. It allows the student to dip into the eternal well of creativity, contentment, and knowing that exists inside. (Ibid.)

Sri Aurobindo & Haridas Chaudhuri

Less recognized than either Krishnamurti or Transcendental Meditation, but seemingly making important statements for all of education, would be the "Yoga for the 20th Century," as developed by Sri Aurobindo and his prominent student Haridas Chaudhuri. Although Yoga has many forms, most American's have associated the concept with the practice of Hatha Yoga, which is the program of physical exercise, stretching, and contortion to bring strength and overall mind-body conditioning. Parallel breathing exercises also increase energy and relaxation. Basic procedures of Hatha Yoga are practiced to ready oneself for the Rundalini Yoga, which is the yoga of energy currents, although many do not master the more basic procedures sufficiently to build upon them (Arya, 1977).

Actually, the term "yoga" means "union," and describes the state of a person when their life of action and thought are in harmony with the very source of their being. In addition to the Hatha Yoga, one can search for that harmony through Bhakti Yoga, the approach of the emotions and encompassing love; Jnana Yoga, the path involving the search for truth and knowledge; or Karma Yoga, which involves growth through action. There is also the approach based on self-analysis, Raja Yoga; and an approach based on the principles of modern psychology involving the expansion of imagination, Novo Yoga (Barth, 1974). The Tantra Yoga involves attention to the levels of being, and spheres of awareness.

Many have noted the experience of partiality in Western Man's scientism, materialism, and rationality; and similar shortcomings in Eastern Man's tendency to withdraw from matter, action, and more concrete thinking. Western Man can split atoms and build rockets to explore in space, and not always know why. Eastern Man can see the need for food production and more farm machinery, and not always know how. There has been recommendation for unification of the philosophies of East and West, and a significant attempt in that direction was that of Sri Aurobindo. Although born in India, he was educated at Oxford in the late 19th century. He offered a system for bringing the major patterns of Yoga together in what he called Integral Yoga. His major translated work was *The Synthesis of Yoga*, in which he suggested that the complexity of the human being warranted variable practices for full development. His orientation was towards a development of body, emotions, and cognitive mind, as well as growth onward to a superconsciousness which implied action within the world (Green, 1974).

Aurobindo taught of inner and outer unification, suggesting that inner growth without action was fragmented. One must start in the sequence of selfobservation, self-understanding, and constant practice of self-control, selfmodification, and self-development—but action must follow. Aurobindo, himself, was not simply a teacher and philosopher, but was socially active in India's quest for independence. He also noted that different people needed different points of departure in their search for "union," and by integrating all the various approaches of Yoga he thought that everyone could find the path most meaningful for their personal growth and development.

A major student of Aurobindo was Haridas Chaudhuri, who taught at colleges and universities throughout the world, including the United States. In an interview shortly

106

before his death in 1974, Chaudhuri outlined his own expansions and interpretations of Aurobindo's Integral Yoga, which he saw as quite parallel to some of the teachings of Tantra. He noted that there are five different levels or dimensions of consciousness:

...the "physical" or biological, which involves basic body awareness...

...the "vital" or domain of the instincts and of basic sensory awareness...

...the "rational" which involves the cognitive domain, basic cognitive awareness...

...the "aesthetic" which includes emotional states and perceptual functions, or emotional awareness...

...the "intuitive" which is purely spiritual and transcendental, or spiritual awareness.

> Naturally, all these different functions or aspects of the psyche are interrelated and interpenetrating—one cannot completely separate them. They are as ways to self-realization, and people can use different styles of yoga—or combinations—depending on their basic psychological type. (Chaudhuri, 1974)

Like his teacher, Chaudhuri also argued that there must be overt behavioral involvement in the world for full realization of the potential of the self.

> Self-actualization is not the end. It must then be supplemented by humanistic participation in evolution." (Ibid.)

These viewpoints support the arguments of the challenge education theorist that every person has unique learning patterns, and that curricula must vary to have impact on all students. Some learn best from seatwork and textbooks, but others require activity and opportunity for direct experience in the learning sequences. Some learn best alone, but many require social interaction to maximize their knowledge and performances. Challenge educators and psychologists also argue against viewing the development of the selfconcept as an endpoint for education or counseling. The individual must use the improved self-concept to effect behavioral changes and improved adjustment to the world. Chaudhuri also gives support to the concept of the person as process, with there never being an ending to growth and learning. He admits that people should set personal goals and that teachers should guide students toward meaningful choice of strategies to help them attain goals for themselves and for all humankind. He concludes:

> However high man goes, there's still beyond. The absolute is the process. All experiences are but partial manifestations of the absolute. The absolute isn't even evolution; it includes evolution. Man is a process. All life is a process. (Op.Cit.)

P. R. SARKAR

Many have suggested that there is an emerging paradigm shift for our whole culture, resulting, in part, from the emergence of an alternative view of reality via a new scientific model (Capra, 1975; Zukav, 1979; Holbrook, 1981). Indian philosopher P. R. Sarkar described the new scientific models in relation to the historic teachings of Tantra Yoga, and developed a theory of "Neo-Humanism" (Sarkar, 1987). Drawing on the concept of existence in a unified field of five levels of awareness, on the new approaches to earth awareness as reflected in Norwegian philosopher Arne Naess's "Deep Ecology," and on the strengths of traditional humanistic theory, Sarkar offered a holistic, ecological philosophy.

Students of Sarkar have extended his philosophy and developed models for "neohumanistic education" (Ananda-mitra, 1986; Hatley, 1988). It is noted that the theory of neohumanistic education bears a relationship to the work of Maria Montessori and Rudolph Steiner. There is emphasis on the "process" of curriculum, rather than the "product." Most importantly, there is attention paid to the "ecstasy" of learning, with recognition that maximal growth and cognitive enrichment occur when the student is enthusiastically involved in the whole learning process. Unfortunately, much of modern education fails to recognize the importance of having students joyfully participate in their learning, but actually programs such state of consciousness out of learning.

Children are born with the proclivity for ecstatic interaction with their environment, and much of what has passed for education until now has actually been the programming-out of this joyful relatedness. ...an early emphasis on categorization, abstraction, classification, and generalization inhibits the child's natural tendency toward perceptual wholeness, and thus prevents the orderly expansion of the higher faculties of mind. (Hatley, 1988)

The neo-humanistic model emphasizes balance between the "inner-directed" and the "outer-directed" activities, and thus advocates strategies of relaxation, guided imagery, creative fantasy, and metaphoric problem solving. In the Tantra Yoga, the highest level of the mind is that of experiencing the oneness with all of creation, and the development of that level of awareness should be the goal of all education. Accordingly, the academic units of the neo-humanistic curricula would be:

...multi-dimensional, integrated, and limited only by the teacher's and student's imaginations. Every element on the "wheel of knowledge" is approached from all levels of the child's being—physical, emotional, imaginative, intellectual, intuitive and spiritual. For example, a unit on Air and Wind might include a story and dramatic play about a "wind spirit" who takes the children on a wind journey, a wind dance with some flying colored streamers, lying on the soft grass to look for shapes in the clouds, guided fantasy about flying on the back of the wind (possibly to view a variety of geographical terrain), songs and finger-plays about the wind, construction of pinwheels and wind mobiles, flying kites, sailing boats, constructing of weather vanes, study of windmills and wind energy, and a look at the changes in the environment brought about by the changing personality of the wind. (Ibid.)

Neo-humanistic education suggests a philosophy and working model for the development of wholeness, and was early summarized:

It is a harmonious synthesis of freedom and responsibility, mysticism and practicality, challenge and relaxation, self-reliance and interdependence. Through it, students will attain both self-knowledge and objective knowledge; for it develops mastery of the world on the one hand, and transcendence of it on the other. It is not only an intellectual education—which often simply makes people more selfish—it is an education of the heart. (Anandamitra, 1986)

EXPERIENTIAL EDUCATION

At the middle of the twentieth-century, four different educational philosophies dominated the American schools. They were:

1. Pragmatism-progressivism, as rooted in the philosophy of William James (c.f., James, 1907), and developed by John Dewey and William Kilpatrick (c.f., Dewey, 1916 1938, 1943, 1956; Kilpatrick, 1934).

2. Perennialism, tied to the absolutist philosophies of Aristotle and Aquinas, and advocated by Mortimer Adler and R. M. Hutchins (c.f., Adler, 1939; Hutchins, 1953).

3. Essentialism, which criticized most of modern education and offered a rallying point for a diverse group whose common denominators included a desire for relevance and content orientation in the curriculum, and an authority model for the classroom teacher. Most of the literature of essentialism appeared in the journal *School and Society*, edited by one of the leaders of the movement, William Brickman (c.f., Brickman, 1948, 1958).

4. Reconstructionism, which attempted to rejuvenate the philosophy of John Dewey as the progressive education movement stalled. The main emphasis was on the social responsibility of the school, drawing on Dewey's ideas not previously related to education (Dewey, 1922). Theodore Brameld was the defining spokesman for this educational orientation (c.f., Brameld, 1950, 1956, 1965).

These educational philosophies have been discussed, compared, and critically reviewed by many others (c.f., Horne, 1927; Kandel, 1938; Butler, 1957; Wynne, 1963; Kneller, 1964; Morris, 1969).

It has been said of philosophy that after Plato, all thinking was in defense of, argument against, alternative to, or reaction against the ideas he expressed. The same can be said of the philosophy of education in America after the writings of John Dewey. Certainly, it was well into the late 1960's and early 1970's before the alternatives of Existential, Humanistic, and Holistic educational philosophy were recognized—and each of those orientations would accept Dewey's ideas on education as paralleling their own on two or three counts:

...emphasis on the role of experience in learning...

...emphasis on the uniqueness, wholeness, integrity, and potential of each student...

...emphasis on the necessity of relationship between education and the democratic process..

Dewey's impact on all educational thought was due, in part, to his pragmatic and functional approach which spoke directly to educators. Most of those concerned with a philosophy of education tended to put more emphasis on defining education, debating about the appropriate goals for education and discussing the meaning of education in civilization. They were "philosophers" dealing with abstract principles and writing in traditional philosophical terminology. Consider, for example, Horne's offering of a definition for education (albeit, a good one), followed by page after page of careful explanation and elaboration of the meaning of each and every word.

Education is the eternal process of superior adjustment of the physically and mentally developed, free, conscious, human being in God, as manifested in the intellectual, emotional and volitional environment of man.... No man is ever all he can be. Age does not wither, nor custom stale, the philosopher's love of truth, the artist's love of beauty, or the saint's love of virtue. There is always more to know, and to love, and to do. Man does not limit his will to know, to enjoy, to achieve to his life's unknown term of years. (Horne, 1927)

Even William James, the essential father of the pragmatism philosophy upon which Dewey's ideas on education are based, was a difficult-to-read and deeply philosophical writer. Few classroom teachers or school administrators were directly influenced by his writings. The notable exception was *Talks to Teachers*, in which he did try to discuss his ideas on education in terms of relevance to teachers (James, 1899). His classic work on *Principles of Psychology* was basically a philosophy of human experience, rather than a textbook on psychology; although it certainly did have impact on educational philosophy and the system unfolded by John Dewey, who was twenty years younger (James, 1890).

Because John Dewey wrote much more clearly, and because he wrote much more on educational theory and practice, it is he who is most often considered the father of the progressive education movement. The relevance of some of James' concepts has been infrequently noted, but was discussed in an article by Donaldson and Vinson (1979). They noted statements from James that were in support of the tenants of experiential education:

1. Experiential Education Principle, as noted by Donaldson & Vinson: "Sensory Experience is Basic."

Quotation from James: "The more different kinds of things a child thus gets to know by treating and handling them, the more confidence grows in his sense of himself within the world in which he lives."

2. Experiential Education Principle, as noted by Donaldson & Vinson: "Interest is of Signal Importance to Learning."

Quotation from James: "In teaching you must simply work your pupil to such a state of interest in what you are going to teach him that every other object of attention is banished from his mind."

3. Experiential Education Principle, as noted by Donaldson & Vinson: "Good Education is Holistic."

Quotation from James. "Man is too complex a being for light to be thrown on his real efficiency by measuring any one mental faculty taken apart from its consensus in the working whole."

4. Experiential Education Principle, as noted by Donaldson & Vinson: "Effective Learning is Interdisciplinary."

Quotation from James. "When the geography and English and history and arithmetic simultaneously make crossreference to one another, you get an interesting set of processes all along the line of learning."

Donaldson and Vinson, after review of James' *Talks to Teachers* suggest that he would wholeheartedly support their own conclusion about the value of experience in learning:

Teachers and youth leaders who truly believe in teaching the whole person in

110

and about the whole environment in which life is lived will provide every learner with many direct experiences. These experiences may take place anywhere people are in the modern world—classroom, community, natural areas, schoolyards, parks, farm, inner city—anywhere! Helping the young to live in a wider and wider continuum of reality experiences is exactly what experiential education is all about. (Ibid.)

As the twentieth century unfolded, many educators were ready to rebel against the excessive formalism of most traditional schools. John Dewey's first major work was published in 1916, taking the pragmatist view that the basis of reality is change, thus offering the suggestion that education should emphasize process, experiment, the dynamically changing child, and learning by experience in the real world. He wrote:

> There is no such thing as genuine knowledge and fruitful understanding except as the offspring of doing. Men have to do something to the things they wish to find out about; they have to alter conditions. This is the lesson of the laboratory method, and this is the lesson which all education has to learn. (Dewey, 1916)

Kneller has summarized six assertions of Dewey's progressive education philosophy as it evolved through time and the interpretations of others. Most experiential educators, and most of those who advocate the theory and practice of challenge education, would find agreement with these six points:

1. Education should be life itself, not a preparation for living.

2. Learning should be directly related to the interests of the child.

3. Learning through problem solving should take precedence over the inculcating of subject matter.

4. The teacher's role is not to direct but to advise.

5. The school should encourage cooperation rather than competition.

6. Only democracy permits the free interplay of ideas and personalities that is necessary as condition for true growth. (Kneller, 1971)

In their acceptance of the basic philosophy of progressive education, contemporary experiential and challenge educators should seek to avoid an error resulting from a misinterpretation of Dewey that was often made. This error is best exemplified by the "child activity movement" of the 1930's and 1940's, which gave the impression that a selfselected free activity was sufficient to the learning of the child. Such stretching of the tenants of Dewey's point caused negative reaction against the whole progressive education movement. Dewey would certainly argue that all experiences make a contribution to learning, but he would also argue that it is not proper for the educator to simply stimulate free activity and personal interest experiences. It is the responsibility of the teacher to help each student identify appropriate goalpoints, and then guide the student toward significant learnings which move them toward those goals, even though those goals may be modified and redefined as experiences unfold through time. Dewey would argue that growth cannot be self-justifying; while the process is of the utmost importance, there must be attention to direction and the basic sequence of the unfolding experiences.

> Growth is not enough; we must specify the direction in which growth takes place, the end toward which it tends.
> Every experience is a moving force. Its value can be judged only on the ground of what it moves toward and into.

They (students) should know how to utilize the surroundings, physical and social, that exist so as to extract from them all that they have to contribute to building up the very experiences that are worthwhile.

The belief that all genuine education comes about through experience does not mean that all experiences are genuinely or equally educative. Experience and education cannot be directly equated to each other. For some experiences are miseducative. Any experience is miseducative that has the effect of arresting or distorting the growth of further experience. An experience may be such as to engender a callousness; it may produce lack of sensitivity and of responsiveness. Then the possibilities of having richer experience in the future are restricted.

An experience may be immediately enjoyable and yet promote the formation of a slack and careless attitude; this then operates to modify the quality of subsequent experiences so as to prevent a person from getting out of them what they have to give.

Again, experiences may be so disconnected from one another that, while each is agreeable or even exciting in itself, they are not linked cumulatively to one another.

The central problem of an education based upon experience is to select the kind of present experiences that live fruitfully and creatively in subsequent experiences. (Dewey, 1938)

Many of the "free schools," "open classrooms," and "self-selection" learning programs did not attend to the full details of Dewey's arguments. He certainly advocated self-direction, and allowing the students choices, but he argued that it was the responsibility of the teacher to guide the student to awareness of meaningful goals and towards defining personal goals in terms of their contribution to future functioning. Teachers should be very involved in the education of their students. They should help them recognize the difference between experiences which can contribute to goal attainment and experiences which may have negative effect. All in all, Dewey's orientation is similar to that delicate balance with which the adult supports the infant child during first steps. The infant does have to experiment and experience, to fall down and then stand up to try again, and finally to master the task in his/her own way. However, adults should be there to guide the child to appropriate time and place for the practice, to encourage the whole adventure, and to reach out with support and comfort after the tumble.

In any case, the first half of the twentieth century brought increasing exploration of and experimentation with, educational approaches that were purportedly grounded in the tenants of progressive education. There were periodic reactions against the movement, misinterpretations of the underlying philosophy, and debates about the wisdom of such a "child-centered" educational system. A major burst of criticism came shortly after America was shocked by the fact that the Russians had sent Sputnik into space. The situation was summarized by George Kneller, as follows:

Progressivism always attracted a lion's share of criticism, but never more than during the days of mingled amazement and humiliation that followed the launching of the first Soviet sputnik. Americans had been convinced that the Russian education was undemocratic and authoritarian and; therefore, ineffective. But how then could such success in science and technology be explained? Could it be that American schools were paying too much attention to the children they taught and too little to the subjects they taught them? There was a revulsion against the "child-centeredness" identified with progressivism. Americans, it was said, had pandered to their children too long; the nation was going soft; the rot must be stopped.   (Kneller, 1971)

It appeared that the more liberal educational philosophies and practices were outdated; the era of the educational conservative arrived. There was recommendation for "back to basics," increased scientific and technological curriculum, and arguments against the work of the humanistic and holistic educators in the schools. The content orientation of the curriculum led James Coleman to suggest that our youth were "information rich, but experience poor."

In the late 1970's, interest in experiential learning was rekindled, with special attention from professionals in adventure education and outdoor learning and recreational pursuits. A small but enthusiastic young organization formed to support experience as the basis of significant learning. The Association for Experiential Education (A.E.E.) soon expanded to include professionals interested in outdoor education, urban experiential adventures, sensory awareness as a key to learning, and the facilitation of personal growth through experiential adventure sequences. The new era of experiential education once again based itself on the works of John Dewey. Most of the early articles in the *Journal of Experiential Education*, published by A.E.E., sought definition and philosophy by focus on Dewey (Crosby, 1981; Joplin, 1981; Hunt, 1981). In the mid-1980's, A.E.E. published a collection of papers dealing with the theoretical basis of experiential education, and the major thread of influence was Dewey (A.E.E., 1985).

As experiential education broadened its scope, recognizing its overlap with the humanistic educators, the affective educators, and the personal growth facilitators, the scope of the philosophical questions also widened. Jim Kielsmeier offered "a challenge for experiential education" to "grow with the times." He asked experiential educators to examine the predominant human problems of the times and consider developing programs that would steer young minds toward solutions. He asked, quite simply: "What are today's generative themes? Do you care about the earth, poor children, conflict among nations, or issues of race and gender?" (Kielsmeier, 1989).

Certainly, Kielsmeier's suggestion for new focus for experiential education was in line with John Dewey's ideas. The pragmatist views change, not permanence, as the essence of reality. Progressivism argues that education must be viewed as always in the process of development. Educators must be ready to modify methods, policies, curricula, in response to new knowledge and new goals. The social problems to be tackled vary from time to time, and they need to be educationally defined and attacked. Education should provide students with visions and with methodology for dealing with the problems they will face in life. Dewey wrote:

We thus reach a technical definition of education: it is that reconstruction and reorganization of experience which adds to the meaning of experiences, and which will widen the ability to direct the course of subsequent experience. (Dewey, 1916)

According to Dewey, education must teach children how to solve problems, not the solutions to problems, for the problems they will face in their lives will unfold differentially. Teachers should guide students toward recognition and utilization of their own resources, not direct them in time-worn authoritarian models of learning. Students should learn to identify the problems that are important to their society and their world, then they will be motivated to learn more about the nature of those problems and the procedures for solution. If educators are successful, they will guide the student toward a vision of the future, a motivation to move sequentially towards that future, a readiness to face the problems that will be encountered along the way, and the knowledge to develop solutions to those problems which are compatible with the goals ahead.

Challenge education places strong emphasis on experiential learning, and has been considerably influenced by the experiential education movement as reflected in A.E.E. through the 1980's. Certainly, the philosophical foundations of experiential education, the future directions of this orientation to schooling, and the philosophical and social questions considered, should offer much to a developing philosophy of challenge education.

TRANSFORMATION THEORY

Humankind, as an integral part of the whole process that is called earth, has evolved, is evolving, and will continue to evolve. The latter half of the twentieth century marks a very significant point on the spiral of evolution, for it was then that human beings fully discovered the complex and unfolding nature of their own evolution. This awareness was first cited as important by the Jesuit priest Pierre Teilhard de Chardin, whose major thesis was that as the human mind has been changing and evolving through time, it has finally reached that critical point of discovery of its own evolution. His position was so controversial that his writings were banned by the church, and he spent almost twenty years working as a geologist and paleontologist, quietly observing the world from the viewpoint of the evolutionary anthropologist, studying the nature of the relationships between evolution, the nature of religious experience, the human personality, and the totality of the universe.

His classic work, *The Phenomenon of Man*, was first published in 1938, but was limited to private distribution because of the church's ban. His thinking was often discussed in the writings of other evolutional theorists, but his book did not become available to the general public until after his death in the 1950's (Teilhard de Chardin, 1959).

Teilhard's writings became influential on all scientific thinking, on religious philosophy, and perhaps most impactfully, on the complex body of thinkers and doers who were influential in unfolding the "human potential movement." In fact, in her survey for determination of the individuals who had influence on the whole human potential movement, Marilyn Ferguson found that Teilhard de Chardin ranked at the very top of the list (Ferguson, 1980). In her significant summarization of the movement, which she called

"The Aquarian Conspiracy," Ferguson gave this overview to Teilhard's theory:

> This new awareness—evolving mind recognizing the evolutionary process—is the future natural history of the world. It will eventually become collective. It will envelop the planet and will crystallize as a species-wide enlightenment he called "Omega Point." Certain individuals, attracted to a transcendent vision of the future and to each other, seemed to be forming a spearhead in the "family task" of bringing humanity into this larger awareness." She quoted Teilhard: "The only way forward is in the direction of a common passion, a conspiracy."   (Ibid.)

According to Teilhard, the whole universe is in a continuous process of becoming, of attaining new levels of existence and organization. Man is one of the significant phenomena of the total universe, a delicate part of the whole process. All of the evolutionary processes, including the phenomena of man, are processes which cannot be described solely in terms of their origins; they must also be defined in terms of their directions, their inherent capabilities, and their unfolding potentialities. Under such vision, the whole process of evolution takes on new meaning; humankind is now responsible for visioning and directing the journey. According to Teilhard "omega" is both process and product, and is now determined by increasing knowledge of man and the universe, the development of a meaningful perspective on things, and movement in the most appropriate direction. It is time for combining our best visions with our best actions.

> We don't need new facts (there are enough and even embarrassingly more than enough) so much as we need a new way of looking at and handling facts. We need a new way of seeing, combined with a new way of acting; that is what we need... What we have to do is make up our minds, and get to work—right now. (Teilhard de Chardin, 1959)

Teilhard also emphasized a higher order evolution or transformation, the spiritual journey of man, based on his own experience through time. He wrote of how his attention to the more physical evidences of evolution, from his geologist/paleontologist orientation, led to discovery that there is parallel evolution toward a harmony of man-men-earth-universe-God. It was to this spiritual transformation of all things to which man must put his energies. He wrote:

> To be in communion with Becoming has become the formulae for my whole life.
> The sun is rising ahead...the past is left behind...the only task worthy of our efforts is to construct the future. (Teilhard, quoted in Mortier & Aboux, 1966)

Teilhard was not alone in expansion of the concepts of evolutionary theory beyond biological boundaries. Many other evolutional scientists were attending to the broader complexity of the human species, and thus to the broader scope of evolution. In a scientist's celebration of the 100th anniversary of the publication of Charles Darwin's *Origin of Species,* a consensual statement on contemporary evolutionary theory was issued:

> Evolution is definable in general terms as a one-way, irreversible process in time, which during its course generates novelty, diversity, and higher levels of organization. It operates in all sectors of the phenomenal universe, but has been most fully described and analyzed in the biological sector. (Land, 1959)

By that time, the general ideas of evolutionary theory had withstood the criticisms from the fundamentalist biblical scholars, and from both the Lamarckian and neo-Lamarckian emphasis on behavioral influences on evolution. Actually, Darwin also emphasized the behavioral influences on biological change, with less attention to the underlying genetic influences. By the middle of the twentieth century, after some years of intellectual debate about the "chicken-or-egg" issue, the most widelyheld position on evolutionary processes was that attempting reconciliation of the naturalist's emphasis on behavior and the geneticist's emphasis on inherent structures. George Simpson summarized the reconciliation as between the "naturalist's hen-evolution" (an egg is a hen's way of producing another hen), and the "geneticist's egg-evolution" (a hen is an egg's way of producing another egg). The whole process of evolution, after a century of scientific study, had turned out to be "something broader than, and in some respects different from, Darwin's concept" (Ibid.).

Early in the century, Kropotkin had argued for attention to the social factors in evolution. (It is interesting to note that this was about the same time that neo-Freudians and behavior scientists began to suggest that Freud's biological orientation to personality and human development should be expanded to include the influence of social factors.) Kropotkin posited the concept of "mutual aid," and suggested that the definition of "fit" in Darwin's "survival of the fittest" must not be solely defined in terms of physical capabilities. He cited evidence from animal research which showed that those who could establish the behaviors of social cooperation and developed ways of working together were often the more successful (Kropotkin, 1902). His arguments made little impact on the more biologically-oriented evolutionists of his time, but were recognized later when the image of humankind was broadened to attend to the complexity and totality that was obvious.

By the 1960's, evolutionists were recognizing the need to focus on all the "sectors of the phenomenal universe." Theodosius Dobzhansky, who was an early president of the American Teilhard de Chardin Association, and one of those who recognized the forthcoming emphasis on "transformation," noted:

> Man has not only evolved; for better or worse he is evolving. Our not very remote ancestors were animals, not men; the transition from animal to man is, on the evolutionary time scale, rather recent. But the newcomer, the human species, has proved fit when tested in the crucible of natural selection; this high fitness is a product of the genetic equipment which made culture possible... Now man's future inexorably depends on the interactions of biological and social forces. (Dobzhansky, 1962)

Actually, the psychological and cultural factors were long at work in man's history. Rene Dubos has noted:

> From Cro-Magnon time on, the evolutionary development of humankind has been almost exclusively sociocultural rather than biological. Humanity has transcended animality. (Dubos, 1981)

Many would debate Dubos' argument, suggesting that man still often behaves like a "crazy ape." Albert SzentGyorgi, biologist and Nobel Laureate for Medicine, recognizes that human-kind was going through a critical period of evolutional history, "which could

116

very well end with his extinction in the not too distant future." The fact that humans are still biological entities, often regressing to hedonic choices that are inappropriate in the long-range picture warrants concern.

Of course, the ultimate question is: will mankind be able to survive the machinations of present-day men who often appear to act more like crazy apes than sane human beings? ...Why does man behave like a perfect idiot? ...Nature is big, man is small; the quality and level of human life has always depended on man's relation to nature. ...Mankind has now reached a crossroads, and is confronted by two road signs that point in opposite directions. One of these can be symbolized by the happenings at My Lai. It points to a dark world, dominated by militaryindustrial complexes and conducted by fear, hatred, and distrust. It features terror and the building of monstrous instruments of murder—atomic bombs and submarines, napalm, defoliants, nerve gases, etc. This road leads to doomsday, to the deserved disappearance of man from his polluted little globe. The other road sign points in the opposite direction. It would lead man to a sunlit, peaceful, and clean world, marked by good will, human solidarity, decency and equity, and free of hunger and disease, with a place for everyone. Man can waste no more time in making a decision as to which road he is going to take. It seems like such a simple decision. Or is it? (Szent-Gyorgi, 1970)

Transformation theory is essentially optimistic. Human beings, with new awareness of their own role in the evolutionary process, will meet the challenge of evolution to a higher order of existence. George Leonard, an active participant and chronicler of the human potential movement, subtitled his book on the transformation of man, "A Guide to the Inevitable Changes in Humankind." His basic

proposition was that man is on the verge of grasping his responsibility for his own future, and that "the transformation is underway," since awareness is the initial step in the necessary growth forward. He is optimistic and hopeful, declaring:

The new species will evolve, for man has already recognized the need to dismantle the walls between ourselves and our sisters and brothers, and dissolve the distinction between flesh and spirit, and to transcend the present limits of time and matter.

For those who are willing to overcome fear and learn through pain, there is the delight of high adventure in store, travels of the spirit, festivals of our accomplishment in realms now hidden from our senses.

And after all the journeying, all the pain and joy, we may discover that the Transformation was difficult to grasp, not because it was so far away but because it was so very near.   (Leonard, 1972)

Rene Dubos, in *Celebrations of Life*, presents a view of the richness, and humanness of all societies, arguing that "trend is not des-

tiny," and that the human being's capacity for change gives reason for optimism:

In the final analysis, the welfare of Humankind may well depend upon our ability to create the equivalent of the tribal unity that existed at the beginning of the human adventure, while continuing to nurture the individual diversity which is essential for the further development of civilization.

This is not the best of times, but it is nevertheless a time for celebration because, even though we now realize our insignificance as parts of the cosmos and as individual members of the human family, we know that each one of us can develop a persona which is unique, yet remains part of the cosmic and human order of things. Human beings have been and remain uniquely creative because they are able to integrate the pessimism of intelligence with the optimism of Will. (Dubos, 1981)

Lionel Tiger also advocates optimism, arguing that man has the potential for the process of "equilibration," which involves the capability to "inhibit present responses in order to achieve the future goals." Tiger notes that our evolution has brought us to a level where our consciousness is now augmented by an elaborate ability to think things through and think ahead. He feels that man has enough consciousness of his own evolution to meet the challenge of transformation to the future; because, he argues, it is the natural human tendency to choose the positive, the track that will bring greater joy to one's being. Although he is an anthropologist, his study of "the Biology of Hope" suggests that the tendency toward positive growth has both biological and social bases (Tiger, 1979).

Transformation theory is also supported by the works of the prominent psychological theorists. Abraham Maslow, whose theoretical constructs have been most often associated with personality theory and the human potential movement, might best be considered for his ideas on human motivation. In a 1955 article for the classic Nebraska Symposium on Motivation, Maslow outlined his views on

the innate tendency of human beings to grow in a positive direction, toward a higher order of personal humanbeingness. He opened the article with statements of his personal orientation, and of the development of the humanistic tradition in psychology. It should be noted that these thoughts were presented during the years of formulation of his more comprehensive "psychology of being."

Hans Zinsser has described the difference between philosophical and scientific theorizing by comparing the latter to a trellis which one builds out just ahead of the growing vine in the direction of its growth and for the sake of its future support....

I am very definitely interested and concerned with man's fate, with his ends and goals and with his future. I would like to help improve him and to better his prospects. I hope to help teach him how to be brotherly, cooperative, peaceful, courageous, and just.

In recent years more and more psychologists have found themselves compelled to postulate some tendency to growth or self-perfection to supplement the concepts of equilibrium, homeostasis, tension-reduction, defense and other conserving motivations... The humanistic task of psychology is that of constructing a scientific system of values to help men live the good life; i.e., a humanly usable theory of human motivation... If we define growth as the various processes which bring the person toward ultimate self-actualization, then this better conforms to the observed fact that is going on all the time in the life history. (Maslow, 1955)

Maslow defines need as basic or "instinctual," as its satisfaction is essential to the health of the organism, but notes that satisfaction of the basic life needs only serves to release the motivation to grow, rather than maintain equilibrium. He does not differentiate between the "basic needs" and the "growth needs," noting that the basic needs are more typically similar across the whole species, whereas the "selfactualization" needs are unique for each person both in terms of goals and the behavior patterns chosen to attain those goals (Ibid.).

Maslow's theory was parallel to that of Carl Rogers, whose basic theory of personality and behavior presented a few years earlier had extended as one of its propositions:

> The organism has one basic tendency and striving—to actualize, maintain, and enhance the experiencing organism... We are speaking of the tendency of the organism to move in the direction of maturation, as maturation is defined for each species. This involves self-actualization, though it should be understood that this too is a directional term... (Rogers, 1951)

Some evolutionists have also pointed up the human being's choice at many points in evolution. Bjorn Kurten, in a discussion of the long-time differences between the human species and the apes, notes:

> Our ancestors were not forced to leave the trees by some kind of crisis, such as death of the forest by desiccation. They came down to the ground to invade a new, favorable life zone. (Kurten, 1972)

Marilyn Ferguson, in her overview of the transformation, notes that the idea of an intrinsic motivation to grow to the demands of the future is certainly not a temporary flash in human consciousness. The "lightning" of this awareness has been reported by others, but the central idea is always the same:

> Only through a new mind can humanity remake itself, and the potential for

such a new mind is natural.(Ferguson, 1980)

Her review of the "premonitions of transformation and conspiracy" includes reference to over one-hundred figures from contemporary history who spoke with foresight of the forthcoming transformation. For example:

> In the 1920s, Jan Christian Smuts, the Boer general who was twice prime minister of South Africa wrote a book, *Holism and Evolution*, in which he argued for existence of a powerful organizing principle in all of nature and a drive toward ever higher organization.
>
> In 1927, Nikos Kazantzakis, the great Greek novelist, envisioned a union of individuals—those who might create for earth a brain and a heart. What we have called God is the evolutionary drive of consciousness in the universe.
>
> H. G. Wells proposed that the time was nearly ripe for global change. All this world is heavy with the promise of greater things, and "a day will come, one day in the unending succession of days, when beings who are now latent in our loins shall stand upon this earth." (Ibid.)

As the human potential movement and the unfolding new orientations of the sciences has developed theories and practices based on a new paradigm, and we have recognized the latent potential of all persons to become, Ferguson suggests:

> Transformation is no longer lightning, but electricity. We have captured a force more powerful than the atom, a worthy keeper of all our powers. (Op.cit.)

George T. Lock Land, one of the early contributors to a unifying theory of the transformation, suggested that the drive toward growth is a biological-genetic process. He posited a very reductionist view of the transformation, arguing that the key to understanding individual and social behavior, and the whole of the evolution-transformation process, is to be found in the behavior of atoms, molecules, and cells. Still, his thesis is not a deterministic prognostication of the future, for he feels that the human species can utilize the basic laws of nature to choose the direction of future evolution. He states the problem:

> This book is about Man: a creature who fouls his own nest while flying to the moon, an ambivalent being who grasps the future with one hand while clinging to the past with the other; who does all these things with a mind powerful enough to continually expand his domination of Nature but who is unable to explain why. Rather than engage in a fruitless dispute of the many theories about our nature, this book outlines a theory on the origin, nature, and nurture of Man that sees apparently conflicting achievements and failures as integral parts of the whole of Man and his mission. We call the theory that begins to integrate these relationships, Transformation.   (Land, 1973)

Land offers the postulates of his version of transformation theory, and presents scientific data to support them. He argues that human behavior has naturally evolved from biological behavior, and that the behavior of all living things is growth-directed behavior. (Note, his argument is quite similar to that of the famous biologist, Albert Szent-Gyorgi, about "drive in living matter to perfect itself.") As knowledge of the principles that govern evolutional growth become known, humans have a new responsibility and a new challenge:

> Spurring the natural process of growth to ever higher forms is the direct responsibility of Mankind, the most effective agent of evolution and natural selection in life's history... As the evolved

mechanism for evolution, Man is therefore the sole responsible agent to and for his species and environment. As an emerging megamutualistic species, we can continue to transform our environment through new growth processes and new products and select out nonmutual expressions of our technology and society at ever-increasing rates. We can safely assume that in our evolution there is no finite or visualizable end to growth or transformations to unique levels of growth on the part of each person and of a total culture.   (Ibid.)

The responsibility for defining the nature of the desirable future, and for guiding the evolution-transformation energies of the species, has two important implications. First, it means that there must be more attention to the relationship between evolution and ethics. As evolutionary theory began to focus on the totality of the human being, and the seeds of transformation theory were being sewn, prominent anthropologist George Simpson noted that the traditional biological emphasis on evolution was essentially amoral (Simpson, 1953). Only a few years later, as the scope of evolutional theory was broadening to include those factors which would soon define transformation theory, C. H. Waddington discussed the concept of man as *The Ethical Animal* (Waddington, 1960). For transformation theory, in which people must choose between alternative destinies and alternative strategies, the questions of ethics are extremely important. Teilhard de Chardin, who can certainly be considered the first and foremost of the transformation theorists, noted that we need to explore our ethics in relationship to our evolution. He wrote:

> The boldest of tomorrow's navigators will set out across the mysterious ocean of moral energies, which they will have to

explore and humanize.   (Teilhard, in Hefner, 1970)

The second major implication of transformation theory is that concerning education. First the human species evolved towards the development of culture, and thereafter culture became a part of evolution. Culture then flows down the evolutional trails through teaching and learning. The very problems and issues placed before our children, and the very methodologies by which we teach them, are reflective of all that we are and can be. There is, quite obviously, need to attend to the practices of education. Szent-Gyorgi notes that:

> What we call education is nothing but the programming of the brain at an early age when it is still quite malleable. The future of mankind depends on education, a system of programming which can be changed. We need an educational system based on the real understanding of moral, esthetic, and spiritual values. (Szent-Gyorgi, 1970)

Land gives suggestions for parents, teachers and counselors, noting that the appropriate orientation should be toward:

> ...providing the freedom for safe exploratory play with the environment, and incrementally granting responsibility to the growing child; providing a belief in dignity, respect, and self-affirmation by being willing not only to educate but to learn from and mutualize with our children; and allow the expression of their growth through creatively affecting their environment. (Land, 1973)

Michael Brown has recently summarized the challenge for experiential educators, but the challenge is certainly applicable to those who consider themselves challenge educators, and to all those who understand the nature and demands of transformation theory.

As experiential educators, we are challenged to teach people how to live deliberately, to confront the central facts in their lives, and to learn what they can about themselves, each other, and the natural world. We guide people on journeys which often lead to personal growth, positive change, and more effective ways of thinking and behaving. From the highest point of view, we are attempting to facilitate a process of transformation for those in our charge.

The concept of transformation is complex, and can convey a wide spectrum of meanings. At the low end, it can imply a simple change in form or outer appearance. At the high end, however, it can imply metamorphosis—a permanent shift to a higher level of operating. (Brown, 1989)

Whether one speaks of the transformation of persons, cultures, or the whole human species, the process and the product are the same. Evolution has brought us to a point of illumination of our own potentialities, and now lights the way to the future. As Marilyn Ferguson has noted, "The transformation is underway" (Ferguson, 1980).

> Blind indeed are those who do not see the sweep of a movement whose orbit infinitely transcends the natural sciences and has successfully invaded and conquered the surrounding territory—chemistry, physics, sociology, and even mathematics and the history of religions. One after the other all the fields of human knowledge have been shaken and carried away by the same underwater current in the direction of the study of some development. Is evolution a theory, a system, or a hypothesis? It is much more; it is a general condition to which all theories, all hypotheses, all systems must bow and which they must satisfy henceforward if they are to be thinkable and true. Evolution is a light illuminating all facts, a

curve that all lines must follow. (Teilhard de Chardin, 1959)

CONNECTEDNESS AND BELONGINGNESS THEORY

It is possible to cluster a number of thoughts about the human being and the world into an overview of what could be called a theory of connectedness. Basically, such a theory would rest on two propositions. The first proposition is that all things of the universe are living and are a part of the whole; they are bio-spiritually connected and interdependent. Second, when human beings become aware of this connectedness, their natural tendency is to care for, nurture, and belong to all other things—to actualize the beauty, the wisdom, and the love of this connectedness through belongingness. While the specific nature of both the connectedness and the belongingness warrant greater attention than can be given at this time, it should be recognized that the supportive ideas have a long history, and have been discussed by major thinkers as well as lived in the lives of peoples. Many have recognized the connectedness of all things; and quotations of relevance can be traced through the past fifty years.

The deeper we look into nature, the more we recognize that it is full of life, and the more profoundly we know that all life is a secret and that we are united with all life that is in nature. Man can no longer live his life for himself alone. We realize that life is valuable and that we are united to all this life. From this knowledge comes our spiritual relationship to the universe. (Schweitzer, 1934)

We take a tiny colony of soft corals from a rock in a little water world. And that isn't terribly important to the tide pool. Fifty miles away the Japanese shrimp boats are dredging with overlap-ping scoops, bringing up tons of shrimps, rapidly destroying the ecological balance of the whole region. That isn't very important in the world. And six thousand miles away the great bombs are falling on London and the stars are not moved thereby. None of it is important or all of it is. (Steinbeck and Ricketts, 1941)

Consciousness stretches up through time from the placid mass of cells on the drying mud, through reptiles that browse on the branches of trees and the little mammals peeping on them through the leaves, up to proust in his exquisite agonizing web consciousness must surely be traced back to the rocks—the rocks which have been here since life began and so make a meeting place for the roots of life in time and space, the earliest and the simplest. (Hawkes, 1951)

Cosmic awareness differs from self-awareness in that it goes beyond being present at the moment and provides an experience of contact with the universe that differs from the one usually presented to the senses....a new way of perceiving the world and one's relationship to it. (Mann, 1972)

A human being is a part of the whole, called by us the universe, a part limited in time and space. He experiences himself, his thoughts and feelings, as something that is separated from the rest—a kind of optical delusion of his consciousness. This delusion is a kind of prison for us, restricting us to our personal desires and to affection for only a few persons nearest to us. Our task must be to free ourselves from this prison by widening our circle of compassion to embrace all living creatures and the whole of nature and its beauty. (Einstein, 1972)

The words EARTH AND HEART, graphically, are composed of the same letters of the alphabet; the difference is the placement of the letter "H". Symbolically, the two words express a relationship. The letter H ending one word and beginning the other depicts a linkage... To experience EARTH is to experience HEART. With the Earth as our classroom, we learn to relate to ourselves, others, and the World through our Heartfelt relationships, our EARTH-HEART. (Hill, 1984)

We are where we are now because of certain deeply-rooted assumptions we have made, more or less consciously, about the nature of the world and our place in it. Everything depends on who we think we are, and it's no secret that we have our conceits. Our intelligence exalts us, we believe; all other species are subordinate. We alone have cosmic destiny; we alone are perfectible. Having known, at times, great hardship, we have fixed on material development as the measure of our progress and call it the pursuit of happiness. Economic growth is our mission, the earth our heathen to convert... The sky's the limit. And the soil. And the water. How forgiving the earth has been until now—its capacity to give as resource and take back as waste so great our economics have assumed it away.

But now we overcome one limit only to find another more formidable than the last. The effect is cumulative. Could it be that far from transcending limits we've merely been blind to them? Have we misperceived our place in the scheme of things? Our central task will be to find these things out. But who will teach us? The earth is our teacher, always has been, but the gift of seeing does not come unbidden. We must go into the future with our eyes open—and our hearts, and our minds. (Barrett, 1990)

Over the past few decades, as awareness of negative effects of humankind's actions toward the earth has increased, there has been much attention to the cosmological philosophy of the Native American Indians. It may be that some of their beliefs and practices have even been glamorized to illustrate appropriate points. Still, most recognize that there is validity in their teachings about the spiritual relationship between humans and the earth. They did, indeed, reflect an awareness of "connectedness."

You ask me to plough the ground. Shall I take a knife and tear my mother's bosom? You ask me to dig for stone. Shall I dig under her skin for her bones? You ask me to cut the grass and make hay, and sell it to be rich like the white man. But dare I cut off my mother's hair? (Smohalla, Medicine Man of the NezPerce)

Our teachers tell us that all things within this universe know of their harmony with every other thing, and know how to give away one to the other, except man. All things of the Universe Wheel have spirit and life, including the rivers, rocks, earth, sky, plants, and animals. But man is a determiner. Our determining spirit can be made whole only through learning of our harmony with all our brothers and sisters, and all the other spirits of the Universe. To do this we must learn to seek and perceive. (Storm, 1972)

In his history of psychotherapy, Walter Bromberg notes that the Native Americans did not make a distinction between mental and physical disorders, because they did not make a distinction between biophysical existence and the realm of spirituality. He quotes a Pit River Indian: "All animals, plants, land, and peoples were placed here by the Great Spirit—hence manipulation of one injures the other." Sickness, therefore, was the result of the person being "out of harmony" with nature (Bromberg, 1975).

This same idea has been revised by holistic health experts in recent years, as evidenced in a book on the ecology of nutrition.

The complex interplay of animate and inanimate systems on the surface of the earth—soil, air, water, plants, and animals—has come only recently to be appreciated as a delicate but fundamental factor in the welfare of the planet. We have just begun to recognize that our unthinking interaction with these systems —air, soil and water—multiplied by families and groups and cities and crowds can burden them and shift them from a state of equilibrium, the thrust of which can recoil, damaging our food supply and our health in turn. The movement of certain minerals and plant-made compounds into the body of the human, a phenomena we call "nutrition," is but one small part of the overall ecological whole. We must understand the nature of the human cell and the nature of the plant cell; we must grasp the relationship between the quality of cellular life and the quality of the soil from which it springs.   (Ballentine, 1978)

Frank Waters, a Navajo, noted that one of the healing rituals was a "Sing," a ceremony of chant and dance that lasted up to 100 hours, which attempted to bring the sick person back into harmony with others, the world, and the universe (Waters, 1973). Rituals for harvest, burial, and celebration were also consistent with a perspective of the wholeness and interrelatedness of the universe. There have been a number of publications which can contrib-

ute to a broader understanding of this cosmological view of life by the Native Americans (e.g., Highwater, 1981; Brown, 1982).

The *I Ching* (Book of Changes) originated three thousand years ago and is a basis for both Taoist and Confucian philosophies.

One of the primary teachings of the *I Ching* is that of the wholeness and interrelatedness of all things, which has been translated as the principle of "synchronicity" (Wilhelm, 1967). The Taoist philosophy expresses the same principle, as the very word Tao implies the creative principle that orders the universe.

> In the universe we have four greatnesses, and man is but one. Man is in accordance with earth. Earth is in accordance with heaven. Heaven is in accordance with Tao. Tao is in accordance with that which is.   (Wing-tsit Chan, 1963)

In Eastern philosophies, there is also the Law of Ahimsa, which stresses the importance of reverence for all that is. Ghandi often referred to Ahimsa, for it advocated cooperation, unity, and nonviolence to every form of life. Like the Native Americans, the Eastern philosophies have generally avoided the trap created by division of mind and matter, spiritual existence and material existence.

> The Eastern philosophies have not categorized mind and matter, soul and body, in the same way as the Western. Departmentalization is foreign to them... there is no separation of the spiritual and material.   (Watts, 1961)

In Greek Mythology, the Gods and their families were often interrelated. Zeus was in charge of the sky, his brother Poseidon of the sea, and his brother Hades of the underworld. Zeus wed Hera, who began as an Earth Goddess, and became the Goddess of Marriage— the first goddess of a blessed pattern of connectedness and belongingness. Poseidon was to become the consort of Ge, the earth, who became Gaia, the motherearth—thus also the guardian of that beautiful pattern of connectedness and belongingness. Poseidon also fertilized Demeter, the Goddess of crops; and he also seeded Leto, mother of the twins, Apollo and Artemis. Apollo became the force against evil—and perhaps the greatest evil was to become the human beings' violations of the desired love of each other and of the earth (Guthrie, 1950).

"Gaia," thus represents the earth as a living system, and was therefore the name chosen by James Lovelock for his theory of knowledge and awareness which humankind must recognize if the choice is for survival (Lovelock, 1987). The hypothesis has been summarized by Michael Cohen, who subtitled his most recent book, "Regenerating Kinship with Planet Earth" (Cohen, 1986).

> The Gaia Hypothesis scientifically confirms an ancient truth found in most non-western cultures which are environmentally and socially sound. Planet Earth organizes, perpetuates, and regenerates itself, suggesting that it is a living organism (Gaia), for only living entities demonstrate these properties. Earth's pulsating global life community (Nature) is a seamless continuum that biologically envelops and embodies all entities including rocks and people. (Cohen, 1989)

We are all children of the earth, umbilically linked to Gaia. Lovelock's basic theory has been summarized in a book about the 1988 Earth Conference, "Sharing a Vision for Our Planet."

> The critical insight Lovelock offered us was the importance of learning again to be part of the Earth, and not separate from it. While we saw ourselves as separate from the Earth we could behave badly towards it, as if the damage we did to it didn't matter in itself and didn't rebound on us. Blinded by this illusion, we were able to pollute rivers, stain the sea and the air; we could strip the fields of their fertility and tear down the forest trees think-

ing all the while only of our immediate profit, our "high productivity." But as soon as we saw the Earth and ourselves as part of the same whole, then we could see that we can no more strip the Earth and remain unaffected than we could strip off our skin and not feel the pain. (Vittachi, 1989)

Lovelock's mandate for the future was to put "spiritual awareness" back into scientific knowledge. Basically, he seeks an acceptance of knowledge as both scientific and spiritual, in parallel to that of the ancient philosophies of the East and the American Indian. His suggestion for reintegration of spirituality and science, his recognition of the value of both rational knowledge and the lessons of intuition and spiritual awareness, has been an often-tackled problem in the history of philosophy.

One example would be that of Giardano Bruno, who has been recognized as influential in the development of "Unitary Thinking." Writing in the 16th century, he postulated a "universal intellect," which "illumineth the universe and directeth nature." His basic argument was that the ignorance of man is the failure to perceive in things "the harmony between substances, motions, and qualities" (Hoffding, 1955). Bruno's thought was influential on Baruch Spinoza, who wrote in the 17th century shortly after Rene Descartes had posited the dualistic view of mind and body. For Spinoza, there is but one substance in the universe, and that is God. God is nature, is the universe, is substance, is all; and is at one time both mental and material. All is God, all is therefore connected. His pantheism included a distinction between the mental and the physical, but they must always be recognized as interactional. This psycho-physical parallelism influenced much early psychological theory, but would be considered inadequate for the "third force" holistic/humanistic psychologies. Still, his writings address issues that are of concern for the modern philosopher.

Consider, for example, his concept that human freedom and peace of mind must follow from an awareness and acceptance of the totality of the Universe. He argued against the authority of the State, in favor of a world-view consciousness. Reason is not enough, humans must also trust basic intuitive knowledge— and that will lead to vision of the connectedness of all things (Wright, 1950).

Lovelock warned that failure to attend to Gaia would mean continuation of human narcissism, and continual destruction of our earth. Of course, it is difficult to see how humankind cannot attend to Gaia. The ecological crises of the past few decades have brought awareness of the limits at hand. There are limits to how much the human population can increase. There are limits to converting forest land to agricultural usage. There are limits to the quantities of waste that can be dumped into the land or the oceans. There are limits to the land itself, to its resources, and to the energy available. At the 1988 Earth Conference, all participants at the general assembly sat under a gigantic blowup of the famous photograph of Earth from space. Lovelock later wrote:

> Over the past few decades we have come to realize that we have one home, our planet. It was significant that the hall was dominated in a visual sense by that stunning vision of a blue sphere wrapped in cloud, so unlike any other planet, which enthralled the eyes of those first astronauts, and all of us vicariously... We can no more ignore the symbolism of the living planet seen from above than we can ignore the Cross or even the Mona

> Lisa....(That vision) has sustained us and set our minds and our hearts on the true task ahead; to ensure not just human survival, but the survival of all life through living in harmony with the Earth itself. (Lovelock, 1989)

Not so long ago, Aldo Leopold called for a "land ethic," which focused on the need for all people to expand one's sense of community beyond human beings and include the land and the nonhumans within one's sense of basic responsibility (Leopold, 1949). He suggested balance between the needs of man and the needs of the environment, recognizing their interdependency. In discussion of Leopold's ideas, it was noted:

> Such an ethic does not demand that the natural physical environment be given top priority in every human decision. It simply means that the concerns of the environment will be recognized when ethical decisions are made. (Simpson, 1985)

The recent "ecophilosophy" of Norwegian Arne Naess differentiates between "ecology" and "deep ecology," in pattern similar to Spinoza's two processes for knowledge. Whereas "ecology" is essentially a scientific study, emphasizing rational understanding and cognitive awareness of the balance of nature, "deep ecology" includes, indeed requires, heartfelt and spiritually-accepted awareness. His distinction is also quite similar to that of Abraham Maslow, humanistic psychologist, who recognized both "scientific theorizing" and "philosophical theorizing," with the latter including knowledge and awarenesses that rational-empirical scientific methodology did not include (Maslow, 1955). For Naess, the whole ecology movement must attend to the broader, more encompassing overview.

In so far as ecology movements deserve our attention, they are ecophilosophical rather than ecological. Ecology is a limited science which makes use of scientific methods. Philosophy is the most general forum of debate on fundamentals, descriptive as well as prescriptive and political philosophy is one of its subsections. By an ecophilosophy I mean philosophy of ecological harmony or equilibrium. A philosophy as a kind of sofia wisdom, is openly normative; it contains both norms, rules, postulates, value priority announcements and hypotheses concerning the state of affairs in our universe. Wisdom is policy wisdom, prescription, not only scientific description. (Naess, 1973)

An ecophilosophy appropriate for the present, and mandatory for the Twenty-First century would certainly seem to include the Gaia hypothesis at its very core. Our awareness of the connectedness of all things cannot be denied, and the task is now to turn to establishing an interactional love for mother-earth and all that is, self-otherplanet.

Indeed, it can be argued that human survival depends upon recovering an erotic relatedness to the total environment. Love or perish! It is clear that man's alienation from and carelessness of nature must come to an end or man will destroy both himself and the world. Either we learn that we are a part of natural ecology which must be reverenced and loved or we will not survive.   (Keen, 1970)

Recently, in a provocative overview of the necessary blending of holistic education and ecological ethics it was suggested that the appropriate directions for humankind is "The Way of Ecopiety." This is because when ecophilosophy leads to an awareness of the nature of the person in the modern world, the person possesses a characteristic of "Ecopiety."

By ecopiety, we wish to convey a deeply abiding sense of care and reverence for coexistence among all beings and things whether they be human or not. "Piety" refers to the absolute reciprocity of giving and receiving that is at once mental and bodily.   (Jung & Jung, 1989)

The way of ecopiety leads to a redefinition of the good life, and provides a regulatory principle of conduct towards all things of the earth, and all other beings. Ecopiety is a quality of being, a characterological trait. It involves loving concern for fellow human beings and all that is of the earth; it can be represented by the equation:

ECOPIETY=HOMOPIETY + GEOPIETY

The second proposition of a theory of connectedness and belongingness suggests that the nature of the human being is to seek and develop loving relationships with those things to which they are connected. There is a drive toward attachment or "belongingness." The motivation towards this belongingness is not based on need-reduction, it is not a primary biological need; but is rather a higher-order motivation toward self-actualization, which might well be considered as a spiritual need.

Early American psychological theory was dominated by the biological–scientific model, and this resulted in postulation of motivational theory based on need reduction, and tied directly to basic biological drives, such as hunger, thirst, and sex. More complex behavioral patterns were usually considered "secondary" or "instrumental" drives, developed to meet the underlying "primary" motivations.

As psychological theory moved through the middle years of the twentieth century, there were significant developments in the theory of motivation. From the "third force" psychologies of Goldstein (1939), Fromm (1941), Snygg and Combs (1949), Rogers (1951), Maslow (1954), and Allport (1955), came the ideas that there were higher-order motivations toward creative expression and self-actualization. It was suggested that there was a built-in drive toward certain activities and accomplishments; not everything could be related to basic internal imbalances. Psychoanalyst Charlotte Buhler, summarized:

> In the fundamental psychoanalytic model, there is only one basic tendency, that is toward need gratification or tension reduction. Present-day biologic theories emphasize the "spontaneity" of an organism's activity which is due to builtin energy. These concepts will require a complete revision of the original principle of homeostasis.   (Buhler, 1959)

Ludwig von Bertalanffy, a biologist, concluded that "living things have intrinsic activity. The very definition of living being is that of a self-maintaining, self-repairing, self-moving system" (Bertalanffy, 1967).

Humanistic psychologist Gordon Allport wrote:

> The healthy child and adult are continually building up tensions, in the form of new interests, and are going way beyond the basic, safely established level of homeostasis; acquiring knowledge for its own sake, creation of works of beauty and usefulness, love, a sense of duty, etc., cannot be reduced to basic drive psychology.   (Allport, 1961)

Although Maslow's famous "hierarchy of needs" suggests that the person must attend to the basic needs first, there are drives toward higher-order goals that are quite independent of the primary needs. The human desires for love and belongingness were recognized.

In Maslow's model there really is no "need" for love. The person reaches out for attachment, affection, sharing, caring, and belonging, not as a means to an end, but as an end itself. Maslow does suggest a distinction between "Blove" (i.e., love of the other's very Being), and "A-love" (i.e., deficiency love or selfish, narcissistic love) (Maslow, 1955).

About the same time that the "third force" psychologies were emerging, there were some significant laboratory findings that were to influence later theories of motivation. In the primate labs of Harry Harlow at the University of Wisconsin, studies showed that rhesus monkeys would work their way through complex locks and latches for the simple reward of a cage door opening and providing them with "a peek at the world" (Harlow, 1953; Butler and Harlow, 1954). With reservations, the behaviorists postulated a drive of "curiosity," although many attempted to relate the results of the research to a basic drive for sensory stimulation.

Harlow soon expanded his perspectives on research problems, and began the classic series of studies on "the Nature of Love." He showed how the early experiences of bonding with a nurturing mother figure could contribute to later capacity for meaningful love with others (c.f., Harlow, 1958, 1971). His overview of love suggested four patterns (maternal, infant, agemate, and paternal). With contemporary awareness of the desirable bond between the human being and the earth, there should perhaps be a fifth pattern recognized. If the human-earth relationship was so defined, perhaps empirical studies could help us understand ourselves better.

Soon after the classic work with the "Butler Box," R. W. White examined the whole concept of motivation, and offered the construct of "competence" to motivational theorists. He suggested that human activities are sometimes motivated by "effectance," the production of environmental change which provides a sense of "competence" or "effectiveness." Many psychologists have viewed White's classic review and postulation as a turning point in all motivational theory (White, 1959).

In any case, as the 1960's unfolded, it was becoming appropriate to recognize the higher order drives of humans toward "love," "creativity," "growth," "self-actualization," "connectedness," and "belongingness." Through the 1970's and 1980's, as the scope of psychological theory broadened from the impact of the "third force," the holistic perspective recognized the complexity of the human being. It is now appropriate to consider that there is a drive in human beings to belong, to develop a sharing-caring reciprocal relationship with others and with the earth.

Early in the century, Kropotkin, who was a social evolutionist, suggested that "mutual aid" (the process of helping each other) was a more appropriate concept of the "fitness" in the Darwinian model of survival of the fittest, than was the notion of aggressive domination (Kropotkin, 1902). It may well be that with the expansion of awareness to understanding of the connectedness of all things, and the recognition of the interdependency of humans and the earth, Kropotkin's argument should be expanded. Survival means survival of both human-kind and the world, as they are but

one, it is time to change our behavior from taking from the earth to a giving-and-taking exchange. What has been called "human chauvinism" or "anthropocentricism" should not give way to the reverse error of "ecocentricism," placing the human being in an inferior perspective. We must not subsume the needs of the human to the needs of "mother earth." Instead, there needs to be a consciousness of the connectedness and the belongingness of all.

In terms of their discussion of "ecopiety," Jung and Jung suggest: "What dominative and utility are to anthropocentricism, harmony and reverence are to the ethics of ecopiety" (op.cit.).

A theory of connectedness and belongingness has implications for ethical theorizing, which must now address the interrelationship of human beings and the earth, as well as the interactions between human beings. There are also some obvious implications for education, which might start with the seven propositions proposed for "earth-centered learning" as outlined by David Orr.

1. All education is environmental education.

2. Environmental issues are complex and cannot be understood through a single discipline or department.

3. The study of place is a fundamental organizing concept for education.

4. For inhabitants education occurs in part as dialogue with place and has the characteristics of good conversation.

5. The way education occurs is as important as its content.

6. Experience in the natural world is both an essential part of understanding the environment, and is also conducive to good thinking.

7. Education relevant to the challenge of building a sustainable society will enhance the learner's competence with natural systems.

(Orr, 1989)

Of course, as it has been outlined, any theory of connectedness and belongingness is broader than basic environmental education or ecological education. In order to enhance the development of an awareness of the oneness of self-otherearth, education will have to be a multidisciplinary, multi-modal and multiexperiential situation. Connectedness and belongingness theory should provide challenge educators with a good many ideas for exploration in building a significant philosophy.

ADDITIONAL IDEAS FOR A PHILOSOPHY OF CHALLENGE EDUCATION

1. TRUST LEVEL THEORY. "Trust" is one of the frequently-discussed concepts in challenge education. There should be value, accordingly, in attending to a theory of trust in human interaction, as developed by Jack Gibb and his associate (Gibb, 1971, 1972, 1978). In his professional career as a psychologist, Gibb was involved with the N.T.L. (National Training Laboratory), which developed the famous T-Group methodology for industrial and educational leaders. He was also active in the human potential movement, and became a consultant to transforming business, industry, and educational organizations. Through the 1970's, together with his wife, his colleagues, his friends, and a number of his students, Gibb formed a network community of sharing, caring, supporting, creating, and growing. The basic overview of this community gave foundation to his TORI theory.

Gibb calls it "Trust Level Theory," and the acronym TORI stands for the four cornerstones of the orientation:

Trusting-being,
Opening-sharing,
Realizing-growing,
Interdependency-teaming.
(Gibb, 1972)

In summarizing the theory, he states that, unfortunately, "trust is not a part of the American, global, political way of life" (Gibb, 1978). Fortunately, he argues, trust is a basic human characteristic, and it can be seen in some families, some social groups, and some organizations. Trust can be viewed as bipolar to the feelings of suspicion, fear, and the lack of confidence others that is often found in interactional and international relationships. When trust is evident:

...people and people systems function well...
...it is an integrating and wholing force...
...it is a releasing process...it gives freedom... (Ibid.)

Basically, trust can be seen as the process of discovering.

To trust with fullness means that I discover and create my own life. The trusting life is an interflowing and interweaving of the process of discovery and creation. These processes have four primary and highly-interrelated elements:
...discovering and creating who I am, tuning to my own uniqueness, being aware of my own essence, trusting me—being who I am.
...discovering and creating ways of opening and revealing myself to myself and to others, disclosing my essence, discovering yours, communing with you—showing me.

130

...discovering and creating my own paths, flows and rhythms, creating my emerging and organic nature, and becoming, actualizing or realizing this nature—doing what I want.

...discovering and creating with you our interbeing, the ways we can live together in interdepending community, in freedom and intimacy—being with you.

Use of such words as "discovering" and "creating" may suggest to some that I am talking here of largely cognitive and conscious processes. I do not mean to imply this at all. I am referring to organic, holistic, body mind, total person processes that have the quality intuitive and instinctual about them. Each process is both a discovering and a creating—indistinguishable in fusion. I think of the person, the group, and the organization as a total organism that develops these processes, especially under climates of high trust. (Op.cit.)

Gibb's concept is that trust begets trust, that it overcomes fear, and that it provides a flowing, growing, creative, sharing, supporting format for any relationship or any group. Trust develops when individuals open themselves to others, becoming personal and authentic. The defensive blocks and the fears that are so typical can be overcome when individuals risk sharing and cooperative experiences. "When trust transcends fear, all things are possible." (Op.cit.)

His presentation includes a scale for individuals to "self-diagnose" their capacities on the four TORI factors, and a parallel version for teams or groups to judge themselves. Gibb's collection of ideas may well have many applications to the practice of challenge education, and the underlying analysis of trust and group interaction should help in understanding these very complex human dynamics.

2. THEORETICAL FOUNDATIONS FOR OUTDOOR ADVENTURE PURSUITS. In a recent survey of the foundations, models, and theories which underlie the contemporary interest in outdoor adventure activities, including risk recreation, high adventure journeys, and adventure education, Alan Ewert discusses some of the theoretical models which have been applied (Ewert, 1989). He notes that the systematic development of theoretical foundations for adventure pursuits has a relatively short history. Therefore, that search parallels the situation for challenge education. Ewert lists the following as having possible application to outdoor adventure:

A. OPTIMAL AROUSAL (Duffy, 1957). This concept refers to the individual seeking arousal in relationship to a survival instinct that desires information in order to gain mastery over the environment. The challenge of new problems tends to raise the motivational level of the person to seek solution. Performance satisfaction is ultimately related to the level of arousal in curvilinear manner, as excessive levels of arousal tend to create anxiety and less adequate performance.

B. COMPETENCE-EFFECTANCE (White, 1959). This concept also involves a need to practice behaviors which lead to environmental control. The reward is a feeling of self-satisfaction, and the individual becomes motivated to ever more complex and challenging tasks to gain greater "competence." Ewert relates this to the idea that balance between the problems, the activities, the challenges, the person's feelings of competence-effectance, and the success of the experience creates a congruence which evidences itself as a "flow" of joyful activity (Csikszentmihalyi, 1975).

C. SELF-EFFICACY THEORY (Bandura, 1977).

Self-efficacy theory refers to personal judgments about capability and performance requirements. Basically, the concept is that the individual seeks accomplishment because it produces an inner state of self-satisfaction; feelings of mastery or control of the environment are not necessary. It has been noted that the individual often tends to seek out the problems that contain ambiguous, unpredictable, and stressful features, because they hold the most promise for greater self-satisfaction (McGowan, 1986).

D. ATTRIBUTION THEORY (Iso-Ahola, 1976).

People make assumptions about the cause of events, and their relationship to them. This leads to a pattern of participation, or limited participation, or non-participation, as a function of those attributations. When the individual feels personally responsible for the actions and outcomes, motivation and involvement are the highest. On the other hand, if the person assumes that the situation and the outcome are out of personal control, in the hands of nature, leaders, or others in the group, there would be less drive to accomplishment. Also, when the whole situation is attributed to the phenomenological self, there will be greater satisfaction and greater transfer to life in general.

E. EXPECTANCY THEORY (McAvoy, 1978; Progen, 1979).

This concept is parallel to that of attribution theory, arguing that the individual tends to develop attitudinal expectancies about endeavors. These expectancies may be with regard to skill development, personal growth, improvement of social relationships, or physical fitness, and they will influence the whole process. If the person has a psychological "set" for learning, or growth, or "excitement," or "challenge," then the subsequent perception of the task will be colored accordingly. The hypothesis of "expectancy" suggests that adventure leaders need to be aware of the diverse orientations of various individuals in any adventure group facilitation.

F. ATTITUDINAL AND BEHAVIORAL MIX (Fishbein and Ajzen, 1975).

It is possible, of course, to "mix" some of the above concepts. The whole sequence of behavioral activity in the outdoor adventure pursuit will be a complex blend of the individual's beliefs, attitudes, emotions, and intentions. Their personal expectancies, their personal perceptions of the situation, and their personal reactions to the unfolding process make for a complex and changing predisposition to the adventure. Furthermore, when there is a whole group of people, the complexity increases. Ewert proceeds to offer his own "causal model" of outdoor pursuits, based on these many ideas, in an attempt to analyze the nature of participation.

By exploring the theories that can glue our observations together, the field will be better able to explain how outdoor adventure activity impacts on individuals...the field will move closer to realizing its ultimate goal: a healthier, more vibrant individual and society. (Ewert, 1989)

3. RIGHT-BRAIN/LEFT-BRAIN, MULTIMIND, WHOLE LEARNING.

The holistic perspective of challenge educators would appear to be given support by the abundance of contemporary theory and research regarding the complex functioning of the brain/mind. One of the considerations which has already been recognized by many educators as very important is that proposing differential functions of the brain's two hemispheres. Research by neuropsychologists and physiologists in the 1950's identified the separate functioning of the two sides of the brain. The young scientist, Robert Ornstein, worked in laboratories with some of that pioneer research involving split-brain preparations in animals. Ornstein also began to delve into the philosophies and practices of the East. As an educator-theorist, he early recognized the potentials of the "esoteric traditions," such as Zen, Sufism, Yoga, and especially the meditation practices that were part of most every Eastern religion/philosophy. He recognized that such practices could provide a counterbalance to Western psychology's emhasis on the biological aspects of the human. One of his first publications was a book on meditation, pointing up its educational value (Naranjo & Ornstein, 1971).

At that time he was already developing his theory of consciousness, which advocated different functions for the two hemispheres of the brain. In an early summarization of his ideas, Ornstein wrote:

> The right side of the cortex primarily controls the left side of the body, and the left side of the cortex largely controls the right side of the body. The structure and the function of these two "half-brains" influences the two modes of consciousness. The left hemisphere is predominantly involved with analytical thinking, especially language and logic. That part of the brain seems to process information sequentially, which is necessary for logical thought since logic depends on sequence and order. The right hemisphere, by contrast, appears to be primarily responsible for our orientation in space, artistic talents, body awareness, and recognition of faces. It processes information more diffusely than the left hemisphere does, and integrates material in a simultaneous, rather than linear function. (Ornstein, 1973)

In that same publication, Andrew Weil offered a summarization of Ornstein's ideas, noting that there was now "light on the dark side of the brain."

> There exists within us two major modes of consciousness; one analytic, the other holistic; one rational and linear, the other intuitive and nonlinear. One of them—the dominant, verbalintellectual, rational one (Ornstein calls it the "day" side of consciousness) has at times been paid great attention by orthodox psychologists. The other—the "night" side of our conscious life, the mode of the dreamer, the artist, the mystic—has been largely ignored except by the "esoteric psychologists," that is, persons trained in such systems as yoga, Buddhism, and Suffism. There must be a complementary interaction of the two modes of our consciousness if man is to realize his highest potential. It is not that intuition is better than intellectual, or that verbal knowledge is worthless, but rather that the two modes of knowing must go together. The "night" side of consciousness must be acknowledged as real, experienced, and integrate into the obscuring brilliance of the "day." (Weil, 1973)

When he published the complete theory in 1975 there was an immediate impact on the educational scene. His thesis supported affective education, confluent education, transpersonal education, and humanistic education, and gave biological validation to their suggested strategies (Ornstein, 1975).

As educators debated the whole issue of the duality of consciousness and the need for appropriate educational strategies for both, Ornstein proceeded to scientifically study the phenomena of consciousness in general. It was suggested by some educators that Ornstein's emphasis on "right-brain" and "leftbrain" was metaphorical, not physiological—but still valuable as a stimulant for educational theory (Roberts and Clark, 1976). The transpersonal psychologists used Ornstein's theory to support educational and counseling work with "guided imagery" (Hendricks and Fadiman, 1976). The humanistic educators and the holistic educators cited Ornstein's work to advocate "whole-brain learning." It was suggested that traditional educational approaches "may miss training or developing half the brain" (Springer & Deutsch, 1981).

While the controversy raged, and educational programs were developed to provide "whole learning," Ornstein and his colleagues published a volume of brain drawings, showing how the various parts of the brain function and which activities take place in which parts of the brain (Ornstein, et al.,1984). Already, his mind was developing even broader concepts of the brain, consciousness, and human behavior. A year later, he published *Multimind.*

The brain developed over a period of more than 500 million years. It is composed of quite separate structures that seem to be laid on top of each other, like a house being remodeled. So we do not have one single brain but a multilevel brain, built in the different eras for different priorities. Many of these separate brains have, loosely speaking, "minds of their own": minds for alertness, for emotions, for danger, for comparing sensory information, for avoiding scarcity.

We are much more complex and much more integrate than we imagine. There is a different structure to the mind than we think, and there are many different levels of operation of the mind. Some are quite fixed and rigid, some flexible, some innate, some learned. Some have direct access to consciousness, some do not. No wonder we have been so confused and have asked questions about the mind that pertain to different levels. The multimind view is a multilevel or hierarchical view of the mind.   (Ornstein, 1986)

Robert Ornstein is a creative thinker, and his multimind model should stimulate psychologists and educators to even greater exploration of various patterns of learning. As with his earlier ideas, the model may be metaphorical, but it may still create meaningful dialogue and exploration of alternative learning strategies. It can perhaps be related to the developing theories of "multiple intelligence," which are being explored in terms of educational application (Gardner, 1983). Parallel ideas on wholebrain learning have been reviewed by Bob Samples. He notes:

By ignoring the realms of fantasy, dreaming, and feeling, and emphasizing rationality and logic, our culture has chosen to define learning and intelligence in amazingly limited ways. (Samples, 1987)

Ornstein himself recommends greater attention to the whole science of brain, mind, consciousness, intelligence, and learning patterns.

Our understanding of the nature of the mind is, I believe, the current barrier to solving many of the problems that are now seen to have only political or administrative solutions. We are a more danger-ous animal than we would like to think, but we can change more than we might have dreamt by calling on, and calling out some of the very many diverse mental abilities within ourselves. (Ornstein, 1986)

4. A PHILOSOPHICAL CRITIQUE OF PURE MODERNITY.

Philosophy involves attention to critiques and oppositional viewpoints. Many of the ideas which seem supportive of the whole practice of challenge education, and which have been reviewed here as possible contributions to development of a meaningful philosophy of the challenge orientation, can be viewed as reflecting major "paradigm shifts." They seem to represent alternative views of humanity and the world, alternative models for education, counseling, science, medicine, spiritual development, and all of existence. They seem to argue for a change so radical as to be interpreted as bipo-lar—what has been black must become white, what has been past must become future, what has been is wrong and what must be is right. It might appear that the arguments are for a brand new human being in a brand new world.

While there is reason to argue for change, and reason to be optimistic about humankind's capacity for transformation, it should be recognized that there can be no radical flip-flop into the future, leaving all the traditions and history of our species and our world behind.

Some philosophers have considered the new orientation as "modernity," with atten-tion to individuality as a major focus. Subjec-tivity, the emphasis on a world which pro-vides for the enrichment of the individual, and the attention to personal choice are the hall-marks of modernity. Philosopher David Kolb

has presented a "critique of pure modernity." Essentially, his argument is that the world is not all that different now than it ever was, or ever will be; and that human beings may not be nearly so flexible as described. He tackles the philosophies of Hegel, who considered reality a living, evolving process, and Heideg-ger, the existential thinker who saw the person as the center of the ever-changing reality, to accomplish his goal, which he summarizes as: "...dispelling a theoretical and practical illu-sion about the uniqueness and the unified character of the modern world" (Kolb, 1986).

Kolb's work is certainly more tradition-ally philosophical than many of the theoreti-cal ideas suggested in this chapter; and it may seem both difficult to analyze and less rele-vant to challenge education theory. Still, his arguments seem important, for they bring the overly idealistic and hopeful thinker to care-fully analyze expectations. He admits that his argument may lead to a degree of pessimism.

We see one implication that the view we have been exploring might have for our life: there can be no liberating hope for a brand new world. There can be no change of the world as a whole, since there is no world as a whole constituted by a unitary granting of presence or a single basic shape of spirit. There are too many different rhythms and fields and possibilities for all to come to a climax or completion at once, nor are they totally unified within themselves. This may seem to imprison us in the modern age, but in fact it questions whether the modern age should be so sharply walled off from what has gone before or might come after.

Is this modern age as unique as it has described itself to be? If what I have been suggesting were thought out more fully, one effect would be to change our vision when we look backward. The modern age could no longer be thought of as different in one unified fundamental way, because there would be no one fundamental way for each age to exist. The very division of ages would become questionable. This might eliminate hopes for total change, but it would encourage a sense of belonging and fellowship with those who have struggled in the past with the very multiple inhabitation that made them what they were. (Ibid.)

Kolb's arguments tell us that we must carefully attend to our past, and to our present, in any projection to the future. Our values are tied to our history, and who we are is related to who we were; this must be attended to as we become. Rather than lead to pessimism or fatalism or a sense of personal and humankind impotency, Kolb's argument challenges us to base growth, learning, and our future on a more solid perspective of the reality, the complexity and the disconnectedness of what we are.

Much of the "power" of the world does, indeed, exist outside ourselves, and much happens over which we, as individuals, have little control. We must be cognizant of this reality.

None of this means that we should accept without challenge what we find we are within. There will be some movements over which we have little control even though we are intimately shaped by them... Our choices will be exercised for goals and basic activities that we already find ourselves among. New goals and standards may become available, but they will simply not always be our creations. We cannot distance ourselves from everything at once, because we cannot bring to a totality everything in which we are already involved. (Op.cit.)

If nothing else, Kolb's thinking forces us to an acceptance of the way things are, and

would suggest that our dreams and motivations be keenly tempered with patience. Challenge group leaders have often suggested that the appropriate starting point for growth facilitation of any group is to "take them where they're at, and move forward from there." Kolb's arguments would seem to suggest that we accept all those institutions which we wish to change—education, mental health, business and industry, government, etc., as well as society at large—and then proceed with efforts to introduce them to alternative strategies, alternative goals, alternative visions, and alternative ways of being.

One is reminded of Schumacher's "Small is Beautiful," and tends to recognize that "Slow is Beautiful, Too."

CONCLUSIONS

At the outset of this discussion of philosophical thought that would appear to have relevance for a developing theory of challenge methodology, it was noted that the presentation was not intended to provide a philosophy of challenge education—and certainly that has not been accomplished. However, there would certainly appear to be a number of points of conclusion that should be considered in any developing philosophy for challenge education. These conclusions can be summarized under three interrelated categories:

1. THE CHALLENGE EDUCATION OVERVIEW OF THE PERSON.

(a) Human beings are extremely complex organisms, existing biologically, psychologically, socially, and spiritually (certainly in the sense of identityawareness and some higher-order consciousness, if not in the traditional sense of "soul").

(b) The person has no true existence apart from the dynamic, flowing, changing process that is the nature of life. Humankind is process!

(c) Each human being is a unique, ever-changing individual; there is, within each person, a drive toward becoming. Each person is a special person, blending all the many biological, social, and spiritual experiences of their past and present into a phenomenological whole that is unlike any other. There may, indeed, be some common denominators and similarities of persons and processes, but the uniqueness of each individual far outweighs any of these.

(d) All human beings are connected one to the other, and to all other living things, including the planet Earth. In the evolving flow toward tomorrow, all living things are complexly interdependent.

(e) Humankind is at an evolutionary crossroads, having evolved to a point of awareness of the very nature of those basic evolutionary processes. Therefore, human beings now have the potential, and the awesome responsibility, for manifesting their own destiny.

(f) Optimism and hopefulness are basic characteristics of the human being. When the biological, social, and spiritual environment that make up the phenomenological field of the individual provide safety and security, inner balance and wisdom follow to facilitate positive choices and positive growth. Individuals may struggle with value orientations and ethical dilemmas, but they most often choose rightly and positively; such is also the case for

the totality of the human species. In spite of moments of confusion, anxiety, depression, and periodic feelings of futility and hopelessness, the nature of humankind is to seek positive vision and a direction appropriate for survival and speciesactualization. Awareness of the basic optimism of humankind is a basis for even more optimism.

2. THE CHALLENGE EDUCATION OVERVIEW OF HUMAN PROBLEMS.

It must be recognized that the journey of humankind is not without obstacles. There will always be temporary blockages from without and from within; there will always be decisions to make, new strategies to learn, and problems to solve. At this point in time, the important problems confronting the human expedition through the wilderness of life would appear to be:

Environmental Problems. One of the major problems facing humankind is that of the impending destruction of the environment. This can be viewed as a trend toward self-destruction. Even if one does not accept the hypothesis that the phenomenological field and the phenomenological self are a totality (i.e., the world is as our body, and to destroy any part of it is as severing a limb or vital organ), there certainly must be recognition of the never-ending interdependence of the human being and the earth. If the earth is as our mother, then even severance of the umbilical cord only separates us from, but does not make us independent of the nurturing warmth and wisdom of her. There must be attention to the fact that the survival of humankind and the survival of the earth are one and the same.

137

Interactional Problems. A second set of human problems warranting great attention, and which has been a problem throughout history, is that of humankind's interaction with each other. Whether the attention is on interpersonal or international relationships, we face the problem of learning about the interconnectedness and/or interdependency of all people. In many cases, it is obvious that we must transform from the way we have been to the way we ought to be. That means finding our inner potentials for trust, tolerance, sharing, caring, supporting, enriching, and loving. As each gives that to others, more and more will become all that is their potential.

Personal Problems. Another of the chronic problems of humankind throughout history is that of the internal moods, attitudes, values, character traits, emotions, and personal philosophies that are negative and tend to block natural growth toward self-actualization. These are the feelings of anxiety, depression, fear, anger, mistrust, suspicion, cynicism, and pessimism, all of which may well be part of the natural process of living, but none of which should dominate the intrapsychic world of any person. Perhaps most damaging of all is the internal cognitive, emotional, and spiritual state of personal impotency—a feeling of insignificance, unimportance, helplessness, powerlessness, and hopelessness. The key is to provide all people with a safe and secure world, wherein trust, openness, honesty, support, and concern prevail, and to provide all people with opportunity to explore personal potentials and share creative problem solving and joyful experiences with others. It is in such environment that the person can grasp more fully a sense of what they can become, and of what all of humankind can become.

Personal Growth Problems. While the natural tendency of the human organism is to grow, to become, to actualize, each person faces problems of understanding, directing, and releasing their personal energies. People need to better understand the complexity of their being, the nature of their personal responsibilities, and the potency they have for creative solution to problems. The individual needs to explore alternative strategies, to uncover new awarenesses and collect the cognitive information that will help them in their growth. The problem is that the world provides all too few opportunities for the individual to explore the nature of his being, and to begin the process of becoming. The demands of the modern world, for "fitting in," following the mandates of authoritarian institutions, and becoming productive materialistically often seem to be defining both strategy and goals for the individual. Many become aware of alternatives, and yet do not know how to proceed to explore and move toward self-actualization. Priorities are often determined by societal attitudes. For example, in recent decades, many have developed more positive attitudes about the health and well-being of their biological being, and so there is less smoking, better eating, and increased attention to physical conditioning; whereas there is less social support for cultivating the spiritual being, and those who struggle in that sphere of existence do not know where to turn. This problem of personal growth must be recognized as both personal and social, for individuals must have the support of others, and of their whole society, when they turn to the issues of personal growth.

Ethics. Perhaps, all of the above problems of the person in the modern world are related to the questions of Ethics. Socrates, the first great moral philosopher, suggested that, "the unexamined life is not worth living." Certainly, flowing beneath every human action is the current of ethical significance, and people of all ages and places have often turned to questions about moral conduct and moral principles. Our environmental problems, our

interactional problems and our personal problems all contain significant ethical issues and all are interrelated. "To be or not to be—that is the question." Unless we learn to live in peace and harmony with others, then we do not live. If we do not learn to love our earth as we love ourselves, then we do not live. Unless we find meaningful personal answers to the questions of ethics, we exist but do not live. The inter-relationship of the problems is obvious. It has been noted in an argument for development of earth wisdom that "to recover the moral sense of our humanity, we would need to recover first the moral sense of nature." (Kohak, 1984) Ethical philosophizing is no longer for the philosophers alone; every human being must attend to Ethics. We must take the time to think deeply and honestly

about who we are and what we ought to become.

3. THE CHALLENGE EDUCATION OVERVIEW OF EDUCATION.

Summarization of the challenge education perspectives on education is best left to the reader, and to those who develop the appropriate basic philosophy of challenge education. However, since the challenge education philosophy may well incorporate a number of the concepts and overviews presented in this review, there would appear to be value in maintaining some familiarity with the following words, phrases, and concepts:

...small is beautiful... ...transformation... ...omega... ...ecopiety... ...law of Ahisma... ...confluent education... ...perceptual psychology... ...the biology of hope... ...lebenswelt... ...earth-heart... ...paradigm shift... ...spiritual worldview... ...the courage to be... ...mutual aid... ...TORI... ...the phenomenon of man... ...competence-effectance... ...the freedom to learn... ...multimind... ...ontology... ...general systems theory... ...personal growth... ...integral yoga... ...guides... ...land ethic... ...studentcentered... ...meditation... ...drive in living matter... ...third force psychology... ...flow... ...neo-humanism... ...psychosynthesis... ...holistic education... ...phenomenological field... ...Gaia... ...progressivism... ...affective education... ...multiple intelligence... ...the nature of love... ...unitary thinking... ...I and thou... ...split-brain... ...reconstruction of experience... ...the Great Spirit... ...inner certainty... ...optimal arousal... ...life skills... ...ecophilosophy... ...the act of Will... ...live classroom... ...transpersonal education... ...whole brain learning... ...existentialism... ...self-validation... ...modernity... ...peak experiences...

139

...spiritual worldview... ...the Aquarian conspiracy... ...values clarification... ...eigenwelt... ...self-actualization... ...essentialism... ...ethical reflection... ...connectedness... ...open mind... ...belongingness... ...slow is beautiful...

No doubt, what has been covered in this brief overview of ideas for a philosophy of challenge education is but a small portion of what could, and should, be attended to. The above list of concepts will need to be expanded tenfold as professionals attend to the task of philosophizing about the whole challenge approach. The reference list which follows will provide a starting point for further reading.

REFERENCES

Adler, M. (1939, Feb.). The crisis in contemporary education. *The Social Frontier, V.*

Allport, F. (1937). Telenomic description in the study of personality. *Character and Personality, 5* (2).

Allport, F. (1953). *Theories of Perception and the Concept of Structure.* New York: John Wiley & Sons.

Allport, G. (1950). *The Nature of Personality.* Cambridge, MA: Addison-Wesley.

Allport, G. (1955). *Becoming: Basic Considerations for a Psychology of Personality.* New Haven: Yale University Press.

Allport, G. (1961). *Pattern and Growth in Personality.* New York: Holt, Rinehart, & Winston.

Anandamitra, A. (1986). *Neo-Humanistic Education.* Philippines: Amanda Morgan Publishing.

Armstrong, T. (1987). *In Their Own Way.* New York: J. P. Tarcher.

Arya, U. (1977). *Philosophy of Hatha Yoga.* Honesdale, PA: Himalayan Institute.

Assagioli, R. (1974). *Psychosynthesis.* New York: Viking Press.

Assagioli, R. (1973). *The Act of Will.* New York: Viking Press.

Assagioli, R. & Servan-Schreiber, C. (1974). A higher view of the man-woman problem. *Synthesis: One.* Los Angeles, CA: Psychosynthesis Press.

Baldwin, R. (1989). *You Are Your Child's First Teacher.* Berkeley, CA: Celestial Arts Press.

Ballentine, R. (1978). *Diet and Nutrition: A Holistic Approach.* Honesdale, PA: Himalayan International Institute.

Bandura, A. (1977). Self-efficacy: Toward a unified theory of behavioral change. *American Psychologist, 37* (2).

Barrett, T. S. (1990) The sky's the limit. *Earth Ethics: Evolving Values for an Earth Community, 1* (2).

Barth, G. F. (1974). *Nova Yoga: The Yoga of the Imagination.* New York: Mason & Lipscomb.

Bedford, M. (1972). *Existentialism and Creativity.* New York: Philosophical Library.

Bertalanffy, L. (1950). "An Outline of General Systems Theory," *British Journal for Philosophy of Science, 1* (2).

Bertalanffy, L. (1955). General systems theory, *Main Currents in Thought, 11* (1).

Bertalanffy, L. & Rappaport, A. (1956). General Systems. *Yearbook of the Society for General Systems, 11.*

Bertalanffy, L. (1967). *Robots, Men and Minds.* New York: George Braziller.

Bingswanger, L. (1956). Existential analysis and psychotherapy. In Fromn-Reichman, F. & Moreno, J. (Eds.). *Progress in Psychotherapy.* New York: Grune & Stratton.

Bohm, D. (1980). *Wilderness and the Implicate Order.* London: Routledge, Kegan Paul.

Bradley, D. (1948). *No Place To Hide.* Boston, MA: Little, Brown & Company.

Brameld, T. (1950). *Patterns of Educational Philosophy.* Yonkers, NY: World Books.

Brameld, T. (1956). *Toward a Reconstituted Philosophy of Education.* New York: Dryuden.

Brameld, T. (1956). *Education as Power.* New York: Holt, Rinehart, & Winston.

Brickman, W. W. (1948, May). Essentialism—ten years after. *School and Society, XLVII.*

Brichman, W. W. (1958, October). The essentialist spirit in education. *School and Society, LXXXVI.*

Bromberg, W. (1975). *From Shaman to Psychotherapist.* Chicago, IL: Henry Regnery.

Brown, G. (1971). *Human Teaching for Human Learning.* New York: Viking Press.

Brown, G. (1974). Conversations on Gestalt Therapy. *Synthesis: Two.* Los Angeles, CA: Psychosynthesis Press.

Brown G., Yeomans, T., & Grizzard, C. (1975). *Live Classroom: Innovation Through Confluent Education with Gestalt.* New York: Viking, Esalen Books.

Brown, J. E. (1982). *The Spiritual Legacy of the American Indians.* New York: Crossroads Press.

Brown, M. (1989). Transpersonal psychology: Facilitating transformation in outdoor experiential education. *Journal of Experiential Education, 12* (3).

Buber, M. (1937). *I and Thou.* Edinburgh, Scotland: T & T Clark.

Buhler, C. (1959). Theoretical observations about life's basic tendencies. *American Journal of Psychotherapy, 13* (6).

Butler, R. & Harlow, H. (1954). Persistence of visual exploration in monkeys. *Journal of Comparative and Physiological Psychology, 47.*

Butler, J. (1957). *Four Philosophies and Their Practice in Education and Religion.* New York: Harper.

Canfield, J. & Wells, H. (1976). *100 Ways To Enhance Self-Concept in the Classroom.* Englewood Cliffs, NJ: Prentice-Hall.

Capra, F. (1975). *The Tao of Physics.* New York: Random House.

Carson, R. (1962). *Silent Spring.* Boston, MA: Houghton-Mifflin.

Chaudhuri, H. (1974). The meeting of East and West: A conversation with Haridas Chaudhuri. *Synthesis: Two.* Los Angeles, CA: Psychosynthesis Press.

Child, I. (1973). *Humanistic Psychology and the Research Tradition: Their Several Virtues.* New York: Wiley.

Clark, E. (1988). The search for a new educational paradigm. *Holistic Education Review, 1* (1).

Cohen, M. (1986). *How Nature Works: Regenerating Kinship With Planet Earth.* New York: World Peace University.

Cohen, M. (1989). Earth kinship: The fabric of personal and global balance. *Journal of Experiential Education, 10* (1).

Combs, A. & Snygg, D. (1959). *Individual Behavior: A Perceptual Approach to Behavior.* New York: Harper & Row.

Combs, A. (Ed.). (1962). *Perceiving, Behaving, Becoming: A New Focus for Education.* Washington, DC: National Education Association.

Combs, A., Richards, A., & Richards, F. (1976). *Perceptual Psychology: A Humanistic Approach To The Study of Persons.* New York: Harper & Row.

Combs, A. (Ed.). (1978). *Humanistic Education: Objectives and Assessment.* Washington, DC: National Education Association.

Crosby, A. (1981). A critical look: The philosophical foundation of experiential education. *Journal of Experiential Education, 4* (1).

Csikszentmihalyi, M. (1975). *Beyond Boredom and Anxiety.* San Francisco, CA: Josey-Bass.

Dewey, J. (1916). *Democracy and Education.* New York: Macmillan.

Dewey, J. (1922). *Human Nature and Conduct.* New York: Philosophical Library.

Dewey, J. (1938). *Education and Experience.* New York: Macmillan.

Dewey, J. (1943). *The Child and the Curriculum.* Chicago, IL: University of Chicago Press.

Dewey, J. (1956). *Philosophy of Education.* (Originally *Problems of Men*, published in 1946). New York: Littlefield, Adams, & Company.

Dobzhansky, T. (1962). *Mankind Evolving.* New Haven, CT: Yale University Press.

Donaldson, G. W. & Vinson, R. (1979). William James, philosophical father of experience based education, *Journal of Experiential Education, 2* (3).

Dubos, R. (1972, July). A theology of the earth. *Audubon.*

Dubos, R. (1981). *Celebrations of Life.* New York: McGraw-Hill.

Duffy, E. (1957). The philosophical significance of the concept of arousal and activation. *Psychological Review, 64* (3).

Einstein, A. (1972). An Einstein letter. *New York Times*, March 29.

Ewert, A. (1989). *Outdoor Adventure Pursuits: Foundations, Models, and Theories.* Columbus, OH: Publishing Horizons, Inc.

Ferguson, M. (1980). *The Aquarian Conspiracy.* Los Angeles, CA: J. P. Tarcher.

Forem, J. (1973). *Transcendental Meditation.* New York: E. P. Dutton & Co.

Fromm, E. (1941). *Escape From Freedom.* New York: Rinehart.

Gang, P. (1988). Holistic education for a new age. *Holistic Education Review, 1* (1).

Gardner, H. (1983). *Frames of Mind.* New York: Basic Books.

Gayer, N. (1961, Oct.). Will existentialism triumph over pragmatism? *Phi Delta Kappan.*

Gibb, J. (1971). TORI Community. In Egan, G. (Ed.). *Encounter Groups: Basic Readings.* Belmont, CA: Brooks/Cole.

Gibb, J. (1972). TORI Theory and Practice. In Pheiffer, J. W. & Jones, J. E. (Eds.). *1972 Annual Handbook for Group Facilitators.* Iowa City, IA: University Associates.

Gibb, J. (1978). *Trust: A New View of Personal and Organizational Development.* Los Angeles, CA: Guild of Tutors Press.

Giorgi, A. (1970). *Psychology As A Human Science: A Phenomenologically Based Approach.* New York: Harper & Row.

Goldstein, K. (1939). *The Organism.* New York: American Book Company.

Green, A. (1974). The integral yoga of Sri Aurobindo. *Synthesis: Two.* Los Angeles, CA: Psychosynthesis Press.

Greenem M. (Ed.). (1967). *Existential Encounters for Teachers.* New York: Random House.

Guthrie, W. K. C. (1950). *The Greeks and Their Gods.* Boston, MA: Beacon Press.

Harlow, H. (1953). Motivation as a factor in the acquisition of new responses. In Brown, J. (Ed.) *Current Theories and Research in Motivation: A Symposium.* Lincoln, NE: University of Nebraska Press.

Harlow, H. (1958). The nature of love. *American Psychologist, 13.*

Harlow, H. (1971). *Learning To Love.* New York: Albion Publishing Company.

Harman, W. W. (1970). Two contrasting forecasts. In Piele, P. & Eidell, G., (Eds.). *Social and Technological Change: Implications For Education.* Eugene, OR: University of Oregon.

Hatley, K. (1988). A neo-humanistic model of education. *Holistic Education Review, 1* (3).

Hawkes, J. (1963). *The World of the Past*. New York: A. A. Knopf.

Hawkes, J. (1974). *The New Archeology*. New York: A. A. Knopf.

Hefner, P. (1970). *The Promise of Teilhard*. New York: J. P. Lippincott & Co.

Hendricks, G. & Fadiman, J. (Eds.). (1976). *Transpersonal Psychology*. New York: Prentice-Hall, Spectrum Books.

Highwater, J. (1981). *The Primal Mind*. New York: Harper & Row.

Hill, T. (1984, March). *Earth-Heart*. Newsletter of the Association for Humanistic Psychology.

Hoffding, H. (1955). *A History of Modern Philosophy*. New York: Dover.

Holbrook, B. (1981). *The Stone Monkey: An Alternative Chinese-Scientific Reality*. New York: Wm. Morrow & Company.

Horne, H. (1927). *The Philosophy of Education*. New York: Macmillan.

Hunt, J. (1981). Dewey's philosophical method and its influence on his philosophy of education. *Journal of Experiential Education, 4* (1).

Husserl, E. (1936). *The Crisis of European Sciences and Transcendental Phenomenology* (H. L. Van Breda, Trans.). New York: Marlins Nyhoff Publishing.

Hutchins, R. M. (1953). *The Conflict in Education*. New York: Harper.

Iso-Ahola, S. (1976). On the theoretical link between personality and leisure. *Psychological Reports, 39* (1).

James, W. (1890). *Principles of Psychology* (Two Volumes). New York: Rutledge.

James, W. (1899). *Talks to Teachers*. New York: Rutledge.

James, W. (1907). *Pragmatism: A New Name For An Old Way of Thinking*. New York: Longman, Green, and Company.

Jones, R. M. (1968). *Fantasy and Feeling in Education*. New York: New York University Press.

Jung, X. & Jung, P. (1989). The way of ecopiety: Holistic education for ecological ethics. *Holistic Education Review, 2* (3).

Kandel, I. (1938). *Conflicting Theories of Education*. New York: Macmillan.

Keen, S. (1970). *To A Dancing God*. New York: Harper & Row.

Kellner, G.E. (1964). *Introduction to the Philosophy of Education*. New York: John Wiley.

Kielmeier, J. (1989) Growing with the times: A challenge for experiential education. *Journal of Experiential Education, 12* (3).

Kilpatrick, W. (1934, Oct.). The essentials of the activity movement. *Progressive Education, 2.*

Kline, P. (1988). *The Everyday Genius—Restoring Children's Natural Joy of Learning—and Yours, Too*. New York: Great Oceans Publishing Company.

Knapp, C. & Goodman, J. (1981). *Humanizing Environmental Education*. Martinsville, IN: American Camping Association.

Kneller, G. (1964). *Introduction to the Philosophy of Education*. New York: John Wiley & Sons.

Kneller, G. (1965). *Existentialism and Education*. New York: John Wiley & Sons.

Kolb, D. (1986). *The Critique of Pure Modernity*. Chicago, IL: University of Chicago Press.

Kohak, E. (1984). *The Embers and the Stars*. Chicago, IL: U. Chicago Press.

Krathwohl, D., Bloom, B. & Masia, B. (1956). *Taxonomy of Educational Objectives: Handbook II, Affective Domain*. New York: David McKay.

Krishnamurti, J. (1974). *On Education*. New York: Harper & Row.

Krishnamurti, J. (1981). *Education and the Significance of Life*. San Francisco, CA: Harper & Row.

Kropotkin, P. (1902). *Mutual Aid: A Factor in Evolution*. Boston, MA: Sargent Publishing.

Kuhn. T. (1962). *The Structure of Scientific Revolutions*. Chicago, IL: University of Chicago Press.

Kumar, S. (Ed.). (1984). *The Schumacher Lectures: Vol. II*. London: Sphere Books.

Kurten, B. (1972). *Not From The Apes*. New York: Random House.

Lederman, J. (1969). *Anger and the Rocking Chair*. New York: McGraw-Hill.

Leonard, G. (1968). *Education and Ecstasy*. New York: Dell Publishing Co.

Leonard, G. (1972). *The Transformation*. New York: Dell Publishing Co.

Leopold, A. (1949). *A Sand County Almanac*. Oxford University Press, Inc.

LePage, A. (1987). *Transforming Education: The New 3R's*. New York: Oakmore House.

Levine, P. (1972, Dec.). Transcendental Meditation and the science of creative intelligence. *Phi Delta Kappan*.

Lewin, K. (1935). *A Dynamic Theory of Personality*. New York: McGraw-Hill.

Lock Land. G. (1959). *Grow or Die: The Unifying Principle of Transformation*. New York: Random House.

Lovelock, J. (1988). *GAIA—A Way of Knowledge*. New York: W. W. Norton.

Lovelock, J. (1989). Introduction. In Vittachi, A. *Earth Conference One: Sharing a Vision for Our Planet*. Boston, MA: New Science Library.

Lutyens, M. (1984). *Krishnamurti: The Years of Awakening*. London: Rider.

Lutyens, M. (1985). *Krishnamurti: The Years of Fulfillment*. London: Rider.

Lutyens, M. (1988). *Krishnamurti: The Open Door*. New York: Farrar Straus Giroux.

McAvoy, L. (1978). Outdoor Leadership Training. *Journal of Physical Education, Recreation, and Dance, 4*.

McGowan, M. (1986). Self-Efficacy: Operationalizing Challenge Education. *The Bradford Papers Annual, Vol. 1*. Indiana U. Press.

Mann, J. (1972). *Learning to Be: The Education of Human Potential*. New York: Macmillan Publishing.

Maslow, A. (1954). *Motivation and Personality*. New York: Harper & Row.

Maslow, A. (1955). Defining motivation and growth motivation. In M. R. Jones, (Ed.). *Nebraska Symposium on Motivation*. Lincoln, NE: University of Nebraska Press.

Maslow, A. (1968). *Toward A Psychology of Being*. New York: Van Nostrand.

Maslow, A. (1970). *The Further Reaches of Human Nature*. New York: Viking.

May, R. (Ed.). (1958). *Existence*. New York: Basic Books.

May, R. (Ed.). (1969). *Existential Psychology* (2nd Ed.). New York: Random House.

Mead, G. H. (1935). *Mind Self, and Society*. Chicago, IL: U. Chicago Press.

Merleau-Ponty, M. (1945). *Phenomonology of Perception*. New York: Humanists Press, Inc.

Miller, J. P. (1988). *The Holistic Curriculum*. Ontario, Canada: Institute for Studies In Education.

Miller, R. (1988). Two hundred years of holistic education. *Holistic Education Review, 1* (1).

Miller, R. (1989). Defining holistic education. *Holistic Education Review, 2* (4).

Miller. R. (1989). *What Are Schools For? Holistic Education in America*. **please supply info on publisher**

Montessori, M. (1949). *Education and Peace*. Chicago, IL: Henry Regnery Co.

Montessori, M. (1973). *The Absorbent Mind*. New York: Montessori Society.

Morris, V. (1966). *Existentialism and Education*. New York: Harper & Row.

Morris, V. (Ed.). (1969). *Modern Movements in Educational Philosophy*. New York: HoughtonMifflin.

Mortier, J. & Aboux, M. (Eds.). (1966). *Teilhard de Chardin Album*. New York: Harper & Row.

Moustakas, C. (Ed.). (1956). *The Self*. New York: McGraw-Hill.

Murphy, G. (1947). *Personality: A Biosocial Approach*. New York: Harper & Row.

Murray, E. (1989). Krishnamurti, education, and wholeness. *Holistic Education Review, 2* (2).

Naess, A. (1973). The shallow and the deep: Long-range ecology movement: A summary. *Inquiry, 16*.

Naranjo, C. & Ornstein, R. (1971). *On the Psychology of Meditation*. New York: Viking Press.

Ornstein, R. (1973, May). Right and left thinking. *Psychology Today*.

Ornstein, R., Thompson, K., & Macaulay, D. (1984). *The Amazing Brain*. Boston: Houghton-Mifflin.

Ornstein, R. (1986). *Multimind: A New Way of Looking at the Brain*. Boston, MA: Houghton-Mifflin.

Orr, D. (1989). Ecological literacy: Education for the twenty-first century. *Holistic Education Review, 2* (3).

Page, H. (1987). William James: An ethical philosopher for experiential education. *Journal of Experiential Education, 10* (1).

Perrone, V. (1989). *Working Papers: Reflections on Teachers, Schools, and Communities*. New York: Teachers College Press.

Progen, J. (1979). Man, nature, and sport. In Gerber, E. & Nillian, M. (Eds.). *Sports and the Body: A Philosophical Symposium*. Philadelphia: Lea & Febyer.

Raths, L., Harmon, M., & Simon, S. (1966). *Values and Teaching: Working With Values in the Classroom*. Columbus, OH: Charles Merrill.

Ricoeur, P. (1967). *Husserl: An Analysis of His Phenomenology*. Evanston, IL: Northwestern University Press.

Riesman, D. (1950). *The Lonely Crowd*. New Haven, CT: Yale University Press.

Roberts, T. & Clark, F. (1976). Transpersonal psychology and education. In Hendricks, G. & Fadiman, J. (Eds.). *Transpersonal Psychology*. New York: Prentice-Hall, Spectrum Books.

Rogers, C. R. (1951). *Client Centered Therapy*. Boston, MA: Houghton-Mifflin.

Rogers, C. R. (1961). *On Becoming A Person*. Boston, MA: Houghton-Mifflin.

Rogers, C. R. (1969). *Freedom to Learn*. Columbus, OH: Charles Merrill.

Rogers, C. R. (1977). *On Personal Power*. New York: Delacorte Press.

Rogers, C. R. (1980). *A Way Of Being*. Boston. MA: Houghton-Mifflin.

Rogers, C. R. (1981). Communities. In Villoldo, A. & Dychtwald, K. (Eds.). *Millennium: Glimpses Into the 21st Century.* Los Angeles, CA: J. P. Tarcher.

Rozak, T. (1978). *Person/Planet: The Creative Disintegration of Industrial Society.* Garden City, NJ: Anchor/Doubleday.

Rozman, D. (1975). *Meditating With Children.* Boulder Creek, CA: University of the Trees Press.

Samples, B. (1987). *Openmind/Wholemind.* Rolling Hills Estates, CA: Jolmar Press.

Sarkar, P. R. (1987). *Neo-Humanism in a Nutshell.* Calcutta: Manasi Press.

Sartre, J. (1947). *Existentialism.* (Frechtman, B., Trans.). New York: Philosophical Library.

Schumacher, E. F. (1973). *Small Is Beautiful: Economics as if People Mattered.* New York: Harper & Row.

Schumacher, E. F. (1977). *A Guide for the Perplexed.* New York: Harper & Row.

Schweitzer, A. (1934). Religion and modern civilization. *The Christian Century, 51* (47). (reprinted in Joy, C.R.(Ed.). *A. Schweitzer: An Anthology.* Boston, MA: Beacon Press)

Scobey, M. & Graham, G. (Eds.). (1970). *To Nurture Humaneness: Commitment for the '70's.* Washington, DC: National Education Association.

Shiflett, J. & Brown, G. (1972). *Confluent Education: Attitudinal and Behavioral Consequences of Confluent Teacher Training.* Ann Arbor, MI: University of Michigan Monograph Series.

Simon, S., Howe, L., & Kirschenbaum, H. (1972). *Values Clarification.* New York, A & W Publishers.

Simon, S., Howe, L., & Kirschenbaum, H. (1978). *Values Clarification. A Handbook of Practical Strategies for Teachers and Students.* New York: Hart Publishing.

Simpson, G. (1953). *The Major Features of Evolution.* New York: Columbia University Press.

Simpson, G. (1958). The study of evolution: Methods and present status of theory. In Roe, A. & Simpson, G. (Eds.). *Behavior and Evolution.* New Haven, CT: Yale University Press.

Simpson, S. (1985). Short term wilderness experiences and environmental education. *Journal of Experiential Education, 8* (3).

Snygg, D. & Combs, A. (1949). *Individual Behavior: A New Frame of Reference For Psychology.* New York: Harper & Row.

Springer, S. & Deutsch, C. (1981). *Left-Brain, Right-Brain.* New York: W. H. Freeman.

Steinbeck, J. & Ricketts, E. (1941). *Sea of Cortez.* New York: Viking.

Steiner, R. (1923). *The Child's Changing Consciousness and World of Education.* Hudson, NY: Anthroposophic Press.

Steiner, R. (1924). *The Kingdom of Childhood.* Hudson, NY: Anthroposophic Press.

Storm, H. (1972). *Seven Arrows.* New York: Ballantine Books.

Sullivan, H. S. (1953). *The Interpersonal Theory of Psychiatry.* New York: W. W. Norton.

Szent-Gyorgi, A. (1970). *The Crazy Ape.* New York: Grosset & Dunlap.

Szent-Gyorgi, A. (1974). Drive in living matter to perfect itself. *Synthesis: One.* Los Angeles, CA: Psychosynthesis Institute Press.

Tielhard de Chardin, P. (1951). *The Phenomenon of Man.* New York: Harper and Row. (2nd edition, 1965)

Tielhard de Chardin, P. (1964). *The Future of Man.* New York: Harper & Row.

Tiger, L. (1979). *Optimism: The Biology of Hope.* New York: Simon & Schuster.

Tillich, P. (1952). *The Courage To Be.* Boston, MA: Little and Company.

Turner, F. (1986, Sept.). Design for a new Aaademy. *Harpers.* 273:1636.

Untermeyer, L. (1955). *A Treasury of Great Poems.* New York: Simon & Schuster.

Vargu, J. (1974). Subpersonalities. *Synthesis: One.* Los Angeles, CA: Psychosynthesis Institute Press.

Vishnudevananda, S. (1960). *The Complete Illustrated Book of Yoga.* New York: Bell Publishing Company.

Vittachi, A. (1989). *Earth Conference One: Sharing A Vision For Our Planet.* Boston, MA: New Science Library.

Waddington, C. (1960). *The Ethical Animal.* London: George Allen & Unwin.

Waters, F. (1973, May). Lessons from the Indian school. *Psychology Today.*

Watts, A. (1961). *Psychotherapy East and West.* New York: Pantheon.

Weil, A. (1973, June). Light on the dark side of the brain. *Psychology Today.*

Weinstein, G . & Fantini, M. (1970). *Toward Humanistic Education: A Curriculum of Affect.* New York: Prager.

Wild, J. (1963). *Existence and the World of Freedom.* Englewood Cliffs, NJ: Prentice-Hall.

Wilhelm, R. (1967). *The I Ching Book of Changes.* (Baynes, C., Trans.). Princeton, NJ: Princeton University Press.

Wilson, C. (1984). Peak experience. In Kumar, S. (Ed.). *The Schumacher Lectures, Vol. II.* London: Sphere Books.

Wing-Tsit, Chan. (1963). *A Source Book of Chinese Philosophy.* Princeton, NJ: Princeton University Press.

White, R. W. (1959). Motivation reconsidered: The concept of competence. *Psychological Review, 66* (3).

Worth Commission. (1972). *A Future of Choices: A Choice of Futures.* Edmonton, Canada: Huity Publications.

Wright, W. K. (1950). *A History of Modern Philosophy.* New York: Macmillan.

Wylie, R. C. (1961). *The Self-Concept: A Critical Survey of Pertinent Research Literature.* Lincoln, NE: University of Nebraska Press.

Wynne, J. (1963). *Theories of Education.* New York: Harper & Row.

Yogananda, A. (1981). *Autobiography of a Yogi.* Los Angeles, CA: Self-Realization Press.

Yogi, M. (1965). *The Science of Being and Art of Living.* New York: Interstate SRM Publishing.

Zaner, R. & Ihde, D. (1973). *Phenomenology and Existentialism.* New York: G. P. Putnam's Sons.

Zukav, G. (1979). *The Dancing Wu-Li Masters.* New York: Morrow.

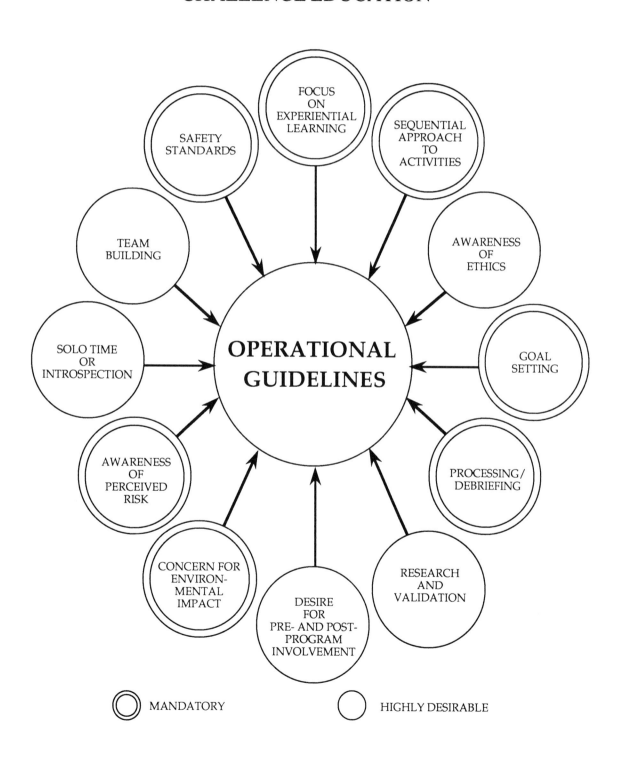

CHAPTER THREE

OPERATIONAL GUIDELINES FOR
CHALLENGE EDUCATION

Chapter Three

Standard Operational Procedures for Challenge Education

The unfolding programs of challenge methodology include a variety of strategies, facilitated by professionals from many different backgrounds, for a diversity of client populations. In spite of this, there are a number of commonly accepted operational guidelines. Whether the challenge sequences are offered as part of a broader program, or as a packaged program of service, the challenge facilitators tend to follow general standard procedures.

The Standard Operational Procedures (S.O.P.'s) for Challenge Education can be viewed in two groups as shown on page 149.

First, there are those programmatic guidelines which are essentially mandatory. These are procedures and principles which must be incorporated if the program sequence is to be considered as Challenge Education. Second, there are those operational procedures and guidelines which are highly desirable in challenge programming, but which may or may not be adopted by the programming professional. In the first grouping are those principles which should be followed by all challenge facilitators all of the time. The second grouping involves guidelines that should be followed by most educators most of the time.

Any list of required S.O.P.'s for professionals facilitating challenge sequences is subject to discussion and debate. While some challenge education leaders would argue for certain guidelines as mandatory, others might suggest those same guidelines are desirable but not mandatory for challenge sequences. On the other hand, guidelines that are deemed as desirable by some would be considered as quite mandatory by others. The present listing of required/mandatory programming procedures has been developed from the perspective of the author and his subsequent use of two "tests" that any operational procedure was required to pass in order to be listed as mandatory.

1. The "Test" of Professional Acceptance: During the past five years, the authors have discussed the ideas shown on page 157 with a wide range of experienced challenge educators. Reactions were not quantitatively summarized, but the authors took careful note of any patterns of disagreement. Through time, the ideas on mandatory operational procedures were "tested," causing some principles to be lowered to the desirable classification. For example, the authors initially thought that the S.O.P. involving evaluation might be considered mandatory. Certainly, there is a need to validate the challenge methodology and program outcomes. However, other professionals noted that while validation evaluation

and research is highly desirable, not all challenge facilitators have the time, the resources, or the expertise to conduct even the most basic program evaluation. When adequate evaluation and research methods are available, it may well be that S.O.P. of evaluation/research could be considered mandatory in challenge programming. For now, however, it remains a highly desirable program procedure.

2. The "test" of "no expectation": Again, in discussion with challenge program leaders, and by inspection of various challenge sequences and situations, the S.O.P.'s that were considered mandatory for challenge facilitators were "tested." Could one find situations, programs, or challenge sequences in which the suggested mandatory S.O.P. be discarded? For example, is there any situation or program activity which does not require attention to the S.O.P. of safety? Or, is there any justification for "immersion" into more complex activities without proper warm-up and sequencing?

The S.O.P.'s shown as mandatory for challenge programs have passed both of these informal "tests." It is recognized that such a designation of any operational guideline might not have 100% endorsement from challenge facilitators, but the list provided does seem to reflect the attitudes of the vast majority of experienced challenge leaders as the 1990's unfold.

I. MANDATORY STANDARD OPERATIONAL PROCEDURES

A. Focus on Experiential Learning

The first and most obvious mandatory operating procedure is the focus on experiential learning. Although obvious, this focus does not necessarily take place in some programs! For example, the authors have observed some challenge programs, including workshop presentations, that consisted mainly of lecture and handouts. At one national conference, a workshop was presented on "An Introduction to Adventure Education." For 60 minutes, the workshop participants sat and listened and asked a few questions. The presenter failed to make the session experiential—how contradictory!

For one to focus on Experiential Education, one needs to define Experiential Education. Herbert (1981) states,

> In the experiential model, the learner is actively involved in his/her education. Decisions are made by the learner that have a direct bearing on what is learned and how it is learned. The teacher's role is that of guide, resource person, and clarifier. Their attention is on both the content of what is being learned, as well as the process of learning that is taking place. (pp. 1-2)

There are numerous Experiential Education models. One example is the model by Gager (1977).

This model suggests that the learner be impelled and not compelled into the "demanding reality context." Facilitators, teachers, and trainers put this theory into practice by encouraging, reasoning, laughing, and placing gentle pressure on the learner. This "demanding reality context" is a situation that can cause people to act, to be responsible to themselves, and to be responsible for others; it can represent the wilderness environment, a low or high ropes course, or a problem solving simulation. The "new skills" are sequential and incremental and are necessary to function effectively in the immediate environment. The final stage of the process, critical analysis and reflection, is explained by James (1980):

> ...should be supportive of the action and should lead to further responsible action; it should provide a sense of closure and a synthesis of experience, linking practice with theory, suggesting ways of

transferring knowledge and skills to other situations in the life of the learner.(p. 119)

B. SAFETY STANDARDS

Challenge facilitators must be keenly aware and attentive to the issues of safety. Due to the historical overlap with high-risk recreation and high adventure programming,

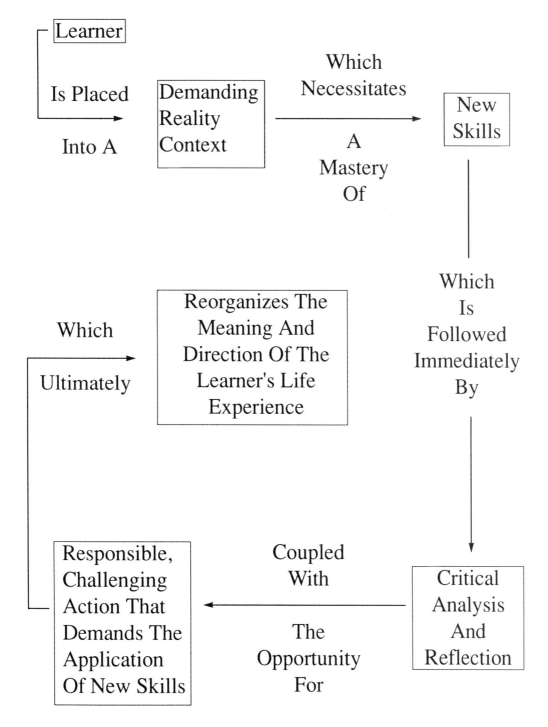

the whole question of safety and leadership liability has been brought to bear. In their 1983 article "Risk or Reckless?" Morganthau, Frons, & Smith query the safe practice of numerous challenge activities, especially those taking place in the wilderness and on the sea. Our program activities may well involve risk taking, but there should be every effort to make the activities 100% safe. The Association for Experiential Education (AEE) has addressed this issue in their publication of Safety Practices in Adventure Programming (1990). Recommended risk management forms, medical forms, etc. are included. In addition, the National Safety Network (Bellefonte, Ohio) continues to compile statistical information regarding safety in a wide range of challenge pursuits. For example, Hale (1990) reports a ropes course accident rate of .00032 accidents per 10,000 hours of programming. This is an impressive figure and one that can even be lower if safety practices are strictly adhered to.

C. AWARENESS OF PERCEIVED RISK

Challenge facilitators must be aware that for some clients a trust fall, or a drop over a cliff on a belay line, may be relatively easy, whereas eye contact, or the touching of another person's face might be filled with fear and anxiety. For example, Keyes (1985) interviewed the famous aerialist, Philipe Petit. He admitted that the mere presence of a snake presented significant amount of stress and anxiety, whereas balancing on an elevator cable strung between New York's twin towers, presented minimal stress. From a challenge facilitator's viewpoint, the perception of risk is critical when working with students. Leroy (1983) explained:

[A Challenge Education student] begat my interest in the nature of adventure by teaching me a valuable lesson. Back on the glacier, what I perceived as a simple stroll, Priscilla perceived as high adventure, full of danger, difficulty and the unknown. Priscilla taught me that when we try to understand "adventure," the physical magnitude of the peak, pole, lake, or trail is no more important than the emotional response the task elicits. (p. 18)

To conclude this mandatory S.O.P. are some quotes taken from *Issues in Challenge Education and Adventure Programming* (1985):

Greg Lais: "...As [participants] develop their skills and confidence, greater degrees of real risk can be introduced as long as the participants understand the ramifications. These risks must be explicitly stated. Perceived risk is a useful tool for building confidence, but if misapplied it can backfire. Perceived risk techniques often can be easily recognized by the participants. These efforts can undermine the very goal they set out to accomplish" (pp. 46-47).

Tom Smith: "Since we know that perceptions of risk can change, and that perceived risk is influenced by confidence in self and others, it behooves us to attend proper sequential build-up for individuals and groups" (p. 82).

Anthony Richards: "...when designing an adventure/challenge program it is essential that each participant has an opportunity to increase or at least be on the edge of, their own adventure threshold" (p. 63).

John Dewey, in *Experience and Education*, summarizes this section by stating that "...growth depends upon the presence of difficulty to be overcome by the exercise of intelligence" (p. 79). The difficulty Dewey is referring to can be the physical, social, emotional, or intellectual.

D. GOAL-SETTING

Facilitation of challenge education activities and events require the development of goals as they relate to the participant's and group's needs. Goalsetting is dependent upon appropriate leadership (Buell, 1978). Facilitators need to have sufficient knowledge and experience on the wide range of leadership approaches, including situation, trait, behavior, and shared function as well as leadership styles (autocratic, democratic, laissez-faire).

Strategies of goal setting can be informal, with the facilitator simply conducting a "Go Around" asking each person standing in a circle for a personal and/or a professional goal. Goal setting can also be fairly structured. For example, in the psychiatric hospital setting, therapists will often discuss with their clients specific goals that relate to their individual and group needs. The therapist then selects appropriate challenge activities that directly relate to the stated goals. The following gives an example of a goal-setting sheet used in the clinical setting.

GOAL SETTING
Directions: Listed below is a list of goals for the Challenge Program group. You are to check any goals that you feel you need to work on. After checking the ones that apply to you, select the three goals that you need to work on the most and number them 1, 2, 3.
I would like to work on:
__ My level of faith and trust in myself.
__ My level of faith and trust in others.
__ Leadership skills and abilities
__ My self confidence.
__ My sense of humor.
__ Solving problems.
__ Working well with others.
__ Taking risks (healthy, positive ones).
__ Asking for help when I need it.
__ Participanting without horsing around.
__ My self-esteem.
__ Expressing my thoughts and feelings
__ Accepting criticism (constructive).
__ Listening better.
__ A more positive attitude.
__ Accepting compliments
__ Trying new things.
__ Trying new things without drugs/alcohol.
__ Taking responsibility for me.
__ Finishing what I start.
__ Challenging myself.

Goal Setting in the corporate environment often requires additional preparation prior to program implementation. Often, consultants will travel to the organization two to three weeks prior to the challenge program to discuss goals with the organization's training director. Often, corporate goal-setting takes the form of a needs assessment. Consultants will often use custom designed and/or commercial instruments. An example of the latter is the Zenger-Miller Needs Analysis for Managers/Supervisors. This instrument is divided into the three main areas of Leadership, Relationships, and Personal Skills.

E. SEQUENTIAL APPROACH TO ACTIVITIES

The need for activity sequencing has been recognized as one of the critical mandatory S.O.P.'s. Roland & Havens (1981) explained:

> Participants need to be introduced to the concept of [challenge] activities before more challenging activities are attempted. Experts believe that by providing lead-up activities, participants are more likely to become involved and thus benefit from the program. There is also the greater possibility that participants will become more involved in the higher levels of adventure through the sequential process. (p. 9)

Although there are programs that offer an "immersion" approach (i.e., introducing participants to a high level challenge activity on the first day of programming), professionals in the field today believe that regardless of ability level, participants need to be introduced to a careful sequential approach. In addition, emphasis appears to be on the process (e.g., how a group worked together and solved a problem) versus the product (e.g., how many people can be facilitated through a challenge course in eight hours.

Sequence Models

In essence, every program requires a unique sequential paradigm in order to meet its diverse goals and needs. However, one generic model appears to have application to numerous programs. Roland, Keene, Dubois, & Lentini (1989) developed the Activity Process Model shown above:

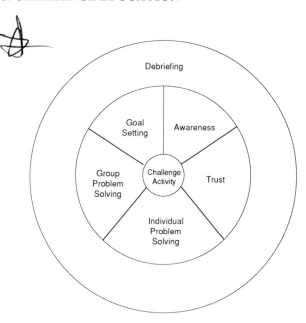

This model includes the following five major programming categories:

1. Goal-Setting. Without specific goals, the potential impact of the program cannot be realized. It is an on-going process throughout the challenge program in which participants, with the assistance of the facilitator, re-establish both short and long term goals. In order for optimum participant growth, it is important that participants clearly understand the goals for each session. The goal-setting process can be implemented in three ways: (1) the facilitator working individually with the participants, (2) the facilitator working with a small group of participants, and (3) the facilitator working with dyads.

2. Awareness. Activities in this level are relatively basic and passive. They are designed to promote an initial awareness towards oneself and one's environment. The awareness activities are also excellent tools to help evaluate each participant and continue the goal-setting process. Smith (1981) stated,

> ...In the case of "awareness education" it is the enhancement of the heart and soul of the [participants] which is the goal...The students' basic concepts of "self" and of "environment" and of the interaction between self and the environment are the focus. (p. 45)

3. Trust. These activities help the participant enhance a trust relationship between his/her facilitator as well as between other participants. Trusting new environments, especially the outdoor environment is also of great importance. Smith (1986) added,

> ...In his classic *On Becoming a Person*, [Rogers] also talks of the person of tomorrow having "trust in their own experience...they are process persons welcoming the risk-taking changes that are always there...for life is change. (p. 67)

4. Group Problem-Solving. Groups of participants, typically six to twelve per group, are given a problem or "initiative" that no one individual can solve. Many problems are encountered on the indoor or outdoor Teams Challenge Course. A complete group effort is

required in order to arrive at a solution. Roland & Havens (1981) remarked,

> An initiative task...is success oriented. It teaches people to deal with the anxiety that precedes any new adventure, to cope with uncertainty and to survive with increased confidence while developing a more positive concept of self. (p. 45)

5. Individual Problem Solving: The Low/High Challenge Course. These indoor and outdoor courses involve a series of events which challenge individual participants phys-

155

ically, cognitively, and emotionally. This gross motor equipment has been designed to be utilized indoors or outdoors. Benefits to participants have included increases in self-concept and locus of control. Although innovative and exciting, the equipment need not be available in order for challenge programs to be effective. Monies must be appropriated not only for Course materials but also for thorough staff training. If an agency is considering the development and implementation of a Course, it is strongly advised that professionals be consulted. Referring to the benefits of challenge courses in general, Smith (1981) stated,

> ...[Challenge course] sequences... require...resolution of interpersonal conflict, personal risk-taking and basic commitment. The intensity of the experiences, therapeutically, is very great, as they require the students to deal with stress, trust levels, fears, personal limitations and a range of powerful emotions. (p. 175)

F. DEBRIEFING

Debriefing challenge activities appears to be a critical ingredient in the Challenge Education process. By merely facilitating a group through an activity and then immediately moving to another activity makes the program recreational and diversionary. Challenge Education facilitators concur that group discussion needs to follow most activities. Discussion can focus on leadership styles, group involvement, problem solving styles, etc. Highly skilled facilitators will often spend more time on debriefing than those facilitators with minimal experience. Flip charts, VCR units, and transfer of learning models are typically the norm with experienced facilitators.

Debriefing is an open-ended interview conducted with the participant(s) at the conclusion of challenge activities (Darst & Armstrong, 1980). This process is intended to allow the participants to verbalize their behaviors, reactions and feelings. Learners are encouraged to reflect, describe, analyze, and communicate in some way that which was recently experienced. Debriefing can be considered an internal, self-directed, reflective form of reinforcement. It is a process which strongly relies on the sensitivity and knowledge of the debriefer toward the participants.

In 1956 Bloom outlined a taxonomy of cognitive processing or thinking levels which can be helpful in the planning of debriefing activities. The following six levels of thought

are listed from the most basic to the most complex thinking levels:

KNOWLEDGE (memory level: remembering information by recognition or recall)

COMPREHENSION (understanding level: interpreting or explaining knowledge or learnings in a descriptive literal way)

APPLICATION (simple usage level: correct use of knowledge, e.g., to solve rote problems or answer rote questions)

ANALYSIS (relationship level: breaking knowledge down into component parts and detecting relationships between them, e.g., identifying causes and motives)

SYNTHESIS (creative level: putting together pieces to form a whole, e.g., to formulate a solution)

EVALUATION (opinion level: making judgements about the value of ideas, solutions, events)

In 1984 Quinsland & Van Ginkel made the following suggestions on how to prepare for a debriefing session:

1. What are the most important questions to which I want participants to respond?

2. At what level are these questions?

3. What questions should I use to lay the foundation for the important questions to be more easily answered?

Processing with individuals and groups is a definite challenge for the facilitator. But much frustration can be avoided if the leader begins with the most basic level—KNOWLEDGE. Asking participants such questions as "What did you just do?" or "Who said what?" or "Did you see that too?" are much more effective than questions like "How did you feel about that?" (EVALUATION level)

Smith (1985), writing in *Issues in Challenge Education and Adventure Programming,* stated,

> I have long advocated some "alternative" methodologies for [debriefing], which require less counseling or group work skill on the leader's part...Some of the processing methods that I find valuable can be incorporated as group-building and warm-up experiences themselves ... Examples of this sort of early experience that later helps in processing include:
> A. Centering, relaxation, meditational time
> B. Guided fantasy, used as interactional warm-up and can include mental rehearsal of later experiences or follow-up reliving of experience past.
> C. Dyads, triads and reflective listening exercises
> D. Structured group sharing, adjective cards, topic talk
> E. Journaling

Debriefing Topics

There are numerous topics that can be integrated in the debriefing process. Included are:

157

1. Involvement Level

2. Trust — between group members; between participants and facilitator

3. Strengths & Weaknesses — Utilization of newsprint and easel help with outlining a group's progress. Summaries can be used for future sessions.

4. Success/Failure — It is important to analyze a group's failures as well as their successes. If a group is having difficulty with any event (e.g., tired, not spotting properly), the leader should terminate the activity and debrief. At this time he/she needs to make a decision if the group is then able to continue. Sometimes it is appropriate for the group to make the decision. Processing or debriefing can be one of the most important parts of the entire challenge experience. It takes a thorough understanding of the debriefing process and much practice to have participants gain all the benefits of a particular challenge experience.

G. Concern for Environmental Impact

As more and more people utilize the outdoors as part of their challenge education experience or program, there is a concern for the impact on earth's environment. Anyone who has walked parts of the Appalachian Trail can attest to what hundreds of feet can do to the soil, tree roots, etc. And anyone who has recently visited Yosemite can also attest how thousands of visitors can transform a mountain village to a crowded city with its crime, pollution, etc., etc.

The Ropes/Challenge Course: Environment Friend or Foe?

The ropes/challenge course is often closely linked with challenge education. Certainly, challenge courses are not an absolute necessity for successful challenge programming (in some cases, they should not be used at all!). But with literally thousands of courses installed in the United States, Canada, England, Australia, New Zealand and a host of other countries world-wide, this maze of cables, bolts, ropes and wood simply cannot be overlooked.

Inspect the Environment

Too often, organizational decision-makers fail to realize that a challenge course and the environment in which it sits, require careful maintenance and upkeep. Although it appears that numerous challenge courses are professionally inspected each year, a certain percentage of the inspectors neglect the immediate environment. For example, trails leading to and from a challenge course are often eroded; this erosion is often carried to the trees supporting the challenge course. Program leaders and challenge course coordinators need to be aware of the wide-range of tree care techniques. Shingo (1982) noted,

> Proper tree care procedures require a great amount of basic knowledge about trees and a great amount of skill in working with a variety of materials under all types of conditions.

For example, one tree care procedure that is beginning to be more commonplace with challenge courses is the installation of lightening protection devices. Since most challenge courses consist of galvanized aircraft cable, chances of lightning strikes are enhanced.

Today, organizations are being advised to have at their disposal a consulting arborist to answer questions and make recommendations before, during and after a challenge course is installed, especially if there is no one on staff with tree care and ground care skills.

Facilitators and participants alike need to share their insights, thoughts and feelings about the fragility of our environment. Whether walking in the High Sierras or balancing on a challenge course cable, basic concepts such as "leave only your footprints and take nothing but pictures" can be a simple beginning to the inclusion of environmental awareness throughout all challenge education programming.

H. Ethics

An understanding of ethics and an awareness of ethical dilemmas need to be in the back pocket of every challenge educator. Havens (1985) explained that the "discipline of ethics is of core concern to all human service fields, and is that part of philosophy which deals with the study of what people 'ought' to do" (p.75). Practitioners are thus often faced with ethical issues or dilemmas and have a need for guidelines to help them in their choice of action (Levey, 1974).

As challenge education programs multiply, so will the ethical considerations and ethical dilemmas. An example of an ethical dilemma was given by a reader of *The Roland Report* (1988):

> I am an Adventure Education facilitator at an outdoor center primarily serving "normal" children. The center has an excellent reputation with an extremely (almost non-existent) accident rate (the Director gets upset if a student gets a splinter!). For the record, I am a certified adventure leader, having attended all of Project Adventure's trainings. I have led for Outward Bound, the local school system and a number of recreation programs.
> One Friday, we had a regular staff meeting, reviewing the programs for the following week. I was assigned to a group of retarded teenagers from a special school. Because of the good press our center has received, especially with our

high ropes course, teachers from this school requested high adventure activities. Well, since I have no experience with the retarded, I expressed my concerns with my director. All he said was, "You are an extremely safe leader. Give them the program they want, and if you have any questions, just ask one of their teachers." I appreciated this assurance, but I still didn't feel comfortable. I know if I had refused to lead this group, my job might have been in jeopardy (ethical dilemma #1).

So, on Monday, the group arrived and we began trust activities. The first problem was the trust fall—many of the retarded didn't want to do it, and those that did sat down! At this point I really wanted to just play games, but the pressure was on to do otherwise (dilemma #2).

One dilemma all facilitators must face is what to do when a particular challenge activity or intervention is so powerful that it opens up a participant so he/she is left raw and vulnerable. Without advance counseling skills, the facilitator may find him/herself

helpless, leaving the participant in a less-than-positive condition.

Challenge educators need to remember that any activity, intervention or simulation that is powerful enough to help is also powerful enough to hurt. By being aware of and sharing ethical dilemmas with our colleagues and students. The chance for negative challenge experiences will greatly diminish.

II. HIGHLY DESIRABLE STANDARD OPERATING PROCEDURES

A. PRE & POST PROGRAM INVOLVEMENT

Program Coordinators may decide to include a pre-program and/or post program segment. Unfortunately, many programs do not have the luxury of these options; lack of funding is often cited as the major obstacle. Yet, many training organizations are realizing the need for pre/post involvement—without this intervention, one may be sacrificing the potential impact. The following are examples of pre/post involvement:

Pre-Program

1. Lecture, slide show or videotape of program's components
2. Discussion regarding "What is Challenge?"
3. Lecture of the evolution of challenge education
4. Facilitation of indoor initiatives

Post-Program

1. Facilitation of additional experiential activities
2. Review of videotape from the outdoor session.

3. Discussion of whether the group goals were met or in the process of being met; new goals may need to be developed.
4. Conferences with each participant. Many professionals believe this S.O.P. needs to become mandatory. The potential for individual and group growth appears to be heightened when there is pre and post program involvement. Research data from a challenge program at a major government installation indicate enhanced group cohesion and group clarity when pre and post sessions were included (Wagner & Roland, 1991). Unfortunately, such sessions may be costly and therefore prohibitive to implement. This situation reveals an interesting question: "If experts agree that a 'challenge education' program involves pre and post segments, then those programs that do not include the discussed segments would need to be identified differently, e.g., therapeutic challenge program, adventure education, etc.

B. TEAM BUILDING

A common goal in many Challenge Education programs is team building. Wagner, Baldwin & Roland (1990) report 90% of corporate clients cite team building as the main program goal. Burke (1988) gives the following definition of team building: "When a work group has at least one common goal that is common to all members and when accomplishment of that goal requires cooperative interdependent behavior on the part of all group members." Beckhard (1972) gives four purposes of team building:

1. To set goals or priorities,
2. To analyze or allocate the way work is performed according to team members' roles and responsibilities,

3. To examine the way the team is working—that is, its processes, such as norms, decision making, communications, and so forth,
4. To examine relationships among team members. (p. 3)

Obviously, all Challenge Education programs do not focus on team building; however, one program outcome, whether written as an initial goal or not, is the enhancement of the group/team process. Program Coordinators are sometimes surprised to hear a program participant remark, "We came here to learn about problem solving—and we did—but what we also learned was how to make our team more productive."

Other aspects of team building that challenge programs often accentuate are (1) the building of *esprit de corps*, (2) the bridging of cultural gaps, and (3) the developing of interpersonal and organizational communication skills. The power of challenge programs to empower teams is always present; program coordinators need to carefully consider if team building is indeed an appropriate goal for a particular group.

C. EVALUATION & RESEARCH

As mentioned in the introduction to this chapter, the authors, who readily profess they have spent some time in the ivory towers, have a clear bias on the need for research and evaluation. Recent research studies have given the Challenge Education field a substantial boost in credibility. For example, a team building study conducted by Wagner, & Roland (1991) indicated significant growth in group variables including group clarity, and group cohesiveness. However, it is not realistic to expect this type of quantitative study from all programs. Yet many programs can include some alternative evaluative methods that are relatively easy to implement. One method is the implementation of "observer systems."

Observer systems are tools to study "dynamic, ongoing interaction between people" (Simon & Boyer, 1967). They allow an observer to use a coding system in order to divide behaviors (facilitators' and participants') into meaningful and manageable categories. The observer can then record the particular behavior and analyze the resulting data to some method of data analysis.

Common forms of observer systems include anecdotal recording (Cartwright & Cartwright, 1974), dialogue analysis (Hughes, 1982), and participant observation (Cheffers, 1977). During the last decade a reliable observer system that generate detailed information regarding participant involvement has been developed: Individual

Response Gestalt II (I.R.G. II). This instrument will be briefly reviewed.

I.R.G. II is a reliable instrument that measures individual and group involvement. As Cheffers, Brunelle, and Von Kelsh (1979) stated, "The question of involvement is critical to human functioning. The degree to which people commit their attention, interest, and labor determines the ultimate success of the venture at hand."

I.R.G. II was developed out of five years of research at Boston University; it is simple in structure, discrete in categorizations and easy to subscript and postscript. Validation and computerization procedures are continuing at the University's School of Education. The instrument is comprised of six behavior categories which illustrate a continuum of intensity of a person's involvement — from no involvement to intense and out-of-control involvement. These categories are shown on the following page.

The essential procedures for administering this instrument are as follows:

1. Verbal behaviors of individuals are coded with numerals one through six (1-6), which correspond with relevant behaviors.
2. Nonverbal behaviors are coded in the same classifications by utilizing the "teen" equivalent (11-16).
3. When the verbal categories are circled, an individual is expressing verbal and nonverbal behaviors simultaneously.
4. The subscript "N" after a category number indicates that an observed individual is behaving in a negative or hostile manner.
5. A further subscript "V" recorded instead of an "N" indicates that the participant

INDIVIDUAL REACTION GESTALT (IRG) II.
A Description Thermometer Measuring the Involvement of an
Individual Set against the Gestalt of the Total Group
Or Overall Group Involvement.

CATEGORIES

Suggested
Subscripts: V: Violence
N: Negative Conotations
G: With group or another individual

V NV 1 11	V NV 2 12	V NV 3 13	V NV 4 14	V NV 5 15	V NV 6 16
No Apparent Involvement	Distracted	Spasmodic Involvement	Engrossed Involvement	Emotionally Involved	Ultimate Involvement
Illustrative Behaviors					
Wandering around the institution or learning area, usually occupied doing something else. Not at all task , oriented.	Present, but not giving the lesson concentration. Asleep, or talking with someone.	No permanent focus. Fluctuates concentration on and off task.	No Apparent emotional release. Leaning forward, eyes never leaving the task.	Strong emotion. Laughing, smiling, frowning, but emotions and reactions are in control.	Strong, excessive emotional release. Reaction to task or environment is not under control.
Concepts					
LOW INVOLVEMENT		SPASMODIC INVOLVEMENT	INTENSE INVOLVEMENT		

is not only acting negatively, but with signs of physical or verbal violence as well.

6. A postscript "G" is used when the participant is interacting with other individuals.

The coder records the appropriate behaviors every ten seconds or whenever there is a change in behavior. Codings are recorded on a horizontal flow chart. The instrument can help program directors and coordinators determine those activities that generate the highest levels of involvement. Thus, I.R.G. II can help document the statement, "Oh, yes. The kids really get involved with that activity."

Highly Desireable Operational Guidelines

D. SOLO TIME OR INTROSPECTION

Many challenge educators believe that participants need to have the opportunity for periodic solo time. Allowing time to be by oneself is often too rare of an occurence. A chance to reflect on the day, to listen to the sounds of nature, or even to listen to one's heartbeat is, for some, a revelation. After a two day solo experience with Outward Bound, one participant exclaimed, "I'm 33 years old, and to this day have not stopped—I mean *really* stopped to process with myself the meaningful things in life."

163

Of course, solos need not always be two days in length or take place in the wilderness.

A form of solo is commonly referred to as "secret spot" or "my place." The objective is to select a spot with which you would like to spend a few minutes. Sitting, standing, with eyes open or closed, you "get to know" your spot. Poems, haikus, drawings, a letter to yourself (that your facilitator mails back to you in 6 months), can all be a part of secret spot.

Journals are often used during a solo experience. For many participants, just a blank notebook or actual bound journal and pen are needed. For young people or persons with disabilities, a more structured journal format is needed. Tom Smith, in his work with youth, is an advocate of the structured journal format. Below are a few pages of one of his creations:

In the corporate training environment, twenty minute solos can be weaved throughout a one, two or three day program. Trainees can be asked to individually process a particular experience or simulation which can then be shared with the large group. Solos can then be changed to diads, triads, etc., allowing a variety of sharing environments. In addition to the opportunity to synthesize and accentuate learning, corporate trainees can find the solo experience especially powerful by allowing themselves a unique opportunity to stop and think—instead of think and stop! Executives from one organization found their solo experience so rewarding that they instituted a solo time in the work place: during one specific hour per day middle managers and executives took no phone calls, visits or interruptions of any kind. Doors were closed for solo, meditation, journalling, etc.

REFERENCES

Association for Experiential Education. (1990). *Safety Practices in Adventure Programming*. Boulder, Co: Author.

Burke, W. (1988). Team Building. In *Team Building: Blueprints for Productivity and Satisfaction*. Alexandria, VA: NTL Institute

Cartwright, C. & Cartwright, G., (1974). *Developing Observation Skills*. New York: McGraw-Hill, 1974.

Cheffers, J. (1977). Observing Teaching Sytematically. *Quest*, 28, 17-28.

Cheffers, J., Brunelle, J. & Von Kelsh, R. (1978). *Measuring Student Involvement*. Paper presented at AIESEP International Conference. Magglingen, Switzerland.

Darst, P. & Armstrong, G. (1980). Outdoor Adventure Activities for Schools and Recreation Programs. Minneapolis: Burgess.

Dewey, J. (1938). *Experience and Education*. New York:

Gager, R. (1977). Experiential Learning Process Flow. *Yoyageur Reports*. The Association for Experiential Education, 1(1), 4-5.

Hale (A.) (Ed.). (1990). *Annual Review-1989*. Bellefontaine, Ohio: National Safety Network

Havens, M. (1985). "Ethical challenges in the outdoor setting." *Therapeutic Recreation Journal*, pp. 75-80.

Herbert, T. (1981). *Experiential Learning: A Teacher's Perspective*. Concord, N.H.: Concord High School.

Hughes, M. (1962). What is Teaching? One Viewpoint. *Educational Leadership*, 19, 251-259.

James, T. (1980). *Education at the Edge*. Denver, Colorado: Colorado Outward Bound School.

Keyes, R. (1985). *Chancing it: Why we take risks*. Boston: Little, Brown & Company.

Leroy, E. (1983). Adventure and Education. *Journal of Experiential Education*. 6, 18 22.

Robb, G. (Ed.). (1985). *Issues in Challenge Education and Adventure Programming*. Bloomington, Indiana: Indiana University.

Roland & Havens (1981). *An Introduction to Adventure: A Sequential Approach to Challenging Activities With Persons Who Are Disabled*. Loretto, Minn.: Vinland National Center.

Roland, C., Keene, T., Dubois, M. & Lentini, J. (1987). Experiential Challenge Program Development in the Mental Health Setting. *The Bradford Papers Annual, Volume III*. Bloomington, Indiana: Indiana University.

The Roland Report (1988). "An ethical challenge from the field," 2(3), p. 7.

Shingo, A. (May/June 1982). "Cabling & Bracing. How to minimize internal injury." *Arbor Age*. pp. 16-19.

Simon, A. & Boyer, G. (1967). *Mirrors for Behavior*. Philadelphia: Research for Better Schools.

Smith, T. (1985). Real vs. Perceived Risk. In G. Robb (Ed.) *Issues in Challenge Education and Adventure Programming*. Bloomington, Indiana: Indiana University.

Smith, T. (1981). *Wilderness Beyond ... Wilderness Within*. Madison, WI: Printing Plus.

Quinsland, L. & Van Ginkel, A. (1984). How to Process Experience, *Journal of Experiential Education*. 7(2), 8-13.

Wagner, R., Baldwin, T. & Roland, C. (1991). Outdoor Training: Revolution or Fad? *Training & Development Journal*. 51-56.

Wagner, R. & Roland, C. (1991). *Does Outdoor-Based Training Really Work? An Empirical Study*. Manuscript submitted for publication.

Wagner, R. & Roland, C. (in press). Outdoor-Based Training: Research Findings and Recommendations to Trainers. *Training & Development Journal*.

CHAPTER FOUR

CONTEMPORARY ISSUES IN CHALLENGE EDUCATION

A. **Introduction:** Mark Havens, Ed. D., President, Accessible Adventures, Sisters, Oregon

B. **Program Accessiblity for Persons with Disabilities:** Chris Roland, President, Roland & Associates, Inc., Keene, New Hampshire

C. **Environmental Ethics:** Gary Robb, M.S., Director, Bradford Woods Outdoor Center, Indiana University

D. **Realizing Human Values:** Mike McGowan, Re.D., Assistant Professor, Western Illinois University

E. **Leadership Development**: Tom Smith, Ph.D., Founder, The Raccoon Institute, Cazenovia, Wisconsin

F. **Societal Impact:** Warren Schumacher, J.C.D., CFLE, Associate Professor University of Massachusetts and Judith Hoyt, Ed.M., CFLE, Independent Consultant, Holland, Massachusetts

G. **Higher Education**: Dan Creely, M.S., Associate Professor, Northeastern Illinois University and Bill Quinn, Ed.D., Assistant Professor, Northeasetern Illinois University

H. **Corporate Outdoor Experiential Training and Development:** Richard Wagner, Assistant Professor, Dept. of Management, University of Wisconsin–Whitewater; Gail Ryan, B.S. Research Assistant, University of Wisconsin–Whitewater and Chris Roland, President, Roland & Associates, Inc., Keene, New Hampshire

I. **Interdisciplinary Communication and Networking:** Chris Roland, Ed.D., President, Roland & Associates, Inc.

J. **Urban Issues:** Steve Proudman, M.S., Director, Voyageur Outward Bound School's Chicago Center

K. **Research:** Tom Smith, Ph.D., Founder, The Raccoon Institute, Cazenovia, Wisconsin

Chapter Four

Introduction

By Mark Havens

Contemporary issues, in any field of practice, are often perceived as negative—problems to be addressed, barriers to overcome, or simply, conflicts to be resolved. Challenge education has evolved so quickly, it is not surprising that issues have evolved. We can, however, view these conflicts in a positive light. In fact, Thomas Crum, in his book, *The Magic of Conflict*, suggests that:

> Instead of denying conflict, this book is an invitation to embrace it and understand it. When we do, it becomes one of the greatest gifts we have for positive growth and change, an empowering and energizing opportunity. There is truly a magical quality about conflict which can call out the best in us, that which is not summoned under ordinary circumstances. (Crum, 1987)

Perhaps we should then celebrate the fact that there are many contemporary (timely) issues to address during the emergence of challenge education. If the use of challenge curricula was not important or a current trend in education, business, and rehabilitation, then the need for this chapter would not exist. The authors of this book embraced the issues in this chapter and see their inclusion as a means of stimulating positive growth among all practitioners of adventure/challenge education.

Issues

As stated above, the papers solicited for this chapter were chosen because of the timeliness of the issue and the diversity represented. **"Program Accessibility for Persons with Disabilities,"** by Chris Roland reviews the evolution of accessible challenge programs. He focuses on how the ubiquitous ropes/challenge course has been made accessible to a wide-range of populations including persons who use wheelchairs and persons who are seventy years and older. With the passing of the Americans with Disabilities Act (ADA) in July 1990, many, if not most, "traditional," nonaccessible ropes courses will require some level of adapatation.

Gary Robb, writing about **Environmental Ethics**, poses the question: What role will challenge educators play in the environmental crisis? This paper defines existing boundaries between challenge and outdoor educators and offers both a strategy for dialogue and call for a psycho-educational model to address the issue. **"Realizing Human Values,"** by McGowan, implores the reader to consider the need to develop "affective capacity" as leaders, or run the risk of becoming truly destructive in practice. Technocratic training and cognition are not discounted in this paper; however, McGowan challenges us to help both ourselves and participants focus on affective capacity and spiritual potential.

"Leadership Development" by Tom Smith is both a historical review and a comprehensive synthesis of leadership issues in challenge education. Smith clearly dissects the nature of technical and facilitation skills in leadership development and draws on literature from related fields of practice, including metaphysical and Native American sources. In **"Societal Impact,"** Schumacher and Hoyt suggest that challenge education may begin with the individual but "ripples" out to family, community and world systems. The authors advocate the use of challenge curricula to foster the togetherness–connectedness "we" paradigm shift that may reflect the trend of the 90's. Creely and Quinn address the integration of challenge education in higher education. This paper, **"Higher Education,"** suggests that despite the "specialists" trend in higher education today, there is a place for challenge education under the guise of interdisciplinary education. A pragmatic example is outlined in the paper, emphasizing both the successes and struggles involved in impacting higher education.

Richard Wagner, Gail Ryan and Chris Roland collaborated in the popular topic, **"Corporate Outdoor Experiential Training & Development."** After reviewing the history of corporate outdoor training and looking at the question "Why is outdoor training attractive to business?" the authors review four models, including an "indoor-outdoor-indoor" model. Finally, the issue of the effectiveness of outdoor training is critically reviewed.

In **"Interdisciplinary Communication and Networking,"** Roland provides a rationale and model for successfully integrating the professional practice of challenge education with more established fields of practice (e.g.,

Special Education, Psychology, Corporate Training and Development). Concrete examples are cited and "processes" are highlighted for successful communication and networking, including electronic media, cooperative presentations and collaborative writing. In **"Urban Issues,"** Proudman provides an informative paper on creating challenge education experiences in urban and community settings. The author suggests a conceptual framework of transposing a traditional "wilderness" program model into an inner city construct of reality. Finally, in **"The Challenge of Research for Challenge Education"** paper, Smith encourages the challenge education facilitator to consider alternative methodologies for getting the "data," so often asked for in order to validate programs. Smith reviews the notion of scientism and discusses new paradigms for research in the 1990's.

It should be obvious to the reader that the issues selected for this chapter are not all-inclusive. "Ethics" and "safety" are two issues which would naturally fit with the papers presented. It was determined by the editors that these two areas have and are continually being addressed in the field of challenge education. We refer you to Alan Hales' National Safety Network and Jasper Hunts' books on ethical issues in experiential education (available from the Association For Experiential Education).

An Overview

Issues in experiential education can resonate around four major theme areas: professional competence, obligation to the client, responsibility to colleagues and accurate representation of services to society. Professional competence is a common conflict among adventure/challenge educators: What are the necessary technical and facilitation skills required of the challenge educator? To address the heart of the issue, consider this analogy from *The Magic Of Conflict* by Thomas Crum:

> Many of us have had the negative experience of a close friend who has just undergone some major change in his thinking and become an "evangelical pest," speaking of nothing but his new religion, vitamin, exercise program, or guru, to the point where we feel guilty and angry and frantically search for a bag to tie over his head. We wonder, who is this strange alien disguised as our friend and pretending to be a mother, father, priest all rolled into one insensitive authority?
>
> As we become enthusiastic about something new of great value to ourselves, there is an initial tendency to keep persuading ourselves of the validity of it. Unfortunately, our method of doing this often seems to involve persuading someone else. So off we go on our "mission from God." We proceed up our friends' sidewalks, wondering why we hear doors being bolted and window shades dropping. (Crum, 1987)

This observation from Crum can be used as an important metaphor for the status of professional competence within the context of adventure education. It should not be surprising that the technical and facilitation skills required for the adventure leader are not well defined. Moreover, it should not be surprising that adventure leaders go to workshops or training programs and hurry back to colleagues with the news that, "we finally figured out what we need to know and practice to be competent," only to have someone else suggest new competencies gleaned from a new source. We should be confused and should be struggling with professional competence.

The American Psychological Association (APA) struggled for 35 years with the development of a code of ethics for their membership and continues to welcome the process as "ongoing" (Havens, 1986). Throughout the history of developing professions, a basic pattern can be identified which has led to understanding necessary technical and facilitation skill competencies. The steps in this "process" include: (a) an initial collection of unique ethical dilemmas faced by practitioners in the field, which led to an understanding of the moral philosophical foundation for the field; (b) the establishment of a "code of ethics" to guide practitioners; (c) from this code of ethics, or moral philosophical base, came "standards of practice," competencies; and (d) the establishment of accredited institutions to deliver the competencies agreed on by the professional membership.

It may not be prudent to copy or embrace the "processes" established by other fields of practice. It is clear that all professions have problems and gray areas concerning the content of knowledge/skills required of practitioners. However, it would be wise to include these "processes" in the development of competencies within the adventure education field. More importantly, it would be valuable to embrace the "conflict" with an attitude that allows "ongoing" dialogue and a willingness to value and consider many "schools" of thought regarding professional knowledge and skills (competence).

Assuring the physical, emotional, and intellectual safety of participants in adventure programs is a common goal for many challenge education service providers. In fact, it is not uncommon for agencies/ organizations to advertise that trust, group cooperation, team building and risk taking can be addressed—even practiced—in a safe and supportive environment. The word often used is "perceived" risk. For example, participants can glean the many benefits from adventure experiences while only taking "perceived" versus "real" risks. Our obligation to clients (participants of adventure programs) becomes an area that requires close scrutiny. Obviously, if there is such a power to impact clients in a positive manner, there is a chance to impact them, just as powerfully, in a negative way. Consider these ideas:

1. There may be a real contradiction in terms if we say that our adventure experiences or services are (real) risk free. The term "adventure" implies risk and even danger. There is some chance or even opportunity for danger in our programs. Without it, there is no "real" adventure.

2. There is nothing more "real" than a "perceived" risk. While we take great care to study physical safety (we even have the National Safety Network), we lack the same concern about emotional well-being. Yes, there are significant research findings that indicate it is possible to scare yourself to death.

3. As indicated throughout this chapter, "Contemporary Issues In Challenge Education," the increase in numbers and diversity of participants in adventure programs are staggering. The passage of the Americans With Disabilities Act (1990), alone, will stimulate access for 40,000,000 citizens in adventure and other related programs.

With these ideas in mind, it is not difficult to conclude that our obligation to clients becomes even more difficult to define, articulate and defend. However, if we embrace this

surprising popularity for the use of adventure programs with persons who are disabled, at-risk youth, corporate managers, gifted and talented students, college freshmen, chemically dependent persons—as a welcome issue or conflict—proaction can be the "battle cry," not reaction.

It was not long ago that adventure/ challenge educators went into this field of practice with the understanding that the allocation of resources for programs and services were minimal. Some of the benefits one had to look forward to included, (a) a chance to inspire individuals to consider their connectedness with the natural environment, (b) an opportunity to facilitate a "process" that was consistent with a chosen lifestyle (live what you teach), and (c) a notion of "newness," a chance to explore a field that was focused on networking, pluralism and collegial camaraderie. The common struggle among practitioners resided in the promotion of adventure education as an alternative to traditional services, whether it be education, business or rehabilitation. There was an "aura" of strong *esprit de corps*.

This notion of struggle brought with it positive and powerful efforts by adventure educators throughout the United States. However, it was not uncommon to witness leaders who became skilled and knowledgeable facilitators, leave the field of practice at the peak of their careers (low wages, long hours and a need for security forced a rethinking of future goals). In spite of the turnover, one characteristic that remained constant was a willingness and even excitement for sharing among colleagues—information, technical advice and marketing strategies.

With the popularity and acceptance of adventure learning as a viable medium for rehabilitation, education and training, it is now possible to acquire financial resources from work well done. This opportunity for "making a decent living" has brought both comfort and discomfort to the adventure education community. It is not uncommon to hear a comment like, "I used to call my colleagues for advice on a new activity and would immediately get assistance. Now when I call, I get put off. I suppose no one wants to share any secrets of the trade."

Philosophers who study professions would probably advocate that there is an obligation a member of a profession has to his/her colleagues; that obligation being a willingness to share information. Currently, we do this by presenting at conferences and publishing our ideas. Perhaps if we viewed our profession within the same context as we convey one of the principles of our field, "the fact that there is enough resources to go around if we share," then this issue of responsibility to our colleagues would simply pass.

I heard a comment once that sounded like this: "professions work hard to develop a language that confuses the public, which allows job security for the professionals providing the service." Most professions develop in response to a "felt need" by society. It is clear, from the response by the public, that adventure/challenge education is responding to a "felt need" by society at large. It is the responsibility of professionals to advertise the service provided in an accurate and truthful way to society. Several factors make this difficult, including:

- There is a paucity of research information to give us a clear picture of the impact adventure programs have on participants.

- There is a tendency, by leaders, to still be in the "I've got to sell this adventure program any way I can" state of mind.

- The tremendous number of requests for programs, from diverse groups, places professionals in an "I can do that" posture.

- There is an attitude of "I'd better hurry up and get as much money as I can while this adventure topic is hot."

Adventure/challenge education has always been an exciting profession (or field of practice) to be involved in. The conflicts have changed as well as our response to such issues. We have handled the stage of being the "alternative" or "new kid on the block" quite well, with determination and commitment. The present challenge seems to be: How well will we handle success? The papers which follow represent a response to this question. I hope you find them as enlightening and timely as I did.

REFERENCES

Crum, T. (1987). *The Magic Of Conflict*. New York: Simon and Schuster, Inc.

Havens, M. (1986). *Professional Ethics In Outdoor Adventure Education*. Unpublished doctoral dissertation, Boston University, Boston, MA.

Program Accessibility For Persons With Disabilities

by Christopher C. Roland

On July 26, 1990, President George Bush signed into law the Americans with Disabilities Act of 1990. The Act, affecting more than 43 million Americans with disabilities, will be known as the most sweeping civil rights legislation in 25 years. The ADA will have a direct impact on most profit and nonprofit challenge education programs in the United States. Agencies with 25 or more employees must comply by July 26, 1992, while those agencies with less than 25 employees and more than 15 employees must comply by July 26, 1994. This paper (1) presents the historical development of the ADA, (2) discusses the section of the ADA that is most applicable to challenge education programs: Title III: Public Accommodations and (3) presents an historical development of how ropes/challenge courses, a popular component to challenge education, have become accessible to a wide-range of populations.

Historical Development of the ADA

In 1986, the National Council on Disabilities (NCD), an independent federal agency to establish disability policy for federally funded programs, completed a two year study on disabilities. The agency's report recommended that a comprehensive civil rights law be enacted that would require equal opportunity for individuals with disabilities throughout the United States.

Two years later, former Senator Lowell Weicker, Jr. and former House Democratic Whip Tony Coelho introduced legislation that failed to pass the Senate Labor and Human Relations Committee as well as the House Public Works Committees. However, in May 1989, legislation was reintroduced in Congress, with the Bush administration supporting the ADA through Attorney General Dick Thornburgh's public testimonies before the Senate Committee on Labor and Human Relations and the House Judiciary Committee. After a number of changes were made, and after extensive negotiations between the bill sponsors and the White House, conference Committee deliberations and floor debates, legislation was unanimously passed in July 1990 (Holland, 1990).

Who is Disabled?

Bartholomew (1991) summarized the ADA's definition of disability to include persons:

1. With a mental or physical condition that affects some major life activity, such as walking, talking or breathing;
2. With a record of impairment, such as a history of mental illness, chemical dependency, heart disease or cancer. In this case, the concern is that a person could face discrimination because he or she had such a condition in the past, whether or not the illness is a current problem;
3. Who is regarded to have an impairment, for example, a significant facial disfigurement that causes the person to

be shunned and discriminated against. (p. 45)

The ADA and Challenge Education

The ADA involves four titles: (I) Employment, (II) Public Transportation & Services, (III) Public Accommodations and (IV) Communications. Of these four titles, Title III - appears to have the most applicability to challenge education programs. The following are the highlights of the title (Lotito & Pimentel, 1990):

1. Public accommodations offering services may not discriminate against people with disabilities.
2. Establishments must modify policies and procedures, provide auxiliary aids and remove architectural barriers in existing facilities that are easily achieved.
3. New facilities and alterations to existing ones must be made accessible.

Holland (1991) defines accessibility to accommodations as "any site, building, facility, or portion thereof that complies with the guidelines and can be approached, entered, and used by individuals with disabilities. For example, entrances, corridors, bathrooms, water fountains, and other amenities should be accessible to people with disabilities" (p. 19). There appears to be little debate that challenge education programming, including the use of ropes/challenge courses indeed fits under the labels of "public accommodations," "facilities," and "site." Many of today's present and future challenge education programs will come under close scrutiny—entire mission statements may change as a result of the ADA.

The ADA and Ropes/Challenge Courses

From this legislation, all public facilities (with at least twelve employees) that provide challenge programming will be forced to comply with making their buildings and programs accessible. Obviously, there will be limitations regarding the degree of program accessibility. For example, an organization that sponsors a program that includes backpacking into the high Sierras would not be expected to pave a trail into the mountains or expect staff to wheel a participant in his/her wheelchair. However, one "facility" that will indeed be impacted by the law is the ropes/challenge course. This type of challenge education facility is either indoors or outdoors (though outdoors is often preferred) and is constructed from cable, ropes and wood. The traditional ropes course has evolved over many years with origins from Outward Bound (Fischesser, 1991). The "Tension Traverse," "Nitro Glycerin Crossing," and "Hickory Jump" are just three of dozens of elements that are very challenging to participants who are able-bodied; however, they are not accessible to persons with disabilities, especially those individuals who use wheelchairs. Fortunately, it did not take the arrival of ADA to begin the process of making challenge courses accessible.

The Historical Development of Accessible Challenge Courses

There were, no doubt, various efforts in the 1970's to include people with disabilities on challenge courses. But one of the first documented efforts (Roland & Havens, 1982) was in 1977 at Camp Allan in Bedford, New Hampshire, a facility that provided year-round programs for persons with physical disabilities. The camp had been awarded a federal grant to develop and implement Project Torch—an outdoor education inservice training program for special education teachers. One group that was involved with the grant was a special education class from Derry, New Hampshire. The head teacher and teacher aides brought eight students to camp for introductory outdoor education activities. The day ended with the students and teachers waiting for a bus that was late. As some of the children began to exhibit their periodic acting-out behavior, the head teacher, on an impulse, grabbed a climbing rope, some webbing, and a couple of carabiners. He then located a ladder, climbed to a branch approximately 15' above ground, and set up a "tree climb." Every student became extremely quiet and patiently waited for his/her turn. Thirty minutes later, the bus finally arrived-the children hopped into the bus enthusiastically sharing their experiences in the tree.

The camp director, Gary Robb, marveled at the change in behavior of these students as well as their ability and risk taking propensity to climb the tree. In a few days he made the decisions to include the "Tree Climb" as part of his summer camp program. A large platform was constructed in a white pine tree, a staff person hired and trained, and program begun. During that first summer, more than 125 campers experienced the tree climb with the help of a special hoist system.

The Next Step

In 1980, a special educator (Chris Roland), psychologist (Tom Smith), a recreation therapist (Mark Havens), an adapted outdoor equipment consultant (John Galland), an architect (Larry Orr) and a staff member of the Minnesota Outward Bound School (now

known as the Voyageur Outward Bound School) (Gordon Opel) met at Vinland National Center in Loretto, Minnesota to develop health and fitness programs. One informal discussion centered on Camp Allan's Tree Perch program and whether more traditional "ropes courses" could be made accessible to persons with physical disabilities. Since there were some questions regarding the appropriateness of high ropes elements, only low adaptations were initially considered.

During a two week period, this team brainstormed ideas and began experimenting with the construction of a few partially accessible elements. Using only hand tools and one battery-powered drill, a "tree traverse," "scoot bridge" and "inclined parallel balance beams" were constructed. Two of the professionals who used wheelchairs attempted the challenges with positive results.

From these simplistic beginnings, the design of accessible challenge events continued to be refined. The following is a chronology (with highlights) of this challenge course development process:

1977   Camp Allan: The Tree Perch Program
Highlight: rated as one of the most
exciting and popular activities.
Campers with muscular dystrophy,
cerebral palsy, and muscular
sclerosis were able to climb a tree
for the first time in their lives.

1979   Minnesota Outward Bound: An
Integrated Adventure
Highlight: Chris Roland and John
Galland met and discussed the
various barriers that confronted
persons with disabilities in their
quest for challenge and adventure.

1980   Camp Riverwood, Winchendon,
Massachusetts: A Ropes Course
Experience for Campers with
Moderate to Severe Mental
Retardation
Highlight: Many campers attempted
low as well as high elements with
varying degrees of success (Frant,
Roland & Schempp, 1982). Leaders
began to realize the need for
elements that met the needs of those
with balance and coordination
difficulties.

1980   Vinland National Center: The First
Accessible Challenge Course
Highlight: The course was very
primitive, yet it represented the
foundation of accessible challenge
An initial training manual was
published by Vinland, *An
Introduction to Adventure: A
Sequential Approach to Challenging
Activities with Persons who are
Disabled* (Roland & Havens 1981).

1982   Bradford Woods Outdoor Center,
Martinsville, Indiana
Highlight: By this time, Gary Robb
had migrated south to Indiana. From
his experiences at Camp Allan in
New Hampshire, he contracted for
an accessible course. This course
was a bit less primitive, but
difficulties with nonadjustable
balance beams, floppy bridges and a
wheelchair that wouldn't stay on
two cables created some frustration.

1983   Mt. Hood Kiwanis Camp,
        Rhododendron, Oregon
        Highlight: Next to a rushing river,
        this course proved to be much more
        accessible. Gym mats were used for
        the first time in the Burma Bridge
        with positive results. The "Parallel
        Web Beams" and the "Forbes
        Traverse Seat" as created by Kathy
        Forbes. However, parallel balance
        beams that could not be adjusted
        continued to be a problem.

1985   Massachusetts Hospital School,
        Canton, Massachusetts
        Highlight: The first attempt at
        integrating a challenge course at a
        rehabilitation hospital. Adjustable
        parallel balance beams were
        incorporated in the design as well as
        an accessible "Swinging Log."

1986   Mansfield Public Schools, Mansfield,
        Ohio
        Highlight: A course was designed to
        meet the needs of Grades 6-8,
        including students with physical
        disabilities. Included was a tree
        perch program adapted from the
        Camp Allan days.

1987   Association for the Support of
        Human Services, Westfield, Mass.
        Highlight: An accessible challenge
        course, installed in 1985, became a
        key program for a summer camp
        (Kamp for Kids), an after-school
        program, and a family challenge
        program. Accessible indoor
        elements were developed by the
        Association's staff at a nearby
        facility.

1988   National Park Service, Chesterton,
        Indiana
        Highlight: Once the necessary
        paperwork for approval was
        completed, a course was installed to
        meet the needs of all students in
        Porter County.

With each course , the level of accessibility increased, allowing more and more individuals with disabilities to participate. By the late 1980's, this evolution included the adaptation of some "traditional" ropes course events. Many organizations began to realize that even if just one person with a disability comes through the doors each year, it was reason enough to make a few elements accessible. This process of adapting existing traditional, nonaccessible courses will become increasingly evident as a result of the

Americans with Disabilities Act (Havens, 1982).

Integrating the Accessible Challenge Course in Rehabilitation Hospitals

In November 1989, a health care organization made the commitment to include accessible challenge courses in three of its hospitals. Due to the specific needs of the rehabilitation hospital, many changes in the design of the course were made; in fact, completely new designs with new materials were orchestrated by consultant Don Rogers. Some of those needs included:

- installing equipment as close to the hospital as possible allowing for easy in-out access to the equipment;
- designing portable indoor equipment that can be easily stored in the often-crowded physical therapy gym;
- designing equipment to be used by only one therapist with one or two patients;
- including familiar equipment, but outdoors (e.g. parallel bars);
- designing equipment to accommodate a wide-range of disabilities and ages (including the geriatric population); and
- designing an interdisciplinary curriculum for physical therapists, occupational therapists, psychologists, recreation therapists and family therapists/social workers.

Finally, a new name was created to give special meaning to challenge programming in this setting: TRACS: The Rehab Accessible Challenge System. Today, TRACS appears to be developing into an accepted therapeutic modality supported by administrators, therapists and physicians. Some physiatrists are now prescribing TRACS to many of their patients. One medical director remarked, "TRACS allows therapists to observe and to work with patients in a new light. With the help of TRACS, therapists have greater opportunities to see how their patients function in challenging indoor and outdoor environments. These environments, in fact, represent challenges patients may face in the community and at home."

Summary

We are well on our way to making challenge education programs accessible to all, regardless of age or ability. Making accessible challenge courses is obviously not the only area needing attention. In the early 80's, Vinland National Center published an array of manuals that addressed the needs of other challenge education area including: *Pulk Skiing, Sled Skiing, and Ice Sledding for Persons with Mobility Impairments* (Orr, 1981), *Health Promotion, Wellness and Medical Self-Care* (Sehnert, 1981), *Cross Country Skiing for Persons with Disabilities* (Opel, 1982), *An Introduction to Kayaking for Persons with Disabilities* (Galland, 1981), and *An Introduction to Fitness with Persons who are Disabled* (Roland & Partridge, 1985).

Today, the accessible challenge and adventure movement is steadily gaining momentum. Organizations such as Wilderness Inquiry II (Minneapolis), S'Plore (Salt Lake City), Accessible Adventures (Sisters, Oregon), and Roland & Associates, Inc. (Keene,

New Hampshire) are taking the lead to providing accessible challenge programming. With the help from the Americans with Disabilities Act, the 1990's will be a decade of increased accessibility to challenge and adventure throughout our nation. The "doors" of ropes courses, rivers, lakes and the wilderness are slowly, but surely, opening for one and for all.

References

Bartholomew, D. 1991). "Opening your door to the disabled." *Your Company,* pp. 42-48.

Fischesser, M. (1991). "The evolution of the ropes course." *Adolescent Counselor.*

Frant, R., Roland, C. & Schempp, P. (1982). "Learning through outdoor adventure education." *Teaching Exceptional Children.* pp. 146-151.

Galland, G. (1981). *An introduction to kayaking for persons with disabilities.* Loretto, Minn.: Vinland National Center.

Havens, M. (1992). *Bridges to accessibility.* Hamilton, Mass.: Project Adventure, Inc.

Holland, C. (March/April 1991). "ADA: Americans with disabilities act 1990." *The Building Official and Code Administrator,* pp. 18-37.

Lotito, M. & Pimentel, R. (1990). *The Americans with disabilities act: Making the ADA work for you.* Northridge, CA: Milt Wright & Associates, Inc.

Opel, G. (1982). *Cross country skiing for persons with disabilties.* Loretto, Minn.: Vinland National Center.

Orr, L. (1982). *Pulk skiing, sled skiing and ice sledding for persons with mobility impairments.* Loretto, Minn.: Vinland National Center.

Roland, C. & Havens, M. (Jan. 1982). "Tree climbing: Handicapped find "perch" exciting." *Camping Magazine,* pp. 36-37.

Roland, C. & Havens, M. (1983). *An introduction to adventure with persons who are disabled.* Loretto, Minn.: Vinland National Center.

Roland, C. & Partridge L. (1985). *An Introduction to fitness with persons who are disabled.* Loretto, Minn.: Vinland National Center.

Sehnert (1981). *Health promotion, wellness and medical self-care.* Loretto, Minn.: Vinland National Center.

Environmental Ethics

By Gary M. Robb

Challenge Education and Our Fragile Environment

With all the glitz, glamour and rapid development that has and currently surrounds Challenge Education, we often forget about one of the primary tenets of our beginnings—the environment in which we work and our ethic towards that environment. Aldo Leopold (1949), a noted environmental educator once said, "It is inconceivable to me that an ethical relation to land can exist without love, respect, and admiration for the land and a high regard for its value." He also noted that, "The extension of ethics to (the land) is...an evolutionary possibility and ecological necessity."

Aspiring Challenge Education professionals often have little interest in "teaching and learning" traditional outdoor education concepts. We find them anxious to rush off to the nearest ropes course and "go for it." This is unfortunate because as the decade of the nineties emerges our nation finds itself at an all-time low in respect to environmental consciousness, with many serious environmental problems at hand.

Yambert (1985) quotes Peckett: "We are between a death and difficult birth." The quote could easily be referring to the current state of development in challenge education. The question is, what role will challenge educators play in this environmental crisis? Aldo Leopold was known and respected internationally for his essays on conservation and a "land ethic." He said of education, "Education, I fear, is learning to see one thing by going blind to another" (1949). In some respects, this quote has meaning for many challenge educators today. We have opened up this new and exciting world of challenge education, but in doing so we must ask ourselves if we are raping the mother of our creation.

In recent years, heeding the warnings of Rachel Carson's *Silent Spring* (1957), and the teachings of other naturalists, there has been increasing emphasis on teaching people to appreciate the requirements of the delicate balance between man and his world. All of us must begin to experience the earth as suffering and become a part of the community that includes suffering people, plants and animals (Fritsch, 1990). If only we could break out of our sterile, boxed-in identity as invincible beings living on top of nature! The managerial ethos is dangerous folly. Our goal should not be to stretch out our "resources" and let the rest of the earth community be damned, but to fill our vital needs with minimal damage to the biosphere and with awe and humility toward the great unfolding of the earth story of which we are a part (Spretnak, 1990). We must internalize the basic ecological concept that all things are connected including, in particular, humans and nature. Honoring nature is the key to our survival; nature must be our model. Rather than dominion over the earth, we must remember that we are tenants. Our landlords are our children, and their children (Viederman, 1990).

One of the underpinnings of the Challenge Education movement has been the concept of developing the inner self, expanding our horizons and inner limits and tolerances. Challenge educators have prided themselves on being ethical in their relationships with clients and participants. This same notion can and should be a part of our environmental ethic. By far the most pressing challenge before us is to stretch our human imagination and our capacity to expand our moral responsibility towards the environment. In the Western world we have become accustomed to manipulating the external world to support our sustainable habits. This type of manipulation cannot work for much longer in our finite eco-system (Weiskel, 1990). Knapp (1987) has aptly quoted Stuart Chase's, *The Proper Study of Mankind*, which posed two great questions: "How shall we come to terms with nature?" and "How shall we come to terms with our own kind?" Part of the answer to these questions hinges upon a

recognition that humans and the rest of nature are integrally connected.

The Challenge Sequence*& Environmental Quality: Problems and Solutions

Item	Years to Decompose
Cigarette Butts	1-5
Plastic Film Container	20-30
Nylon Fabric	30-40
Leather	50
Aluminum Can	200-500
Plastic 6-Pack Ring	450
Glass Bottles	1,000,000

(Sources: *USA Today* and *Earth Ethics*)

Many Challenge Education programs offer a sequence of activities or experiences which include goal setting, awareness, trust building, cooperation, problem solving and high adventure. Often, these experiences are introduced in the above order, depending on the length of time with the group.

As proponents of the Challenge Education Sequence, we include activities that are designed to develop awareness, trust, cooperation, communication, problem solving skills and increasing levels of group cohesiveness through a carefully developed sequence of challenges. We should and must begin including in this sequence, not only activities that will heighten environmental awareness but those that will also place challenge educators along side other environmental proponents in attacking some of the serious problems we face today.

Some examples: At the initial sequence level, goal-setting, we need to include goals that will not only advance human growth, but those that include environmental stewardship as well. Perhaps each Challenge Education experience should include a group signature project. The longer the experience, the more significant the project. Signature projects could range from simply giving each participant a trash bag and having them pick up trash to and from the challenge area(s), to more extensive projects such as creating checking, refurbishing trails or creating wildlife habitat on longer experiences.

The awareness level of the challenge sequence most often focuses on the development of intra- and interpersonal awareness. Just as significant is the need for environmental awareness. In many challenge programs, environmental awareness has been included simply to make participants feel comfortable in the new environment. This is not enough! We need to educate our participants about the significance of picking wildflowers or throwing away a Pepsi can. The fact is that in the real ecological world there are tens of thou-

sands of ramifications down the line. Commoner's (1972) first law of ecology is that everything is connected to everything else, yet our thinking is often limited to only the first one, two or three ramifications. We need to educate ourselves about these things. As an example, Yambert (1985) has pointed out that at one time we thought that using colored toilet paper on the trail was not proper since it had dye in it and could pollute streams and ground water. Later we learned that the bleach used to make toilet paper white is more ecologically harmful than the type used to make colored paper. As educators, we need to make informed, environmentally sound choices in our programs.

When environmental awareness activities *are* provided as an early part of the challenge sequence, we must be certain to pay attention to the delicate nature of the environment that we are intruding upon. For example, wildlife populations are good indicators of the state of the environment. Wildlife management efforts over the years have been mixed with success and failure, but one factor appears most critical: habitat. Given proper habitat, populations will do well; deprived of its necessary habitat, a species will decline (Carman, 1986). So, when we take a group through a marshland for sensory experiences, we would do well to first consider the impact on the cattails, bulrushes, sedges and other wetland plants that produce food and habitat for wildlife. We need to fully understand that we should not pursue personal growth at the expense of environmental integrity.

When we move our challenge education participants into the trust and cooperation levels of the sequence, there are numerous analogies and metaphors that we can draw upon to include environmental ethics. A popular trust development activity is what is commonly termed the "Blind Trust Walk." This activity can also provide an excellent opportunity to teach environmental awareness through heightened use of smell, hearing and touch. Leaders should also insure that these walks do not adversely effect meadows, trees, flowers and other natural vegetation in the course of accomplishing "personal or group trust." In developing group trust and cooperation, communication is an integral component. We could include activities from bird watchers to enhance our communication, i.e. distinguishing varying bird sounds will heighten our listening skills. Discriminating similarities and differences among bird calls or looking at the similarities, yet differences, of deciduous trees can be translated back to the development of trust and cooperation, in the sense that understanding each person as an individual is essential in the development of positive interpersonal relationships. We can foster the development of interdependency among group members by realizing that

pesky insects feed trout that are caught by fishermen who support a multi-million-dollar fishing industry. We can realize that flowers are dependent upon insects that pollinate them while insects are dependent upon flowers that nourish them (Ford, 1985). The popular activity of "Bird Lofting" or "Blanket Lofting" is often used at this level of the sequence to develop both cooperative skills and group trust. Another goal of the activity could also be to heighten sensitivity of the group towards birds and how we can successfully co-inhabit the same area.

The problem solving and challenge sequence levels can similarly include numerous considerations related to environmental ethics. Problem solving challenges often center around the use of ropes courses, challenge courses, and solo experiences. The concern for the environment becomes paramount if we think in terms of soil compaction created by ropes courses. By understanding soil characteristics we can minimize these problems. Tree scarring and damage caused by the construction of ropes courses provides an excellent opportunity for problem solving. Research on positive and negative impact on trees can be an excellent opportunity for the development of both an environmental ethic and the development of individual and group problem solving skills. Fire building and fire scarring of the earth during solo experiences and the ramifications of privies and latrines can be considered a part of this sequence. For example, we have latrine kits with nicely designed shovels so that the barrel is just the correct length to indicate how deep you should dig to stay within the biologically active layer of soil, i.e. if it's too shallow the skunks will dig it up; if it is too deep the bacteria won't work on it. If you have a roll of toilet paper and matches in the kit, you can burn the toilet paper but will sacrifice a little air pollution while saving a little land and water pollution, or vice versa (Yambert, 1985). As challenge educators we can, in very concrete and meaningful ways, create the problem-solving atmosphere, decision-making opportunities and join in the effort to solve environmental problems at the same time.

Group challenge can be enhanced by using environmentally-oriented projects as part of a sequence. Many possibilities exist including (1) construction of nesting boxes that could be placed and left at locations that will enhance the development of wildlife (Carman, 1986) and at the same time meet the objectives of the group challenge sequence; (2) creating openings in heavily wooded areas; (3) constructing brush piles or planting berry-producing shrubs, herbarium cover or food plots of grain. Openings in the woods means more sunlight reaching the forest floor. This stimulates growth of the seedlings and other small plants, thus providing more food and cover for wildlife. Brush piles are like natural magnets for wildlife. Piles of sorghum and buckwheat will help assure a source of winter food and cover; (the metaphor for the group and its human growth potential is obvious); trails surfaced with wood chips can be designed and constructed by participants marked along the way with interpretive stations; a tree planting project that would benefit both participants and the area itself in the establishment of a windbreak.

These are not new ideas. Leopold and many others for decades have been advocating responsible environmental ethics as critical to our future. Roszak (1979) stated, "that the needs of the planet are the needs of the person. Therefore, the rights of the person are

the rights of the planet." We cannot continue to be smug about the role of challenge educators in environmental ethics. As Engle (1986) has stated, "we must approach eco-justice with the same regard as we approach social justice." Eco-justice describes the application of a global philosophy. Every effort to achieve economic, racial, political and gender justice involves solving the problems of the earth's resources. Our efforts as challenge educators must be synergistic with those of environmental educators. Many challenge educators are already conscious of this need and are taking proactive roles in this regard. We should look to the environmental literature to assist us in these efforts. Activities from Project Learning Tree (1975), Project Wild (1983) and innumerable other sources can easily be applied to our challenge education sequence and applied nicely.

As challenge educators develop an environmental consciousness, we must be creative in our efforts to assist in the resolution of such environmental problems as energy consumption, global warming and overcrowded landfills, etc. We must realize, for example, that the greenhouse effect is not the result of something done wrong, like illegal dumping of toxic wastes or nuclear accidents. It is a result of normal everyday life (The P.E.A.C.E. Connection, 1990).

We must initiate dialogue with outdoor educators and develop a "psycho-ecological model" that has relevance for both practices. A crossbreeding of ideology, knowledge, concerns and methodologies can lead to significant progress. We need to incorporate the teachings of sage outdoor educators into challenge education training and practice. We can even learn from the Boy Scouts who recently published their new handbook that stresses low-impact camping (1990). We must also remember as Williams (1988) stated, "You don't make time for nature study; you incorporate it into reading social studies, math, history..."

REFERENCES

Carman, S. (1986). Making your school site an environmental smorgasbord. In G. Robb (Ed.), *The Bradford Papers Annual*, *1*, 39-44.

Carson, R. (1957). *Silent Spring*. New York: Harper & Row.

Commoner, B. (1972). *The Closing Circle: Nature, Man and Technology*. New York: Alfred A. Knopf.

Donaldson, G.W. (1985). Converging concerns: Recreation education, some imperatives for our third century. In G. Robb (Ed.), *The Bradford Papers*, *5*, 41-51.

Engle, R. (1986). Eco-justice: Burning word for our time. *Unitarian Universalist World*, *17* (2), 4-5.

Ford, P. (1985). Making the world your oyster. In G. Robb (Ed.), *The Bradford Papers*, *5*, 1-11.

Fritsch, A. (1990). Entering the 1990's. *Earth Ethics*, *1* (2), 11.

Knapp, C. (1987). Connecting people and planets. In G. Robb (Ed.), *The Bradford Papers Annual*, *2*, 91-98.

Leopold, A. (1949). *A Sand County Almanac*. New York: Oxford University Press.

Outdoor Ethics. (1990). Vol. 9, No. 1. The Izaak Walton League.

The P.E.A.C.E. Connection. (1990 Jan./Feb.). Newsletter of the people for ecological awareness and conservation ethics.

Project Learning Tree. (1975). The American Forest Institute.

Project Wild. (1983). Western Regional Environmental Education Council.

Roszak, T. (1979). *The Creative Disintegration of Industrial Society*. Garden City: Anchor Press/Doubleday.

Spretnak, C. (1990). Entering the 1990's. In *Earth Ethics*, *1* (2), 11.

Viederman, S. (1990). Entering the 1990's. In *Earth Ethics*, *1* (2), 12.

Weiskel, T. (1990). Entering the 1990's. In *Earth Ethics*, *1* (2), 11.

USA Today and *Washington Citizens for Recycling*. (1990).

Williams, T. (1988). Why Johnny shoots stops signs. *Audubon*.

Yambert, P. (1985). Outdoor education—the next fifty years. In G. Robb (Ed.), *The Bradford Papers*, *5*, 22-32.

Realizing Human Values

By Michael McGowan

To teachers who have had one experience in challenge education it seems simple to put a group of participants through the paces on the teams or ropes course. The impulse to rush out and build their own course, so that they too can provide high impact experiences for all their students, is quite attractive. However, one quickly learns that if he or she approaches challenge education as a group of activities and techniques they inevitably fail. One simply cannot apply mass production approaches to challenge education and obtain even satisfactory results. Such attempts inevitably lead to administrative compromise and the dilution of the program which results in wholly different outcomes than were originally intended.

When designing the challenge experience it is necessary to consider the fundamental nature of the experience, not just the techniques and activities to be included in a program. Challenge education certainly involves teaching how to handle equipment and how to act and interact safely in the environment. However, challenge education facilities do not teach outdoor skills and recreational activities as their primary focus. By definition, they design and facilitate human experiences. Personal experience is that intimate sphere of being where human values emerge to take on the intrapersonal substance which influences and colors lives.

We are at once enabled and constrained by the inherent affective capacities of our humanity. If we defer to develop our affective capacity because of ignorance, that is unfortunate and we are crippled by it. Indeed, all of our conceptions of the immature, the weak, and the crippled contain this element of unrealistic capacity or deferred potential. If we purposefully focus on one aspect of our being and defer holistic development of our capacities and potential we are crippled at best and truly monstrous at our worst. If our focus is extreme, we become truly "unnatural and twisted" more closely resembling cunning beasts or cybernetic monsters than human beings. All our conceptions of the monstrous contain this element of volitional bent or willfully deferred affective capacity and potential.

Affective Development: Problem Solving and Valuing

The question of having moral beliefs at all or not having them, is decided by our will. Are our moral preferences true or false, or are they only odd biological phenomena, making things good or bad for us, but in themselves indifferent? How can your pure intellect decide? If your heart does not want a world of moral reality, your head will assuredly never make you believe in one. (James, 1898)

Virtually all activities utilized in challenge education involve problem solving in some form. Problem solving outcomes provoke personal awareness of values. The competitive and paradoxical nature of values becomes real only when students are forced to

Once a student has adopted the outcome/reward perspective, transferability of learning, skill, and understanding to other problem solving situations becomes extremely difficult. Cognition based problem solving mastery does not transfer readily or easily because of the limited nature of it's method and focus. Neither does mastery of cognitive derived problem solving techniques relate well to problems that require insight into human values and capacities for broader and deeper perceptions of focus, efficacy, relationship, intimacy and value.

Human Values

The principles of honesty, justice, courage, self sacrifice, sensitivity, awareness and self control, stand out as a culturally universal, albeit transitional, human values. Unlike the outcome oriented values of efficacy, predictability and congruence, they are not cognitively derived as problem solving outcomes and then pursued. They arise naturally from our inherent human organism. Honesty, justice, self sacrifice, courage, sensitivity, and self control were not invented as logical procedures and techniques for solving problems. They exist in each of us as inherent human potentials pointing toward our capacity for solving problems by developing as affective human beings. Consequently, they qualify as holistic values and constitute valid processes of being and becoming and therefore are principles that may be used for judging growth and quality in human experience. Indeed, our maturity as a human being is judged by our ability to engage these valuing capacities and to grow and develop in them toward our potential.

choose between outcomes in problem solving. During problem solving students often utilize efficacy, predictability and congruence as cognitive tests of reliability and validity for judging the value of outcomes within the situation. Because efficacy and predictability are cognitive measures they give rise to the logical identification of concrete values such as safety and security, prestige and power that may be congruent with individual logic but that are disassociated from aggregate human values. When perceived as outcomes these values come to be viewed as rewards for mastery in problem solving and are cognitively differentiated from the affective values that were actually engaged to solve the problem. Consequently, the students' understanding of the problem solving process is confounded by cognitive fragmentations of value. They focus upon safety, security, power and stability as problem solving outcomes to be obtained rather than focusing upon affective human values of doing, being and becoming.

The goal of challenge education is not limited to mastery of logical cognitive problem solving skills. Rather the focus is upon facilitating the awareness and emergence of inherent human values by providing planned opportunities to discover and realize them. Problem-solving initiatives are used to provide opportunities to focus, exercise and condition our capacity to value through incremental situational challenges in the context of concrete consequential relationships. Initiatives are laboratory tools that develop insight and perspective into human values and ones personal affective condition.

During problem solving initiatives, challenge education facilitators diagnose the group's and individual's use of values. They then guide the students, through the use of pertinent questions, helping the students to examine their understanding and their use of values. It is not enough to tell the students: You weren't fair, You weren't compassionate, You didn't put others first. Students must discover and explore their capacity to value for themselves. It is their examination of outcomes in consequential situations that allows them to realize them.

Facilitator guidance enables the students to access group knowledge during group processing. Processing questions must, therefore, encompass a holistic examination of the situation and facilitate recognition of the values involved. Holistic group processing focuses upon values beyond efficacy, predictability, and congruence. The group examines decisions and actions, the meaning and purpose attributed to them, and their understanding of the consequences in relation to their personal values. Are they attending to outcomes only or are they attending to the values selected as means in solving the problem? Are personal actions reflective of personal values? Are they growing in their valuing capacities? Are they

growing in their capacity for tackling more sophisticated valuing problems? Are they using problemsolving situations as the means of obtaining power, security, safety, and prestige in the group? Are they being ruled by ends rather than means?

Honesty

To obtain accurate knowledge of process and outcomes, student's must engage their capacity for honesty. To be honest is to attempt to perceive the situation as it is rather than as they would have it be. Indicators of students' honesty in group processing is linked to accuracy, in memory, in perception, and in evaluation. Without honesty in regard to events and consequences, students' knowledge of values is confounded by self serving perceptions regarding outcomes. Facilitators must help students to make use of accurate/honest information as a basis for judging outcomes. They must model and demand honesty so that the students may learn to think critically, honestly and to focus upon the values with which they operate.

Justice and the Emergence of Mercy

Personal freedom demands for one's self the right to meet needs and strive toward personal goals. Problem-solving initiatives confront students with others who are themselves emotionally empowered to exercise their freedom in striving toward their goals. If students are to seek personal fulfillment within a healthy and peaceful community of persons the opportunity to meet needs and strive for value must be accorded as the due of each individual. In order to accommodate and maximize each person's potential for affective development, an obligation must be

189

placed upon both members of any interpersonal interaction. If choice is viewed as being an inalienable right of the individual, then opportunities to choose must be accorded the due of each person. Each person in order to choose for their own benefit must render to the other that same privilege. This we call justice. Justice on the material level during problem solving is easy to perceive: breach of the belayers contract, taking turns at emptying the portapotty, theft or destruction of personal property, etc. Unless honesty is present in the group, the need for safety provokes the formulation and enforcement of arbitrary rules of behavior by the facilitator and other group members.

Lack of honesty reduces justice in the group to rules and regulations regarding overt behavior. Problem solving interactions and transactions become mechanistic, legalistic, extrinsically motivated and facilitator-directed if honesty does not direct the individuals exercise of personal freedom. However, unless student decisions are freely made during problem solving, individual responsibility for negative values can be denied. It is only through the acceptance of responsibility for personal, interpersonal and environmental consequences that the group's conception of justice is realized. If the individual fails to exercise justice responsibly, he will be avoided or censured by others, and his freedom will be restricted for the safety of the group.

Interpersonal justice arises out of the individual's responsible actions upon themselves. They become just and consequently justice prevails in the group. Agreement to be just in the group provides the catalyst for the emergence of trust and tolerance which engenders affection and expression between group members. It is the exercise of personal responsibility in seeing that the rights of all group members are upheld during problem solving that the characteristic spirit of the community within their fundamental agreement concerning justice. If they are honest concerning their human capacity for failure, they may also experience a family-like intimacy that provokes in them the ability to move beyond justice and practice mercy.

Courage and Self Sacrifice

Central to the understanding of problem solving and affective development is recognition of the emotional power that arousal provides to the individual during valuing actions and interactions. The intensity of emotional arousal is an adequate test for measuring the strength of a personal value. However, strong emotion may arouse one to strive for and implement values that are destructive to self, other people, community, the environment and that defers personal growth and development. Emotional strength associated with valuing, therefore, is not a reliable indicator of the validity of the value being enacted.

For emotional strength to be used constructively, honesty and justice must direct the action empowered by the emotion. Without the direction of honesty and responsible justice, powerful emotion gives rise to brutish and selfserving actions in the extreme. Honesty and justice must transform the raw power of emotion into purposefullydirected fortitude if action is to be of benefit and not result in damage to self and others.

Descriptors of fortitude such as courage, endurance, perseverance, stick-to-it-tiveness, staying power, self sacrifice, commitment, personal conviction and strength approximate

190

but do not encompass the totality of the value. Its relationship to honesty and justice must be realized if the individual is to apply it toward growth and development rather than to merely further self-centered aims that are neither honest nor just. Strong feeling, guided by honesty and justice, empowers the individual to endure hardship and difficulty, to be courageous, to sacrifice sensibly, and to experience enjoyment and accomplishment by moving the individual to powerful, constructive and healthy actions.

Sensitivity, Awareness and the Emergence of Self Control

Sensitivity is a prerequisite condition to awareness. Level of awareness determines the individual's ability to define problems and bring volitional selfcontrol to problem solving. Awareness enables the individual to recognize fragmented evaluations based on power, predictability and congruence used in the group during problem solving. With practiced sensitivity the individual becomes aware of the ramifications of applying cognitive discounts to emotional issues raised during problem solving evaluation. They become aware of their rigid adherence to covert personal expectations and their stubborn pursuit of personally desired outcomes regardless of the personal, interpersonal, and environmental consequences. Sensitivity that provokes awareness during problem solving facilitates the development of volitional control of behavior and sentiment to mediate the powerful emotional and intellectual inputs to problem solving that arise from severe environmental or challenging situational conditions.

Cognitive descriptions of self control—patience, tolerance, knowing when enough is enough, balance, the ability to defer immedi-

ate gratification, and moderation—approximate but do not encompass the value. Self-control is patently not a process of merely depriving oneself of pleasurable experiences. Rather it is a process of exercising sensitivity which provokes awareness that enables discrimination, selection and volitional action during problem solving. It is the sensitive ordering of personal perception and action toward purposeful implementation of appropriate behaviors and ordinate feelings that are congruent with the situation encountered during problem solving.

Human Expressions of Value

Personal realization of human values is demonstrated through the emergence of characteristically human and therefore meaningful expressions that arise naturally out of our human organism: worship, volitional self-development, positive gender relationships, family, community, and the creative endeavors of service, leadership, stewardship, craftsmanship and art. These expressions are, in and of themselves, effective, predictable and congruent and yet holistically human in character. They are the inherent and natural paths of becoming aware of, realizing and expressing human values.

In the challenge education view of problem solving, the student is seen as acting primarily upon his inner (affective) self. It is his adjustment of his internal affective condition that brings about the solution, not the conditions of the situation that allow him to solve the problem. He, himself becomes responsible, caring, self-disciplined, patient and courageous and that solves the problem. Concrete affective growth is demonstrated by his creative service and leadership, by his stewardship of group resources, by his nurture of group members, by his focus upon both means and ends, and by his aesthetic attention to interpersonal nuance. Safety, security, efficacy and stability outcomes arise in the group because of his fulfillment of his affective capacities and his realization of human values.

On the teams course, for example, a student is confronted with the competing values of freedom and obedience. Cognitively he perceives the group initiative forcing him to choose between freedom and obedience. If he chooses obedience he violates personal freedom but perceives a degree of personal control. He expects to trade his current obedience for some future privilege of getting his own way. If he chooses freedom, the group does not receive his help but he still perceives a reward for his actions—a perception of personal control in the situation. In reality the situation has controlled him by forcing him to choose between extremes in value and expression. It is cognitive shortsightedness that keeps his eye upon the either/or outcome/reward and thus blinds him to the nature of brotherhood as a human value that transcends the freedom and obedience, leader and follower paradox. His experience is one of smug superiority or one of begrudging compliance. Either way the experience of brotherhood has escaped him.

> Discovery and exploration imply transcendence, a going beyond the known, a stretching of one's self toward new dimensions of skill and competence. (Csikszentmihalyi, 1975)

If, however, the student goes beyond logical argument into affective valuing, he realizes the need to exercise an aggregate human value in solving the problem. Such a perspective enables him to choose to act upon himself by engaging his capacity for affective growth.

He acts for the benefit of all through his ability to give help and the group's need to receive it. He exercises the value of brotherhood and, in so doing, transcends the paradox between personal freedom and obedience. The logical cognitive paradox between doing as he wishes and doing for others is transcended through the qualities of trust, sensible self-sacrifice and compassion synthesized in the aggregate human value: brotherhood. Rendering help becomes an intimate and joyful act of servant leadership contributing to a familial atmosphere both for him and the group. It is not logical, but it works. This is because it is essentially an individual action based upon affective human insight rather than an application of an outcome-oriented problem solving strategy. Such an insight into the human condition points up the salience of human values inherent in every problem. Transferability of learning is enhanced, a process of recognizing the paradoxical nature of cognitively derived values and transcending them by exercising aggregate human values.

With insight, affective values no longer compete with cognitively derived values. Rather they cooperatively provoke solutions that enable the individual to transcend linear valuing paradoxes. With such an holistic perspective, worship, growth and gender cease to be expressed as competitive spheres of endeavor and become complimentary sources of purpose and power. Art, craftsmanship, service, leadership and stewardship are realized not as rigidly distinct endeavors but as necessary and complimentary expressions of the process of being maturing as human beings.

The logical complaint that such a balanced perspective will bring mediocrity is ludicrous. Balanced development expands our capacity for accurate focus, positive growth and complimentary gender realization in family and community, and provokes creative expression in art, craftsmanship, stewardship, personal service and leadership through a synthesis of meaning and purpose. Anything less than balance fragments the individual and defers cognitive and affective maturity by deferring personal transcendence of valuing paradoxes.

Holistic Valuing

Ideas produce insight and understanding, and the world of ideas lies within us. The truth of ideas cannot be seen by the senses but only by that special instrument referred to as "The Eye of the Heart," which in a mysterious way, has the power of recognizing truth when confronted with it. (Schumacher, 1977)

Human beings hang together in balance or in fragments, creating affective cripples or intellectual monsters, depending upon the direction and extent of individual fragmentation. Students cannot choose cognitive values over affective values and not defer their ability to mature and fulfill their affective human capacities. If they focus on cognition and they awake to find affective function atrophied. This atrophy of human affective capacity and potential is the source of value fragmentation and subsequent experiences of anxiety and alienation. Valuing safety by itself becomes precaution and stifles the individuals ability to act. Predictability alone leads to a rigid and mechanistic existence. The exercise of personal power becomes licentious. Absolute congruence with logic is antithetical to our human nature making us guilt ridden because of our illogical selves. Inevitably, the individual who pursues the exercise of efficiency, predictability and congruence as being more valuable than intimacy, relatedness and ordinance awakens one day to the loneliness and

isolation of his or her fragmented focus. One must focus and grow in all of his or her human capacities or suffer the alienation and anxiety of personal deferment and atrophy of his or her human capacity and potential.

Growth toward maturity as a human being requires faith and hope in one's personal capacity and potential. Having faith and hope in our potential provokes exploration of what it means to become fully human. Exploration, in turn, provokes the discovery of affective values which enlarge our cognitive, affective and physical capacities and potential and widens the scope of our valuing. Experiential exploration of human capacities provokes recognition of a synthesizing, holistic, affective human principle of human valuing: Love. It resolves the freedom versus obedience paradox. It resolves the growth versus decay paradox and the action versus inaction paradox, not just by understanding them, but also by transcending them.

Love cannot be operationalized in fragmented forms and remain love. Disproportionate attention to justice as an aspect of love denies mercy and forgiveness. Focus upon sensory sexual gratification reduces cognitive and affective dimensions of intimacy and gender realization. Love without honesty results in indiscretion; without self control it becomes promiscuity; without courage it becomes trivial and shallow; without justice it becomes auto-erotic and egocentric; without sensitivity it becomes brutish. However, when operationalized with love, negative states of being are transformed into positive growth; anger is transformed into courage, lust into affection, sloth into hope, gluttony into satisfaction, pride into humility, envy into admiration, and covetousness into generosity and compassion.

Striving to love holistically is characterized by a transformation of personal expression in worship, personal growth, gender relationships, family, community, stewardship, service, leadership, art, and craftsmanship. Love as it is expressed, empowers all human endeavors and gives them a sacred quality. This is the principle that distinguishes pedantic ritual from meaningful, purposeful human worship. As it is played out through all human endeavors it is identified as the quality that distinguishes the craftsman from the technician, the beloved from the sex object, the parent from the caregiver, the artist from the boor, the helper from the servant, the good steward from the resource exploiter, the true friend from the social climber, and the responsive community from an apathetic society.

It is faith and hope in the student's affective capacity and spiritual potential that provokes facilitators to plan opportunities for students to recognize and realize these thematic Human Values. They are cross cultural and universal capacities and potentials for each individual human being. When they are encountered in consequential relationships and examined with honest attempts at understanding they provoke growth and change in students that is impactful and far reaching in its consequence.

To have a clear perception (rather than a purely abstract and verbal philosophical acceptance) that the universe is all of a piece and that one has his place in it, one belongs in it, can be so profound and shaking an experience that it can change that person's character and his Weltanschauung forever after (Maslow, 1974).

REFERENCES

Csikszentmihalyi, M. (1975). *Beyond Boredom and Anxiety*. San Francisco, CA: Josey-Bass, Inc.

Maslow, A. (1964). *Religions, Values, and Peak-Experiences*. Middlesex, England: Penguin Books.

Schumacher, E. (1977). *A Guide for the Perplexed*. New York: Harper & Row Publishers, Inc.

Leadership Development

Technical Skills, Peoplework Skills, Character Traits, Personal Growth, and Challenge Leadership

by Thomas E. Smith

This paper is concerned with the requirements for leadership of challenge therapy and/or adventure counseling programs. A review of the history of adventure/challenge methodology's explorations in mental health, corrections, rehabilitation, special education, and personal growth leads to the conclusion that challenge therapy is now accepted as a viable therapy/ counseling alternative. It follows that the leaders of challenge sequences should be considered as therapists, counselors, and personal growth facilitators. This raises, in new light, the question of the nature of effective leadership for challenge programs. It is argued that the requirements for challenge therapy leadership can be viewed as fourfold:

First, there is a need for training and experience with a variety of technical skills.

Second, there is a need for training and experience with human relationships and peoplework skills.

Third, the challenge therapist should possess or seek to cultivate certain character traits.

Fourth, and most important of all, the challenge group facilitator should have personal experience with, and ongoing concern for, their own personal growth.

Challenge therapists must now recognize that...

There is the outside challenge...and there is the inside challenge...

Most professionals who facilitate adventure/challenge sequences recognize that they have considerable psychological and social impact on clients. Many programs are specifically designed and implemented as alternatives for, or as adjuncts to, traditional psychotherapeutic and rehabilitative procedures. Even those professionals who view their offerings in terms of outdoor education, therapeutic recreation, management training, or as basic adventure vacationing, recognize that there is psychosocial impact on the participants. Almost every program of challenge education makes reference to goals or outcomes such as "enhancement of self concept," "improvement of interpersonal relationships," "development of leadership potential," and "increasing problem solving skills." The descriptions "challenge therapy," or "outdoor therapy," or "adventure-based counseling," are often used, and many would argue that these are the more appropriate designations for the challenge/adventure program since the experiences are so unquestionably in the psychosocial realm.

This was not the case in the early years of adventure programming, as there was considerable reluctance to accept the whole challenge sequence as a viable therapeutic alternative. In part, the caution was an attempt to avoid any confrontation with the professional therapists of society. Leaders in the field also recognized that adventure/challenge facilitators seldom had background in psychology, social work, counseling, or groupwork, and therefore could hardly be considered therapists. There were attempts to involve more professional psychologists and social workers in the adventure movement, but only a few responded (Kaplan, 1979; Smith, 1977, 1978, 1979a, 1979b, 1979c). There was early recognition of the guidance and counseling potentials of the adventure experience (Lovett, 1971; Collingswood, 1972; Dowd, 1972; Smith, 1978). Some of the adventure programs and residential outdoor programs arranged for psychological and psychiatric consultation to oversee therapeutic impact of the experiences, but that involvement was typically of an "on paper" nature, as the professionals seldom accompanied groups on the adventures.

In spite of this reluctance and caution, the 1970's brought about a significant exploration of challenge/adventure methodology as a therapeutic alternative. The Outward Bound programs explored the possibilities of their methodology as an alternative in the treatment of juvenile delinquency and youth-at-risk (Kelly & Baer, 1968, 1969, 1971; Brown & Simpson, 1976; Cardwell, 1976; Golins, 1978; King & Harmon, 1979; Riddick & Meisinger, 1979). The lack of supportive validation research was often noted, but explorations continued (Kelly, 1974; Wichmann, 1976; Gaston & Wichmann, 1979).

There had also been recognition of the potentials of "therapeutic camping." Camp-

bell Loughmiller's classic *Wilderness Road* (1965) had summarized a program of outdoor adventure for troubled youth. His second book, *Kids In Trouble* (1979), appeared in the same year as two critical reviews of the whole process of wilderness camping as therapy (Byers, 1979; Gibson, 1979). Outdoor residential treatment centers were also recognized as a developing trend, but the research validation was lacking (Behar & Stephens, 1978). The developing Project Adventure program published a paper, "Counseling on the Run," which contributed to their "Adventure Based Counseling" model (Schoel, 1976). There was also attention paid to the impact of wilderness survival training on the personality and adjustment of participants (Clifford & Clifford, 1967; Adams, 1970; Heaps & Thorstenson, 1974; Robbins, 1976; George, 1979). However, as the 1970's ended there was still very cautious advocacy of the challenge/adventure experience as therapeutic.

Early in the 1980's stronger arguments for the adventure experience as a therapeutic alternative appeared (Bagby & Chavarria, 1980; Kimball, 1980; Chase, 1981; Plakun, et.al.,1981; Smith, 1981; Stich & MacArthur, 1981; Stich & Sussman, 1981; Stich, 1983; Gass, 1983; Kimball, 1983; Wright, 1983; Wichmann, 1983). There were also suggestions for challenge programs as having therapeutic and rehabilitative potentials for the physically challenged and other special populations (Roland & Havens, 1981, 1982; Smith, 1981, 1982; Kirkpatrick, 1983; Robb, et al.,1983).

As in the 1970's, there were a few psychologists and social workers supporting the adventure/challenge therapeutic process; and one clinical psychologist wrote, "My Couch

Is Made Of Pine Needles" (Smith, 1981). However, there was still not widespread acceptance of the challenge sequence as a therapeutic alternative.

It was in the last half of the 1980's when further exploration of the concept of adventure therapy and challenge sequences for personal growth resulted in a broader acceptance of the methodology (Brannan, et al., 1984; Lappen, 1984; Smith, 1984; Stich, 1984; Stich & Senior, 1984; Young & Crandall, 1984; Castle & Eastman, 1985; Mobley, et al., 1985; LaCasse, 1985; Stanley, 1985; Kimball, 1986; Ziven, 1986; Robb & Ewert, 1987; Roland et al., 1987; Teaff & Kablach, 1987; Wittman, 1987; Kidder, 1988; Roland et al., 1988; Voight, 1988). A strong statement for the counseling potentials of adventure/challenge came in 1988, with publication of the immediate classic in the field, *Islands of Healing* (Schoel, et al, 1988). Alan Ewert contributed a review of the psychosocial benefits of outdoor sequences (Ewert, 1989).

When the 1990's opened, there were thousands of professionals across the nation and around the world who recognized and advocated challenge programming as a meaningful counseling intervention. This acceptance of the counseling and personal growth potentialities of adventure/challenge sequences can be attributed to two factors. First, there was that "internal factor," which was the faithful exploration and development of adventure therapy by many of the challenge movement's leaders. While they continued to develop challenge therapy sequences, there were attempts to deal with the issues of needed research, improvement of safety considerations, the leadership needs for "peoplework" skills, and ongoing education of other professionals. These innovative and persistent pro-

fessionals must be credited for their persistent efforts through the 1970's and 1980's. Second, there were those "external factors," which involved developments and changes in the field of psychotherapy, and the whole system for delivery of human services in our society. There were a number of trends that can be shown to have influence on the final legitimatization of adventure/ challenge therapy.

Trends of Significance: There were a number of trends in psychology and mental health which unfolded in parallel to the development and acceptance of challenge therapy.

(1) There was the trend away from psychoanalytic psychotherapy. Although the psychoanalytic theory of personality development and functioning during periods of emotional distress and behavioral breakdown continues to have wide acceptance among professionals, the therapeutic treatment methodology of psychoanalysis has very few advocates. Counseling via the full psychoanalysis is simply too expensive and too long to be of value to the majority of people in need. It could be argued that this decline started with greater recognition of the humanistic therapies of Rogers, Maslow, May, Perls, Allport, and others in the 1950's. There was further rejection of the psychoanalytic model in the 1960's as the reality therapies of Glasser, Ellis, Berne, and others impacted; and near disappearance of psychoanalysis as a mode of therapy in the 1970's as the behavior therapies of Bandura, Wolpe, Lazarus and others developed. As psychoanalysis declined, the field of psychotherapy greatly expanded, and there were a wide variety of methodologies accepted as legitimate psychotherapy. The boundaries of the therapeutic profession expanded into psychology, social

work, counseling, psychiatric nursing, and other human services.

(2) Psychiatry, in general, tended to move away from the whole practice of psychotherapy as the knowledge and effectiveness of psychotropics increased. Partly because of their biomedical backgrounds, and partly because of the vast numbers of patients they were called upon to serve, the psychiatrists became advocates of treating most patients with medications. As there was considerable societal resistance to this trend, those professionals who advocated therapeutic intervention as opposed to psychotropic containment gained some support. Even within psychiatry there was recognition of the need of many people for counseling intervention in addition to, or in place of, the medications, and thus some support to the efforts of others.

(3) There was also a trend in psychotherapy and counseling to move away from the more traditional one-to-one procedures and toward the group process. This trend had a long historical basis. Early in the century, colleagues and students of Freud suggested that he had not placed enough emphasis on the social factors in personality dysfunction. Alfred Adler argued that most neurosis was the result of improper social interactions, and Karen Horney introduced the idea that "basic anxiety" (as opposed to basic security) was conditioned by social factors. Harry Stack Sullivan emphasized "interpersonal theory" in both development and treatment of personality disorders. The founder of the group technique called "psychodrama," J. L. Moreno, predicted the increasing importance of groups in therapeutic treatment (Moreno, 1946, 1951). In one egotistical commentary, Moreno was purported to claim that his "discovery" of the group therapy process was

more significant than Freud's attention to one-to-one analysis. In any case, by the second half of the century, psychologists, psychiatrists, social workers, and psychiatric nurses were most often trained in group counseling methods as well as individual therapy procedures (Dreikurs, 1955).

(4) The evolution of the adventure therapies was also influenced by that major societal trend called the "Human Potential Movement," which began in the late 1950's, peaked in the 1960's, leveled off in the 1970's, and became a rather stable and significant minority force in the 1980's. The basic founders of the movement were humanistically oriented professionals in psychology, sociology, counseling, education, medicine, philosophy, and religion. The human potential movement has often been mistakenly considered as advocating self-fulfillment and an emphasis on "me." It is more appropriate to see the movement as suggesting that there is a need for each person to look inward, to find the energy and wisdom that will enable reaching out to all persons in need. Basically, the human potential movement is quite optimistic, believing that the nature of the human species is to care, share, and grow forward in community.

The human potential movement recognized that there are many strategies for personal and social growth, and many techniques that can stimulate people to new awareness and new energy. The movement brought a wide acceptance of alternatives in therapy, education, recreation, medicine, and spiritual development. Marilyn Ferguson summarized this disjointed movement as "The Aquarian Conspiracy," noting that growth could be facilitated in a multiplicity of ways (Ferguson, 1980). Although there was some deceleration of the human potential movement in the

1980's, many of the professionals who had been influenced were at work in human services and the helping professions. In many ways, the movement therapies, the relaxation methodologies, the visualization techniques, and many other strategies which are often incorporated into the adventure/challenge sequence were first given recognition as therapeutically relevant by the human potential movement.

(5) In close alliance with the human potential movement, and also influenced by the increasing emphasis on group methods, there was the trend of "personal growth groups," "sensitivity groups," "encounter groups," and "lab groups." Their origin can be traced, in part, to Kurt Lewin, a famous social psychologist, who first introduced concepts about group dynamics which had little to do with therapy, counseling, or personal growth. His "field theory" was influential in the development of training laboratories for business leaders and educators, sponsored at MIT and the University of Michigan.

Meantime, at the University of Chicago, Carl Rogers and his colleagues were exploring the "client-centered" approach to group counseling. By the end of the 1950's there was a societal explosion of groups for growth, groups for therapeutic intervention, groups for stimulating creativity, groups for developing leadership, groups for solving racial conflicts, and groups for the sake of groups. Rogers called the new group movement "the most significant social invention of this century" (Rogers, 1970). Certainly, the group movement was a significant force in replacing the "medical model" for psychotherapeutic intervention with the alternative "growth model." This made it possible for therapeutic help to be provided to many people in many settings

besides the hospital, clinic, or private consultation office.

(6) Finally, there were the interwoven societal trends considered as the "community mental health movement" and "deinstitutionalization." In hopes of improving the quality of life for patients, and to relieve the overcrowding at the large centralized hospitals and state residential units, there was an effort to move clients back to the community. Mental hospitals, residential centers of the criminal justice system, and state homes for the retarded and disabled were closed or greatly reduced population. There was an effort to make early intervention into the world of youth-at-risk, and to provide mental health services to the community. Placement problems were extreme, but solutions were developed through foster homes, group homes, half-way houses, and community residential centers. For the school-aged, special education programs developed within the schools. The greatest problem created by the decentralization of treatment and residential services was that of providing services to clients. There simply were not enough psychiatrists, psychologists, social workers, nurses, recreational therapists, and other trained professionals to deliver the services which had been available in the large institutions. This resulted in a search for, and development of, viable alternative treatment methodologies. The advocates of challenge/adventure counseling were among many to respond. Even though there was still no adequate validation of the methodology, a market had developed for challenge therapy. Adventure based programs were developed for youth-at-risk, the chemically dependent, psychiatric patients, special education populations, the physically challenged, and a host of other populations.

Challenge methodology was given recognition as a viable way to accomplish, or assist in accomplishing, goals of recreational, rehabilitative, educational, and therapeutic professionals.

As the 1980's ended, these complex "external factors," coupled with the "internal factors" of adventure leaders' persistence in exploring the therapeutic impact of the challenge sequences, brought the challenge/adventure ideology to widespread acceptance. Advocates of the methodology emphasized the potency of the group process, the power of the challenge sequence for enhancing personal growth, and the potentials for guiding clients toward better interpersonal adjustment. Granting the early reluctance of many professionals to give full credence to the therapeutic potential of the challenge program, and granting that the methodology still needs research validation, it seems safe to say that there is, in fact, a viable therapeutic and counseling methodology which can be called "challenge therapy" or "adventure based counseling."

Challenge Therapists: As the challenge methodologies have come to be accepted as counseling alternatives and stimulants for the personal growth of participants, a number of questions regarding the leadership are raised. While it opens a giant can of semantic worms, it seems appropriate to raise the question as to whether challenge sequence leaders are, in fact, therapists. Traditionally, a professional psychotherapist would be a psychiatrist, psychologist, social worker, counselor, or clergyman trained in pastoral counseling. Typically, to be a psychotherapist one must have appropriate undergraduate and graduate training, and also pass professional qualifying examination for some sort of state or national certi-

fication. Those therapists without appropriate certification are obliged to work in a setting where they have supervision and/or affiliation with an acknowledged professional. However, in spite of such monitoring of the professional identification of psychiatrists, psychologists, and psychiatric social workers, there is much less control or standardization for the label of "psychotherapist" or "counselor." It is still possible in many parts of the country to advertise oneself as a "family therapist," "marriage counselor," or "counselor," without having the desirable professional background; although professional organizations are continually working to change that.

Many years ago, in recognition of the need for qualified therapists, there was some discussion about developing a profession of "psychotherapist." The advocates argued that the medical training or the scientific psychology coursework, or the study of sociological theory was really unnecessary for the future work of the psychotherapist. In fact, the argument unfolded, it would be more desirable to give the future therapist more training in human values, group dynamics, communication skills, and peoplework sensitivity. This idea did not come to reality, or there might have now been a professional identification as "psychotherapist," and thereby stricter limits on the usage of that professional identification. A major barrier to that movement was the argument by many professionals that psychotherapy was not a profession, but a variety of methodologies that could be applied by many different professionals in their work with people. Discussions as to whether or not there is a profession of "adventure education" or "challenge education" have focused on the same argument: There is, indeed, a complex methodology which can be considered as the

200

"adventure/challenge methodology," but it is available to a wide variety of professionals at work in a wide variety of settings with a wide variety of populations (Brannan, et al, 1984; Robb, 1985). As with the psychotherapies, challenge education is best considered as a methodology, and with emphasis on the counseling and personal growth aspects of adventure/ challenge, it may be that the challenge therapy methodology is one variety of psychotherapeutic methodology.

A distinction is usually made between psychotherapy and counseling, with the former being considered for persons who are emotionally disturbed or "mentally ill," and the latter being applied when the clients are more "normal," with situational problems. Some have suggested that counseling differs from psychotherapy in another respect, as it usually requires only a limited number of contacts with the client, whereas psychotherapy involves more contacts over an extended period of time. It has been suggested that adventure counselors need to recognize the difference between counseling and therapy so they can carefully stay "within their level" (Buell, 1983). However, the distinction is hard to maintain, as when considering "family therapy," as opposed to "family counseling," or "marriage therapy" as opposed to "marriage counseling." It may even be that the distinction between therapy and counseling has essentially disappeared through the years as the whole process of facilitation of growth and learning in others has been expanded to include a wide range of strategies.

In the 1960's and 1970's, as the human potential movement unfolded with attention to growth and enrichment groups for everyone, many professionals began to identify themselves as "group leaders," or "growth facilitators" in order to stay clear of any identification with the process of psychotherapy or counseling. Again, as time passed, these distinctions became more difficult to maintain. When is an experience "group therapy," as opposed to "group counseling," or to a "personal growth group?" Certainly, the adventure group experience can be considered as therapy, or counseling, or a personal growth journey.

There may still be value in some of those early attempts to distinguish the offerings. If one uses challenge programming for drug-dependent youth, or for the patients of a psychiatric clinic, then it may be best to consider the method as "challenge therapy." If the clients are special education students, or a group of delinquents, then the term "challenge counseling" may be more appropriate; and if offering an adventure/challenge sequence as part of a college orientation program, or for a group of executives, then it may best be considered "personal growth experience." The distinctions may be difficult to maintain, but they also seem valuable in defining the role of the group leader. With therapy, the aim is usually to bring about some basic changes in the personality and behavior patterns of the client. In such case the leader needs more background in psychodynamics, abnormal behavioral adjustment, and personality development. In counseling, the chief focus is more typically a particular life problem, or seeking to improve human relationships. Then the leader needs less knowledge of psychodynamics and psychopathology and more skill in communication, sensitivity to the emotional states of the clients, and awareness of the nature of the problems and decisions faced. Facilitation of personal growth groups may require more basic monitoring of group interaction, skill in creating open and honest communication, and ability to develop a situation of trust within which the person can risk newness. On the other hand, all of these skills are desirable for any leader dealing with group processes.

Italian psychiatrist Roberto Assagioli has suggested that the appropriate term for all therapists and growth facilitators may well be "guide" (Assagioli, 1973). He advocates that the leader's role is to be flexible and creative in steering the client to awareness of his/her own holistic unfolding, and to help them grow in their own natural patterns. This label for the facilitator of individual or group processes may have some special appeal for adventure/challenge professionals, as they often move toward outdoor sequences as "guides" for the group. Some have even proclaimed that experiential challenge outdoor leaders may have an important role as "therapists for humankind."

There is certainly a need for what has been called "the Transformation"—the process of people evolving to a higher order of humanbeingness (Leonard, 1972; Lock Land, 1973). This growth and learning process may even involve an "evolutionary leap to planetary consciousness" (Russell, 1983). Challenge facilitators may well be viewed as "midwives" or "societal therapists" to the extent that they are a part of:

> A crusading band of spiritually connected peopleworkers who do all they can to prevent and cure the troublesome cancers of the human condition, and attempt to guide people in the most desirable evolutionary paths.   (Smith, 1983)

Outdoor educators with vision have also suggested that there is challenge for all teachers, counselors, and environmentalists:

> Environmental educators are futurists. We seek positive conditions for the future life. Outdoor education's challenge is to gain a perspective on the human role in the mechanism called Earth. (Link, 1981)
>
> Imagine, if we all had the kind of education which helps us put things together as well as take them apart. Our programs would teach us the connections between the earth, sky, and people and how to feel a sense of personal power and to have ideas about how to care for themselves, others, and the planet. (Knapp, 1987)

This role as a guide for the transformation of humankind towards the best that he can become may not even be in consciousness awareness for many outdoor adventure/challenge teachers, counselors, and facilitators. Instead, there may be a "latent" transmission of this goal from leader to client in the adventure sequence (Smith, 1983).

In any case, there is great semantic confusion in searching for appropriate identification of the leaders of the challenge therapy sequences. As there is now recognition of the efficacy and potentialities of "challenge therapy" or "adventure counseling," it must be recognized that those who lead the challenge/adventure sequences are indeed therapists, counselors, growth facilitators and guides for individuals, small groups and perhaps even society in total. However we identify the leader, the conclusion is obvious: Challenge sequence facilitators are leading individuals and groups through powerful and potent psychological, social and spiritual adventures. It is of utmost importance that we attend to the questions of leadership training.

Leadership Requirements for the Challenge Therapist: It has often been argued that good leaders are "born" not "made" (Johnson & Johnson, 1982). If this is the case, then attention and concern for appropriate leadership training for challenge facilitators is for naught; the emphasis should be on selection, not cultivation. However, a conclusion that we need to "discover," not "develop," leaders may result from an erroneous interpretation of the "born" vs. "made" argument. If we accept the humanistic growth model's notion that each of us is "born" anew each moment, each day, then there is a different conclusion to be drawn. Furthermore, an understanding of the whole process of personal growth and self-discovery would suggest that people are indeed capable of giving birth to new energies, new patterns of thought and behavior, and new potentials to be quality leaders. While we cannot "make" leaders, nor develop full leadership potential from without, it is entirely possible for persons to evolve to leadership from within.

The requirements for appropriate leadership of the challenge/adventure group cannot be understated. It has been suggested that challenge leaders may be even more than interventionists for individuals and small groups, but are perhaps "guides for the necessary evolutionary transformation of the human species toward a higher order of human-beingness" (Smith, 1983). Even in less noble perspectives, the role as facilitator of growth and learning journeys for individuals and small groups suggests a major responsibility for the challenge therapist. It is possible to oversee the leadership requirements for challenge/adventure counselors as four dimensional:

1. TECHNICAL SKILLS
2. PEOPLEWORK SKILLS
3. CHARACTER TRAITS
4. PERSONAL GROWTH

The central thesis of this paper is that the training of therapists, counselors, and growth facilitators for the challenge sequence must put major emphasis on the process of personal growth and development. Yes, there is need for learning appropriate technical skills, but all the knowledge that can be collected is of little value if the leader does not possess and cultivate a pattern of personality and behavior that is appropriate, or, as Carl Rogers called it, "a way of being." Yes, there is a need for developing appropriate peoplework skills, but these cannot be mimicked and patterned from a technique orientation. The important character traits that have been emphasized for the adventure/challenge leader cannot be taught, but they can be learned. Emphasizing personal growth programming for future challenge therapists is mandatory.

It is difficult to distinguish between the outdoor adventure leader and the challenge therapist/counselor. It might be that there is relevance in the distinction between two patterns of leadership orientation. It has been noted that there are task-oriented or goal-oriented leaders, and process-oriented or people-oriented leaders. However, it has been noted that there is usually a complex interplay of attention to task and attention to people in most leadership situations. Hersey and Blanchard (1982) have suggested that there is a relationship between the leader's basic job assignment and the desired balance of attention to task or people, goal or process.

It is also possible to view the leadership role for some outdoor adventure pursuits as paralleling that of the expedition leader, with the primary goal of accomplishing the journey safely and as preplanned. Unfortunately, too many facilitators of ropes and teams courses, initiatives, and challenge sequences tend to adopt that orientation, and thus become overly task-oriented. Fortunately, as more adventure facilitators have come to recognize the therapeutic and personal growth potentials of the adventure sequence, there has been greater attention to process. Still, when the adventure program does involve an outdoor journey or a significant number of days or weeks in an unfolding challenge sequence, the leader must often attend to logistics and timetables. The challenge for leaders is to blend attention to task with careful attention to the people in process. It has been suggested that as an adventure group evolves through a sequence or journey the leader often changes emphasis from task to people dependent on the group's development and the nature of the situations at hand (Phipps, 1986).

Certainly, when the development of the adventure/challenge program is for therapeutic impact or personal growth facilitation, then primary attention must be on the people in process. It matters little if the group gets over the wall or not, there is learning in the process. Still, most of the literature on the training of adventure leaders has been concerned with task, and there has typically been an emphasis on learning "skills" for leadership, as opposed to cultivation of a potential leader's humanbeingness.

(1) Technical Skills: The "hard skills" required for adventure and challenge leadership were the first given attention by the professionals. More than ten years ago, when more and more people began facilitating outdoor adventure and challenge education programs which involved risks, the issues of safety, risk management, liability, and appropriate leadership qualifications were discussed (Meyer, 1979; Van der Smissen, 1979; James, 1980). The Association for Experiential Education (AEE) had working committees by the end of the 1970's which were attempting to develop professional standards and guidelines. The final summarization of *Common Practices in Adventure Programming* offered recommendations for facilitation of groups in various adventure activities (Johanson, 1984). Basically, the general guideline for group leaders is quite straightforward. Those who lead groups should have adequate training and considerable experience with the tasks they facilitate. In other words, if you facilitate groups at rockclimbing, you need solid background in the technical skills involve with rockclimbing; if you facilitate groups through teams courses and ropes courses, then you should have experience and training in that methodology—and be familiar with the spe-

cifics of each particular teams or ropes course; and if you utilize initiative games, or relaxation and movement exercises, then you should have solid experience with those strategies (Buell, 1981; Green, 1981; Swiderski, 1981; Stich & Gaylor, 1984; Ewert, 1984; Phipps, 1986).

This recommendation was voiced throughout the 1980's, and was summarized in *Islands of Healing*:

> ...leaders should have training and experience necessary to lead each specific group and should not lead a group that is beyond their scope of training and experience...leaders need to be aware of the boundaries of their professional competence...   (Schoel, et al., 1988)

Leaders of adventure sequences should also have knowledge of rescue techniques and emergency procedures appropriate for the activities they facilitate, and most adventure/challenge professionals should also have regular first aid and CPR certification. The AEE publication has become a standard for challenge leaders, in spite of criticisms and controversy about the simplicity and/or idealism of many of the recommendations. It certainly does provide a detailed breakdown of technical skill requirements for many of the more commonly used outdoor adventure activities.

Obviously, there are other dimensions to the hard skills involved in challenge leadership. Leaders need the skills involved in program organization and administration. This may include knowledge of appropriate equipment and equipment repair, the logistics of guiding a group through hours or days of adventure, and the selection and training of associate leaders. In his careful study of out-

door leadership, Simon Priest noted that the leader's ability to teach others the complexity of skills for the adventure may be a highest-order technical skill itself (Priest, 1987).

The hard skills required for effective leadership need to be learned experientially, for there are so many variations in situations. One can read volumes about whitewater canoeing, but know very little until there are some direct experiences.

Furthermore, there are very different hard skills for each outdoor pursuit. Although the whitewater canoeing has been learned, there are few applications to the rock climbing bluff or the cave experience.

There are, however, some general hard skills that need be learned by all adventure leaders. One of the earliest overviews to hard skills in adventure and challenge programming suggested a five-fold subclassification, as shown below:

1. **Physiological Skills—knowledge of health, proper clothing and shelter, first aid, medications, etc.**
2. **Environmental Skills—knowledge of weather systems, geography, environmental ethics, ecological balance, etc.**
3. **Safety Skills —knowledge of ropes, rescue methodology, supervision of the clients, etc.**
4. **Technical Skills—training and adequate experience with the activities before the group, etc.**
5. **Administrative Skills—paperwork abilities, organizational skills, staff selection and training, etc.**

Michael Swiderski has argued that because the hard skills are "the most visual of

leadership skills, and the skills most easily taught and evaluated, they are often over-emphasized within outdoor leadership training programs" (Swiderski, 1987). Perhaps this is so, for the hard skills have been given considerable attention by the major outdoor leadership training programs (Outward Bound, National Outdoor Leadership School, Wilderness Education Association, etc.). However, one must be careful to say that these skills have been "over-emphasized" in the training of adventure/challenge leaders. After all, issues of health, safety, adequate client training, and adequate client supervision are extremely important for the adventure leader. Granting the need to expand leadership training, there should certainly not be any deemphasis on the acquisition of the technical skills.

The hard skills required for leadership of the various adventure and challenge programs provide those leaders with a unique identification among human service professionals. It is this knowledge of special outdoor activities, wilderness treks, facilitating safe and growth-producing group interaction on the ropes and teams course, and guiding people through challenge sequences which defines the adventure/challenge leader as offering a special pattern of counseling.

Through the years, as the profession gave attention to the hard skill requirements of adventure leadership, there was discussion and debate about the necessity and possibility of "certification." The work of the AEE committees through the late 1970's and early 1980's was seen as an effort to put forth some standards for outdoor adventure leadership which could lead to a certification process. However, because of the broad range of activities and procedures which make up outdoor challenge programming and the diverse number of professionals who were utilizing the methodologies, there has not been an end to the "debate" over certification (Cockrell & LaFollette, 1985; Hunt, 1985). The difficulty in reaching any sort of consensus about leadership requirements resulted in the AEE project finally being summarized as "acceptable peer practices," with notation that the guidelines provided for various adventure activities were not hard and fast rules, and did not imply any sort of certification. At the end of the 1980's the emphasis had shifted to attempt to find alternative ways for monitoring the adventure/ challenge leader, or procedures for certification of particular skills involved in outdoor pursuits (Priest, 1987, 1988).

(2) Peoplework Skills: In recognition of the many psychological and social aspects of the challenge group experience, there was also early attention given to the challenge leaders' need for "Soft Skills."

> In selecting instructors we need to look beyond their technical skill ability and background, and seriously look at their human relations or soft skills... including observation and listening skills. (Weider, 1979)

In spite of this recognition, there has been considerably less discussion about, and delineation of, the requirements of such leadership. In the AEE publication of nearly two hundred pages there is less than a page devoted to peoplework skills. The recommendations are quite broad:

> Instructors should be able to: demonstrate appropriate interpersonal communication skills and relationships; offer and accept feedback; acknowledge and resolve conflicts; exhibit cooperation, compromise, and compassion.
> Instructors should be able to demonstrate knowledge of basic group dynamics and group facilitation techniques.
> Instructors should be perceptive to individual needs, personalities, limitations, potentials, and capacities for work, and be able to make decisions in a group context.
> Instructors should be able to debrief program activities and teach problem solving in order to promote decision making and cooperation.
> Instructors should demonstrate respect for others' rights, standards, and styles.   (Johanson, 1984)

Many challenge education leaders have noted the difficulty in defining the exact nature of these complex peoplework skills (Brannan, et al., 1984; Robb, et al., 1985; Priest, 1987). Swiderski (1987) suggests that the soft skills could be subdivided into the following three areas:

1. Psychological Skills—understanding personality dynamics and individual differences, working with client fears, problems
2. Social Skills—understanding group dynamics, skills for the resolution of conflicts, knowledge of cultural differences, etc.
3. Communication Skills—good listening skills, knowledge of non-verbal

language, capability to lead debriefing sessions, giving clear messages, etc.

Much of the attention to development of the soft skills needed for good challenge group facilitation has focused on the task of debriefing or processing the group experiences. It has been recognized that good leaders should be able to facilitate profitable sharing discussions and group meetings that guide participants towards personal and interpersonal growth (Quinsland & Van Ginkel, 1984; Knapp, 1986; Hammel, 1986; Jordan, 1987; Roland, 1987).

Challenge counselors must be able to demonstrate sensitive listening, and be able to guide many different individuals toward new awareness and personal insights. It has also been suggested that good processing leadership may involve the facilitation of alternatives to the group sharing circle. At times, there may be advantage of cultivating dyads or triads, spending time in a 1-1 interaction, or steering participants toward an introspective "solo" time (Smith, 1987). The value of the leader structuring time for individuals to selfprocess their experience was earlier noted by Thomas James, as he asked the question, *Can the Mountains Speak for Themselves?* (James, 1980).

Methodologies from small group theory have been suggested for application to the challenge group process (Jensen, 1979; Gass, 1983; Kerr & Gass, 1987; Schoel, et al., 1988). There have also been numerous references to values clarification methodology (Simon et al., 1972), exercises for the enhancement of self-concept (Canfield & Wells, 1976), and fantasy games (Otto, 1972). Techniques for relaxation (Stevens, 1971; White & Fadiman, 1976; Fensterman, 1981), and cen-

tering (Hendricks & Wills, 1975, 1980) have been considered valuable for challenge leaders. It has been suggested that challenge leaders should, in fact, go outside the adventure/challenge movement to find soft skill methodologies that work with their groups.

Instead of reinventing the wheel to meet our professional needs, we should borrow from those professions which are adept in soft and conceptual skills. A selected list of professions includes the fields of education, psychology, philosophy, counseling, sociology, speech communication, military sciences and business management. By tapping into these interdisciplinary resources, their literature and textual references, we can expand our awareness of soft skill components and integrate them into our current leadership training curriculums. (Swiderski, 1987)

Unfortunately, even though soft skills have been recognized as being important for challenge group facilitation, there has been misinterpretation of the need by leaders in the field. Many saw the problem as one of needing a second set of skills, or techniques, in parallel with the hard skills. Leaders had learned appropriate knots for belay lines, safety considerations for whitewater, proper instructions for "trust falls," and procedures for the organization of "new games" or "sun exercises" for warm-up and group building.

They had taken the first aid courses, and obtained CPR certification. Now the task was to learn how to ask appropriate processing questions, structure group interactions that would resolve conflicts, and offer exercises for value clarification. All too often, the field leader sought out a "cookbook" of appropriate activities and debriefing questions. All too often, the young leader asked for help in developing a new "bag of tricks" that could be easily incorporated into the challenge group process.

And, all too often, the leadership responded. Perhaps a few "unreferenced" statements from leadership manuals, professional publications, and idea notebooks will serve to exemplify:

The following questions, organized by specific program objectives, are designed to assist leaders in more effectively processing experiential activities...
To guide the group toward deferring any judgement of others, ask: "Can you think of examples of when you judged others in the group today?"
To explore issues of trust, ask: "How do you increase your level of trust for someone?"

Or, from a training manual, specifications for the facilitator's role:

Observe body language...give appreciation to others...establish the fact that each individual is unique and different...watch your posture and body language...if you look interested, so do they.

Or, "some tactics for dealing with conflict are:"

Keep a sense of humor, and have fun...remove a group member...be a good actor...if the group needs to know you are disappointed, then be disappointed...with-hold...we will go no further until we get a grip on ourselves...

"Men of good will should not have formulas" (Krishnamurti). It was a good many years ago that Carl Rogers suggested that there really was no "technique" for facilitating the clientcentered counseling group. He gave the suggestion that there was only a "way of being," and often argued against having his ideology included in books on "techniques of psychotherapy." In one of his last writings, he suggested that the label "person-centered approach" might be most descriptive, although he continued to maintain that there were no formula or cookbook prescriptions for development of such an approach (Rogers, 1980).

In spite of those reflections, people frequently suggest that the "techniques" of the client-centered approach have application for groupwork in a variety of settings. For example, in reference to development of "effective helping" practices in recreation leaders, Okum writes, "Many of the skills of client-centered therapy may be applied in the daily practice of therapeutic recreation" (Okum, 1976). Many of those seeking to develop good training programs for adventure/challenge leaders with attention to the soft skills fall into the same trap.

Developing the skills necessary for appropriate growth group facilitation is more than a cognitive exercise, and our goals will not be met by the mimicking of peoplework skills as summarized by someone else. Both the trainers of challenge leaders and the field facilitators need to know that there is much more to the development of soft skills than learning a few new techniques for one's "bag of tricks." Basically, what is required is a cultivation of one's personal human-beingness. For Rogers,

a basic key to application of the person-centered approach is the "authenticity" of the person. One cannot "be a good actor," nor "look interested" if that is not the case. One cannot take out a list of the appropriate processing questions and lead group discussion. The important thing to do is to be.

(3) Character Traits: Through the past decade, there has been identification and discussion of a number of basic personality, attitudinal, and character traits desirable for the challenge/adventure leader. Any discussion of character traits for challenge facilitators should definitely be prefaced by noting that there is very little research to support claims that particular characteristics do contribute to more effective leadership. Some of the suggested characteristics for effective leadership might have a consensual validation within the adventure/challenge leadership, but some others may not. The diversity of recommended competencies for outdoor leaders is obvious in a table of summarization offered by Ewert, and shown in Table 1.

There are competencies that are representative of both hard skills and soft skills, but also reference to various personality and character traits.

Obviously, competencies in the domain of "judgment," "empathy," "environmental ethic," and other personality and character traits are very difficult to clearly define. It should be recognized that such characteristics of leadership are not "skills" which can be easily taught to the prospective challenge facilitator. Certainly, they are not learned by future challenge therapists; they are character traits of the person. They are attributes, attitudes, value orientations, and qualities which have developed, or need to be devel-

209

AN OUTDOOR LEADER SHOULD BE COMPETENT IN:					
McAvoy 1978	Green 1981	Swiderski 1981	Buell 1983	Ewert/Johnston 1983	Priest 1987
Decision making	Analyzing risks	Outdoor techniques	Evaluation	Judgment	Judgment
Judgment	Judgment	Navigation	Outdoor skills	Outdoor skills	Awareness empathy
Outdoor skills	Risk management	Shelter building	Human growth	Human resources	Teaching
Group skills	Minimum impact	Clothing equipment	Safety skills	Medical skills	Group skills
Safety skills	First-aid		Program planning	Personality	Problem solving
			Environmental ethics		

TABLE 1: Reported Competencies of Outdoor Leaders (after Ewert, 1989)

oped, over a long period of time. While they are modifiable and capable of cultivation, they most typically require a learning and experiential process through a long period of time.

There has also been recommendation for leaders to be "charismatic," "self-confident," "sensitive," "genuine," "warm," and "supportive." Such characteristics are not only difficult to define, but difficult to quantify for any validation research. However, there has been considerable discussion about some of these character traits.

(A) JUDGMENT: The quality of perceptive, sensitive, and informed judgment was early recognized as a necessary characteristic for adventure leaders. In the early 1980's, when major emphasis was on the hard skills necessary for outdoor leadership, and much attention was given to the development of

standards and guidelines, Jasper Hunt warned of "the dangers of substituting rules for instructor judgment" (Hunt, 1984). In recent years, the leadership training courses offered by Outward Bound, the National Outdoor Leadership School, and the Wilderness Education Association have emphasized the importance of good judgment in outdoor leadership.

In his review of the qualities of effective challenge leadership, Swiderski (1987) suggests that there are a number of "components" to the desired good judgment, including:

...recognizing potential problems...
...perceiving potential dangers...
...analyzing alternatives...
...anticipating the unexpected...
...analytical and creative problem
    solving...

210

(B) CREATIVITY: Swiderski also suggests another clustering of leadership behaviors that have to do with creativity:

...generating new ideas...
...foresee and visualize the
    nonexistent...
...perceive trends...
...improve equipment and shelter...
...make repairs in an emergency...

Simon Priest has offered an analysis of the role of judgment, decision making, and problem solving for outdoor leaders (1988). He attempts to clarify the differences between these important ingredients of adventure leadership, and raises the important question as to whether or not the judgement can be taught, or only cultivated by experience.

(C) GENDER CONSCIOUSNESS: In recent years our society has focused much attention on problems and issues related to gender. This highly desirable trend has helped us identify and develop initial solutions for the inequities and imbalances which have blocked us from becoming highest-quality human beings. It is also important to attend to the issues of gender because they do, in fact, affect the whole group in process of challenge/adventure. Unfortunately, the field of adventure education was too long dominated by males, and a masculinity orientation. Only a few years ago, one summer camp boasted a "100% man award," given to those campers who could successfully meet a series of challenges and risks. No wonder that Cliff Knapp suggested that "escape from the gender gap" may be "the ultimate challenge for experiential educators" (Knapp, 1985).

It has been noted that "the issue of gender is considerably more complex than it might

appear at first sight" (Humberstone, 1986). The issue was given attention by educators in the early 1980's, with arguments about the lack of female role models in the schools (especially in physical education), the desirability of mixed-gender groups, societal prejudices against girls in risk-taking and adventure pursuits, and the responsibility for the whole field of education to recognize and deal with the androgynous nature of people (Marland, 1983; Whyld, 1983; Whyte, 1985).

The whole issue was soon given attention in the specific field of outdoor education and adventure programming (Yerkes, 1985; Ball, 1986; Humberstone, 1986; Henderson & Bialeschki, 1987; Bartley, 1987; Bartley & Williams, 1988; Estes & Ewert, 1988). It was noted that the imbalance of men over women leaders, and of men over women participants, was quite undesirable for the adventure programs. Furthermore, it was suggested that these imbalances, gender prejudices, and misunderstanding of androgyny, changed the potential effectiveness of the whole challenge experience for individuals, and limited the possibilities of adventure group experiences impacting on the gender problems of society-at-large. Estes and Ewert (1988) noted that:

Experiential education organizations have traditionally conducted their programs with little regard to perceived or real differences due to gender. Gender differences can be manifested in differences in expectations, communications, motivations, perceptions, and attributions for success.

They give suggestions for challenge/adventure group leaders:

...recognize that females and males are different not so much in abilities and competencies, but more in motivations and perceptions...

...design program goals and objectives to attain a mix by giving equal attention to masculine and feminine aspects.....

...strive to make instructors and students aware of how sex-role stereotypes influence their behavior... and make conscious efforts to downplay these roles...

...employ male and female staff at all levels of the program... (Estes & Ewert, 1988)

Research on the gender issue as effecting the adventure group is limited, but Bartley has studied the interactions of gender, personality, soft skill training, and leadership style; and the influence of these variables on the outcome of the challenge/adventure sequence. A basic conclusion of that study was that careful training of leader/facilitators in some of the peoplework skills (listening, accepting, supporting, etc.), and cultivating some of the desirable character traits for effective leadership (sensitivity, empathy, regard for the integrity of others, etc.) would help move those facilitators in desirable directions on the gender issues. It was also suggested that pairing group facilitators, male and female, might be quite beneficial for both leaders and the participants in group adventure (Bartley, 1987; Bartley & Williams, 1988).

As there has been attention to the gender issues in relationship to adventure/challenge programming, a recommendation for leadership emerges. The challenge facilitator/therapist should possess, or develop, a character trait that can be considered "gender consciousness." This implies awareness of, and attention to:

...personal gender schema and androgyny...

...the gender schema and androgyny of others...

...the influence of gender schema and androgyny on the groups facilitated.....

...the desirability for the whole profession of challenge therapy to pay close attention to the issues of gender.....

(D) PLANETARY CONSCIOUSNESS: Another character trait desirable for the challenge group facilitator is that of keen awareness of, and attention to, the interrelationships and interdependencies of all things. For many years, the professionals in outdoor education, environmental education, experiential education, and adventure education have attended to the issues of ecological balance and psycho-ecological harmony. The past quarter century has brought about new explorations and new understanding of the world beyond our world, the universe. As we expand our interactional boundaries, reaching out to the very limits of space, it is obvious that we must not only give more consideration to the nature of our relationship to the earth and all that it is, but we also must expand our consideration to the universe. The nature of planetary consciousness is such that it includes the heretofore-considered "earth wisdom" and a broader vision of the cosmos and a search for a personal cosmology.

There are a number of ways to cultivate this pattern of consciousness, many of which have already infiltrated the ideology and practices of the adventure leadership. A prime example is the thought, ritual, and cosmological orientation of the Native American Indians. Although there was diversity in belief and ceremony from tribe to tribe, there were some common themes reflected in most of the

Native Americans. In fact, many of these themes and belief systems are also reflected in other primitive cultures. Certainly, some of the desirable patterns of consciousness about the connectedness of all things have been voiced by the Native Americans:

> All things of the universe have spirit and life, including the rivers, rocks, earth, sky, plants, and animals....... Our teachers tell us that all things within this Universe know of their harmony with every other thing, and know how to give away one to the other, except man... It is we alone who do not begin our lives with knowledge of this great harmony...(and)...our determining spirit can be made whole only through the learning of our harmony with all the other spirits of the Universe... To do this we must learn to seek and to perceive. We must do this to find our place within the medicine wheel. Any idea, person, or object can be a medicine wheel, a mirror for man. The tiniest flower can be such a mirror, as can a wolf, a story, a touch, a religion, or a mountain top...
>
> The medicine wheel is the total universe... We must all follow our vision quest to discover ourselves, and to find our relationship with the world around us. (Storm, 1972)
>
> We haven't yet comprehended, as have the Indians, the psychical ecology underlying physical ecology. As I see it, we must graduate to this belief, to attune ourselves to both inner and outer realities of life if we are to close the widening rupture between our minds and hearts. By rupture, I mean this: In ruthlessly destroying nature, man, who is also part of nature, ruptures his own inner self... So it seems to me we've got to learn from the Indians. We've got to listen to the voice of the secret and invisible spirit of the land itself. (Waters, 1973)
>
> Teach us to know and to see all the powers of the universe, and give to us the knowledge to understand that they are really one Power... The first peace, which is the most important, is that which comes

within the souls of men when they realize their relationship, their oneness, with the universe and all its Powers... (Black Elk, 1961)

Many outdoor educators have long recognized the value of incorporating Native American ritual and ceremony into their programs, and many summer camps are formatted after the Indian's appreciation for "Mother Earth." It has been suggested that these practices may also have potential as format for personal growth groups (Smith, 1979a, 1979b, 1979c, 1979d, 1979e, 1981).

The Native American Indians tended to have a conceptual overview to life that stressed man in harmony with the universe, man in balance with the world he was a flowing part of, man in harmony with his fellow man, and man in balance with himself... Some of the rituals and ceremonies of the Native American Indians seem to have potential for modern man...the search for new ways to enhance the growth and learning of others can lead the group facilitator to explore models for workshop or growth sequence that utilize interactional and selfexploratory exercises loosely based on the practices of the Native Americans. (Smith, 1979a)

Challenge education workshops and publications have made a good deal of reference to the cosmological overview of the Native Americans. There are numerous references to

Black Elk Speaks (Neihardt & Black Elk, 1961); *Seven Arrows* (Storm, 1972); *Rolling Thunder* (Boyd, 1974); *Earth Wisdom* (LaChapelle, 1978); and *The Medicine Wheel: Earth Astrology* (Sun Bear & Wabun,1980). Certainly, the cosmological overview of the Native American Indian can guide one to an understanding of the planetary consciousness desirable for all leaders of adventure/challenge sequences.

There is a second body of literature and ideology that can provide cultivation of planetary consciousness. This can be considered "Transformation Theory." Long ago, Teilhardt de Chardin, a theologian and evolutionist, predicted that some people would develop a new state of consciousness, toward which the human species would evolve. Quite simplified, his argument was that humankind has evolved to a crucial point of awareness of his own evolution, which would be reflected in a consciousness of his place in the universe (Hefner, 1970).

Other forecasters of this inevitable transformation of the very consciousness of man have been summarized and reviewed by Marilyn Ferguson in *The Aquarian Conspiracy*. Her historical review includes reference to the following:

> *Cosmic Consciousness*, written in 1901, by Richard Bucke, an American physician, described the experience of an electrifying awareness of oneness with all life...
>
> Ludwig von Bertalanffy, a German biologist, framed a view of science he first called perspectivism, later General Systems Theory, which sees all of nature— including human behavior—as interconnected...
>
> In *The Transformation* George Leonard described the current period as unique

in history, the beginnings of the most thoroughgoing change in the quality of human existence since the birth of civilized states...

> In *Person/Planet*, Theodore Roszak states that the needs of the planet are the needs of the person, and the rights of the person are the rights of the planet. (Ferguson, 1980)

Cliff Knapp has noted that part of the answers to those very basic questions of all people about life and living can be seen to hinge on "a recognition that humans and the rest of nature are integrally connected." He summarizes and sets forth a challenge:

> Some visionaries have noted that humankind is integrally connected to the universe. This recognition is critical to our survival on earth. (My) purposes are to illustrate some of the connections that people have with the planet, and to challenge outdoor-environmental educators to promote this concept in their programs. (Knapp, 1987)

Peter Russell has defined the evolutional transformation as development of "the Global Brain," and suggests that the species is, indeed, about to make an "evolutionary leap to planetary consciousness" (Russell, 1983). Transformation theory is filled with hope and challenge for all who are involved in personal journeys along the trails of life, and also for all who facilitate the growth and development journeys of others. Knapp's challenge to the outdoor-environmental educators must certainly be extended to the adventure/challenge growth facilitators and therapists.

The third body of knowledge that can help us cultivate a planetary consciousness is that considered ecology, environmental education, outdoor education, and/or environmental ethics. There is a long history of attention to the manworld interdependency. Some of the significant historical points were noted by Roth, Cantrell, and Bousquet, in an article for *Fifty Years of Resident Outdoor Education: 1930-1980* (Hammerman, 1980).

...Rachel Carson's *Silent Spring*...

...Adlai Stevenson's "Spaceship Earth" address to the United Nations...

...The first "Earth Day" in 1970...

...The United Nations Intergovernmental Conference on Environmental Education, which identified among the guiding principles: "A basic aim of environmental education is to succeed in making individuals and communities understand the complex nature of the natural and built environments resulting from the interaction of their biological, physical, social, economic, and cultural aspects (Roth, Cantrell, & Bousquet, 1980).

There was also significance in the Environmental Education Act of 1970, which gave the following description of the issues to be dealt with by environmental educators:

> Environmental education is an integrated process which deals with man's interrelationship with his natural and man-made surroundings, including the relation of pollution, population growth, resource allocation and depletion, conservation, technology, and urban and rural planning to the total human environment. Environmental education is intended to promote among citizens the awareness of the environment, our relationship to it, and the concern necessary to assure our survival and improve quality of life. (U. S. Congress, 1970. *Environmental Education Act of 1970*)

Roszak's *Person/Planet* made a strong statement for the absolute necessity of humans developing a planetary consciousness: it was simply a matter of survival. This same point had been suggested earlier in the classic *Sand County Almanac* by Aldo Leopold. In his discussion of the ethical sequence, which he saw as unfolding from concern about relationships between individuals, to relationships between individuals and society, and finally to relationships between people and the earth. He wrote:

> There is yet no ethic dealing with man's relationship to land and to the animals and plants which grow upon it. The extension of ethics to this third element in human environment is, if I read the evidence correctly, an evolutionary possibility and an ecological necessity. A land ethic simply enlarges boundaries of the community to include soils, waters, plants, and animals, or collectively: the land. (Leopold, 1949)

It might be hypothesized that Leopold would have expanded his definition of the collective to include the universe, if he had known of the imminent opening of the frontiers of space. Or, perhaps, he would have seen a fourth step to his ethical sequence.

Quite obviously, humankind is not going to wake up one morning filled with a new planetary consciousness and concern for appropriate behaviors. It will most likely be as predicted by Teilhardt de Chardin, that a "conspiracy of individuals" would lead the way. According to Teilhardt, certain individuals, attracted to a transcendent vision of the future and to each other, will lead others forward to this larger awareness.

Challenge facilitators who cultivate their own planetary consciousness will not only model appropriate awareness and behavior for group participants, they may seek out designs and methodologies for experiential sequences which can guide participants towards their personal awareness of earth and cosmos.

John Breeding has suggested that those who become truly powerful survivors in their own right will shake free of the traditional belief of Western science and technology, the belief that "we can bring nature ever more under our control since it is so clearly separate and external to us," and will adopt the awareness that "we are truly connected rather than truly separate." He notes that at the very time that we are creating "horrendous planetary debacles," we are also involved in the creation of an unprecedented movement of personal growth within which many people are transforming themselves and developing new levels of awareness about self, others, and environment. Breeding suggests that this puts a challenge before experiential educators and adventure group facilitators:

> ...Our best chance of survival is through creation of survivors; people who are developing their full potentials as human beings... The earth does need our wisdom to heal...
>
> The people of this planet are moving forward: there is no other way... It is up to us to help emerge new human beings who are synergistic... (Breeding, 1985)

(E) ETHICAL CONSCIOUSNESS: While both gender consciousness and planetary consciousness have ethical components, there is a still broader scope of value and behavior which requires ethical attention. In the past few years, as the whole challenge/adventure movement has matured, there has been a beginning attention to both personal and professional ethics for adventure group facilitators. Although it is not often stated directly, it is certainly always implied that challenge group leaders will be ethical in conduct. Ethical consciousness implies that the field leader will be continually attempting to understand and apply the available code of decision making and conduct of the profession of adventure/challenge programming, and will also be engaged in an ongoing journey of exploration of personal ethics.

The issues of ethics have been discussed under two separate but related orientations. First, it has been suggested that there is need for the development of a code of conduct for adventure/challenge leaders (Fain, 1984; Havens, 1985, 1986, 1987; Havens & Fain, 1986; Smith, 1988). Second, there has been attention to the need for field leaders to examine their own ethical dilemmas and the value-influenced decisions they face in daily program practice, and cultivate their personal ethical orientations (Hunt, 1986; Robb, et al., 1988; Smith, 1988).

The foundations of ethics are often traced to Socrates' comment as he faced death that "the unexamined life is not worth living." It has been suggested that field facilitators of challenge sequences might well consider that "the unexamined practice is not worth practicing" (Smith, 1988). Certainly, as individual practitioners search for personal ethics, they should be influenced by the available code of conduct and standards of their profession. Fain has noted:

> Those who seriously engage in the helping professions—social work, medicine, psychology, or other human service field—discuss, struggle, and learn to live with the discipline of conduct established by peers. (Fain, 1984)

216

Examination of the sequential development of ethical codes by other professions can provide suggestions and models for the adventure program movement (Havens, 1986). Although focusing on the particular field of therapeutic recreation programming in the natural environment, the suggestions for action suggested by Havens have relevance to the whole field of adventure/challenge programming:

(1) Collection of case data relating to the ethical dilemmas faced by practitioners of outdoor programs.

(2) Establishment of procedures for a nationally coordinated effort, allowing for practitioners to report cases of an ethical nature.

(3) Careful analysis and dissemination of data by the practitioners and committees to insure that the moral philosophical foundations of programming in the natural environment is better understood (Havens, 1985).

A more elaborate system for small group discussion and problem solving, considered as Critical Incident Methodology (CMI) has been suggested:

(1) Development of an information survey, to identify personal issues with regard to ethics...and some actual crisis situations faced in the field.

(2) Development of a list of actual field problems that create ethical dilemmas.

(3) Utilization of these field problems and dilemmas in workshop format with adventure professionals.

(4) Summarization of the discussions and decisions of problem solving groups, enabling further development of both the critical situations and the decisions made by professionals.

(5) Utilization of this "improved" list of problems and solutions in further small group workshops. i.e., circling back and through steps 3-4-5 repeatedly.

(6) At some point, leaders in the profession of adventure programming would attempt summarization of the results of the field discussions, in an effort to develop an initial overview to conduct standards (Smith, 1988).

Field workshops have been offered which involve the sort of small group discussion of ethical dilemmas suggested by Havens and Smith (Robb, et al., 1988; Havens, 1989, Havens & Smith, 1989). As such efforts continue, there should be evolution of a code of conduct for professionals in the adventure/challenge programs. In addition, the discussion workshops offered in the field should kindle the fires of ethical reflection in individual challenge sequence leaders.

A significant dimension of ethical consciousness has to do with the individual struggling with the question of how to cultivate ethical consciousness. An early awareness brings up questions such as: How should one seek the right, the good, the moral, the ethical? Does one wait passively for others to set down a code of conduct? Does one find a noble guru to give guidelines for appropriate behavior? Or does one begin by examining personal issues and ethical dilemmas in daily efforts? Does one open the doorways to ethical consciousness by reflections on personal behaviors?

217

Hunt's manual of Ethical Issues in Experiential Education states as goals:

> to encourage experiential education practitioners to reflect carefully about the ethical issues in their profession... and...lead to a clear way of thinking about ethical issues in experiential education... (Hunt, 1986)

His discussion gives the individual field leader opportunity to focus on the ethical issues involved with facilitation of high-risk activities, individual vs. group benefit, environmental impact, secrecy and deception, and other real field concerns.

Certainly, the cultivation of ethical consciousness is not an easy process; and it must be recognized that the individual's journey through reflective thought about the "right" behaviors, attitudes, decisions, and facilitation procedures is never-ending.

> It would be nice if the process of attending to the ethics of challenge programming was simply one of attending to the writings and debates that have gone before, or spending a day atop the mountain in deep meditative search for conduct principles, or copying down the code of conduct of others. Such efforts may give starting points, or enable us to begin the journey a bit further along the road, but there is no substitute for that long and evolutional trek that must unfold. While it may be a new journey for most adventure leaders and challenge facilitators (we have been busy doing, and not always thinking very much about what we were doing), it can be as exciting as any new adventure.   (Smith, 1988)

(4) Personal Growth: There is still another aspect of importance to the training of challenge group facilitators. It could perhaps be considered another character trait for good leadership, as it certainly has similarity with the aforementioned "gender consciousness," "planetary consciousness," and "ethical consciousness." In such case, it would be appropriately considered "personal growth consciousness," and defined as an awareness of, and attention to, one's ongoing personal growth. However, because of its major importance in leadership development, and because it is an essential process for appropriate cultivation of the other desirable character traits and many of the important peoplework skills, it deserves separate classification.

A comprehensive education and training program for challenge therapists must provide students with personal growth experiences. A meaningful component for in-service training and continuing education of leaders in the field would be personal growth sequences. For the adventure group leader at work in a field station with limited in-service programming, there would be recommendation to reach out for a supportive network which includes personal growth opportunities. It is necessary for the facilitator of growth and learning of others to be keenly aware of personal needs, values, conflicts, motivations, and the growth journey within themselves. Challenge therapists need to have experienced the challenges, the fears, the pains—and the excitements, the energies, and the joys—of personal growth. In one's personal journey to the wilderness within, one finds awareness of the vibrant and dynamic growth force that cries out for release in all people.

Christian existential philosopher Soren Kierkegaard long ago described an essential element of the human drama, which was that human beings had untold possibilities for growth, change, and development within themselves. Moreover, these hidden inner possibilities could become more richly and fully realized to the extent that the individual learned to free self from the tyranny of others and the environment (Hanna, 1970).

The humanistic psychologies of Maslow, Rogers, Allport, May, and others have also recognized this growth potential within each person. It exists in all persons, often hidden beneath the defensive armor and avoidance behavior that we develop to protect the self, but which now block the release of growth potential. A poetic description of this inner pattern of vibrancy, awaiting release and transformation, has been offered by George Leonard:

> Of what is the world made? Underlying everything, forming itself into what we call electrons, neutrons, and all the rest, obliterating basic distinctions between matter and energy, substance and spirit, joining all manifestation in common origin and cause, there is the elemental vibrancy. Let us say that substance is vibrancy tending toward transformation. All existence—whether mountain, star, self—is vibrancy. (Leonard, 1972)

The theory and practice of Psychosynthesis, as developed by Roberto Assagioli, also speculates that there is a natural tendency toward growth, and that the person can—and should—attend to and cooperate with this natural tendency toward growth and development through states of awareness. The maximization of growth and learning involves the person actively participating, choosing self-direction and selfdevelopment strategies, and carefully noting personal progress (Assagioli, 1971).

In a journal of theory and practice for psychosynthesis, Albert Szent-Gyorgyi, re-search biologist, twice awarded the Nobel Prize, described his conception of "innate drive in living matter," with remarkable parallel to the words of George Leonard. He outlines research to suggest a process of "syntropy," which involves cells evolving toward "higher and higher levels of organization, order, and dynamic harmony" (Szent-Gyorgyi, 1974).

The chains that would try to prevent full development of the individual cannot be broken from without, but as the person finds awareness of energies and potentialities those chains cannot withstand the vibrant growth force from within. Growth facilitators seek to provide individuals and groups with experiences which will enable them to find that self-awareness. One of the long-suggested guidelines for outdoor leaders has to do with never leading a group over trails or through experiences that they have not previously traveled themselves. This has been called "common grounding" (Schoel, et al., 1988).

Each challenge counselor must, therefore, have a keen awareness of the search (the process), and the energy, potency, and unfolding potential (the product) of personal growth journeys. They must also be aware, of course, of the uniqueness of their own personness, and the uniqueness of their particular growth journey. All of this can only be learned by direct experiences in personal growth sequences.

In spite of the importance of personal growth experiences for challenge/adventure facilitators, there has been but limited attention to this aspect of leadership training. In *Islands of Healing* it is noted:

219

Many effective adventure leaders have never participated in group or individual counseling. Yet, because of the kinds of persons they are, they instinctively provide powerful growth experiences and counseling insights for their clients. But untrained intuition can lead to hunches, projection, or even cultural bias. What conclusions can we draw from this, then? We recommend that practitioners gain experience as participants in counseling or therapy groups. (Schoel, et al., 1988)

Such requirement for the challenge therapist is quite in line with historical traditions for other therapists. It began with Freud and psychoanalysis, for he required the physician or psychologist who wished to become an analyst to undergo a complete analysis themselves. Professionally-trained clinical psychologists and psychiatric social workers also partake of both individual and group counseling experiences as part of their training. In academic programs for psychologists, counselors, and other human service professionals, courses in group dynamics or group counseling often take the form of an experiential unfolding of a group in process. In general, students of therapy and counseling are encouraged to partake of a variety of personal growth experiences, such as retreat weekends, special Gestalt workshops, or values clarification seminars.

Personal Growth experiences enable the challenge therapist to explore gender schemas, ethical orientations, and even relationships to the earth and universe. These experiences can provide one with the opportunity to break down personal barriers to growth and higherorder consciousness.

If we begin with the premise that man is an alien in the cosmos, then all we can do is strengthen the walls that keep us within our self-imposed prisons and learn to cope with our loneliness. But true therapy consists of ridding ourselves of the illusions of individuality and dissolving our egocentricism into cosmic consciousness. (Oscar Ichazo, 1973)

In *Islands of Healing*, after making the recommendation that adventure counseling leaders should have personal growth and/or counseling group experiences, the authors contemplate that the recommendation may not be well-received. They continue:

Resistance to this direct experience can be overcome by viewing the counseling group as a time for learning, rather than "headshrinking." This learning process has to do with emotions, and how those emotions relate to other people. For many people it is difficult to subject themselves to such a process of self-examination. Therefore, if we define our own counseling as acquiring skills that will aid us in our work, perhaps we can strip away the stigma of "headshrinking" that has been attached to it. (Schoel, et al., 1988)

Such a recommendation is really quite inappropriate and unfortunate. The reason for a professional therapist and growth facilitator to seek out counseling group experiences should not be for development of skills. A personal growth group experience may well result in increased knowledge and understanding of group process, group dynamics, and groupwork skills, but that is a supplemental bonus. The primary motivation for taking part in a personal growth experience should be to face the challenges and attain the rewards of personal growth. One should seek to grow, to become, to actualize the person that they are, because that is the nature of the life process. One should recognize that the experience is not one of "headshrinking," but of "heart expanding."

The authors of *Islands of Healing* would seem to be selling short the adventure/challenge facilitator's understanding of the whole process of therapy and therapeutic growth. There may still be some who view counseling and personal growth groups in terms of the old "medical model" of "healthy doctor vs. sick patient," but most now have a full grasp of the "growth model" of "facilitator/guide and growing person," which has certainly replaced the former model. There may well be some adventure therapists whose personal chains and barriers would motivate them to reject the recommendation for partaking in personal growth group experiences. It may even be that some will develop alternative strategies for personal growth. However, most will fully understand and accept the recommendation; many will have already recognized the challenge of personal growth.

The personal growth journey typically becomes an ongoing process for the therapeutic professional. As with many of the challenges that adventure leaders bring to their group, after initial conquest there is much desire for more. The growing person seeks to share personal feelings and confusions, they seek to find open and honest communication, and they seek to continually explore the trails of their own personal wilderness. It is a journey that has no end: it is a part of the life process. It is as noted by Thomas Wolfe, "You can't go home again." It is as a perpetual motion machine: there is no end to the vibrating process of personal growth. It is as those visionary circles of the Native American Indians: life flows as the rivers. The healthy person is a growing person, always seeking deeper understanding of self, others, and environment. The growth journey is the life journey, always

probing personal waters to actualize personal potentials.

The whole process of personal growth is the key to success for the challenge therapist. The person who grows to this special "way of being" will recognize the need for continual growing, continually reflecting on the journey thus far, and continually dreaming of the world the way it ought to be. He will also recognize the needs of others to have someone reach out with support and regard as they seek to break the chains that keep them from transforming toward self-actualization.

There is a great "challenge" for each person who ventures forward on the journey of personal growth. After all, there is an unknown wilderness within, which may require the person to take some risks, deal with some fears, seek out someone else to trust, and sometimes rely on personal strengths. That is the nature of the journey within, but we need not fear. We are used to facing the outside challenges: now it is time to face the inside challenges.

REFERENCES

Adams, W. (1970). *Survival Training: Its Effects on the Self-Concept*. Dissertation Abstracts International, 70-71, 31, 3883.

Assagioli, R. (1971). *Psychosynthesis*. New York: Psychosynthesis Institute.

Bagby, S. & Chavarria, L. S. (1980). *Outdoor Adventure Education and Juvenile Delinquency*. (ERIC Document Reproduction Service No. ED 191 639)

Ball, D. (1986). The outdoors and gender. *Adventure Education, 3* (2).

Bartley, N. L. (1987). *Relationship of leadership style, gender personality, and training of Outward Bound instructors and their course outcomes*. Unpublished Doctoral Dissertation. University of Utah, Salt Lake City, UT.

Bartley, N. L. & Williams, D. R. (1988). Gender issues in outdoor adventure programming. *The Bradford Papers Annual, 3.*

Behar, L. & Stephens, M. A. (1978). Wilderness camping: An evaluation of a residential treatment program for emotionally disturbed children. *American Journal of Orthopsychiatry, 48.*

Boyd, D. (1974). *Rolling Thunder.* New York: Delta Books/Dell.

Brannan, S., Rillo, T., Roland, C. & Smith, T. (1984). Current issues in camping and outdoor education with persons who are disabled. *The Bradford Papers, 4.* Indiana University Press.

Breeding, J. (1985). Hope for the people and the planet: Truly powerful survivors. *Journal of Experiential Education, 8* (3).

Buell, L. (1981). *The identification of outdoor adventure leadership competencies for entrylevel and experienced personnel.* Doctoral Dissertation, University of Michigan, Ann Arbor, MI. (Dissertation Information Service Microfilms)

Buell, L. (1983). *Outdoor Leadership Competency: A Manual for Self-Assessment and Staff Evaluation.* Greenfield, MA: Environmental Awareness Publishers.

Byers, E. S. (1979). Wilderness camping as therapy for emotionally disturbed children: A critical review. *Exceptional Children, 45.*

Canfield, J. & Wells, H. (1976). *100 Ways to Enhance Self-Concept in the Classroom.* Englewood Cliffs, NJ: Prentice-Hall.

Cardwell, G. R. (1976). Adapted Outward Bound program: An alternative for corrections. *Paper at Atlantic Provinces Criminology and Corrections Conference.* (ERIC Document Reproduction Service No. ED 207 746)

Castle, M. & Eastman, J. (1985). Challenge therapy: An innovative treatment for adolescent alcoholics in a residential setting. In M. Gass (Ed.). *Exploring Horizons: The Implications of Experiential Learning Sourcebook.* (ERIC Document Reproduction Service No. ED 261 829)

Chase, N. (1981). Outward Bound as an adjunct to therapy. *Colorado Outward Bound.* (ERIC Document Reproduction Service No. ED 241 204)

Clifford, E. & Clifford, M. (1967). Self-Concept before and after survival training. *British Journal of Social and Clinical Psychology, 6.*

Colan, N. B. (1985). *Outward Bound: An Annotated Bibliography, 1976-1985.* Hurricane Island Outward Bound.

Cockrell, D. & LaFollette, J. (1985). A national standard for outdoor leadership certification. *Parks and Recreation, 20* (6).

Collingswood, T. R. (1972). Survival camping with problem youth. *Rehabilitation Record, 13.*

Dowd, R. S. (1972). The effects on self of a twenty-three day experiential wilderness program: Implications for counseling. (Doctoral Dissertation, Western Michigan University) *Dissertation Abstracts International, 38* (11) 6531.

Dreikurs, R. (1955). Group psychotherapy and the third revolution in psychiatry. *International Journal of Social Psychiatry, 5.*

Estes, C. & Ewert, A. (1988). Enhancing mixedgender programming: considerations for experiential education. *The Bradford Report Annual, 3.*

Ewert, A. (1984). The risk management plan: Promises and pitfalls. *Journal of Experiential Education, 7* (3).

Ewert, A. (1989). *Outdoor Adventure Pursuits: Foundations, Models, and Theories.* Worthington, OH: Publishing Horizons, Inc.

Fain, G. (1984). Toward a philosophy of moral judgment and ethical process in leisure counseling. In E. T. Dowd (Ed.). *Leisure Counseling: Concept and Applications.* Springfield, IL: C. C. Thomas.

Fensterman, K. (1981). *Relaxation: An Introduction to Relaxation Techniques With Adaptations for Persons With Disabilities.* Loretto, MN: Vinland National Center.

Ferguson, M. (1980). *The Aquarian Conspiracy: Personal and Social Transformation in the 1980's.* Los Angeles, CA: J. P. Tarcher, Inc.

Gass, M. (1983). Learning by sharing in the outdoors. *Workshop of the University of New Hampshire Outdoor Education Program.* (ERIC Document Reproduction Service No. ED 242 472)

Gass, M. (1985). *Exploring Horizons: The Implications of Experiential Learning Sourcebook.* (ERIC Document Reproduction Service No. ED 261 829)

George, R. (1979). Learning survival skills and participation in a solo camping experience related to self-concept. *Dissertation Abstracts International, 40,* 106A.

Gibson, P. M. (1979). Therapeutic aspects of wilderness programs: A comprehensive review. *Therapeutic Recreation Journal,* (2nd Quarter).

Golins, G. L. (1978). How delinquents succeed through adventure based education. *Journal of Experiential Education, 1* (2).

Golins, G. L. (1980). *Utilizing Adventure Education to Rehabilitate Juvenile Delinquents*. (ERIC Document Reproduction Service No. ED 207 746)

Green, P. (1981). *The content of a college-level outdoor leadership course for land based outdoor pursuits in the Pacific Northwest: A Delphi Consensus*. Unpublished Doctoral Dissertation. University of Oregon, Eugene, OR.

Hammel, H. (1986). How to design a debriefing session. *Journal of Experiential Education, 9* (3).

Hammerman, W. M. (1980). *Fifty Years of Resident Outdoor Education: 1930-1980*. Martinsville, IN: American Camping Association.

Hanna, T. (1970). *Bodies in Revolt: A Primer in Somatic Thinking*. New York: Delta/Dell.

Havens, M. (1985). Ethical challenges in the outdoor setting. *Therapeutic Recreation Journal* (4th Quarter).

Havens, M. (1986). *Professional ethics in outdoor adventure education*. Unpublished Doctoral Dissertation. Boston University, Boston, MA.

Havens, M. & Fain, G. (1986). *Ethical and moral issues in experiential education*. Seminar tape. Association for Experiential Education Annual Conference, Moodus, CT.

Havens, M. "Learning from ethical dilemmas." *Journal of Experiential Education*, Vol. 10, No. 1, 1987.

Havens, M. (1989). *Ethical dilemmas in challenge education*. Workshop at Northern Illinois University Colloquium on Aspects of Adventure, Lorado-Taft Campus, Oregon, IL.

Havens, M. & Smith, T. (1989). *Ethical Practice in Outdoor Programming*. Workshop at Bradford Woods Institute on Americans Outdoors, Indiana University, Bradford Woods, Martinsville, IN.

Henderson, K. & Bialeschki, D. (1981). Viva la differencia! *Camping Magazine, 59* (4).

Hendricks, G. & Wills, R. (1975). *The Centering Book*. Prentice-Hall, NJ: Spectrum Books.

Humberstone, B. (1986). Issues of gender in outdoor education. *Adventure Education, 3* (4).

Hunt, J. (1984). The dangers of substituting rules for instructor judgment in adventure programs. *Journal of Experiential Education, 7* (3).

Hunt, J. (1985). Certification controversy. *Camping Magazine, 57* (6).

Hunt, J. (1986). *Ethical Issues in Experiential Education*. Boulder, CO: Association for Experiential Education.

Ichazo, 0. (1973, July). In conversation with Sam Keen. *Psychology Today*.

Index of the Journal of Experiential Education, 1978-1987. (1988). *Journal of Experiential Education, 11* (3).

James, T. (1980). The paradox of safety and risk. *Journal of Experiential Education, 3* (2).

James, T. (1980). *Can the mountains speak for themselves?* Paper, Colorado Outward Bound School, Denver, CO.

Jensen, M. (1979). Application of small group theory to adventure programs. *Journal of Experiential Education, 2* (2).

Johanson, K. (1984). *Common Practices in Adventure Programming*. Boulder, CO: Association for Experiential Education.

Johnson, D. & Johnson, F. (1982). *Joining Together Group Theory and Group Skills, 2nd edition*. Englewood Cliffs, NJ: Prentice-Hall.

Jordan, D. (1987). Processing the ropes course experience. *The Bradford Papers Annual, 2.*

Kaplan, L. (1979). Outward Bound: A treatment modality unexplored by the social work profession. *Child Welfare, 58* (1).

Kelly, F. & Baer, D. (1968). *Outward Bound as an alternative to the institutionalization of adolescent delinquent boys*. (ERIC Document Reproduction Service No. ED 032 152)

Kelly, F. & Baer, D. (1969). Jesness inventory and self-concept measures after participation in Outward Bound. *Psychological Reports, 25* (7).

Kelly, F. & Baer, D. (1971). Physical challenge as a treatment for juvenile delinquency. *Crime and Delinquency, 17.*

Kelly, F. (1974). Outward Bound and Delinquency. In *Major Papers Presented at the Conference on Experiential Education*. Colorado Outward Bound School, Denver, CO.

Kerr, P. & Gass, M. (1987). Applying group development theory to adventure education. *Journal of Experiential Education, 10* (2).

Kidder, P. (1988). Challenge programs in the mental health field. *The Roland Report, 2* (2).

Kimball, R. (1980). *Wilderness adventure programs for juvenile offenders*. Prepared for the National Center for the Assessment of Alternatives to Juvenile Justice Processing, University of Chicago. (ERIC Document Reproduction Service No. ED 196 586)

Kimball, R. (1983). The wilderness as therapy. *Journal of Experiential Education, 5* (3).

Kimball, R. (1986). Experiential therapy for youth. *Children Today, 15.*

Kirkpatrick, T. (1983). *Outward Bound as an adjunct to family therapy in the treatment of alcoholics*. Paper. North Carolina Outward Bound and Randolph Clinic, Charlotte, NC.

Knapp, C. & Goodman, J. (1981). *Humanizing Environmental Education*. Martinsville, IN: American Camping Association.

Knapp, C. (1985). Escaping the gender trap: The ultimate challenge for experiential educators. *Journal of Experiential Education, 8* (2).

Knapp, C. (1986). The science and art of processing outdoor experiences. *The Outdoor Communicator, 16* (l).

Knapp, C. (1987). Connecting people and planets. *The Bradford Papers Annual, 2.*

LaCasse, T. (1985). The use of Outward Bound in the treatment of chemically dependent adolescents. In M. Gass (Ed.). *Exploring Horizons: Implications of Experiential Learning Source-book*. (ERIC Document Reproduction Service No. ED 261 829)

LaChapelle, D. & Bourwque, J. (1974). *Earth Festivals*. Silverton, CO: Finn Arts Publishing,.

Lappen, E. (1984). *Outdoor education for behavior disordered students*. (ERIC Document Reproduction Service No. ED 261 811)

Larson, D. (Ed.). (1984). *Teaching Psychological Skills: Models for Giving Psychology Away*. Belmont, CA: Wadsworth.

Leonard, G. (1972). *The Transformation: A Guide To The Inevitable Changes In Humankind*. New York: Delta/Dell.

Leopold, A. (1966). *A Sand County Almanac*. New York: Oxford Press.

Link, M. (1981). *Outdoor Education*. Englewood Cliffs, NJ: Prentice-Hall.

LockLand G. T. (1973). *Grow or Die: The Unifying Principle of Transformation*. New York: Random House.

Loughmiller, C. (1965). *Wilderness Road*. Austin, TX: Hogg Foundation.

Loughmiller, C. (1979). *Kids In Trouble*. Tyler, TX: Wildwood Books.

Lovett, R. (1971). *Outward Bound: A means of implementation of guidance objectives*. (ERIC Document Reproduction Service No. ED 129 520)

McAvoy, L. (1978). Outdoor leadership training. *Journal of P.E., Recreation and Dance, 4.*

Marland, M. (Ed.) (1983). *Sex Differentiation and Schooling*. London, England: Heineman Co.

Meyer, D. (1979). The management of risk. *Journal of Experiential Education, 2* (2).

Mobley, M., Deinema, K, & Rowell, J. (1985). The power and impact of risk recreation for special populations. *Trends, 22* (3).

Moreno, J. (1946). *Psychodrama*. Beacon, NY: Beacon House.

Moreno, J. (1951). Group psychotherapy: Theory and practice. *Group Psychotherapy, 3* (l).

Neihardt, J. & Black Elk. (1961). *Black Elk Speaks*. Lincoln, NE: University of Nebraska Press.

Okum, B. (1976). *Effective Helping: Interviewing and Counseling Techniques*. North Scituate, MA: Duxbury Press.

Otto, H. (1972). *Fantasy Encounter Games*. Los Angeles, CA: Nash Publishing.

Phipps, M. (1986). *An assessment of a systematic approach to teaching outdoor leadership in expedition settings*. Unpublished Doctoral Dissertation, University of Minnesota, Minneapolis, MN.

Phipps, M. (1986). Experiential leadership education: Teaching soft skills of leadership. *Adventure Education, 3* (4).

Plakun, E., Teicher, G., & Harris, P. (1981). Outward Bound: An adjunctive psychiatric therapy. *Journal of Psychiatric Treatment and Evaluation, 3* (l).

Pollak, R. T. (1975). An annotated bibliography of the literature and research on Outward Bound and related programs: 1966-1975. (ERIC Document Reproduction Service No. ED 161 714 76)

Priest, S. (1984). Effective outdoor leadership. *Journal of Experiential Education, 7* (3).

Priest, S. (1987). *Preparing effective outdoor pursuits leaders*. Report. Institute of Recreation Research and Service, Department of Leisure Studies and Services. University of Oregon, Eugene, OR.

Priest, S. (1987). Certification: Always an issue but no longer a trend. *The Bradford Papers Annual, 2.*

Priest, S. (1988). Agreement reached on outdoor leader certification? *The Bradford Papers Annual, 3.*

Quinsland, L. & Van Ginkel, A. (1984). How to process experience. *Journal of Experiential Education, 7* (2).

Riddick, T. & Mesinger, J. (1979). *Adventure bound: Meeting the needs of the disturbed/delinquent adolescent*. Paper to the 57th Annual Meetings of the Council for Exceptional Children, Dallas, TX. (ERIC Document Reproduction Service No. 170 350)

Robb, G., Havens, M., & Wittman, J. (1983). *Special Education Naturally*. Bloomington, IN: Indiana University Press.

Robb, G. (Ed.). (1985). *Issues in Challenge Education and Adventure Education*. Bloomington, IN: Indiana University Press.

Robb, G. & Ewert, A. (1987). Risk recreation and persons with disabilities.*Therapeutic Recreation Journal, 21* (l).

Robb, G., Roland, C., Havens, M. & Smith, T. (1988). *Professional ethics and outdoor programming.* Institute at Midwest Symposium on Therapeutic Recreation, Lake Geneva, WI.

Robbins, S. (1976). *Outdoor wilderness survival and its psychological and sociological effects.* Unpublished doctoral dissertation, Brigham Young University, Salt Lake City, UT.

Rogers, C. (1970, Nov. 9). Human Potential: The Revolution in Feeling. *Time Magazine.*

Rogers, C. (1980). *A Way Of Being.* Boston, MA: Houghton-Mifflin Company.

Rogers, R. (1979). *Learning To Share; Sharing to Lead.* Sudbury, Ontario, Canada: Council of Outdoor Education of Ontario.

Roland, C. & Havens, M. (1981). *Introduction to Adventure: A Sequential Approach to Challenge Activities With Persons Who Are Disabled.* Loretto, MN: Vinland Center.

Roland, C. (1982). Adventure education with persons who are disabled. *The Bradford Papers, 2.*

Roland, C. & Havens, M. (1982). Tree climbing. *Camping Magazine, 60* (l).

Roland, C., Summers, S., Friedman, S., Barton, M., & McCarthy, K. (1987). Creation of an experiential challenge program. *Therapeutic Recreation Journal, 21* (l).

Roland, C., Keene, T., Dubois, M., & Lentini, J. (1988). Experiential challenge program development in the mental health setting. *The Bradford Papers Annual, 3.*

Roszak, T. (1974). *Person/Planet.* New York: Charles Merrill.

Roth, R., Cantrell, D., & Bousquet, W. (1980). Outdoor education: Impact on environmental education. In Hammerman, W. (Ed.). *Fifty Years of Resident Outdoor Education: 19301980.* Martinsville, IN: American Camping Assn.

Russell, R. (1986). *Leadership In Recreation.* St. Louis, MO: Times Mirror/Mosby College Publishing.

Russell, P. (1983). *The Global Brain: Speculations on the Evolutionary Leap to Planetary Consciousness.* New York: J. P. Tarcher, Inc.

Schoel, J. (1974). *Counseling on the run.* Paper from Project Adventure, Hamilton, MA.

Schoel, J., Prouty, D., & Radcliffe, P. (1988). *Islands of Healing.* Hamilton, MA: Project Adventure, Inc.

Simon, S., Howe, L., & Kirschenbaum, H. (1972). *Values Clarification.* New York: Hart Publishing.

Smith, T. (1979a) *Rituals of the American Indians as formats for personal growth workshops.* Paper to Conference on Consciousness, Metropolitan Community College, Minneapolis. [In *Wilderness Beyond...Wilderness Within,* McHenry Press, 1981]

Smith, T. (1979b). *Rituals and ceremonies of the American Indians: Applications to the human potential movement.* Paper to Regional Conference of the Association for Humanistic Psychology, Chicago. [In *Wilderness Beyond...Wilderness Within,* McHenry Press, 1981]

Smith, T. (1979c). *Health and healing practices of the American Indians: Potentials for personal growth and holistic health.* Paper to Regional Conference of the Association for Humanistic Psychology, Minneapolis. [In *Wilderness Beyond...Wilderness Within,* McHenry Press, 1981]

Smith, T. (1979d). *Ghost dances, medicine wheels, and teaching stories.* Paper to Association for Experiential Education Conference, Portsmouth, New Hampshire. [In *Wilderness Beyond...Wilderness Within,* McHenry Press, 1981]

Smith, T. (1979e). *My couch is made of pine needles.* Paper to Illinois Council for Exceptional Children Conference, Chicago. [In *Wilderness Beyond...Wilderness Within,* McHenry Press, 1981]

Smith, T. (1981). *Wilderness Beyond...Wilderness Within.* McHenry, IL: McHenry Press (out of print).

Smith, T. (1983). Outdoor leadership and ''endu consciousness. *The Bradford Papers, 3.*

Smith, T. (1985). *Outdoor therapy: Innovative individual and group methods.* Paper to Conference of Humanistic Psychology, Indianapolis, IN.

Smith, T. (1988). Ethics for adventure programming: Four points of departure. *The Bradford Papers Annual, 3.*

Stanley, L. (1985). *The use of Outward Bound in conjunction with therapy for the chemically dependent.* Paper, North Carolina Outward Bound.

Stevens, J. (1973). *Awareness: Exploring, Experimenting, Experiencing.* Des Plaines, IL: Bantam Books.

Stich, T. & MacArthur, R. (1981). *The Outward Bound mental health project: A three year report.* Paper, Hurricane Island Outward Bound.

Stich, T. & Sussman, L. (1981). *Outward Bound—an adjunctive psychiatric treatment: Preliminary research findings.* (ERIC Document Reproduction Service No. ED 239 791)

Stich, T. (1983). Experiential therapy. *Journal of Experiential Education, 5* (3).

Stich, T. (Ed.). (1985). *Outward Bound in alcohol treatment and mental health: A compilation of literature.* Paper, Outward Bound, Inc., Greenwich, CT.

Stich, T. & Gaylor, M. (1984). Risk management in adventure programs with special populations: two hidden dangers. *Journal of Experiential Education 7* (3).

Stich, T. & Senior, N. (1984). Adventure therapy: An innovative treatment for psychiatric patients. In B. Pepper & A. Ryglewicz (Eds.), *Advances in Treatment: New Directions for Mental Health.* CA: Jossey-Bass.

Storm, H. (1972). *Seven Arrows.* New York: Harper and Row/Ballantine Books.

Sun Bear & Wabun. (1980). *The Medicine Wheel: Earth Astrology.* Englewood Cliffs, NJ: Prentice-Hall.

Swiderski, M. (1981). *Outdoor leadership competencies identified by outdoor leaders of five western regions.* Unpublished doctoral dissertation, University of Oregon, Eugene, OR.

Swiderski, M. (1987). Soft and conceptual skills: The often overlooked components of outdoor leadership. *The Bradford Papers Annual, 2.*

Szent-Gyorgyi, A. (1974). Drive in living matter to perfect itself. *Synthesis One: The Realization of Self.* San Francisco, CA: Psychosynthesis Institute.

Teaff, J. & Kablach, J. (1987). Psychological benefits of outdoor adventure activities. *Journal of Experiential Education,10* (2).

U. S. Congress. *The Environmental Education Act of 1970.*

Van der Smissen, B. (1979). Minimizing legal liability risks. *Journal of Experiential Education, 2* (1).

Voight, A. (1988). The use of ropes courses as a treatment modality for emotionally disturbed adolescents in hospitalization. *Therapeutic Recreation Journal* (2nd Quarter).

White, J. & Fadiman, J. (1976). *Relax.* San Francisco, CA: Confucian Press.

Whyld, J. (Ed.) (1983). *Sexism in the Secondary Curriculum.* New York: Harper and Row.

Whyte, J. (Ed.) (1985). *Girl Friendly Schooling.* London, England: Methuen.

Wichman, T. (1976). *Affective role expectation for delinquent youth in environmental stress challenge programs.* (ERIC Document Reproduction Srevice No. ED 156 394)

Wichman, T. (1983). Evaluating Outward Bound for delinquent youth. *Journal of Experiential Education, 5* (3).

Williamson, J. (Ed.) (1988). Problem solving. Special issue of *Journal of Experiential Education, 11* (2).

Witman, J. (1987a) *Outcomes of adventure program participation by adolescents involved in psychiatric treatment.* Unpublished doctoral dissertation, Boston University, Boston, MA.

Witman, J. (1987b) The efficacy of adventure programs in the development of cooperation and trust with adolescents in treatment. *Therapeutic Recreation Journal, 21* (3).

Wright, A. (1982). Therapeutic potential of the Outward Bound process: An evaluation of a treatment program for juvenile delinquents. (Doctoral dissertation, Penn State University) *Dissertation Abstracts International, 43* (3) 923A.

Yerkes, R. (Ed.) (1985). Experiential education from the male and female point of view. Special issue of *Journal of Experiential Education, 8* (2).

Ziven, H. (1986). *Psychological theories of adventure programs.* Paper. (Available from author, 79 Woodard Road, West Roxbury, MA)

Societal Impact

By Warren Schumacher
and Judith A. Hoyt

The Challenge Education curriculum activates not only the overt behavior of the individuals involved in the program, but also intellect, feelings, attitudes, values and intuitions! Blended together under appropriate supervision, this combination can lead the individual to new insights about self and one's place in the world. Many who experience "challenge" begin to trust their own instincts in ways that previously were impossible; they begin to relate to others with the conviction that "helping you helps me;" "help givers" and "help receivers" establish more creative relationships. These insights and skills naturally generalize to other relationships in which the person is involved: family, close friends, peers, business associates.

The Challenge Education curriculum, used as a teaching tool with family systems, leads the individuals who are participating to find new insights, feelings and attitudes within themselves that have powerful impact in helping them find their place in the world. The people who have participated in challenge programming begin to trust their own instincts in ways that they never thought were possible. They begin to relate in a more positive way to others. Others in their circle of family and friends recognize that a change has taken place and are ready to listen and learn about this "challenge" program that has made such an obvious difference in how they are coping with their situation.

It gets exciting when the impact of challenge education is internalized by family members as individuals. The family members who have experienced the sequence of growth share this with other individuals they touch in their lives. An awareness is created that there is a chance and a way to shift social values.

This same challenge education curriculum is used in the corporate world and in health rehabilitation environments to enable people to rethink their goals and to begin the experience of personal and social growth in a way that stimulates new awareness and new energy. The challenge education sequence model can complement the work of a therapist in the psychiatric setting. It also supports the collaborative effort of team building that is a current focus in the business and education worlds. School systems incorporating challenge methodologies into their curriculum find greater cooperation between classmates.

All human relationships are founded on establishing some kind of balance between individuality and togetherness, separateness and connectedness, "me" and "we." Our competitive society has produced an imbalance emphasizing the "me generation" during the 60's and 70's and the "I've got mine, let the other guy make it on his own" of the 80's. As we begin the 90's the pendulum seems to be swinging toward the togetherness/connectedness/"we" side of the balance. The time is ripe for a change in social values as many people hunger for a sense of community and strive to find experiences or noncompetitive intimacy.

Family structures have changed; various family forms and lifestyles are gaining respect. Abled and disabled are mainstreamed and share the same lifespace. Institutions that used to "house" the handicapped are closing their doors and those who used to be "sheltered from public view" are becoming more integrated into the community. Social values are changing ever so slowly. The laws that reflect those values will ultimately change only after the attitudes and standards of society change. People with differences are finally witnessing the beginnings of community acceptance. This has taken years of battling for their rights. The road ahead leading to a true respect for diversity is still a long one; many obstacles are still in the way.

Challenge can support and facilitate this process of gradual and orderly movement toward "a more gentle society," a society that cares for those who move, speak and act in ways that differ from the majority. The work of Lawrence Kohlberg and Carol Gilligan at Harvard University emphasize the need for people to move through maturing stages of moral reasoning. If our society is to survive, we must mature beyond the conventional

level of valuing at which we simply accept the standards of the past; we must reach for postconventional levels at which we are able to creatively think through what is "right and wrong," "appropriate and inappropriate." Challenge provides those who participate in the curriculum an experience of this kind of creative thinking and acting in new relational patterns!

Through the challenge experience, participants learn the value of individual initiative in the context of relating with and depending on others. As people set goals and learn to trust others in reaching those goals, a balance is established between individuality and togetherness mentioned above. As individuals experience taking the risk of trusting others, these activities establish the basis for a developing insight that "no person is an island." Gradually, participants grow in the wisdom of realizing that we share more in common than are we separated by differences in race or color, sex or age, physical or mental ability or disability. Tangible, hands-on activities of working together to accomplish a goal that is totally impossible to realize by oneself lead people to think differently about sharing and cooperating. Participants become convinced that some people who previously were thought to be incompetent because of their disability are truly very competent individuals. As attitudes are changed and stereotypes are eradicated, new social values tend to emerge. People who had been locked into their individual concerns become more open to thinking about issues which previously had been irrelevant to them, environmental problems which have an impact on the country and world, issues of racism, sexism, ageism, ableism, etc. In our democratic society, eventually these individual and personal changes in attitudes and values should begin to have an impact on the legislation that governs the way social programs are implemented.

An interesting and challenging proposal that would facilitate the process by which the methodology and philosophy of challenge could be introduced into our society is to bring the curriculum to social service agencies through the Executive Boards of these agencies. Once Board members experience the curriculum, they tend to be motivated to introduce it to not only businesses/ companies with which they are involved. The multiplier effect takes over as more professionals and lay citizens recognize the potential of the program.

As the challenge curriculum is introduced to more communities, those personalities emerge who are uniquely suited to become co-trainers who take on the responsibility to conduct the program with other groups. Gradually this cooperative effort in mutual support and sharing becomes generalized to a variety of social interactions. Eventually the "stone thrown into the lake" will produce a series of ripples that will spread over the entire world's pond.

Those who are convinced of the value of this type of collaborative effort among people of various ages and abilities, different sexes and races, begin to appreciate the possibility of a new world view. The term "human family" takes on a significance that was previously a myth. Decision-formers and decision-makers with political influence are beginning to recognize the value of cooperation over confrontation; if they were given the experience of "challenge" they would realize that what is accomplished on a micro level can truly be implemented on the macro level!

Higher Education

By Dan Creely
and Bill Quinn

Introduction

The processes of conceptualizing, developing, selling and implementing outdoor adventure programs at an urban university takes a great deal of time, "positive energy," effort and patience. The faculty within the Health, Physical Education & Recreation Department at Northeastern Illinois University have been involved in making these processes a reality for the past five years. A schedule of carefully planned activities has been pursued in order to acquaint administration with the techniques and power of the process utilized in challenge education. The faculty sought to establish a base of operation at the University to assemble teachers interested in incorporating adventure challenge discipline into their curriculum and further their own education. Interdisciplinary application has also been a prime concern during the promotion of challenge education theory and practice at Northeastern Illinois University.

As part of this undertaking, affiliations with national organizations which have been recognized as quality leaders in the fields of outdoor experiential education have been investigated. The Chicago Center of the Voyageur Outward Bound School and Project Adventure (Massachusetts) have been reliable allies in this process of incorporating the theory and practice of challenge education into our university. Both organizations have become involved with education in the Chicago Metropolitan Area.

The focus of this section is to share the "process" which has occurred for implementing the Adventure/Challenge Program at Northeastern Illinois University. This information is presented under the following four headings:

I. Sequence of activities which helped bring awareness of adventure/ challenge education to the University.

II. Proposal for an Honors Curriculum.

III. Explanation of the Five Year Curriculum Plan.

IV. Master's Proposal Draft.

I. Sequence of activities which helped bring awareness of adventure/challenge education to the University.

Fall, 1985 Title III Grant.

This grant was used to develop the "Introduction to Adventure" course. Teaching one to two sections of this class each semester is intended to be the foundation of the program. The Introduction to Adventure Education course was submitted to the College of Education Academic Affairs (C.A.A.C.) Committee in November, 1985 and approved.

Fall, 1986 Adventure Education Course Taught

Student response to the course has been so positive during the last five years that each section has been filled. Students registering for "Introduction to Adventure Education" major in a wide variety of academic disciplines such as social sciences, elementary education, business, mathematics, environmental education, leisure studies, and physical education. Faculty throughout the University have shown interest in incorporating the adventure education process into their courses.

Consider this example: Dr. Sherman Beverly, a professor (61 years of age) in the educational foundation department, registered for the course. He was affectionately nicknamed "Papa Smurf" by the students because of his gray hair and beard. The students did not discover he was a professor at the University until six weeks into the course. An excerpt from his class journal states:

> Thanks! This course has brought me as close to young people as I have ever been, under conditions to which I never thought I would subject myself. I know now how much they care, how much they love and want to learn, how badly they need to share their knowledge with sympathetic listeners, and how much they have to offer to those who will simply respect them. I have always prided myself on my ability to relate well with young people, but I'll be better now. I owe it to them and to myself. Incidentally, I am now, more than ever, convinced that nothing I want to do is beyond my reach.

Winter, 1987 Faculty Workshops

A follow-up Kellogg Faculty Fellowship was used to design a series of four 90-minute training and development workshops on challenge education for interested University faculty.

Fall, 1987 Teacher Training Workshops

Several requests from elementary and high school teachers were received urging development of interdisciplinary workshops for inservice training and institute days, prompting the staff to develop workshop offerings.

Winter, 1988 Freshman Orientation Program

The Adventure faculty was contacted to help redesign the freshman orientation program. The task was to incorporate team-building and group initiatives into an experience-based program designed to welcome new students to campus.

Spring, 1988 Portable Teams Initiative Course

Ten portable elements were built and stored in the physical education complex. These elements are used extensively on site for classes, workshops, conferences, and for off-site programs. New elements are being constructed and continually added to the existing stock.

Fall, 1988 Teacher Organization Formed

T.E.A.M. (Teachers of Experiential and Adventure Methodology) was organized through the College of Education and the physical education department to meet the increasing demand by educators to learn and understand the process utilized in adventure/challenge education. Interdisciplinary workshops for academic credit were conducted with positive response. In addition, a workshop was designed and delivered at the Illinois State Physical Education Convention.

Winter, 1989 Workshops for the Chicago Teachers' Center

Adventure/challenge team-building workshops were conducted for several Chicago area high schools.

Spring, 1989 First Annual T.E.A.M. Conference

A grant from the Association for Experiential Education (AEE) assisted in conducting the regional AEE and T.E.A.M. conference at Northeastern. One hundred educators participated.

Summer, 1989 Summer Transition Program

The success of the freshman orientation program prompted the administration to integrate the team-building group initiatives into a special six-week summer transition program for incoming freshmen. The response was so positive the coordinator wants to integrate this as a permanent part of the program.

Fall, 1989 Outward Bound Affiliation

Northeastern and Outward Bound took steps toward a working relationship to develop cooperative training programs and internships.

Fall, 1989 Mission Statement and Four Year Plan

The mission statement of the adventure/challenge program was written and submitted to the administration along with a detailed five-year longterm plan. The mission statement reads:

> The mission of the Adventure Education Program is to provide a minor degree with an interdisciplinary emphasis in Physical Education, Special Education, Counselor Education, and Business and Management. A long-range goal is to offer graduate level coursework. The degree and coursework will be useful to educators in traditional and alternative schools, parks/recreation personnel, and corporate training programs.
>
> In addition to the minor degree, the Adventure Education Program is committed to establishing a comprehensive Training Center at Northeastern Illinois University. The Center will develop collaborative partnerships with the surrounding education, business, and social services agencies. The focus is to provide professional development seminars and

conduct quantitative and qualitative re-search.

Fall, 1989 Graduate Proposal

An inter-institutional graduate program in Outdoor Experiential Education between Northeastern Illinois University and Chicago State University was submitted to the Board of Governors as a N.E.P.R. (new and ex-panded program). Approximately seventy percent of the participants who had attended the challenge/adventure workshops indicated an interest in pursuing graduate work in this discipline.

Fall, 1989 Athletics

Intercollegiate teams started using the ad-venture/challenge team building concept. The following teams have participated: men's bas-ketball, women's basketball, women's vol-leyball, and men's baseball.

Winter, 1990 Honors Program

An Introduction to Adventure Education course for freshmen and sophomores was pro-posed and accepted within the University honors program. The first course was taught in the fall of 1991. An Urban Cultural Adven-ture course for juniors and seniors will be developed in the near future, focusing on using the city as a classroom. The honors coordinator has also requested a four-week honors off-campus experiential seminar pro-gram. It is presently being developed and will eventually be integrated into the program.

Spring 1990 Permanent Structures on Campus

A proposed indoor 15-element high ropes course and a 12-station climbing wall are currently being investigated. Outdoor struc-tures are proposed and will be built after the indoor ones are completed.

Spring 1990 Second Annual T.E.A.M. Conference

One hundred fifty educators attended, 54 speakers conducted 90-minute to eight-hour workshops on integrating challenge educa-tion into traditional K–12 curricula.

Fall, 1990 Presentation and Workshops with Local School Boards, Teacher Institute Days, and State Conventions

Work began with local superintendents and principals to develop programs in their schools. The South Cook County Education Center #7 (with 66 school districts) has used the faculty several times this fall. Response has been so positive that a series of ongoing training seminars is being planned. A work-shop titled "101 Ways to Increase Self-Es-teem in Your Program" at the Illinois State Physical Education Convention drew over 200 people for a 60minute seminar. During the last two years, the faculty has worked with over 700 educators on integrating adventure/challenge education methods and techniques into their curriculums.

Fall, 1990 Adventure Education Minor Degree

Students interest during the past five years in the "Introduction to Adventure Education" course has established a need to develop an interdisciplinary minor. Fourteen new courses were developed and have been sub-mitted to the College of Education Academic Affairs Committee (C.A.A.C.). The minor will have three areas of study: core courses, certification courses and skills courses. [This minor was approved in the spring of 1991.]

Listed below is the outline of the courses.

MINOR IN ADVENTURE EDUCATION – 20 HOURS

A. CORE – Select 4

1. Introduction to Adventure Education*
   3 hours
2. Historical and Philosophical Foundations of Adventure Education
   3 hours
3. Adventure Education Curriculum Design
   3 hours
4. Leadership Skills in Adventure Education
   3 hours
5. Wilderness Experience
   3 hours

B. CERTIFICATION – Select 2

1. First Aid and CPR*
   2 hours
2. Lifeguarding*
   2 hours
3. Water Safety Instructor (WSI)*
   2 hours
4. Outward Bound Internship
   2 hours
5. Iowa Mountaineers Internship
   2 hours

C. SKILLS – Select 2

1. Introduction to Winter Skills
   2 hours
2. Introduction of Backpacking
   2 hours
3. Introduction to Rock Climbing
   2 hours
4. Introduction to Initiatives and Group Dynamics
   2 hours

5. Introduction to Nature Awareness and Native American Skills
   2 hours
6. Introduction to Flatwater Canoeing
   2 hours
7. Introduction to Whitewater Canoeing
   2 hours
8. Introduction to Decked Boats
   2 hours
9. Freshwater Fishing for Beginners*
   2 hours
10. Advanced Techniques and Theories in Freshwater Fishing*
    2 hours

courses already approved and being taught

II. Proposal for an Honors Curriculum.

UNIVERSITY HONORS PROGRAM

A Proposal for an Honors Seminar (HNRS 398)

A. Seminar Description

The topic would be experience-based Adventure Education, and would be housed in the Physical Education Department. This honors seminar is unique in that it is directed at personal growth through individual and group experiential activities, the main objective being active, self-directed learning.

B. Rationale

The structure of this honors seminar would be unique because it incorporates a fundamentally different approach from traditional courses. The components that distinguish this seminar from others are that it develops not only cognitive analysis and physical skills, but also addresses the affective domain, or the emotional development of the student. Well-documented research has shown experience-based Adventure Education courses develop positive attitudes and values, with the end result being an enhanced selfconcept. A direct correlation exists between self-concept and cognitive development. Students are complex individuals who need to be challenged intellectually, physically and emotionally. This new and innovative seminar will not only challenge the students, but will also have a positive impact on them.

The content of the seminar will focus on active learning and critical thinking. A progression of the group interaction initiative activities will be utilized as the foundation for the seminar. These activities develop verbal communication skills and a trust-bond between the students that enhances the group's problem-solving ability.

C. <u>Objectives</u>

The objectives of the seminar are as follows:

1. To establish an active learning environment in the seminar that will break down racial, social and sexual barriers. This will be accomplished during the first three weeks of the seminar in the sequential series of activities designed for this specific purpose.

2. To utilize an interdisciplinary educational methodology in the seminar. This will be accomplished by having the students, through assigned reading, critically review topics in Native American history and environmental issues.

3. To enhance the writing and English skills of the students. This will be accomplished by having each student complete a daily reflective personal growth journal.

4. To develop an awareness of the critical need for community service in today's society. Each student will complete a 10-hour community service project at an agency of his or her choosing (with the approval of the instructor) in order to provide an opportunity to apply the cognitive knowledge and physical skills acquired during class. This will be accomplished during a 3-day Adventure/Challenge experience. This can either be a wilderness experience or an urban experience in the City of Chicago.

D. <u>Syllabus</u>

Week 1 Orientation

Communication Initiative Activities

235

Week 2 Development of Community Service Projects

Trust Building Activities

Week 3 History and Philosophy of Adventure Education

Problem Solving Initiatives

Week 4 Discussion of Environmental Issues and Concerns

Critical Thinking Activities

Week 5 Skills Development: Climbing Equipment and Belaying Practice

Select Outside Text for Critical Analysis

Week 6 Skills Development: Rappelling Practice

Week 7 Skills Development: Orienteering and Wilderness Navigation

Week 8 Written and Oral Book Analysis

Week 9 Equipment Use

Week 10 Assignment of Cooking Groups

Food Budget and Nutritional Needs
Final Trip Preparation

3-day Experience

Week 11 Trip Analysis

Processing and Group Discussion

Week 12 Course Analysis

Processing and Group Discussion

Week 13 Final Written Exam

Course Evaluations

COURSE TEXT: Simer and Sullivan, National Outdoor Leadership School, *Wilderness Guide*, Simon & Schuster, New York.

Students will be required to complete the following:

1. A written daily growth journal that describes in detail course activities and discussions, and how you changed as a result of your experiences.

2. Students will write a 5-page summary paper of their 10-hour community service experience. Explain in detail what you did, what you learned, and how it affected you.

3. Write and be able to verbalize a critical book review of a test that investigates discussion topics in the seminar.

4. Submit a written chapter analysis for each discussion chapter in the seminar text book.

5. Take a comprehensive written essay final exam.

6. Attend and actively participate in all class activities including the 3-day adventure experience.

E. Evaluations

The following is a breakdown of the student's work during the seminar, and the percentage of their final grade for each assignment.

1. Personal growth journal...20%
2. Written chapter analysis for each discussion chapter from the seminar text book...20%
3. Five-page written analysis of community service project and oral presentation of your experience in the seminar...20%
4. Three-page critical book review...10%
5. Comprehensive essay final of the course content. (Student must receive 71% or better to pass)...10%
6. Attendance and participation in all seminar activities, including discussions...20%

The following scale will be used for attendance evaluation:

100 - 91% = A
90 - 81% = B
80 - 71% = C
70 - 61% = D
60 - below = F

III. Explanation of the Five Year Curriculum Plan

Year One

<u>Fall 1989</u>

1) Permanent Structures

Build the climbing wall in the Auxiliary Gym. This first phase will be built with the University Architect and the University carpenters.

2) Professional Activities

<u>T.E.A.M. Workshops</u>
a) November 18
Focus — Adventure Education in the classroom. 50 participants
b) December 5
Focus—Adventure Education in therapeutic recreation. 50 participants

3) Professional Affiliations

Develop programs with Outward Bound to begin training Spring, 1990

4) Degree Programs

Proposal for Adventure Education minor in the Physical Education department, an interdisciplinary minor, other teacher trainer programs on campus.

<u>Winter 1990</u>

1) Permanent Structures

Build indoor initiative course in the ceiling of the Auxiliary Gym. Faculty, architect and University carpenters can do all the work.

2) Professional Activities

<u>T.E.A.M. Workshops</u>
a) January 19
Focus—Adventure Education in Use with Special Education Students. 50 participants
b) March 3
Focus — Adventure Education in the Area of Counselling. 50 participants
<u>T.E.A.M. Conference</u>
a) April 22
Second Annual Conference. 200-300 participants

3) Professional Affiliations

a) No date
Outward Bound and Summer Retraining Institute for Chicago Public School teachers
b) No date
Corporate Program. Start the plans on brochure and program for Executive Challenge.

4) Degree Program

a) No date
Advisory Committee for program development and work of Master's Degree in Adventure Education (Cost: meetings, travel, meals)
b) No date
Implement Adventure Education courses in Physical Education curriculum. Approval of Introduction to Adventure class into general education program.

Spring/Summer 1990

1) Permanent Structures

a) No date
Building Low Ropes and High Ropes Initiative Course on-site at Northeastern. Faculty members, architect and University carpenters can build structures. (Note: Outward Bound has money available to contribute to the building of the Challenge Course, in addition to Northeastern funds.)

2) Professional Activities

a) No date
Run a 4-week retraining institute for Chicago teachers using Adventure Education teaching methodologies.

Year Two

Fall 1990

1) Permanent Structures

a) No date
Building wall—Phase 2 in the Auxiliary Gym. University carpenters, architect and faculty can do construction.

2) Professional Activities

T.E.A.M. Workshops
a) October 20
Adventure Education in the Physical Education Curriculum. 50 participants
b) November 17
Focus—Use of Adventure Education with Business and Industry. 50 participants

3) Professional Affiliations

a) No date
Use Outward Bound as an Internship Training Center with Northeastern students. Use as an interdisciplinary program.

4) Degree Programs

a) No date
Implement Adventure Education minor in the curriculum with an interdisciplinary focus.

Winter 1991

1) Permanent Activities

a) No date
Second Phase—Indoor initiative course in the ceiling of the Auxiliary Gym. Faculty, architect and University carpenter can do all the work.

2) Professional Activities

T.E.A.M. Workshops
a) January 1991
Focus—Teacher Training Methodology. 50 participants
b) March 1991
Focus—Sports Teams and Adventure Education. 50 participants
T.E.A.M. Conference
a) April 1991
Third Annual Conference. 400 participants

3) Professional Affiliations

a) No date
Outward Bound and Institute for Excellence in Education, Teacher Retraining Workshops.
Corporate Program
Continue training and bring back first-year companies for Phase II of their training.

4) Degree Program

a) No date
Advisory Committee for Program Development and Advisement on Master's Degree in Adventure Education.

Summer 1991

1) Permanent Structures

   a) No date
   Alpine Tower—Mike Fischesser will be contracted to construct on campus. He is a Safety and Building Consultant for Outward Bound.

2) Professional Affiliation

   a) No date
   40 week Teacher Retraining Institute work with Outward Bound
   b) No date
   Corporate Program—Continue training and bring back first-year companies for Phase II of their training.
   c) No date
   American Canoe Association—become a certification center for canoe instruction and leadership training.

Year Three

Winter 1992

1) Professional Activities

   T.E.A.M. Workshops
   a) January 1992
   Focus—Adventure Education and Outdoor Education. 50 participants
   b) March 1992
   50 participants
   T.E.A.M. Conference
   c) April, 1992
   Fourth Annual Conference. 500 participants

2) Professional Affiliations

   a) No date
   Corporate Programs continued

3) Degree Program

   a) No date
   Advisory Committee for Program Development and Advisement on Master's Degree in Adventure Education

Summer 1992

1) Professional Affiliations

   a) No date
   Corporate Programs—continue through summer
   b)No date
   Sports teams and coaches
   c)No date
   Summer camps

Year Four

Fall 1992

1) Permanent Structures

   a) No date
   Build a personal challenge course on campus. It can be designed and built by all people on campus. Dr. Tom Smith will be consultant.

2) Professional Activities

   T.E.A.M. Workshops
   a)No date
   10 workshops will be planned throughout the year. 50 participants each
   Focus on the following groups:
   Education (physical education, special counselor elementary and secondary)
   Allied Health (physical, occupational, speech therapists and school psychologists)
   Recreation (community, therapeutic, commercial)
   Sports teams and coaches
   Business (managers and vocational specialists)

3) Degree Program

a) No date
Proposal to B.O.G. for Master's Degree in Adventure Education. New faculty, secretary, graduate assistants, equipment

Year Four

<u>Winter 1993</u>

1) Professional Activities

<u>T.E.A.M. Workshop</u>
T.E.A.M. Conference
a) April 1993
Fifth Annual Conference. 500 participants

2) Professional Affiliations

a) No dates
Corporate Programs continued
Sports teams and coaches
Social groups (YMCA, camps, church groups)
School groups (elementary, secondary)

<u>Summer 1993</u>

1) Professional Affiliations

a) No dates
Outward Bound Program working with Northeastern in their program, workshops, teacher institutes.
All programs continue: corporate, sports teams, schools, camps

IV. Master's Proposal Draft
BOARD OF GOVERNORS OF
STATE COLLEGES AND UNIVERSITIES
Springfield, Illinois

PRELIMINARY NEW ACADEMIC PROGRAM REQUEST FORM

1. Name   Northeastern Illinois University and Chicago State Illinois Universities

2. Title   Master's Degree Program: Outdoor Experiential Education

Outdoor Experiential Education is a process that has proved successful in schools and other settings throughout the world. While started in Europe in the 1920's, it was introduced into private schools on the east coast during the 1950's. Since then it has been implemented in myriad settings across the United States. Presently, there are no Outdoor Experiential Education Master's programs in the state of Illinois, and very few others nationwide.

The Outdoor Experiential Education philosophy centers on physically and mentally challenging experiences, trust and cooperative team building exercises, problem solving opportunities, and reflective thinking. Research has proved it develops a "bond" between students that breaks down social, sexual, and racial barriers and develops a sensitivity to those who are culturally different.

Willi Unsold was a pioneer in the national movement to organize an association for experiential educators. He stated there are four unique advantages of outdoor experiential education over traditional education:

1. Formal classroom behavior is very conditionally laid out and structured. Everyone knows the rules. Outdoor Experiential Education places the student in a new environment and gives the student an opportunity to change habit patterns, values and relationships.
2. Traditional education often delays results. They seldom appear practical, and have no immediate use. In Outdoor Experiential Education, the problems are simple, classroom complexities are reduced and an individual can focus on relationships.
3. Traditional education protects us from danger, and seldom gives us a chance to make mistakes. Because of this, students take casually the consequences of their classroom behavior. In Outdoor Experiential Education, the student learns to live with his decisions.
4. Outdoor Experiential Education makes learning more relevant than traditional education. Students learn to cope with stress and fear in an empathetic group environment that has a way of solidifying relationships.

The underlying theme of Outdoor Experiential Education is to use a physically demanding and mentally stressful situation as a catalyst for an experience that enhances self-

241

concept. Research has identified positive selfconcept as one of the key factors for learning to occur. Integrating the outdoor experiential processes into traditional education is vital to help meet the needs of teachers and students in the 1990's.

Program Description

The student needs to complete 33 hours for the degree. Nine hours need to be completed in the required courses. The three required courses are: Foundations of Outdoor Experiential Education, Research Methods and Techniques, and Theory and Practice in Outdoor Experiential Education. The remaining 24 hours will be completed from elective courses. Up to nine (9) hours can be applied from other graduate disciplines: special education, counseling, psychology, business and educational foundations. There will be a thesis and nonthesis option. Internships will be designed by the student with the guidance of a graduate counselor. Final comprehensive exams will consist of two parts, written and oral.

A. Objectives

Six objectives of the inter-institutional Outdoor Experiential Education Masters are incorporated in the degree program:

1. To establish an interdisciplinary graduate degree program that will provide mainstream educational reform and address the problems of urban youth and minority populations.
2. To develop a collaborative teacher training and research program with Outward Bound that addresses the educational and social issues affecting urban youth.
3. To establish a training and certification program that will encourage interdisciplinary graduate study.
4. To involve community service as a vital component in education.
5. To provide experience in, and exposure to, the practical and theoretical use of research in interdisciplinary outdoor experiential programs.
6. To establish the model teacher training and certification program in the metropolitan Chicago Area, as well as the state of Illinois.

Educational reform programs have been successfully implemented in metropolitan public schools in New York, Pittsburgh, and St. Louis. The Outdoor Experiential component has been identified as a key factor contributing to the success of these programs.

Outward Bound chose to direct its efforts toward mainstream educational reform and minority urban youth. The Chicago, New York, and Boston Outward Bound Centers demonstrate commitment to this objective. All three programs seek to address the issues affecting urban youth.

Outward Bound has a long history of development in these areas. As early as 1966, Outward Bound began work with high schools in Colorado and New Jersey. Outward Bound has worked cooperatively with universities and colleges in Minnesota, Arizona, and Colorado to enhance teacher training programs. To date, Outward Bound offers courses to address literacy, retention, racial integration, and substance abuse.

Outdoor Experiential courses and teaching methodologies are intended to be integrated into the following disciplines: guidance and counseling, special education, therapeutic recreation, business and management, and physical/adaptive education. The interdisciplinary degree program seeks to bridge the gap between traditional teacher preparation and Outdoor Experiential Education. Utilizing techniques and strategies from both disciplines can only assist educators with the academic tools necessary to meet the future integrative and diverse needs of our students.

Community service is an integral part of the curriculum model. This component will develop collaborative partnerships with the surrounding educational, business and socialneighborhood communities. Service learning will create opportunities for students to apply their knowledge and skills in cooperative programs that benefit the community.

Collaborative educational research projects will be designed to attract highly qualified faculty and provide an opportunity for students to pursue interdisciplinary studies. Departments working together will augment the ability of the program to successfully solicit grant money from both public and private organizations.

At the present time there are no master's level Outdoor Experiential Education degree programs in the state. Nationally-recognized Outdoor Experiential Education degree programs will be utilized as models in the development of course work, safety policies, procedures and internships.

B. Relationship of the Request to the Mission, Plans and Priorities of the University

Northeastern Illinois and Chicago State are universities that serve metropolitan Chi-

cago and the surrounding areas. The mission and priorities of the universities closely parallel one another. Therefore, developing an interinstitutional collaborative degree program will be an ideal partnership that will serve as a model to be emulated by other institutions.

The interdisciplinary Outdoor Experiential mater's degree program will address the mission and priorities of both universities in the following manner:

1. It will add to the number and diversity of master's degree programs offered through both universities. The collaborative interinstitutional Outdoor Experiential program would be the first available for educators in the state of Illinois.
2. It will provide an interdisciplinary master's degree program that addresses the needs of a multi-cultural student population by integrating various university disciplines around a central core concept.
3. The program will provide public service to the surrounding metropolitan Chicago area through collaborative partnerships with the surrounding educational, business, and local communities.
4. It will enhance a strong integrated program of general education that supports lifelong learning, which will equip students to be more able to meet the educational challenges of the 1990's.

C. Student Demand

During 1989, approximately 355 educators from the metropolitan Chicago area have attended Outdoor Experiential training sessions sponsored by Northeastern Illinois University of Chicago State:

1. November 18, 1989. Participants–30, Northeastern Illinois University.
2. November 9-10, 1989. Participants–100*, Illinois State, Physical Education Convention, Peoria, Illinois.
3. July 5, 1989. Participants–65*, Chicago State University.
4. June 22, 1989. Participants–15, Arlyn School, Skokie, Illinois.
5. May 5-6, 1989. Participants–45*, Chicago State University.
6. April 21-22, 1989. Participants–100, Outdoor Experiential Conference, Northeastern Illinois University.

* A total of 122 participants were registered as Students-at-Large for graduate credit through Chicago State. The remaining 233 participants registered despite the fact no graduate credit was available.

Program evaluations and information surveys were completed by the participants at the conclusion of each workshop. Two significant factors were identified:

1. Approximately 70% (284) of the participants indicated interest in pursuing graduate degree training, or taking course work as a Student-at-Large.
2. All 355 (100%) participants indicated Outdoor Experiential Education should have been <u>required</u> as part of undergraduate teacher training preparation.

The potential for student demand is outstanding. In 1972, an interdisciplinary Outdoor Experiential Education program was started in Hamilton, MA. The school district received a Title III grant to start a program, named "Project Adventure." In the last 17 years, 1.2 million participants have been exposed to adventure challenge programs developed by Project Adventure.

Indiana University's Outdoor Experiential program, at Bradford Woods, has influenced over 10,000 participants. Since 1985, six hundred educators have attended training and certification workshops. Dr. Mark Havens, at Portland State University in Oregon, has 100 educators annually registered for his Outdoor Experiential workshops.

Student demand, both for participants attending programs and for educators seeking training, may well be excellent. Should an approved interdisciplinary Outdoor Experiential master's program be publicized, students from several different curriculum areas will have the opportunity to augment their professional preparation.

D. Anticipated Number of Major and Graduates in the Fifth Year

The Outdoor Experiential master's degree program would be implemented in Fall, 1991. A conservative estimate of students and graduates is indicated below:

Year	Majors	Graduates
1992	10	--
1993	20	2
1994	30	4
1995	45	6
1996	60	10

Students-at-Large
20
30
45
60
75

Majors were estimated by investigating the number of students enrolled in the following master degree programs: counselor education, special education, and physical education. A number of five percent was selected from their total enrollment as an indicator.

Program graduates are based on a statistic provided by the Dean of the Graduate college at Northeastern Illinois University. He stated that only 16 to 20% of students completed their graduate work within a two-year period, because a majority of them work fulltime.

The graduate program will provide a service element to students-at-large. Dr. George Stroia, Chairman of the Physical Education Department at Chicago State University, stated there are approximately 100 students-at-large taking courses in their graduate program. The numbers indicated are an estimate of student interest from other curricular areas.

E. Description of Possible Internships and Clinical Sites

The strength of the Outdoor Experiential degree program lies in its diversity. Students will have the opportunity to become interns at nationally recognized programs, or established programs in and around metropolitan Chicago. Each student will design, with the guidance of his graduate advisor, his own internship and selection of a clinical site in one of the four following categories: national programs, education, recreation or corporate training and development.

The following programs have indicated a willingness to accept our internship students:

1. National Programs

   Voyager Outward Bound School
   Ely, Minnesota

   Iowa Mountaineers
   Iowa City, Iowa

   Outward Bound, Urban Program
   Chicago, Illinois

   S.L.E.E.P. (St. Louis Experiential Education Program)
   St. Louis, Missouri

2. Interdisciplinary Education Programs

   a. Special Education

   Arden Shore
   North Shore Special Education
   District - N.S.S.E.D.
   Lake Bluff, Illinois

   Sunrise Lake Adventure Center
   North Shore Special Education
   District - N.S.S.E.D.
   Bartlett, Illinois

Upward Bound Program
Eagle River, Wisconsin
District 214
Arlington Heights, Illinois

b. Math, Science & Environmental
Education

Outdoor Wilderness Leadership
School - O.W.L.S.
Lake Geneva, Wisconsin

Atwood Nature Center
Rockford, Illinois

Culver Middle School
Morton Grove, Illinois

c. Counseling

Barrington Middle School
Barrington, Illinois

d. Physical Education
Glenbrook South High School
Glenview, Illinois

Lake Forest High School
Lake Forest, Illinois

Conant High School
Schaumburg, Illinois

Deerfield High School
Deerfield, Illinois

Lyons Township High School
Lyons, Illinois

3. Park Districts

Iron Oaks Adventure Center
Olympia Fields, Illinois

Northbrook Park District
Northbrook, Illinois

Atwood Adventure Center
Rockford Park District
Rockford, Illinois

Camp Algonquin
United Charities
Algonquin, Illinois

4. Therapeutic Recreation

Maine-Niles Special Recre-
ation Association
Niles, Illinois
Rogers Memorial Hospital
Oconomowoc, Wisconsin

5. Corporate Training and Development

Arthur Andersen & Company
World Training Center
St. Charles, Illinois

F. Any Cooperative Relationships That May be Developed with Other Public or Private Universities or Community Colleges

The collaborative inter-institutional Outdoor Experiential master's degree program between Northeastern University and Chicago Illinois University may well serve as a model throughout the state. The Physical Education Departments of both universities have collaborated for the past ten years in offering graduate courses. This collaborative inter-institutional program would enhance their working relationship, and the ability to provide graduate-level opportunities in the metropolitan Chicago area.

The Chicago Outward Bound Urban Program has approached Chicago State and Northeastern Illinois Universities to develop a collaborative teacher retraining program. The focus of the program would address mainstream educational reform and the problems of urban youth and minority populations. During the last 21 years, Outward Bound has developed collaborative teacher training programs with a few select universities in the United States, the most recent proposal being developed with Harvard's Graduate School of Education in March of 1989.

Chicago State and Northeastern Illinois University are leaders in academic analysis and research of education. Outward Bound is a leader in the field of experience-based education. These two institutions working together could have the capacity to profoundly impact not only teachers and students, but the entire educational reform movement in the Chicago metropolitan area.

G. Employment Opportunities for Graduates

The employment opportunities for graduates are excellent. It is anticipated that the majority of students enrolling will currently be employed as elementary and high school teachers in the metropolitan Chicago area. Students in this situation will be able to complete the master's degree requirements while maintaining their teaching positions.

An increased demand for teachers with Outdoor Experiential training is anticipated. The Association for Experiential Education (AEE), founded in 1976, is an organization that seeks to advance interdisciplinary outdoor experientialbased learning. The organization discovered there is a tremendous need for leaders with training because there are only a few degree programs available in the country. The Outdoor Experiential master's degree program would fill a void that exists for educators in the metropolitan Chicago area and allow them to receive an advanced degree.

The Outdoor Experiential Education master's degree will provide employment opportunities not only in education but also in the following fields: outdoor education centers, summer camps, YMCAs, therapeutic hospitals, social agencies, and corporate training and development. Corporations are actively seeking leaders with an Outdoor Experiential background to be used in training and development programs. The business community has endorsed outdoor experiential education as a management training tool.

Dr. Tom Smith, a retired clinical psychologist for District 214 in Illinois, who utilizes adventure challenge teaching methodologies recently stated:

"It has been a long gestation period for outdoor experiential education. However, the pregnancy is over and the birth has occurred. Universities need to establish degree programs, and schools need to implement interdisciplinary experience-based programs into their traditional curriculum. The children in today's society need the benefits derived from these programs."

Northeastern Illinois and
Chicago State Universities

Masters' Outdoor
Experiential Education

BOARD OF GOVERNORS OF STATE COLLEGE AND UNIVERSITIES

Springfield, Illinois

Preliminary Budget Form for
New or Expanded Program Requests

Personnel Services

1.3–Full-Time Faculty (10 month)

$ 2,700/month
One faculty will be located at Chicago
State
Two faculty will be located at
Northeastern

2.2–Full-Time Graduate Assistants (10
month) $600/month

3.1.5 –Full-Time Secretary (12 month)

$1,250/month
Half-time secretary will be located at
Chicago State
Full-time secretary will be located at
Northeastern

4.2 –Students Aides (12 month)

$4.00/hour x 20 hours/week

Equipment

1.2 –Personal Computers and Printers

One unit will be at Chicago State
One unit will be at Northeastern

2. –One-Time Only Permanent Structures
to be Built on Campus at Northeastern
Illinois University

15 element low ropes initiative course
10 element high rope initiative course
Alpine Tower team initiative course

Outdoor climbing and rappelling station
12 station indoor climbing wall

Library (to be housed at the Ronald
Williams Library at Northeastern
Illinois University)

Contractual Services

Commodities

*This total includes $48,000 for "one-time-only" structure developments to be built on campus at Northeastern Illinois University. These structures are a vital part of the training and certification in the Masters' program.

Corporate Outdoor Experiential Training & Development

by Richard J. Wagner
Gail M. Ryan
Christopher C. Roland

Introduction

Outdoor experiential training (OET) has been used by many different people for many reasons, and is known by many different names. This type of training has been referred to as: outdoor training, experience-based training, outdoor-challenge training, ropes course training, challenge course training, wilderness training, outdoor experiential training, and a variety of other names. Training has been used by psychiatric and chemical dependency agencies, physical rehabilitation hospitals, youth counselors, and, most recently by corporations. A recent survey of corporate training directors found that 13.8 percent of U.S. companies use some form of OET as a part of their overall training program (Wagner, Baldwin and Roland, 1991). The use of training by corporations appears to be a relatively recent phenomena, having started in the mid-1980's and having grown steadily over the last five years.

History of Training

The concept of outdoor-based training has evolved over the past sixty years. In the 1930's, Kurt Hahn, a German noble who fled Hitler's Germany, developed the forerunner of the Outward Bound School in Wales. During World War II, Hahn noticed that the older sailors often had a greater ability to survive in stressful conditions than the younger and physically stronger sailors. He concluded that the younger men "lacked the self-reliance, confidence and compassionate bond with their fellow crew members that was so essential to meeting the challenge of the crisis" (Broderic, 1989). In the United States, Hahn's model was adapted by the Civilian Conservation Corps (CCC), a New Deal program using unemployed men who worked to restore and build structures on the nation's public lands. In the early 1960's, the Colorado Outward Bound School was formed allowing youth to experience the wilderness environment, sometimes under stressful conditions.

The experiences that took place during the 1970's, helped revolutionize outdoor experiential training to what it is today. In 1971, Project Adventure was created in Hamilton, Massachusetts to offer an on-site adapted Outward Bound experience for high school sophomores. The findings of this project showed that the student's self-concept was increased as a result of the experience. From that point, challenge education programs grew in popularity and were used to train varied audiences. These audiences included individuals with disabilities, troubled teenagers, and a few managers. During the 1970's the programs would push participants to, and often beyond their mental and physical limitations (Bolt, 1990). However, many observers at this time perceived corporate OET as a fad, citing a lack of research as a major factor. A similar problem had been found in the encounter group movement and sensitivity training.

Although a number of agencies experimented with challenge education programming for managers and supervisors in the 1970's, the real momentum did not begin until 1981 with Boston University's Executive Challenge Program. Supervisors from high technology firms initially participated in a three day program and gave it rave reviews. The consensus was that managerial and team-building skills can indeed be enhanced through exposure to a semi-wilderness environment which utilizes both mental and physical abilities in mildly stress-related activities, and problems which require both individual and group effort to solve. These anecdotal comments were supported by a quantitative research study, *The Transfer of an Outdoor Managerial Training Program to the Work Place* (Roland, 1981).

Why is Outdoor Experiential Training Attractive to Business?

Those initial findings served to attract many of today's "blue chip" companies into exploring experience-based training. One reason that OET appears to be successful is because of the location. The outdoor setting takes the trainee away from the sterile corporate atmosphere allowing for more relaxed interactions in a more comfortable setting than the traditional classroom. In this unique habitat, trainees have the opportunity to understand things about themselves and are given the permission to change. Being in the outdoors also appears to reduce the time necessary for training to take place. "In a very short time a crisis

can arise, providing immediate opportunities for developing leadership and teamwork" (Bolt, 1990). OET exercises are designed to reflect what happens in day-to-day office situations. One of the primary objectives of OET is to transfer the knowledge gained in the outdoors to the work place.

OET can also be directed at specific problems. Different corporate needs dictate different types of exercises. Some exercises focus on team building while others are designed to develop leadership skills. "OET is most often used to provide metaphors with lessons about problem solving, communication, leadership, creativity, self-esteem, motivation, decision making, risk taking, and fear reduction" (Thompson, 1991). Experiential outdoor training is designed to improve honesty, trust, self acceptance, personal empowerment, and teamwork. By working in teams, people learn about withholding judgments and mistrusting stereotyped first impressions, about effective allocation of diverse resources, meshing strong personalities toward a mutual goal, and how to accept help and understand people's pleasure in giving it.

An example of how outdoor-training can change a person's usual behavior involves a manager who said that she had never been good at making her needs known to her peers. Her outdoor training group's challenge was to conquer "The Wall." However, the manager had a shoulder that could be easily dislocated and for fear of injury had to make her needs known. As a result, she told her teammates of her weakness and they responded accordingly, allowing the task to be accomplished without injury. This experience was then directly related to the office, with each trainee discussing his/her limitations and how the team could support each other. An action plan was later developed that committed the team to allow time during staff meetings to openly share each other's concerns and problems.

How Organizations Integrate the Outdoors into their Training

Several models for the use of outdoor-training have evolved over the last few years. The term "outdoor training" means different things to different people. Outdoor training can take the form of a wilderness program, in which the participants live and sleep outdoors and participate in highly active events, such

as mountain climbing, sailing, or rafting. Those organizations which use the wilderness model as part of their training are often looking for changes in selected behaviors of individual managers. The behaviors they seek to change commonly include risk-taking, assertiveness, self-esteem, and leadership skills.

A second model used by companies is the "ropes/challenge course." Although both the low and high ropes challenge courses have been used by companies, the low ropes/challenge course appears to be most often utilized. The low ropes courses generally focus on improving "team performance" and emphasize areas such as trust, communications, problem solving, and improving the overall function of a work group. The high ropes/challenge course is often seen as encouraging changes in individual behaviors such as increased risk-taking and improved individual self-esteem.

Some organizations have become so committed to OET that approval has been given

for the installation of a ropes/challenge course on-site, thereby creating a third model. This allows and OET program to be conducted on-site by in-house and/or external trainers. However, the challenge course can be misinterpreted by company employees who have not participated in a program. Instead of a unique and valuable training resource, the outdoor equipment is perceived as nonessential. The following is a segment of an anonymous internal memo from an employee of an organization that installed such a challenge course.

> The placement of this equipment is already a source of emotional stress to employees who want to continue working for [this organization] but do not want to risk being paralyzed or killed just to keep a desk job...Even if, and I think it is a big if, no one is hurt out there, just installing military training equipment sends a message to employees that we are no longer respected by upper management for our intelligence, but only value our ability to do physical labor.

From this feedback, the Organization Development Department made a concerted effort to educate all employees regarding the OET program. Support was received from the president and his officers. Currently, the numerous positive experiences from the participants are outweighing any criticisms.

Indoor-Outdoor-Indoor Model

In this model, no ropes/challenge course is utilized-only simple, easy-to-transport props are needed. Balls, rope segments, blindfolds, and short boards can all be transported to any site including the corporate training room and the resort conference center.

The OET program begins indoors with goals and objectives, introductions, schedules, etc. Indoor experiential activities follow with appropriate discussion or debriefing sessions linking the experience with real work issues. Depending on the design and needs of the group, an outdoor activity is then facilitated immediately outside the training room. Upon activity completion and perhaps a very brief discussion, the group returns to the training room to fully discuss the applications. At this time, the facilitator has at his/her disposal flip charts, overhead projectors, slide projectors, VCR's etc. to accentuate the outdoor learning. The authors have found that this process generates a higher level of discussion and application of the outdoor experience to real work issues.

Facilitators

A second difficulty companies have faced has been the development of qualified trainers (generally called facilitators) for these programs. Recent studies (Wagner & Roland, in press; Wagner & Roland, 1992) have suggested that the facilitator does have a major impact on the effectiveness of these programs. The lack of in-house facilitators trained in the "experiential model" has contributed to the use of programs offered by external consultants. Although many of these external consultants have strong backgrounds in using experience-based activities, they often are unable to directly link these activities to specific work place issues. It is the absence of this link which often causes OET programs to produce less than desired results.

Finally, a fourth model is gaining popularity. This corporate model uses outdoor training as an integral part of an existing corporate training program, facilitated by internal or external trainers. An example is the use of outdoor training to enhance a TQM (Total Quality Management) effort. Indoor and outdoor experiential activities are integrated throughout the program in order to highlight specific points. In the TQM scenario, experiential activities are facilitated to focus on team building.

How Successful is Outdoor Training?

Companies such as NTW and AT&T have shown an increase in profits as a result of adventure training experiences. NTW more than doubled its profits in the year following it's adventure training experiences. AT&T reports that, "We've shown significant improvement in our revenue-to-expense relationships, we've dropped our cost per order; we've improved our quality, accuracy, and timeliness of orders; and we've improved our collections results" (Gail, 1987).

Outdoor-training programs have proved that, "Learning can come from lectures and books, but if you're interested in changing how people behave, newer methods have a unique power" (Bolt, 1990). Outdoor-training programs often provide more than short term financial benefits to a company; for example, they may also improve employees' interpersonal relations and individual behavior. While many claims have been made about the effectiveness of outdoor training programs, it

is only recently that serious research has been done to determine their effectiveness in corporate settings. Both quantitative and qualitative research efforts have demonstrated that these programs have a significant impact on the way in which participants interact with each other at work, after the training program (Thompson, 1991; Wagner & Roland, in press).

Participants often report a reduction of old conflicts and an increase in simply talking to other people at work. This often takes the form of asking other people for help with a problem or input in areas of mutual interest. Best of all, this "sharing" is commonly reported to take place in situations in which there were no communications prior to attending an outdoor training program. Many participants report that they now talk regularly to fellow workers who they previously paid little attention. In addition, many people report that their work group is more open to new ideas and more willing to accept change than they were before attending training. These changes have been reported for as long as two years after the training program and in many instances appear to increase, rather than decrease, over time (Baldwin, Wagner & Roland, 1991).

While outdoor training programs have been successful for many companies, some companies have found that outdoor training did not address their training needs. Several areas of caution appear to be worth noting. As with many "fads", the growth in the use of outdoor training programs has created some problems for the field. We have found that there are three problem areas especially worth noting. These areas are setting clear goals and objectives, selecting participant groups with care, and being sure that the facilitators are properly trained for the program being conducted.

Many companies began using outdoor-experiential training on a whim, with little or no prior planning; thus, no clear-cut goals or objectives were established for the program. As a result, when asked to rate the effectiveness of the outdoor-training program, these organizations are often at a loss to come up with a meaningful answer. Establishing clear objectives prior to the program is the first step in determining effectiveness. If there are no goals for the program, then no meaningful evaluation of the training program is possible. Many excellent programs fail to be renewed simply because no one can demonstrate their success.

Our studies to date have clearly shown that not all groups improve their work performance after attending an OET program. Almost everyone we have talked to has enjoyed attending OET, but this does not guarantee a transfer of their training experience to the work setting. One key method to aid with transfer appears to depend on the composition of the group that attends OET. If the OET group also works together (intact work group), then the likelihood of transfer to the work setting is high. On the other hand, if the OET group does not work together on a regular basis, the likelihood of transfer of training appears to be minimal. Thus, if an organization seeks to maximize the value of the OET program in improving work behaviors, it is important to select OET groups carefully. This includes careful attention to the work relationships of the participants.

The final area of caution concerns the program facilitators. A good facilitator can greatly enhance the value of the OET pro-

gram. The facilitator must be in-tune with the organizational objectives of the OET program and must possess the training and skills to effectively lead the program. Our research suggest that these skills must include more than just knowledge of the activities. The facilitators must also be familiar with human behavior skills, group interaction skills, and also with the actual organizational culture and problems faced by the OET participants.

Summary

Overall, the use of OET by organizations has been found to be an effective means of training employees in many critical skill areas. These include team building (e.g., high performance work teams), empowerment, leadership, diversity, and creative problem solving. Properly designed, implemented, and evaluated, OET can greatly enhance the effectiveness of a company's overall training and development program. OET, in fact, can become a key link in an organization's quest for individual, team, and organizational change.

References

Baldwin, T.T., Wagner, R. J. & Roland, C. C. (1991, April). *Effects of Outdoor Challenge Training on Group and Individual Perceptions*. Paper presented at the Annual Meeting of the Society for Industrial & Organizational Psychology, St. Louis.

Bolt, J. F. (1990). How executives learn: The move from glitz to guts. *Training and Development Journal, 44*(2), 83-87.

Broderick, R. (1989). Learning the ropes. *Training Magazine, 10,* 76-78.

Gail, Adrienne L. (1987). You can take the Manager out of the Woods, but....*Training and development Journal, 41* (3), 54-59.

Roland, C. C. (1981). *The Transfer of an Outdoor Managerial Training Program to the Work Place*. Unpublished Doctoral Dissertation, Boston University, 1981.

Thompson, Brad Lee. (1991). Training in the Great Outdoors. *Training. 28*(5), 46-52.

Wagner, R. J., Baldwin, T. T. & Roland, C. C. (1991). Outdoor training: Revolution or fad? *Training & Development Journal, 45* (3), 51-57.

Wagner, R. J. & Roland, C. C. (in press). Outdoor-based training: Research findings and recommendations to trainers. *Training & Development.*

Wagner, R. J. & Roland, C. C. (1992, January). *Facilitators: One key factor in implementing successful experience-based training and development programs*. Paper presented to the Coalition for Education in the Outdoors Research Symposium, Bradford Woods, IN.

Interdisciplinary Models, Approaches, & Networking

by Christopher C. Roland

As noted in Chapter I and depicted in Figure 1, challenge education has taken its roots from nine identified influences and disciplines, including adventure education, outdoor education, experiential education, and camping education.

These influences and disciplines were instrumental in the development of the "first generation" challenge programs in a variety of initial settings including schools, camps, and colleges. Examples include the Title III Project Adventure grant in 1972 which enabled high school sophomores to participate in a challenge program in place of traditional physical education class.

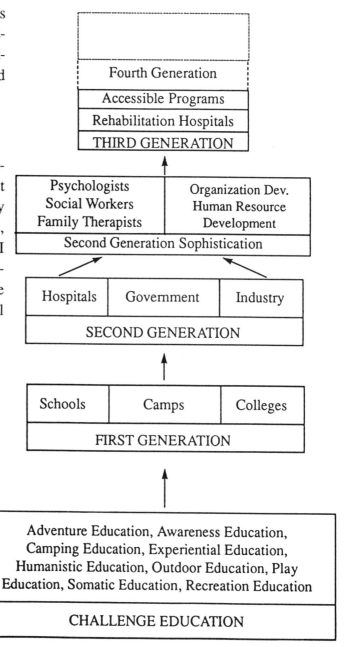

Figure 1

The "second generation" of challenge education was the development of challenge programs in settings including psychiatric/chemical dependency hospitals, special education schools and cooperatives, universities, government, business and industry. This evolutionary process was due to a range of factors, including (1) the level of acceptance in the original settings—challenge education became less and less of a "fad," (2) informal interdisciplinary communication efforts, e.g., between teachers and psychologists, (3) the increasing level of research, including Master's theses, Doctoral Dissertations, and referenced journal articles, and (4) the basic need and desire for more exciting and stimulating methods, materials, and curricula.

Within each of these second generation challenge education programs, staff with backgrounds in experiential education, outdoor education, etc. became the program leaders, facilitators and coordinators. For example in the psychiatric hospital setting, the challenge programs have been typically developed in the Activity Therapy, Adjunctive Therapy or Recreation Therapy departments. In business and industry, corporate groups often traveled to outdoor education centers, with activities being facilitated by professionals with an outdoor/challenge background.

In the past few years, the second generation programs have become increasingly sophisticated. More formalized efforts are being made to communicate between disciplines regarding the value of challenge programs in order to broaden and strengthen how the activities are facilitated. Two examples are given:

1. Psychiatric and Chemical Dependency Hospitals

Hundreds of psychiatric and chemical dependency facilities have made a commitment to challenge education. With a more concerted effort to communicate throughout the hospital, an increasing number of professionals, including psychologists, social workers, and family therapists are becoming involved with challenge programs. As a result, the programs are earning greater respect and recognition and becoming a more meaningful therapeutic intervention.

To encourage interdisciplinary communication, many hospitals are implementing a challenge education orientation program. A main goal is to educate key staff including the medical director, head nurse and psychiatrists. Some orientation programs are conducted prior to installation of challenge equipment, with emphasis being placed on therapeutic value and research data. This allows the key staff to view the program process rather than the ropes equipment. Once there is this level of awareness, the "trickle-down" phenomenon will commence, until the majority of staff will view the program not as "Stress Challenge" or "The Ropes Course Program" but as "The Therapeutically Relevant Challenge Program." Recent research supports this need for staff awareness and support. Gilliam noted

"The issue of support is critical to its widespread utilization. From the five facilities visited, there existed a continuance of support, from those who very much backed it to those who were not supportive." (Gilliam, 1990)

2. Corporations

As noted earlier, an increasing number of corporations are becoming involved with challenge programs. Fortune 100, 500, and 1000 companies are involving their executives, management teams and intact work teams in a wide range of programs. Results from a national survey by Wagner, Baldwin, & Roland (1991) indicated 13% of the companies that responded were involved with some type of challenge program. They also defined two major categories of programming: (1) Wilderness Model, where participants live outdoors and participate in such activities as mountain climbing, rock climbing, whitewater rafting, etc., and (2) Outdoor Centered Model, where participants sleep and eat indoors but are involved with outdoor training activities, including low, teams, and high ropes/challenge courses.

Many corporate programs, especially those which focus on "team building," have been heretofore facilitated by individuals trained in "non-business" disciplines including recreation, outdoor education, counseling and physical education. Although these facilitators do not have a business background, programs are frequently rated highly. This can be attributed to the power of the activities and the overall facilitation skills of the instructor. It can be argued, in fact, that those facilitators with human service skills offer a refreshing non-business oriented approach to training, especially in the team building area. MBA students at a major university who attended an outdoor challenge program concurred. Many noted that the facilitators were indeed refreshing, making the students keenly aware of the need for human interaction skills.

However, an increasing number of the "human service" facilitators are seeking additional training for themselves in training and development, human resources and organizational development. As organizations become more sophisticated in challenge program design and implementation, the facilitators with varied competencies, skills and knowledge are the ones who are being selected as trainers and consultants. Recent research supports this perhaps obvious assumption. Wagner & Roland (1992) analyzed data from one day challenge programs over a two year period. A train-the-trainer program was delivered at the beginning of each year, with the second year's program focusing on transfer of training to the work place. The initial group outcome data indicated that the participants in year two experienced greater gains than those participants in year one.

The aforementioned counselors, outdoor educators, physical educators, etc. are now networking with organizations' Training Directors, Organizational Development Specialists, Human Resource Consultants, etc. Together, they are developing joint programs, including on-site train-the-trainer programs. Everyone is learning from each other and working towards the goal of wide acceptance of challenge programming.

An Evolving Third Generation

Throughout the 1990's, a third generation of challenge programming will continue to evolve. For example, interdisciplinary challenge programs at rehabilitation hospitals will benefit a wide range of patients with head injuries, spinal cord injuries, strokes and amputations. With a focus on interdisciplinary communication and cooperation, physical therapists, occupational therapists, recreation therapists, speech therapists, psychologists and family therapists will all have access to challenge activities in order to make therapy more relevant and fun. For example, a program known as TRACS: The Rehab Accessible Challenge System allows rehabilitation patients to experience Challenge Education as part of their therapeutic routine. As one therapist noted (1991), "We do a lot of esteem building and confidence work. It is especially helpful when working with those who can't get motivated in regular therapy." In addition, with the signing of the American Disabilities Act in July, 1991(Lotito & Pimentel, 1990), there will be greater effort to make existing challenge programs accessible.

ASSOCIATIONS

It is widely acknowledged that the 1300+ member Association for Experiential Education (AEE) is a significant leader in the promotion and validation of challenge education. Based at the School of Education at The University of Colorado in Boulder, AEE publishes books and periodicals, sponsors regional and national gatherings, and serves as a clearinghouse for information about experiential and challenge programs. Many practitioners of challenge/adventure education refer to AEE as their association of choice; since 1974, leaders within the association have acted as experiential pied pipers, teaching and influencing people representing a widerange of fields to the theory and practice of challenge education.

Two new associations have been formed in order to further meet professionals' specific interests and needs. The first, AETD: The Association for Experience-Based Training & Development, was founded in May 1990, with the aim of developing a network of pro-

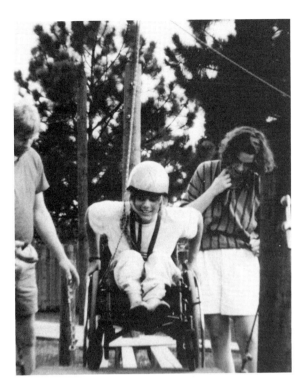

fessionals who are involved, or want to be involved, in experiential programs targeted for corporate personnel.

The first issue of the AETD (1990) noted:

AETD is an association of individuals and organizations who are dedicated to the following:

- facilitating individual and organizational change through experiencebased training and development;
- selecting, developing and maintaining the highest standards for the safe and ethical use of experience-based training and development;
- strengthening the industry through research, evaluation and feedback;
- promoting an accurate and positive image of the industry;
- sharing information to prospective experience-based training users; and
- creating a referral network of providers of experience-based training and development.

The second association is ACCT: The Association for Challenge Course Technology, formed in November 1991. ACCT began as a semi-formal group of challenge course builders meeting for the first time at the Kurt Hahn Leadership Center in North Carolina in 1988. The second meeting was held at the Pecos River Learning Center in 1990.

The primary purpose of ACCT is to focus on technical aspects of ropes course construction with a future goal of developing material and construction standards. Other topics include:

- Accident reports
- Physiological research
- Impact on the environment
- Accessibility issues for persons with disabilities
- New challenge course designs
- Rescue techniques
- Specialty equipment

Plans for the ACCT is to attract a wider audience of both challenge course builders, facilitators and researchers. Information will be disseminated throughout numerous organizations, universities and private companies regarding the next ACCT symposium in San Francisco, California in 1993.

A Need to Network

In order for the benefits of challenge education to be more widely disseminated, it is imperative that the experiential and challenge educators venture periodically from their smaller affiliations to one or more of the grand associations. Workshops and seminars need to be presented and articles need to be accepted for publication. There are tens of thousands of individuals who can learn about the application of challenge programming. For example, a short article by Frant, Roland and

Schempp published in 1982 in *Teaching Exceptional Children* had significant impact on many special education teachers. One teacher wrote explaining, "Thank you for your uplifting article on [challenge education]. As a potentially burnt-out teacher, I have found some of the recommended activities to be exciting and uplifting for both the students and me. I am now searching for money to build one of your "ropes courses" - now this is the way education should be!"

Networking from Within: A Humbling Lesson

One "grand" association is the Council for Exceptional Children. With headquarters in Washington, D.C., CEC has currently over 50,000 members, with at least 12,000 attending the international conference each year. The association has fifteen divisions, including the Division of Mental Retardation, Division of Physically Handicapped and Division of Learning Disabilities. Having received positive evaluations of challenge education workshops during past international conferences, the author coordinated the writing of a proposal to create a new division. Named DACTS: The Division of Alternative Curricula & Teaching Strategies, the aim was to familiarize teachers and administrators with alternative methods of teaching exceptional children.

The process, commencing in early 1988, was long and complex. A total of three years was spent on the overall proposal development. After two rewrites of the original proposal, after numerous lobbying efforts and after meetings in Washington, D.C., San Francisco and Toronto, the proposal was rejected by the Board of Governors. Three years with very little to show—a most humbling experience indeed. Yet, all was not lost. Throughout the three year effort, even more special education teachers and students were introduced to challenge education; as a result, more changes involving challenge education were made to standard curricula. In addition, an increasing level of succinct rationale for the need for challenge education was articulated during this period. As Dr. Herbert Foster of the University of Buffalo wrote in his DACTS support letter:

...Hence, these [special education] students, to a large extent, need a nontraditional curriculum that brings into play cooperative learning, experiential challenge learning, risk-taking, whole language, and a whole host of new and old curricula and teaching strategies not usually practiced in the average regular or special education classroom. Indeed, if more teachers practiced these non-traditional teaching methods, we would have fewer students in special education...

The tackling of such a massive bureaucratic system with the objective to develop an interdisciplinary communication system was unquestionably grandiose. But social change must begin at some place and at some time. Writing to the Director of Membership Services and a DACTS supporter from the beginning, the author noted,

...Naturally we are disappointed; countless hours of work went into the DACTS proposal. Acceptance of DACTS would have meant the opportunity to effect hundreds and possibly thousands of teachers, administrators and parents. Standard, boring, and irrelevant curricula and teaching strategies would have been more subject to review and change. But, alas, social change takes time, lots and lots of time.

Change takes time and requires the support of numerous professionals. Current efforts are underway to continue the change process—not only in CEC but other associations, including American Society for Training and Development (ASTD), Association for Business Simulation and Experiential Learning (ABSEL) and the American Psychological Association (APA). In order for Challenge Education to be truly accepted, professionals from these associations need to be given the opportunity to experience firsthand challenge activities and interventions.

Conclusion

The evolution of challenge education has produced at least three generations of programming. With the initial beginnings at camps and schools, CE has spread its roots to hospitals, Fortune 500 corporations, and government installations. A key to this growth is increased communication among disciplines and professional associations.

As with any "new" movement, challenge education is not without its detractors. The corporate training world, in particular, has seen a number of articles and editorials criticizing challenge programs. "Simply a fad, " "Total waste of time," "No link with real work issues" are but a few recent comments. Ten years ago, it would have been perhaps appropriate to refer to CE as a fad. However, with today's available research and critically acclaimed programs, challenge education appears to be a sound, here-to-stay methodology. Yet the future lies with the need for enhanced interdisciplinary communication efforts: from department to department, organization to organization, and association to association. As these efforts are meshed with other critical needs including program evaluation and qualitative and quantitative research, the viability and relevancy of challenge education will continue to strengthen until challenge education is recognized as the critical intervention for the 21st century.

REFERENCES

Association for Experience-based Training & Development. (1990). 1(1), 1. (Available from AETD, c/o T. Kruse, 10822 W. 28th Place, Lakewood, CO 80215.

Gilliam, N. (1991). *A Qualitative Study of Ropes Courses in Psychiatric Treatment Facilities.* Unpublished Doctorial Dissertation. The Graduate School of the Union Institute.

Making TRACS in rehab. (1991, July/ August). *Team Rehab Report.* pp. 20-21

Lotito, M. & Pimentel, R. (1990). *The Americans with Disabilities Act: Making the ADA Work for You.* Northridge, CA: Milt Wright and Associates, Inc./Jackson, Lewis, Schnitzler & Krupman.

Support Letter from Dr. Herbert Foster. (1990). *The Division for Ancillary Curricula and Teaching Strategies Proposal.* Keene, N.H.: Roland & Associates, Inc.

Wagner, R., Baldwin, T., & Roland, C. (1991). Outdoor Training: Revolution or Fad? *Training & Development Journal.* 51-56

Wagner, R., & Roland, C. (1992, January). *Corporate Outdoor Training: Do Facilitators Make A Difference?* Paper presented at the Coalition for Outdoor Education Research Symposium, Martinsville, Indiana.

Urban Issues

By Steve Proudman

Historically, adventure education has been imagined as a process of learning in a predominantly "outdoor" setting. The complexity and intensity of program models vary from grade school camping trips (which I experienced in my formalized learning) to a six-month odyssey with the National Audubon Society's Expedition Institute. The growth of the adventure/challenge education profession has created a diversity of program models in a variety of settings, such as college freshman orientations, therapeutic uses and corporate management development. Challenge education has matured as a profession realizing a broad range of applications.

It is important to understand the history of our schools and the nature of their surrounding communities in order to gain a clear vision for the integration of adventure education into urban settings. The current models of public schooling were designed by Horace Mann, Barnes Sears and W. R. Harper at the University of Chicago, Columbia Teachers' College and other distinguished institutions. These models were intended to be instruments of scientific management of the mass population. The schools were to produce, through the application of formulae, formulaic human beings whose behavior can be predicted and controlled (Gatto, 1990).

Much of the current national school reform effort is targeting the basic definition of "schooling;" for example, the length of the school year, the control over curricula, the literacy levels of graduating students and the general quality of the educational experience of all public schooled students. Little disagreement exists regarding the need for real changes in our school models.

The President's Education Summit, in the Fall of 1989, called for the "restructuring" of schools in order to close the gap between what youth are learning academically and socially and what they need to be learning for a viable, prosperous and democratic American society in the 21st century (IRE, 1990). Moreover, to create a better future, we must ask ourselves some questions about the current state of schooling. Consider the following:

*Why is it that many young people fail in inner city public schools?

*Why do so many poor and "minority" youth drop out before completing high school? (According to *Cities In Schools*, 1989, over one million young people drop out of school every year in the United States.)

*Why do so many students, from second grade on, find school "boring" and "irrelevant," a place from which they flee at the earliest possible moment?

*Finally, why do many students drop out in school, failing (or refusing) to participate in and thus succeed in the well-intentioned design of the educational process (Clinchy, 1989).

An holistic approach to learning can address these motivational issues which are causing students to disengage from formal schooling. Challenge education in the form of Outward Bound is positioning itself to be an alternative within the "mainstream" of contemporary schooling. The urban Outward Bound programs are the latest chapter in innovations within the adventure education profession.

Outward Bound, seen by some as part of the Human Potential Movement, uses challenge education to teach individuals to explore their own potentials, abilities and humanity in relation to the world around them. Traditionally, the teaching occurs in an outdoor setting using a plethora of methodologies involving the student's cognitive, psychomotor and affective domains in the processing of knowledge. Through challenge/adventure activities, service learning and individual and group experiences, students discover the power they have to choose the paths that define "their" definitions of success and happiness.

Within Outward Bound's fifty-year global history, urban programming has been instituted as a program component. In the case of "City Challenge" in England, the curriculum is centered around the practice of service learning. "City Bound," in Holland, uses the urban setting as a follow-through experience to a wilderness event with the major emphasis being placed on social survival skills for re-employment of the economically disadvantaged (Healy, 1987 & Koekkoek, 1988).

For the past five years, the Outward Bound system in the United States has devel-oped urban centers in many major metropolitan areas in response to a growing urgency for educational reforms. These urban Outward Bound Centers exist in Atlanta, Boston, Baltimore, San Diego, New York, Chicago, San Francisco, Denver and Minneapolis/St. Paul. Each center uses educational models that differ in form and style, yet remain consistent in philosophy. The work in these cities reflect the organizational growth present in the Outward Bound organization as it begins to address social issues of community education and social transformation.

In order to reconceptualize and adapt the familiar Outward Bound wilderness model of adventure education, a shift in paradigms or mental constructs of reality is necessary. Concurrently, an organizational transformation within Outward Bound is taking place to assist in the call for social healing from innercity communities. These changes are seen as strengthening the traditional programs by pushing the educational design potentials. As these changes occur within the organization, additional issues emerge which are concomitant to the process of curriculum and setting adaptations.

Organizational development around the issues of cultural and racial diversity is being addressed both internally and externally in the current Outward Bound system. As the program models move into the urban setting, several issues evolve which affect the management of these programs, including questions of cultural relevancy of the curricula, inclusion of minorities in the staffing process and the openness of the organization's management to collaborative ventures. These issues, along with others, are seen as healthy to the organization in the development process.

Urban Outward Bound has been a part of the international movement that founder Kurt Hahn devised in the 1940's. The model he originally emphasized was that there should be no surrender of responsibility and no denial of the overriding claims of kindness and justice (Welp, 1989). Hahn's concerns were for the students to ignite their sense of responsibility for service to society. Hahn believed Outward Bound should be present in cities. The leadership should make an effort to continually examine its mission and purpose so as to stay relevant to the dynamic needs of people's growth (James, 1990).

Urban Outward Bound represents a fusion of the wisdom of teaching through the wilderness with the street energy of the inner city. The standard educational processes and philosophies remain intact. The adaptations are with the perceptions and assumptions about

what constitutes Outward Bound programming, or in the broader sense, adventure education. Revisiting the essence of Hahn's teaching reveals the beauty of allowing the seeds of his ideas to flower in the concrete of our planet's cultural gardens: the cities. Cross-cultural understanding, self-reliance, community interdependence, compassion, responsibility to the environment, positive attitudes for success, democratic citizen-

ship—these are concepts which come to life through experiential adventure programs in urban classrooms. A review of current research will create a framework for understanding these adaptations.

A passage from Burton and Elizabeth Dyson's book *Neighborhood Caretakers: Stories, Strategies, and Tools for Healing Urban Community* (1986), helps to illustrate this process of individual and organizational change which is imminent, ongoing and fluid:

> The discoveries of science and events in the 20th century have radically shifted our world view and the operating images out of which we live. We no longer see the world as hierarchical, but as interrelated centers of influence. We no longer see reality as objective, but as multiple perspectives, each of which names the reality it points to. To be an educated person today means to be skilled in Life Methods—methods for thinking, for creating one's own destiny (selfhood), and for participating in the global-social process wherever one is. To educate is to enable others to manipulate these skills so that their whole lives are a process of learning and growth. The imaginal educator (motivator, guide) understands that one's images determine one's behavior and therefore intentionally and selfconsciously uses a wide variety of tools and methods to beam methods that challenge a person's or a group's old, limiting images of self and the world in order to open the way for new, enabling images and new, more successful patterns of operating.

The Dyson ideas represent a synthesis of the knowledge being generated in the fields of consciousness research (Harmon & Rheingold, 1984), community mental health, theology (Wilber, 1984 and Cox, 1987) and the Institute for Cultural Affairs. They offer a model for reconceptualizing our views of how social systems transform themselves through individual and group actions. The idea of reconceptualization is an important key in understanding the potential for adventure education in the urban setting. Moreover, Kurth-Schair (1988), offers additional insight on the idea of transformation:

> Today a significant shift in societal context is well under way, and life in nonstationary post-industrial cultures generates new educational imperatives. As stated by Jantsch and Waddington, "We have arrived at a new evolutionary threshold, marked by a novel and unique task...this task amounts to the conscious creation of culture, the conscious design of a life of continuous qualitative changes, pluralism, uncertainty, variability and high fluctuation." (Jadstch and Waddington, 1984) On the assumption that diversity, flexibility and innovation are essential for human survival and progress, it becomes important to assist students in the development of increasingly complex, creative, and socially oriented self-definitions. This task is best accomplished by conceptualizing students as creators, disseminators, and implementors of knowledge. Students are therefore encouraged to assume more active and discriminating roles in shaping their educational experience, in sharing the results of that experience with peers, adults, and in generating and applying new knowledge to benefit themselves and society.

For adventure education to have greater impact on the reconstruction of public education, the profession as a whole needs to question its fundamental assumptions of identity. Is the profession defining itself by activities and working environments, or, is the thinking based on philosophical foundations and learning processes? If we expand the notion that programs must operate in a pristine natural setting, to be a "true adventure," then an open

exploration of the idea of integrating program methodologies in the urban setting can be realized.

Under the rubric of community education, there is ample room for adventure education (Outward Bound) to make a contribution. The idea of an "educative community" as defined by Clinchy (1989), includes all of the non-school or experiential education programs integrated within the school curricula. The perception of "school" needs to include the social networks of the neighboring communities. Shanker (1988) implies that our old definition of "school" limits students in a way that they do not have a "real world" contact with the skills and ideas that enable them to expand their visions of life's possibilities. By reconstructing schools, learning could be organized with team and cooperative projects, apprentice- type programs, peer coaching and counseling, adventure activities, experiential service learning programs, connecting abstract symbols (metaphors) to real things, solving real problems and other-related strategies.

One strategy holding unlimited potential for innovation is the idea of partnerships between schools, parents, students, community agencies, businesses and adventure education service providers. The Institute for Responsive Education (1990) suggests that:

> ...achieving success for all requires schools, families, and community agencies and institutions to forge a stronger partnership, assuming shared responsibility for the social and academic success of each child. To move toward shared responsibility in the real world, schools, families, and community agencies and institutions must change entrenched attitudes and practices.

The IRE's work is based on research from James Comer, Joyce Epstein, David Seeley and Urie Brofenbrunner. Comer (1980, 1989) reports that children develop in many ways simultaneously. Their academic success is tied to concurrent social, emotional and physical development. Adventure education teaches holistically, engaging all parts of "self" simultaneously. Brofenbrunner (1979, 1983) suggests that a child's development and sense of self is the result of complex interactions between the different ecological systems of which he or she is a part including family, peers, neighborhood, school, church and social service agencies. A neighborhood expedition on an urban Outward Bound course places students in direct contact with all these components of "community" through interviewing and by observation and discussion. The educational value of these experiences is reflected in the high level of real and meaningful humanistic interactions that require students' active participation.

Epstein (1984) reports on the critical role played by classroom teachers and the need to train and support teachers who are trying to implement restructuring and innovations such as new ties to families and communities. Teacher training programs, involving adventure education methodologies, are being implemented in urban settings through partnerships initiated by Outward Bound's Urban Centers. To effect systematic change with broader impact potentials, "teacher training institutes" can be conducted, whereby adventure education philosophies and methodologies are taught through a process of empowerment.

Moreover, David Seeley (1985), has developed a partnership model that is defined in terms of "success for all through collaboration for all." Seeley's model does not conceive of education as something delegated by society to one bureaucratic agency called the school, leaving that agency solely responsible for the success or failure of children. The model is collaborative in which parents, students, community organizations, citizens and school staff work together for shared goals in which accountability is shared by all parties. Seeley argues that this collaborative model requires profound changes in the mind-sets of all concerned. Urban Outward Bound Centers are creating community (team) building programs to act as catalyst experiences in the evolution of these change "processes."

Recently, the Voyageur Outward Bound School's Chicago Center presented a workshop, "Building Community Through the Use of Adventure: Outward Bound for Chicago's Schools," at the Citizen Schools Committee's 1990 Leadership Conference which was entitled, "Student Development for the 21st Century: Myths and Realities" (Proudman, 1990). This workshop was presented to teachers, principals and local school council elected officials responsible for localized school-based management. The premise of the workshop was to view schools as communities where creation of a caring and supportive environment is essential to the processes of learning. The community building program utilizes initiatives and mobile ropes course elements to impact the relationships among people concerned with improving the operations and outcomes of schools.

Through the use of Outward Bound activities, adapted to meet the needs of schools, a cooperative and open learning environment is developed. The concepts basic to empowering human relations include: trust, cooperation, communication and respect for self and others. Out of the relationships currently being established, come the comprehensive community-based program models that will mature in the 1990's. Each city has its own unique political realities. The solutions to the social problems must be addressed through a plethora of change agents.

Urban Outward Bound conjures up images of rappelling off buildings, paddling urban waterways, engaging in service learning experiences at shelters for the homeless and camping on rooftops. These images are accurate. The experiences are conducted in the small group "expedition" model of participation that flows from the wilderness programs. However, urban Outward Bound also translates into images of community building programs, modeled after the professional development programs currently being offered to corporate groups. Programs conceived from broader social visions include designing adventure programs to foster race relations and multicultural understanding, cross-culturalism (urban/ suburban, urban/rural), alliance building between many divergent human service professionals and training of teachers as entry level practitioners or for personal and professional renewal after many years of service. The potential is unlimited once a firm understanding of the resources available for programming in an urban environment are developed.

Adventure education in urban settings requires programmers to view the entire city—its natural, physical and human elements—as resources through which a curriculum can be developed. For programs following an "expedition" model (parallel to a wilderness expedition), backpacking on the streets and public transportation systems can be the means of travel. If waterways exist,

canoeing can be instituted. The limits are only in the level of creativity the staff bring to the design process. Commitment, persistence, and detailed study in the design process are essential requirements for staff developing the urban analog to traditional wilderness adventure education.

An advantage of operating adventure programs in the cities is the ability to establish long-term, multi-phased curriculum models that do justice to the follow-through components that require the "climatic" experience. The idea of running "courses" as standalone experiences becomes antiquated when year-long programs can be implemented sequentially. This orientation to designing programs, within the context of partnerships with schools or youth service agencies, versus the single course, becomes a strength of the urban experience. Also, the element of adventure is present through the unfolding process of a group discovering their city's diversity, its complexity and the perspectives they gain by seeing themselves as contributors to the development of their "home" community. It is not surprising that youth respond to the active learning process in a positive way as they begin to explore their unique and creative beings.

Finally, Outward Bound represents one example of adventure education responding to the educational needs of our country's inner cities. Many programs are in operation which are addressing the growth of adolescents into contributing adults. The vision of transforming social reality is not too grand nor too utopian. The profession of adventure education is young and needs to seek visions that are in touch with the social problems that require new ways of thinking and doing. To be on the "cutting edge" means to be willing to take risks, experiment, make mistakes, try new ideas and take steps into the unknown. Adventure education, in the cities, requires a blend of entrepreneurship and creative program design. The potential is unlimited—the challenges are waiting to be met.

REFERENCES

Bronfenbrunner, U. (1979). *The Ecology of Human Development.* Cambridge, MA: Harvard University Press.

Bronfenbrunner, U. (1983). *Children, Families, and Government: Perspectives on American Social Policy.* Cambridge, MA: Harvard University Press.

Cities in Schools. (1989). *Connecting the Disconnected: 1989 Annual Report.* CIS, Inc., 1023 15th St. N.W. #600, Washington, D.C. 20005.

Comer, J. (1980). *School Power.* New York: New York Free Press.

Cox, H. (1984). *Religion in the Secular City.* New York: Simon and Schuster.

Dyson, B. & Dyson, E. (1986). *Neighborhood Caretakers: Stories, Strategies and Tools for Healing Urban Community.* Indianapolis, IN: Knowledge Systems, Inc.

Epstein, J. (1984). Toward a theory of family-school connections. In Hurrelmann, et al. (Eds.), *Social Intervention: Potential and Constraints.* New York: de Gruyter, 13.

Gatto, J. (1990). Why schools don't educate. *The Sun.* Chapel Hill, NC. Issue 175.

Harmon, W. & Rhinegold, H. (1984). *Higher Creativity: Liberating the Uncon-scious for Breakthrough Insights.* Los Angeles, CA: Jeremy Tarcher, Inc.

Healy, L. (1987). *A Report on Urban Outward Bound Programs: City Challenge, England and City Bound, Holland.* North Carolina Outward Bound School.

Institute For Responsive Education, (1990). Success for all children through school-family-community partnerships. *Equity and Choice, VI* (2).

James, T. (1989). *Outward Bound and Public Education.* Unpublished manuscript, Education Department, Brown University.

Kirth-Schair, R. (1988). The roles of youth in society: A reconceptualization. *The Education Forum, 52* (2).

Koekkoek, G. (1988). *City Bound: The Urban Variant of Outward Bound.* Outward Holland, Rotterdam, Holland.

Proudman, S. (1990). *Building Community Through the Use of Adventure: Outward Bound for Chicago's Schools.* Unpublished manuscript, Voyageur Outward Bound Chicago Center, Chicago, IL.

Seeley, D. (1985). *Education Through Partnership.* Lanham, MD: University Press of America.

Shanker, A. (1988). Columns printed in the *New York Times,* "Sunday Week," June 19-22.

Welp, M. (1990). A view from the Potomac: Urban Outward Bound. *MIA Newsletter,* Ely: Voyageur Outward Bound School.

Wilbur, K. (1984). *A Sociable God.* Boulder, CO: Shambala Publications.

The Challenge of Research for Challenge Education

By Thomas E. Smith

The methodology which can be considered "challenge education" has unfolded through the past 25 years. It is a complex, interdisciplinary methodology for facilitating the personal growth and learning of the clients of human service professionals. The challenge methodology has been applied in programs of special education, rehabilitation, counseling, leadership development, college orientation, outdoor education, family enrichment, recreation and executive training. The important issues facing this innovative compilation of strategies have often been discussed (e.g., Robb, et al., 1985). There has been preliminary attention paid to the issues of safety, leadership, ethics, gender consciousness, environmental consciousness, philosophical foundations and theoretical development.

As with any evolving methodology for delivery of human services, there has also been attention given to the issue of research. Some practitioners have been concerned with studying the dynamics of the challenge/adventure sequences in order to improve the practice. However, the major focus of research questions has been validation.

Validation research can be of value for appropriate development and refinement of the methodology, but the primary concern of such study of the challenge methodology has been with regard to marketing. Consumers,

such as schools, hospitals, criminal justice programs, and business and industry, have begun to ask that basic question, "Does it work?"

Challenge/Adventure/Experiential leaders can offer personal enthusiasm, show dynamic slides and videos, and even have graduated clients give personal testimony about the significant impact of their experiences with challenge sequences. Sometimes the most effective answer to that basic question has been, "Try it for yourself." Often, if administrators, advisory boards, and others who hold the "purse strings" are recruited into a sequence of challenge and adventure, they can be "converted" from skeptics to enthusiastic supporters of the approach. Many programs have developed, and continue to develop, because they have the support of administrators and advisory boards. Conversely many good programs have gone under because they did not have that support.

Still, even for the successful programs, the question now faced is that of "Where's the data?" Critics have asked for outcome studies and follow-up research that proves that there are changes in life adjustment, attitude and value orientation, marketplace productivity, and rates of recidivism. The challenge of the 90's will be for professionals in challenge education to deal with these basic questions. As we move forward, there are lessons from

history and philosophical awareness that can guide us. The focus of this section is to provide some thoughts that may contribute to our thinking about the whole question of research validation.

Case Study: The Effectiveness of Psychotherapy

Most often, the goals of the challenge/adventure program can be seen in parallel to those of counseling, psychotherapy, and the facilitation of personal growth. Goals of enhancing selfconcept, improving interpersonal behavior, changing attitudes and values, cultivating creative thinking and problem solving skills, and "empowering" clients with energy, confidence, and risktaking readiness, have often been stated. It is certainly not too great an extension to see the problems of evaluating challenge methodology as similar to those of evaluating counseling and psychotherapy.

As with challenge methodology, it was after two or three decades of rapid development of the therapeutic methodologies that the questions of validation arose. In the early 1950's many began to challenge the counselors and therapists to validate their practice and profession. The challengers noted that a considerable intensity of emotional acceptance prevailed among those who considered themselves counselors and therapists. When it was suggested that there was need for validation research, many therapists reacted as if the suggestion was "to validate the efficacy of prayer" (Teuber & Powers, 1953). When the question of validity arose, one therapist even wrote that "the only wise course with regard to such a challenge is to ignore it" (Sanford, 1952).

Behavioristic psychologists voiced the request for research. A set of minimum requirements for validation research was presented.

The minimum standard for an adequate outcome study includes (a) a control group, (b) pre- and post-therapy evaluation procedures which are either objective, or if judgmental, are uncontaminated, (c) follow-up of both groups, preferably repeated so that exacerbation and remission rates can be estimated and curves extrapolated. (Meehl, 1955)

Many therapists objected to the request for research with control groups. There were arguments about the difficulties of matching individuals from a "treatment" and "non-treatment" group, noting that defined groups would differ on a large number of variables in addition to that of having therapy or not. A major argument against control group studies was one based on ethical considerations, to the effect that it would be unethical to with-hold therapy from clients in need just to create a control group for research purposes.

Some psychologists did attempt to meet those scientific standards (Teuber & Powers, 1953; Rogers & Dymond, 1954; Baron & Levy, 1955). However, their studies were criticized as being flawed and not answering the challenge that had been put forth. In review of over a decade of research on the whole process of psychotherapy, Eysenck (1961) concluded that there was little data to validate the practice. He suggested that the rate of "spontaneous recovery" from personality and adjustment problems, and the complexity of behavioral change through time, meant that well over fifty percent of clients would be different/better in long-term follow-up whether they had therapy or not. Thus, studies reporting 60% to 70% "recovery" or "improvement" were not reporting changes that were much better than chance or "time alone."

Eysenck's general conclusion was that available research on the process of psychotherapy had not lived up to the hopes which greeted its development through the previous decades. He did, however, raise an important question:

> It will be necessary to account for the fact that so many therapists and so many clients believe quite firmly in the efficacy of psychotherapy; this is an undoubted fact which appears to be in contradiction to our conclusion and does require explanation. (Eysenck, 1961)

It had been suggested earlier that:

> The therapist is like a Skinner-box rat on a schedule of intermittent reinforcement, which generates habits which are notoriously resistive to extinction. A sprinkling of even 5%-10% of specific

cures and cases whose shift toward recovery might not have occurred without intervention, could well account for the enthusiasm. (Meehl, 1955)

Many challenge/adventure leaders could be accused of the same blind enthusiasm for their methodology. While they have no real data to support the whole process of challenge and adventure, there are those periodic situations of intensity and observed personal growth that reinforce their personal convictions about the validity of the programming. After facilitation of a difficult tree climb and sharing the sense of accomplishment with the client, watching a troubled group come together cooperatively to conquer the wall or other initiative problem, or reading introspective wisdom in a client's journal report, the challenge leader feels validated, and is ready to argue enthusiastically about the validity of challenge education. It is well to focus on the words of Schoben, writing about psychotherapy:

> The conclusive evidence of therapeutic effectiveness must come not from argument, but from relevant and rigorous research. (Schoben, 1956)

Those who voiced the challenge for validation of psychotherapy were, of course, usually wearing the glasses of Western scientific behaviorism. They were looking for studies of the complex process of psychotherapy, in the rigorous methodology of those Skinner-box rats choosing a black or a white doorway. Thirty years have passed since Eysenck's review, and there is still no validation research on the process of psychotherapy which meets the desired criteria.

A parallel case history could be outlined regarding the strategies and methodologies of the human potential movement, which came under attack from the behaviorists and other scientists in the 1970's, after a decade of rapid expansion and development. Again, the cry was for validation research, and there was much careful thought given to the challenges, the rebuttals, the defensive proclamations, and the discussions about the issue. For challenge education professionals, there is much to learn from review of such case histories. Many of the critics of challenge education, and many of those asking "Where's the data?" come from that same Western scientific orientation. They are asking for validation research, and they are demanding that such research be accomplished according to their methodology. Perhaps Sanford (1952) was partially right. Although we should not ignore the challenge of validating challenge/adventure programming, we probably should ignore their insistence on adopting a methodology that is inappropriate.

Scientism

Throughout the 19th century, and through the first half of the 20th century, American thought was dominated by a pernicious exaggeration of the status, value, and methodology of the "pure" sciences. The orientation that puts scientific methodology on a pedestal near (or even above) God can be called "scientism." One can identify an orientation as "scientism" when there is advocacy for the methods and techniques of the natural sciences as the appropriate way to search for truth. At the extreme, utilization of the scientific methodology becomes both a necessary and sufficient condition for scientific standing.

Psychologists, especially, were caught up early in the mystique of scientific methodology. They made great gains on the road to scientific legitimacy by adopting the methods

of the empirical sciences. Through the 1930's and 1940's the "behavior scientists" made inroads to the great tower of "scientism." By mid-century, some psychologists were even gaining membership in exclusive fraternities such as the American Association for the Advancement of Science. Such gains were made most readily by the experimental psychologists, the comparative psychologists who studied animal behavior, the physiological psychologists who focused on physiological correlates of behavior, and the learning theorists who derived data from rats in mazes. Social psychologists and those studying personality patterns and traits had a greater struggle for scientific acceptance, but did achieve a degree of respectability by careful adherence to the laboratory method in controlled studies of university students.

There were, however, rumblings of discontent. One psychologist of humanistic/holistic orientation noted that "too much of the data of psychology is based on the Wistar albino rat and the college sophomore." The gestalten concepts of the whole being greater than the sum of the parts brought criticism of a reductionistic overview to humankind as a pile of cells. What of the personal framework of the person? What of the self-concept? What of human values, and the domain of the human spirit? What of the whole complex process of growth and development?

Sociologists had even greater struggles in moving toward "scientific" respectability. There were bitter intradisciplinary differences. Some sociologists argued from the perspectives of scientism, seeking to gain acceptance by following the rules of scientific methodology. Others disagreed, in parallel to the humanistic psychologists, arguing that the group, the culture, the society, could not be appropriately studied by the methods of the pure sciences. There were arguments for the development of a research methodology and an approach to sociological truths that was more appropriate for the subject matter. In his study of *The Conduct of Inquiry* (1964), Abraham Kaplan noted, "Many behavior scientists look to methodology as a source of salvation." He pointed out:

> There are indeed techniques to be mastered, but their resources and limitations should be thoroughly explored. But the techniques must be specific to their subject matter, or to distinctive problems, and norms governing their use should derive from the contexts of their application, not from general principles of methodology. The work of the behavior scientist might well become methodologically sounder if only he did not try so hard to be scientific. (Ibid.)

The critiques of "scientism" by those who study more complex behavioral processes are important for the challenge education theorist. Kaplan summarized as follows:

> There is room in behavioral science—indeed there is need—for a variety of theories, models, scales of measurement, and conceptual frameworks. (op. cit.)

Another way to summarize the appropriate criticism of scientism is to note that there are many ways to "study" humankind and that "scientific study" represents but one approach. Almost half a century ago, Max Weber had accepted this position when he advocated a distinction between the "social sciences" and the "empirical disciplines." He suggested:

> The belief in the value of scientific truth is the product of certain cultures, and is not a product of man's nature. (Weber, 1945)

Even Einstein noted that there were differences between "the laws of science" and "the laws of ethics." His discussion focuses on the fact that when working in the area of human values, which includes perceptions and judgments of self, others, environment, the self-other interaction, the self-environment interaction, good and bad, right and wrong and all such complex human dynamics, there are different aspects of "truth." He suggests that there is truth to be found in both areas. For the human qualities, the ethical questions,"*Die Wahrheit liegt in der Beivahring.*" [Truth is what stands the test of experience.] (Einstein, 1950)

Perhaps that has been the dilemma of psychotherapists, and is not the dilemma of challenge methodology professionals. To the extent that we define "truth" solely in terms of scientism, and think of the only appropriate study of humankind as "scientific study," we will struggle with validation. We need to recognize that our dealings are in the area of human values, and then expand our methodology to include broader and more innovative strategies, even though that developing approach to the problem might be criticized by those of "scientistic" orientation.

There may also be wisdom in the existential philosophers' distinction between "truth" and "reality." We may not be able to provide the critics with evidence of the validity of our programming in the sense of scientific proof/truths, although there is certainly merit in continuing attempts to do so. On the other hand, we can provide meaningful data and reports that are very real, and certainly represent proof/truths in their own way.

Paradigm Shifts

Through the past few decades, there has been increasing attention given to alternative orientations to humankind and the environment/universe within which the species exists. Marilyn Ferguson's marvelous book, *The Aquarian Conspiracy*, can be seen as revealing paradigm shifts in education, counseling and growth facilitation, medicine, and even business and industry. She summarizes:

> A paradigm is a framework of thought. A paradigm is a scheme for understanding and explaining certain aspects of reality. A paradigm shift is a distinctly new way of thinking about old problems... The new framework does more than the old. It predicts more accurately. And it throws open doors and windows for new exploration.
>
> The paradigm of *The Aquarian Conspiracy* sees humankind embedded in nature. It promotes the autonomous individual in a decentralized society. It sees us as stewards of all our resources, inner and outer. Human nature is neither good nor bad but open to continuous transformation and transcendence. It has only to discover itself. The new perspective respects the ecology of everything: birth, death, learning, health, family, work, science, spirituality, the arts, the community, relationships, politics. (Ferguson, 1980)

Our attention to paradigms and paradigm shifts is most often dated to the writings of Thomas Kuhn, a science historian and philosopher (1962). Other philosophers had suggested that scientists and philosophers should be keenly aware that what was argued to be truth and reality in one generation was often found or judged to be false and absurd in subsequent generations.

Paradigm shifts occur because new theories, facts, beliefs, values, and unfolding real-

ities are uncovered and discovered. We come to realize that our former perspectives do not fit our present realities. What occurs is a new way of thinking about old problems. There have been a number of scholarly works on shifting paradigms, and outlines for new orientations to humankind and the world (Schumacher, 1973; Capra, 1975; Zukav, 1979; Holbrook, 1981). In the preface to his writings, Holbrook notes:

> This book shows the basic defect in Western science, and explains how it generates negative effects; gives reasons for believing that Chinese science is superior to it, and introduces an alternative world view, science, and potential reality. (Holbrook, 1981)

Challenge education philosophers and researchers would do well to study contemporary thought on paradigm shifts. The overview to humankind, nature, values, truth, reality, and science, has considerable import for questions of appropriate validation research. When a new philosophical/scientific paradigm is adopted, the very ground rules for the study of humankind, and the acceptable methods for research also change.

Challenge education is based on a humanistic/holistic perspective on humankind and all of nature. Many challenge/adventure facilitators have found an attraction to ritual, ceremony, value orientation, and spiritualism of the Native Americans. Quite simply, their personal and cultural cosmological orientation to all that exists makes more sense for our times and the evolutionary requirements for survival. It is interesting to note that there are remarkable parallels between the rituals for awareness, energy, healing, and spiritual discovery of the Native Americans and the traditions of the Orient (Smith, 1990).

Holbrook acknowledges his teacher from China, thanking him for guidance toward "connecting my brain to my heart." (op.cit.) Perhaps that is the greatest thing to be gained from attention to the new paradigms.

It was noted at the start of this subchapter that critics, and those requesting validation data on challenge education methodology, seek more than the enthusiastic testimony of challenge facilitators and clients. Certainly, we should seek to deal with their questions, and the effort to provide answers in terms of traditional scientific standards should continue. However, if we pick up a different set of spectacles than those of scientism and look to new paradigms for understanding ourselves and others, then other "data" become quite admissible.

A recent brochure announcing a hospital's training workshop on "Adventure-Based Counseling for the Mental Health Professional" provides some biographical information on the two program facilitators, and then notes: "Their passion for this field stems from the magic they continually see occurring for those who participate" (Oakwood Hospital, 1991).

Perhaps, after all, challenge/adventure facilitators are really magicians and artists and shamans and ministers guiding clients toward appropriate values, behaviors, and spiritual awareness for the 21st century. Again, it would be helpful to review the psychotherapists' discussions about whether they practice an "art" or a "science." Italian psychiatrist Roberto Assagioli suggested that the most appropriate label for the counselor/therapist/growth facilitator was "guide." (Assagioli, 1965) Challenge education facilitators might well be perceived as a part of a

whole host of people workers who are guiding humankind's transformation.

Personal Values and Evaluation

We need to recognize that our personal values influence our behavior and our impact as challenge education facilitators. Leadership development for challenge education should therefore include a good dose of "personal growth" facilitation. (Smith, 1991) When focusing on the questions of validation research and appropriate study of the challenge methodology, our personal values also influence. Do we accept the orientation of scientism? Do we seek to develop validation methodology that meets the criteria of pure science or the neosocial sciences? Or do we reject the orientation of scientism? Do we accept alternative world views and "study" of human behavior? Do we attempt to convince those who ask about the validity of our methodology to accept the testimony of our leaders and our clients, and to accept summary reports and cumulative data that may not be "scientifically acceptable?"

Because of the interdisciplinary nature of challenge education, and the diversity of background training of contemporary challenge education theorists and researchers, there are no doubt leaders who stand on both sides of the issue. That is our strength, for it means that the problems, the methodology, and the unfolding literature will be reflective of both the historic and the emerging paradigms. In such breadth of thinking we should find maximum understanding of challenge methodology and meaningful answers to the question, "Does it work?"

References

Assagioli, R. (1974). *Psychosynthesis*. New York: Viking Press.

Baron, F. & Leary, T. (1955). Changes in psychoneurotic patients with and without psychotherapy. *Journal of Consulting Psychology (19)*.

Capra, F. (1975). *The Tao of Physics*. New York: Random House.

Einstein, A. (1950). The laws of science and the laws of ethics. *Relativity: A Richer Truth*. New York: Beacon Press.

Eysenck, H. (1961). The effects of psychotherapy. *Handbook of Abnormal Psychology*. New York: Basic Books.

Ferguson, M. (1980). *The Aquarian Conspiracy*. Los Angeles, CA: J. P. Tarcher, Inc.

Holbrook, B. (1981). *The Stone Monkey*. New York: William Morrow & Co.

Kaplan, A. (1964). *The Conduct of Inquiry*. San Francisco, CA: Chandler Publishing Co.

Kuhn, T. S. (1956). *The Structure of Scientific Revolutions, 2nd edition*. Chicago, IL: University of Illinois Press.

Meehl, P. E. (1955). Psychotherapy. *Annual Review of Psychology (6)*.

Oakwood Hospital (1991). Training program brochure. Rockford, IL.

Robb, G. (1985). *Issues in Challenge Education and Adventure Programming*. Bloomington/Bradford Woods, IN: Indiana University Press.

Rogers, C. & Dymond, R. (1954). *Psychotherapy and Personality Change*. Chicago, IL: University of Chicago Press.

Sanford, N. (1953). Clinical methods: Psychotherapy. *Annual Review of Psychology (4)*.

Schoben, E. J. (1956). Some observations on psychotherapy and the learning process. Psychotherapy: *Theory and Research*. H. O. Mower (ed). New York: Ronald Press.

Schumacher, E. A. (1973). *Small is Beautiful*. New York: Harper & Row, Inc.

Smith, T. (1990). Red and yellow: The colors of the sun. *Wilderness Beyond...Wilderness Within*. Cazenovia, WI: Raccoon Institute.

Smith, T., Roland, C., Havens, M. & Hoyt, J. (1991). *The Theory and Practice of Challenge Education*. Lake Mills, WI: Learned Enterprises.

Teuber, N. & Powers, E. (1953). Evaluating therapy: A delinquency prevention program. *Proceedings of the Association for Research on Nervous and Mental Diseases (31)*. Baltimore, MD: Williams & Wilkins.

Weber, M. (1949). *The Methodology of the Social Sciences*. Glencoe, IL: Free Press.

Zukav, G. (1979). *The Dancing Wu-Li Masters*. New York: Morrow.

About the Authors

Tom Smith

Tom Smith, Ph.D., "Raccoon," is a clinical psychologist, challenge educator, and wilderness guide. He has forty years of experience working with alternative approaches to psychotherapy, education, and facilitation of personal growth. For the past five years he has been a consultant for programs of outdoor adventure, experiential education, leadership training, and special education professional energy and personal growth.

Dr. Smith is author of the book *Wilderness Beyond....Wilderness Within....* which is a collection of his papers, including "Health and Healing Practices of the Native American Indians: Potentials for Personal Growth and Holistic Health," "Bringing People Together in the Wilderness: Conjoint Adventure Trips for Special Populations," and "Alternative Strategies for Processing the Outdoor Experience." He also created *The Story of Sundrop*, a storybook/colorbook for "children of all ages," which can be a curriculum overview to challenge education activities.

Christopher C. Roland

Christopher Roland, Ed.D., is Founder and President of Roland & Associates, Inc. He has seven years of experience as a teacher, university professor, and Planning & Training Specialist. For ten years, Chris has worked with a wide-range of organizations in the development, implementation and evaluation of challenge education programs. He has published numerous articles and presented at several national conferences in the areas of corporate training and development and therapeutic challenge programming.

Mark Havens

Mark Havens, Ed.D, is the President of Accessible Adventures, a company which focuses on providing adventure-based activities with persons who are disabled. He recently authored *Bridges To Accessibility*, a primer for including persons with disabilities in adventure curricula. Dr. Havens has presented at several national conferences on such topics as: adventure-based programming, accessibility and ethics in experiential treatment and learning. He is also active in providing adventure-based training with corporations both nationally and internationally.

Judy Hoyt

Judy, an independent consultant, has more than 28 years of experience working with persons with disabilities and their families. She began her career with the birth of her first son who was affected with severe quadriplegic cerebral palsy. This personal experience was the impetus for Judy to become a national spokesperson for discrimination, value systems, respect for families and how to become a change agent.

For fifteen years, Judy directed an integrated camp (Kamp for Kids) and family centre program in Westfield, Massachusetts. She has acted as a member of the National Regional Advisory Committee for the Easter Seal Society and member of the Think Tank on Family Support Issues for United Cerebral Palsy. Judy has also testified in support of the Americans with Disabilities Act (ADA) to the United States Senate and the United States House of Representatives.

ABOUT ROLAND & ASSOCIATES, INC.

Roland & Associates, incorporated in 1983, is an organization development and training firm with three strategic business units:

(1) Corporate experiential "action learning" training and development

> Focus Areas:
>
> Change
> High Performance Work Teams
> Strategic Planning
> Creative Problem Solving
> Quality
> Diversity
> Leadership Development

(2) Therapeutic challenge program consultation and training for mental health settings

> Focus Populations:
>
> Psychiatric
> Eating Disorders
> Chemical Dependency
> Adult Children of Alcoholics
> Dysfunctional Family Systems

(3) Therapeutic challenge program consultation and training for physical rehabilitation settings
> (TRACS: The Rehab Accessible Challenge System)

> Focus Populations:
>
> Head Injury
> Spinal Cord Injury
> Stroke
> Amputee
> Work Hardening

For more information, please contact **Roland & Associates** at:

> 67 Emerald Street
> New Hampshire 03431
> Telephone: (603) 357-2181
> Fax: (603) 357-7992

INDEX